Contents

Peugeot 304 Saloon

Peugeot 304 Estate

Dimensions, weights and capacities

Overall dimensions

Year	Model	Length	Width	Height (unladen)	Ground clearance (fully laden)	Wheelbase	Track Front	Track Rear
1973	Saloon	13 ft 7 in (4.17 m)	5 ft 2 in (1.57 m)	4 ft 7 in (1.41 m)	$4\frac{3}{4}$ in (0.12 m)	8 ft 6 in (2.59 m)	4 ft 4 in (1.32 m)	4 ft 2 in (1.29 m)
1973	Estate	13 ft 1 in (3.99 m)	5 ft 2 in (1.57 m)	4 ft 7 in (1.41 m)	$4\frac{3}{4}$ in (0.12 m)	8 ft 6 in (2.59 m)	4 ft 4 in (1.32 m)	4 ft 2 in (1.29 m)
1973	Coupe	12 ft 4 in (3.85 m)	5 ft 1 in (1.54 m)	–	$4\frac{3}{4}$ in (0.12 m)	7 ft 6 in (2.30 m)	4 ft 4 in (1.32 m)	4 ft 2 in (1.29 m)
1973	Convertible	12 ft 4 in (3.85 m)	5 ft 1 in (1.43 m)	–	$5\frac{1}{8}$ in (0.13 m)	7 ft 6 in (2.30 m)	4 ft 3 in (1.32 m)	4 ft 2 in (1.29 m)
1974	Saloon	13 ft 6 in (4.14 m)	5 ft 2 in (1.57 m)	4 ft 10 in (1.43 m)	4 in (0.10 m)	8 ft 6 in (2.59 m)	4 ft 4 in (1.32 m)	4 ft 2 in (1.29 m)
1974	Estate	13 ft 2 in (3.99 m)	5 ft 2 in (1.57 m)	4 ft 10 in (1.43 m)	4 in (0.10 m)	8 ft 6 in (2.59 m)	4 ft 4 in (1.32 m)	4 ft 2 in (1.29 m)
1975	Saloon	13 ft 6 in (4.14 m)	5 ft 2 in (1.57 m)	4 ft 10 in (1.43 m)	$5\frac{3}{4}$ in (0.14 m)	8 ft 6 in (2.59 m)	4 ft 4 in (1.32 m)	4 ft 2 in (1.29 m)
1975	Estate	13 ft 2 in (3.99 m)	5 ft 2 in (1.57 m)	4 ft 10 in (1.43 m)	$5\frac{3}{4}$ in (0.14 m)	8 ft 6 in (2.59 m)	4 ft 4 in (1.32 m)	4 ft 2 in (1.29 m)
1975	Coupe	12 ft 8 in	5 ft 2 in (1.57 m)	–	$5\frac{3}{4}$ in (0.14 m)	7 ft 6 in (2.30 m)	4 ft 4 in (1.32 m)	4 ft 2 in (1.29 m)
1975	Convertible	12 ft 8 in (3.76 m)	5 ft 2 in (1.57 m)	–	$5\frac{1}{2}$ in (0.13 m)	7 ft 6 in (2.30 m)	4 ft 4 in (1.32 m)	4 ft 2 in (1.29 m)
1976/77	Saloon	13 ft 6 in (4.14 m)	5 ft 2 in (1.57 m)	4 ft 7 in (1.41 m)	4 in (0.10 m)	8 ft 6 in (2.59 m)	4 ft 4 in (1.32 m)	4 ft 2 in (1.29 m)
1976/77	Estate	13 ft 2 in (3.99 m)	5 ft 2 in (1.57 m)	4 ft 10 in (1.43 m)	4 in (0.10 m)	8 ft 6 in (2.59 m)	4 ft 4 in (1.32 m)	4 ft 2 in (1.29 m)
1978/79 /80	Saloon	13 ft 6 in (4.14 m)	5 ft 2 in (1.57 m)	4 ft 7 in (1.41 m)	4 in (0.10 m)	8 ft 6 in (2.59 m)	4 ft 6 in (1.37 m)	4 ft 2 in (1.29 m)
1978/79 /80	Estate	13 ft (3.96 m)	5 ft 2 in (1.57 m)	4 ft 10 in (1.43 m)	4 in (0.10 m)	8 ft 6 in (2.59 m)	4 ft 6 in (1.37 m)	4 ft 2 in (1.29 m)

Weights

maximum permissible laden weights:

Coupe	2750 lb (1250 kg)
Convertible	2387 lb (1085 kg)
Saloon	2932 lb (1330 kg)
Estate 1973 model	3019 lb (1370 kg)
1975 models on	3108 lb (1410 kg)

maximum towing capacities*:

Coupe	1980 lb (900 kg)
Convertible	1760 lb (800 kg)
Saloon and Estate	2205 lb (1000 kg)

*French legal limits

Capacities

Engine and transmission oil	7 pints (4 litres)

Cooling system:

XL3, XL3S and XK5 engines	10.2 pints (5.8 litres)
XL5 and XL5S engines	11.8 pints (6.2 litres)
Fuel tank	11.09 gallons (50.4 litres)
Windscreen washer reservoir	2.54 pints (1.4 litres)

Tyre pressures in bars (lbf in²)

	Front	Rear
145 x 355 (145 SR 14) Saloon	1.8 (26)	2.1 (30)
155 x 355 (155 SR 14) Saloon	1.9 (27)	2.2 (31)
145 x 355 (145 SR 14) Estate	1.8 (26)	2.7 (39)*
155 x 355 (155 SR 14) Estate with reinforced suspension	1.9 (27)	2.8 (40)*

*If driving for extended periods with unladen vehicle, rear tyre pressures can be lowered by up to 0.5 bar (8 lbf/in²)

Buying spare parts and vehicle identification numbers

Buying spare parts

Spare parts are available from many sources. Peugeot have many dealers throughout the UK, and other dealers, accessory stores and motor factors will also stock some spare parts suitable for Peugeot cars.

Our advice regarding spare part sources is as follows:

Officially appointed vehicle main dealers – This is the best source of parts which are peculiar to your vehicle and are otherwise not generally available (eg complete cylinder heads, internal transmission components, badges, interior trim etc). It is also the only place at which you should buy parts if your vehicle is still under warranty. To be sure of obtaining the correct parts it will always be necessary to give the storeman your vehicle's engine and chassis number, and if possible, to take the 'old' part along for positive identification. Remember that many parts are available on a factory exchange scheme – any parts returned should always be clean! It obviously makes good sense to go straight to the specialists on your vehicle for this type of part, for they are best equipped to supply you.

Other dealers and auto accessory stores – These are often very good places to buy materials and components needed for the maintenance of your vehicle (eg oil filters, spark plugs, bulbs, fanbelts, oils and greases, touch-up paint, filler paste etc). They also sell general accessories, usually have convenient opening hours, charge lower prices and can often be found not far from home.

Motor factors – Good factors will stock all of the more important components which wear out relatively quickly (eg clutch components, pistons, valves, exhaust systems, brake cylinders/pipes/hoses/seals/shoes and pads etc). Motor factors will often provide new or reconditioned components on a part exchange basis – this can save a considerable amount of money.

Vehicle identification numbers

Modifications are a continuing and unpublicised process in vehicle manufacture. Spare parts manuals and lists are compiled on a numerical basis, the individual vehicle numbers being essential to identify correctly the component required.

The engine number is located on the top of the flange joining the cylinder block to the transmission just to the right of the coil bracket on the back of the engine.

The engine type is identified by two letters stamped on the front right-hand side of the cylinder block. Their significance is:

S   – XL3 engine with 8.8:1 compression ratio
ZA – XL3 engine with 7.5:1 compression ratio
SA – XL3S engine with 8.8:1 compression ratio
GA – XK5 engine (1127 cc) with 8.8:1 compression ratio
SB – XL5 engine with 8.8:1 compression ratio
ZB – XL5 engine with 7.5:1 compression ratio
SD – XL5S engine wittth 8.8:1 compression ratio

The vehicle type and serial number is stamped on an identification plate riveted to the top of the front right-hand wheel valance under the bonnet. The car serial number is also marked on the engine, if it is the original installed on production, on a printed label stuck on the side face of the timing case.

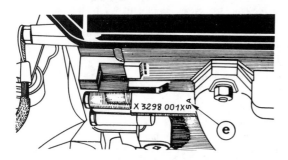

The engine serial number locations at the rear (top) and front (lower). Caption 'e' signifies the engine type identification letter

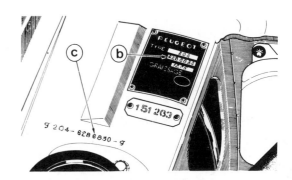

The vehicle serial number location

Tools and working facilities

Introduction

A selection of good tools is a fundamental requirement for anyone contemplating the maintenance and repair of a motor vehicle. For the owner who does not possess any, their purchase will prove a considerable expense, offsetting some of the savings made by doing-it-yourself. However, provided that the tools purchased are of good quality, they will last for many years and prove an extremely worthwhile investment.

To help the average owner to decide which tools are needed to carry out the various tasks detailed in this manual, we have compiled three lists of tools under the following headings: *Maintenance and minor repair, Repair and overhaul,* and *Special*. The newcomer to practical mechanics should start off with the *Maintenance and minor repair* tool kit and confine himself to the simpler jobs around the vehicle. Then, as his confidence and experience grow, he can undertake more difficult tasks, buying extra tools as, and when, they are needed. In this way, a *Maintenance and minor repair* tool kit can be built-up into a *Repair and overhaul* tool kit over a considerable period of time without any major cash outlays. The experienced do-it-yourselfer will have a tool kit good enough for most repair and overhaul procedures and will add tools from the *Special* category when he feels the expense is justified by the amount of use to which these tools will be put.

It is obviously not possible to cover the subject of tools fully here. For those who wish to learn more about tools and their use there is a book entitled *How to Choose and Use Car Tools* available from the publishers of this manual.

Maintenance and minor repair tool kit

The tools given in this list should be considered as a minimum requirement if routine maintenance, servicing and minor repair operations are to be undertaken. We recommend the purchase of combination spanners (ring one end, open-ended the other); although more expensive than open-ended ones, they do give the advantages of both types of spanner.

Combination spanners - 10, 11, 12, 13, 14 & 17 mm
Adjustable spanner - 9 inch
Engine sump transmission drain plug key ($\frac{3}{8}$ in)
Spark plug spanner – use special Peugeot spanner (see Chapter 4)
Spark plug gap adjustment tool
Set of feeler gauges
Brake bleed nipple spanner
Screwdriver - 4 in long x $\frac{1}{4}$ in dia (flat blade)
Screwdriver - 4 in long x $\frac{1}{4}$ in dia (cross blade)
Combination pliers - 6 inch
Hacksaw (junior)
Tyre pump
Tyre pressure gauge
'Mole' wrench – 8 inch
Oil can
Fine emery cloth (1 sheet)
Wire brush (small)
Funnel (medium size)

Repair and overhaul tool kit

These tools are virtually essential for anyone undertaking any major repairs to a motor vehicle, and are additional to those given in the *Maintenance and minor repair* list. Included in this list is a comprehensive set of sockets. Although these are expensive they will be found invaluable as they are so versatile - particularly if various drives are included in the set. We recommend the $\frac{1}{2}$ in square-drive type, as this can be used with most proprietary torque wrenches. If you cannot afford a socket set, even bought piecemeal, then inexpensive tubular box spanners are a useful alternative.

The tools in this list will occasionally need to be supplemented by tools from the *Special* list.

Sockets (or box spanners) to cover range in previous list
Reversible ratchet drive (for use with sockets)
Extension piece, 10 inch (for use with sockets)
Universal joint (for use with sockets)
Torque wrench (for use with sockets)
Ball pein hammer
Soft-faced hammer, plastic or rubber
Screwdriver - 6 in long x $\frac{5}{16}$ in dia (flat blade)
Screwdriver - 2 in long x $\frac{5}{16}$ in square (flat blade)
Screwdriver - 1$\frac{1}{2}$ in long x $\frac{1}{4}$ in dia (cross blade)
Screwdriver - 3 in long x $\frac{1}{8}$ in dia (electricians)
Pliers - electricians side cutters
Pliers - needle nosed
Pliers - circlip (internal and external)
Cold chisel - $\frac{1}{2}$ inch
Scriber
Scraper
Centre punch
Pin punch
Hacksaw
Valve grinding tool
Steel rule/straight-edge
Allen keys
Selection of files
Wire brush (large)
Axle-stands
Jack (strong scissor or hydraulic type)

Special tools

The tools in this list are those which are not used regularly, are expensive to buy, or which need to be used in accordance with their manufacturers' instructions. Unless relatively difficult mechanical jobs are undertaken frequently, it will not be economic to buy many of these tools. Where this is the case, you could consider clubbing together with friends (or joining a motorists' club) to make a joint purchase, or borrowing the tools against a deposit from a local garage or tool hire specialist.

The following list contains only those tools and instruments freely available to the public, and not those special tools produced by the vehicle manufacturer specifically for its dealer network. You will find occasional references to these manufacturers' special tools in the text of this manual. Generally, an alternative method of doing the job without the vehicle manufacturers' special tool is given. However, sometimes, there is no alternative to using them. Where this is the case and the relevant tool cannot be bought or borrowed, you will have to entrust the work to a franchised garage.

Valve spring compressor (where applicable)
Piston ring compressor
Balljoint separator
Universal hub/bearing puller
Impact screwdriver
Micrometer and/or vernier gauge
Dial gauge
Stroboscopic timing light
Dwell angle meter/tachometer
Universal electrical multi-meter

Cylinder compression gauge
Lifting tackle (photo)
Trolley jack
Light with extension lead

Buying tools

For practically all tools, a tool factor is the best source since he will have a very comprehensive range compared with the average garage or accessory shop. Having said that, accessory shops often offer excellent quality tools at discount prices, so it pays to shop around.

Remember, you don't have to buy the most expensive items on the shelf, but it is always advisable to steer clear of the very cheap tools. There are plenty of good tools around at reasonable prices, so ask the proprietor or manager of the shop for advice before making a purchase.

Care and maintenance of tools

Having purchased a reasonable tool kit, it is necessary to keep the tools in a clean serviceable condition. After use, always wipe off any dirt, grease and metal particles using a clean, dry cloth, before putting the tools away. Never leave them lying around after they have been used. A simple tool rack on the garage or workshop wall, for items such as screwdrivers and pliers is a good idea. Store all normal wrenches and sockets in a metal box. Any measuring instruments, gauges, meters, etc, must be carefully stored where they cannot be damaged or become rusty.

Take a little care when tools are used. Hammer heads inevitably become marked and screwdrivers lose the keen edge on their blades from time to time. A little timely attention with emery cloth or a file will soon restore items like this to a good serviceable finish.

Working facilities

Not to be forgotten when discussing tools, is the workshop itself. If anything more than routine maintenance is to be carried out, some form of suitable working area becomes essential.

It is appreciated that many an owner mechanic is forced by circumstances to remove an engine or similar item, without the benefit of a garage or workshop. Having done this, any repairs should always be done under the cover of a roof.

Wherever possible, any dismantling should be done on a clean, flat workbench or table at a suitable working height.

Any workbench needs a vice: one with a jaw opening of 4 in (100 mm) is suitable for most jobs. As mentioned previously, some clean dry storage space is also required for tools, as well as for lubricants, cleaning fluids, touch-up paints and so on, which become necessary.

Another item which may be required, and which has a much more general usage, is an electric drill with a chuck capacity of at least $\frac{5}{16}$ in (8 mm). This, together with a good range of twist drills, is virtually essential for fitting accessories such as mirrors and reversing lights.

Last, but not least, always keep a supply of old newspapers and clean, lint-free rags available, and try to keep any working area as clean as possible.

Spanner jaw gap comparison table

Jaw gap (in)	Spanner size
0.250	$\frac{1}{4}$ in AF
0.276	7 mm
0.313	$\frac{5}{16}$ in AF
0.315	8 mm
0.344	$\frac{11}{32}$ in AF; $\frac{1}{8}$ in Whitworth
0.354	9 mm
0.375	$\frac{3}{8}$ in AF
0.394	10 mm
0.433	11 mm
0.438	$\frac{7}{16}$ in AF
0.445	$\frac{3}{16}$ in Whitworth; $\frac{1}{4}$ in BSF
0.472	12 mm
0.500	$\frac{1}{2}$ in AF
0.512	13 mm
0.525	$\frac{1}{4}$ in Whitworth; $\frac{5}{16}$ in BSF
0.551	14 mm
0.563	$\frac{9}{16}$ in AF
0.591	15 mm
0.600	$\frac{5}{16}$ in Whitworth; $\frac{3}{8}$ in BSF
0.625	$\frac{5}{8}$ in AF
0.630	16 mm
0.669	17 mm
0.686	$\frac{11}{16}$ in AF
0.709	18 mm
0.710	$\frac{3}{8}$ in Whitworth; $\frac{7}{16}$ in BSF
0.748	19 mm
0.750	$\frac{3}{4}$ in AF
0.813	$\frac{13}{16}$ in AF
0.820	$\frac{7}{16}$ in Whitworth; $\frac{1}{2}$ in BSF
0.866	22 mm
0.875	$\frac{7}{8}$ in AF
0.920	$\frac{1}{2}$ in Whitworth; $\frac{9}{16}$ in BSF
0.938	$\frac{15}{16}$ in AF
0.945	24 mm
1.000	1 in AF
1.010	$\frac{9}{16}$ in Whitworth; $\frac{5}{8}$ in BSF
1.024	26 mm
1.063	$1\frac{1}{16}$ in AF; 27 mm
1.100	$\frac{5}{8}$ in Whitworth; $\frac{11}{16}$ in BSF
1.125	$1\frac{1}{8}$ in AF
1.181	30 mm
1.200	$\frac{11}{16}$ in Whitworth; $\frac{3}{4}$ in BSF
1.250	$1\frac{1}{4}$ in AF
1.260	32 mm
1.300	$\frac{3}{4}$ in Whitworth; $\frac{7}{8}$ in BSF
1.313	$1\frac{5}{16}$ in AF
1.390	$\frac{13}{16}$ in Whitworth; $\frac{15}{16}$ in BSF
1.417	36 mm
1.438	$1\frac{7}{16}$ in AF
1.480	$\frac{7}{8}$ in Whitworth; 1 in BSF
1.500	$1\frac{1}{2}$ in AF
1.575	40 mm; $\frac{15}{16}$ in Whitworth
1.614	41 mm
1.625	$1\frac{5}{8}$ in AF
1.670	1 in Whitworth; $1\frac{1}{8}$ in BSF
1.688	$1\frac{11}{16}$ in AF
1.811	46 mm
1.813	$1\frac{13}{16}$ in AF
1.860	$1\frac{1}{8}$ in Whitworth; $1\frac{1}{4}$ in BSF
1.875	$1\frac{7}{8}$ in AF
1.969	50 mm
2.000	2 in AF
2.050	$1\frac{1}{4}$ in Whitworth; $1\frac{3}{8}$ in BSF
2.165	55 mm
2.362	60 mm

A Haltrac hoist and gantry in use during a typical engine removal sequence

Jacking and towing

A pantograph type of jack is supplied with the car but this is only suitable for changing a wheel in an emergency. Under no circumstances work under the car when it is only supported on this jack; additional support is essential and the car should have axle stands or substantial blocks located under the sub-frames whenever it is necessary for you to get underneath.

When using the wheel-changing jack, position it under the jacking point adjacent to the wheel to be changed with the screw spindle pointing towards the diagonally opposite wheel. This will allow the jack to tilt safely as the car lifts through an arc as it is jacked up. The vehicle must always be jacked up on firm level ground. If removing or changing a wheel, loosen off the retaining nuts of the wheel concerned before raising the jack. Then when the vehicle is clear of the ground the wheel nuts can be removed. When refitting the wheel hand tighten the nuts, lower the jack and then tighten the nuts fully to the specified torque setting.

Front and rear anchorage points are provided for tying the vehicle down when being transported. These can be used for towing or being towed in an emergency (photo).

If fitting a tow-bar at the rear of the vehicle, it is recommended that the official Peugeot type be used since it is tailor made for your vehicle type.

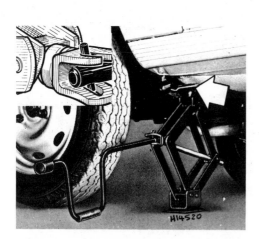

Jack location – front

Jack location – rear

Rear end tie down point which can be used for emergency towing

Front tie down points can be used towing in an emergency

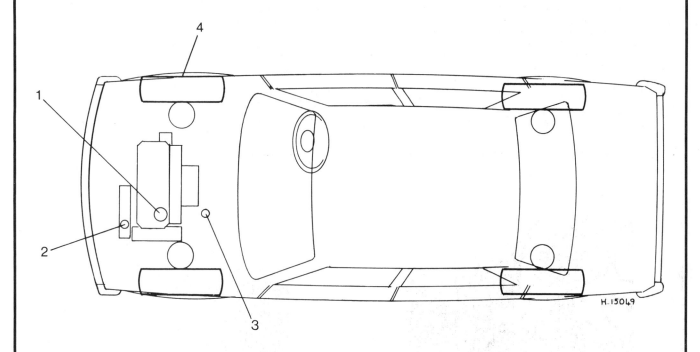

H.15049

Recommended lubricants and fluids

Component or system	Lubricant type or specification	Castrol product
1 Engine/transmission	Multigrade engine oil SAE 10W/40	GTX
2 Cooling system	Antifreeze to Peugeot PN 9730.70 BS 3151 or BS 3152	Anti-freeze
3 Brake hydraulic system	Hydraulic fluid to SAE J1703	Castrol Girling Universal Brake and Clutch Fluid
4 Wheel bearings	Multi-purpose grease	LM grease
Battery terminals	Petroleum jelly	No equivalent
Distributor (sparingly)	Multigrade engine oil	GTX
Hinges, catches, pivots etc	Light machine oil	GTX or Everyman Oil

Safety first!

Professional motor mechanics are trained in safe working procedures. However enthusiastic you may be about getting on with the job in hand, do take the time to ensure that your safety is not put at risk. A moment's lack of attention can result in an accident, as can failure to observe certain elementary precautions.

There will always be new ways of having accidents, and the following points do not pretend to be a comprehensive list of all dangers; they are intended rather to make you aware of the risks and to encourage a safety-conscious approach to all work you carry out on your vehicle.

Essential DOs and DON'Ts

DON'T rely on a single jack when working underneath the vehicle. Always use reliable additional means of support, such as axle stands, securely placed under a part of the vehicle that you know will not give way.

DON'T attempt to loosen or tighten high-torque nuts (e.g. wheel hub nuts) while the vehicle is on a jack; it may be pulled off.

DON'T start the engine without first ascertaining that the transmission is in neutral and the parking brake applied.

DON'T suddenly remove the filler cap from a hot cooling system — cover it with a cloth and release the pressure gradually first, or you may get scalded by escaping coolant.

DON'T attempt to drain oil until you are sure it has cooled sufficiently to avoid scalding you.

DON'T grasp any part of the engine, or exhaust without first ascertaining that it is sufficiently cool to avoid burning you.

DON'T syphon toxic liquids such as fuel, brake fluid or antifreeze by mouth, or allow them to remain on your skin.

DON'T inhale brake lining dust — it is injurious to health.

DON'T allow any spilt oil or grease to remain on the floor — wipe it up straight away, before someone slips on it.

DON'T use ill-fitting spanners or other tools which may slip and cause injury.

DON'T attempt to lift a heavy component which may be beyond your capability — get assistance.

DON'T rush to finish a job, or take unverified short cuts.

DON'T allow children or animals in or around an unattended vehicle.

DO wear eye protection when using power tools such as drill, sander, bench grinder etc, and when working under the vehicle.

DO use a barrier cream on your hands prior to undertaking dirty jobs — it will protect your skin from infection as well as making the dirt easier to remove afterwards; but make sure your hands aren't left slippery.

DO keep loose clothing (cuffs, tie etc) and long hair well out of the way of moving mechanical parts.

DO remove rings, wristwatch etc, before working on the vehicle — especially the electrical system.

DO ensure that any lifting tackle used has a safe working load rating adequate for the job.

DO keep your work area tidy — it is only too easy to fall over articles left lying around.

DO get someone to check periodically that all is well, when working alone on the vehicle.

DO carry out work in a logical sequence and check that everything is correctly assembled and tightened afterwards.

DO remember that your vehicle's safety affects that of yourself and others. If in doubt on any point, get specialist advice.

IF, in spite of following these precautions, you are unfortunate enough to injure yourself, seek medical attention as soon as possible.

Fire

Remember at all times that petrol (gasoline) is highly flammable. Never smoke, or have any kind of naked flame around, when working on the vehicle. But the risk does not end there — a spark caused by an electrical short-circuit, by two metal surfaces contacting each other, or even by static electricity built up in your body under certain conditions, can ignite petrol vapour, which in a confined space is highly explosive.

Always disconnect the battery earth (ground) terminal before working on any part of the fuel system, and never risk spilling fuel on to a hot engine or exhaust.

It is recommended that a fire extinguisher of a type suitable for fuel and electrical fires is kept handy in the garage or workplace at all times. Never try to extinguish a fuel or electrical fire with water.

Fumes

Certain fumes are highly toxic and can quickly cause unconsciousness and even death if inhaled to any extent. Petrol (gasoline) vapour comes into this category, as do the vapours from certain solvents such as trichloroethylene. Any draining or pouring of such volatile fluids should be done in a well ventilated area.

When using cleaning fluids and solvents, read the instructions carefully. Never use materials from unmarked containers — they may give off poisonous vapours.

Never run the engine of a motor vehicle in an enclosed space such as a garage. Exhaust fumes contain carbon monoxide which is extremely poisonous; if you need to run the engine, always do so in the open air or at least have the rear of the vehicle outside the workplace.

If you are fortunate enough to have the use of an inspection pit, never drain or pour petrol, and never run the engine, while the vehicle is standing over it; the fumes, being heavier than air, will concentrate in the pit with possibly lethal results.

The battery

Never cause a spark, or allow a naked light, near the vehicle's battery. It will normally be giving off a certain amount of hydrogen gas, which is highly explosive.

Always disconnect the battery earth (ground) terminal before working on the fuel or electrical systems.

If possible, loosen the filler plugs or cover when charging the battery from an external source. Do not charge at an excessive rate or the battery may burst.

Take care when topping up and when carrying the battery. The acid electrolyte, even when diluted, is very corrosive and should not be allowed to contact the eyes or skin.

If you ever need to prepare electrolyte yourself, always add the acid slowly to the water, and never the other way round. Protect against splashes by wearing rubber gloves and goggles.

Mains electricity

When using an electric power tool, inspection light etc, which works from the mains, always ensure that the appliance is correctly connected to its plug and that, where necessary, it is properly earthed (grounded). Do not use such appliances in damp conditions and, again, beware of creating a spark or applying excessive heat in the vicinity of fuel or fuel vapour.

Ignition HT voltage

A severe electric shock can result from touching certain parts of the ignition system, such as the HT leads, when the engine is running or being cranked, particularly if components are damp or the insulation is defective. Where an electronic ignition system is fitted, the HT voltage is much higher and could prove fatal.

Routine maintenance

Maintenance is essential both for safety and for obtaining the best in terms of performance and economy from your vehicle. Over the years, the need for periodic lubrication – oiling, greasing, and so on – has been drastically reduced, and this has led some owners to think that the various components either no longer exist or will last forever. This is a serious delusion. It follows, therefore, that the largest initial element of maintenance is visual examination.

The following routine maintenance summary is based on the manufacturer's recommendation, but is supplemented by certain checks which we think will add up to improved reliability and an increase of component life. For further information concerning service checks and procedures, refer to the Chapter concerned.

Every 250 miles/400 km, weekly, or before a long journey

Engine
Check the engine oil level with the car standing on level ground and, if necessary, top up to the upper mark on the dipstick (photos).

Cooling system
Check the coolant level in the radiator or expansion tank if fitted.

The level should be within 5 cm (2 in) of the filler orifice. Check for leaks if the level is low (photo).

Brakes
Check the reservoir fluid level. If it requires topping up use an approved fluid and examine the brake pipes and hoses for fluid leaks (photo), referring to Chapter 7.
Check the effectiveness of the brakes including the handbrake.

Steering and suspension
Check the tyre pressures, including the spare, and adjust them as necessary.
Examine the tyres for wear and damage (Chapter 7).
Check the steering for smooth and accurate response.

Electrical system
Check battery electrolyte level and top up with purified water if necessary (photo) referring to Chapter 10.
Check the operation of all the lights, the wipers (wet the screen first), the horns, instruments and gauges.
Check the windscreen washer reservoir fluid level and top up as required (photo).

Check the engine oil level

Check the engine coolant level

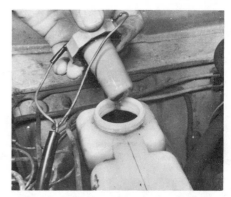
Check the brake system hydraulic fluid

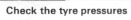
Check the tyre pressures

Top up the battery electrolyte level (but only if necessary)

Check the windscreen washer fluid level in the reservoir

Renew the engine oil

**Steering tie-rod outer balljoint with
grease nipple (earlier models)**

**Renew the engine oil filter – remove
using a clamp wrench as shown if
necessary**

Every 5000 miles/7500 km, or six months

In addition to the work listed for the weekly servicing

Engine

Drain the engine oil when hot. If this is the first 5000 miles/7500 km servicing, renew the oil filter cartridge (refer to Chapter 1) and refill with new oil (photo).
Clean and adjust the spark plugs (Chapter 4).
Check, clean and adjust the contact breaker points (Chapter 4).
Wipe clean the distributor cap, coil and HT leads.
Examine for oil, coolant or fuel leaks.
Check the exhaust system for damage and security (Chapter 3).

Steering, suspension and driveshafts

Inspect all rubber gaiters for leaks, damage and deterioration.
On earlier models, lubricate the steering tie-rod outer balljoint on each side (photo).

Brakes

Inspect the disc pads and drum linings for excessive wear (see Chapter 8).

Every 10 000 miles/15 000 km, or annually

In addition to the work listed for the six-monthly servicing

Engine

Renew the oil filter cartridge on draining the engine oil (photo).
Renew the spark plugs and contact breaker points as given in Chapter 4.
Lubricate the distributor.
Check and adjust the ignition timing (Chapter 4).
Check and adjust the carburettor idle setting (Chapter 3).
Check and adjust the valve clearances as given in Chapter 1.
Check and adjust the fanbelt.
Where an oil bath air filter is fitted, remove the top cover, extract the element and wash it clean in petrol, allow it to dry and soak it in clean engine oil. Also clean out the container and then refill this with engine oil so that it comes up to the level marking. This requires approximately 0.44 pint (250 cc) of oil.
Refit the cover.
With the normal paper element type air filter, change the filter if the vehicle is used in dusty conditions.
Check all nuts and bolts for tightness, but don't exceed torque loads where these are specified.

Electrical

Clean the battery, its stowage and the battery terminals.

Cooling system

Check the radiator, heater and carburettor hoses for deterioration and tightness of their clips.

Brakes

Check the clearance of the foot pedal when the brakes are applied. Check the hydraulic pipes and hoses of the system for signs of leakage and/or severe corrosion. See Chapter 8 for details.

Suspension and steering

Inspect all the joints for excessive play and the bushes for wear.
Check the shock absorber struts for security and fluid leaks.
Check the steering rack for security.
Inspect the condition of the steering column flexible coupling.

Clutch

Check and adjust the clutch cable. On models with a hydraulically actuated clutch, check the hydraulic lines for condition. Check clutch adjustment (Chapter 5).

Lights

Check and if necessary adjust the headlight beam alignment as given in Chapter 10.

Bodywork

Lubricate all door locks and hinges including the bonnet and boot.
Check the seat belts for security and wear.

Every 20 000 miles/30 000 km, or two years

In addition to the work listed for the annual servicing

Engine

Drain and flush the cooling system, and refill with fresh antifreeze mixture, referring to Chapter 2 for details.
Change the air cleaner filter (Chapter 3).
Clean the fuel pump and filter (Chapter 3).

Brakes

Clean out the rear brakes, removing all dust, but take care not to inhale it. Whilst the drums are removed, clean and regrease the rear wheel hub bearings prior to refitting the drum/hub units.

Front wheel hubs

Have your front wheel hub bearings cleaned and regreased by a Peugeot dealer. Special tools are required. See Chapter 7, Section 4.

Every 30 000 miles/45 000 km or three years

In addition to the work listed for the annual or two-yearly servicing, as applicable

Brakes

Drain and renew the hydraulic fluid.

Fault diagnosis

Introduction

The vehicle owner who does his or her own maintenance according to the recommended schedules should not have to use this section of the manual very often. Modern component reliability is such that, provided those items subject to wear or deterioration are inspected or renewed at the specified intervals, sudden failure is comparatively rare. Faults do not usually just happen as a result of sudden failure, but develop over a period of time. Major mechanical failures in particular are usually preceded by characteristic symptoms over hundreds or even thousands of miles. Those components which do occasionally fail without warning are often small and easily carried in the vehicle.

With any fault finding, the first step is to decide where to begin investigations. Sometimes this is obvious, but on other occasions a little detective work will be necessary. The owner who makes half a dozen haphazard adjustments or replacements may be successful in curing a fault (or its symptoms), but he will be none the wiser if the fault recurs and he may well have spent more time and money than was necessary. A calm and logical approach will be found to be more satisfactory in the long run. Always take into account any warning signs or abnormalities that may have been noticed in the period preceding the fault – power loss, high or low gauge readings, unusual noises or smells, etc – and remember that failure of components such as fuses or spark plugs may only be pointers to some underlying fault.

The pages which follow here are intended to help in cases of failure to start or breakdown on the road. There is also a Fault Diagnosis Section at the end of each Chapter which should be consulted if the preliminary checks prove unfruitful. Whatever the fault, certain basic principles apply. These are as follows:

Verify the fault. This is simply a matter of being sure that you know what the symptoms are before starting work. This is particularly important if you are investigating a fault for someone else who may not have described it very accurately.

Don't overlook the obvious. For example, if the vehicle won't start, is there petrol in the tank? (Don't take anyone else's word on this particular point, and don't trust the fuel gauge either!) If an electrical fault is indicated, look for loose or broken wires before digging out the test gear.

Cure the disease, not the symptom. Substituting a flat battery with a fully charged one will get you off the hard shoulder, but if the underlying cause is not attended to, the new battery will go the same way. Similarly, changing oil-fouled spark plugs for a new set will get you moving again, but remember that the reason for the fouling (if it wasn't simply an incorrect grade of plug) will have to be established and corrected.

Don't take anything for granted. Particularly, don't forget that a 'new' component may itself be defective (especially if it's been rattling round in the boot for months), and don't leave components out of a fault diagnosis sequence just because they are new or recently fitted. When you do finally diagnose a difficult fault, you'll probably realise that all the evidence was there from the start.

Electrical faults

Electrical faults can be more puzzling than straightforward mechanical failures, but they are no less susceptible to logical analysis if the basic principles of operation are understood. Vehicle electrical wiring exists in extremely unfavourable conditions – heat, vibration and chemical attack – and the first things to look for are loose or corroded connections and broken or chafed wires, especially where the wires pass through holes in the bodywork or are subject to vibration.

All metal-bodied vehicles in current production have one pole of the battery 'earthed', ie connected to the vehicle bodywork, and in nearly all modern vehicles it is the negative (–) terminal. The various electrical components – motors, bulb holders etc – are also connected to earth, either by means of a lead or directly by their mountings. Electric current flows through the component and then back to the battery via the bodywork. If the component mounting is loose or corroded, or if a good path back to the battery is not available, the circuit will be incomplete and malfunction will result. The engine and/or gearbox are also earthed by means of flexible metal straps to the body or subframe; if these straps are loose or missing, starter motor, generator and ignition trouble may result.

Assuming the earth return to be satisfactory, electrical faults will be due either to component malfunction or to defects in the current supply. Individual components are dealt with in Chapter 10. If supply wires are broken or cracked internally this results in an open-circuit, and the easiest way to check for this is to bypass the suspect wire temporarily with a length of wire having a crocodile clip or suitable connector at each end. Alternatively, a 12V test lamp can be used to verify the presence of supply voltage at various points along the wire and the break can be thus isolated.

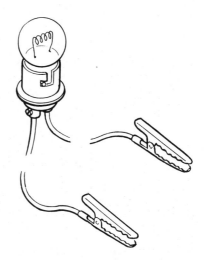

A simple test lamp is useful for tracing electrical faults

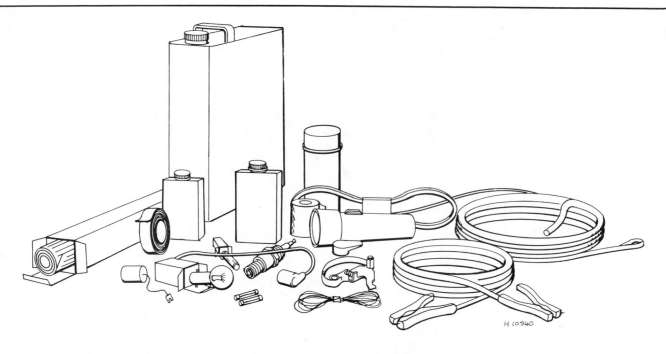

Carrying a few spares can save you a long walk!

If a bare portion of a live wire touches the bodywork or other earthed metal part, the electricity will take the low-resistance path thus formed back to the battery: this is known as a short-circuit. Hopefully a short-circuit will blow a fuse, but otherwise it may cause burning of the insulation (and possibly further short-circuits) or even a fire. This is why it is inadvisable to bypass persistently blowing fuses with silver foil or wire.

Spares and tool kit

Most vehicles are supplied only with sufficient tools for wheel changing; the *Maintenance and minor repair* tool kit detailed in *Tools and working facilities,* with the addition of a hammer, is probably sufficient for those repairs that most motorists would consider attempting at the roadside. In addition a few items which can be fitted without too much trouble in the event of a breakdown should be carried. Experience and available space will modify the list below, but the following may save having to call on professional assistance:

Spark plugs, clean and correctly gapped
HT lead and plug cap – long enough to reach the plug furthest from the distributor
Distributor rotor, condenser and contact breaker points
Drivebelt(s) – emergency type may suffice
Spare fuses
Set of principal light bulbs
Tin of radiator sealer and hose bandage
Exhaust bandage
Roll of insulating tape
Length of soft iron wire
Length of electrical flex
Torch or inspection lamp (can double as test lamp)
Battery jump leads
Tow-rope
Ignition waterproofing aerosol
Litre of engine oil
Sealed can of hydraulic fluid
Emergency windscreen
'Jubilee' clips
Tube of filler paste

If spare fuel is carried, a can designed for the purpose should be used to minimise risks of leakage and collision damage. A first aid kit and a warning triangle, whilst not at present compulsory in the UK, are obviously sensible items to carry in addition to the above.

When touring abroad it may be advisable to carry additional spares which, even if you cannot fit them yourself, could save having to wait while parts are obtained. The items below may be worth considering:

Clutch and throttle cables
Cylinder head gasket
Dynamo or alternator brushes
Fuel pump repair kit
Tyre valve core

One of the motoring organisations will be able to advise on availability of fuel etc in foreign countries.

Engine will not start

Engine fails to turn when starter operated
Flat battery (recharge, use jump leads, or push start)
Battery terminals loose or corroded
Battery earth to body defective

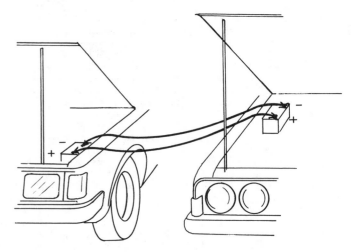

Correct way to connect jump leads. Do not allow car bodies to touch!

Engine earth strap loose or broken
Starter motor (or solenoid) wiring loose or broken
Ignition/starter switch faulty
Major mechanical failure (seizure)
Starter or solenoid internal fault (see Chapter 10)

Starter motor turns engine slowly
Partially discharged battery (recharge, use jump leads, or push start)
Battery terminals loose or corroded
Battery earth to body defective
Engine earth strap loose
Starter motor (or solenoid) wiring loose
Starter motor internal fault (see Chapter 10)

Starter motor spins without turning engine
Flat battery
Starter motor pinion sticking on sleeve
Flywheel gear teeth damaged or worn
Starter motor mounting bolts loose

Engine turns normally but fails to start
Damp or dirty HT leads and distributor cap (crank engine and check for spark)
Dirty or incorrectly gapped distributor points (if applicable)
No fuel in tank (check for delivery at carburettor)
Excessive choke (hot engine) or insufficient choke (cold engine)
Fouled or incorrectly gapped spark plugs (remove, clean and regap)
Other ignition system fault (see Chapter 4)
Other fuel system fault (see Chapter 3)
Poor compression (see Chapter 1)
Major mechanical failure (eg camshaft drive)

Engine fires but will not run
Insufficient choke (cold engine)
Air leaks at carburettor or inlet manifold
Fuel starvation (see Chapter 3)

Engine cuts out and will not restart

Engine cuts out suddenly – ignition fault
Loose or disconnected LT wires
Wet HT leads or distributor cap (after traversing water splash)
Coil or condenser failure (check for spark)
Other ignition fault (see Chapter 4)

Engine misfires before cutting out – fuel fault
Fuel tank empty
Fuel pump defective or filter blocked (check for delivery)
Fuel tank filler vent blocked (suction will be evident on releasing cap)
Carburettor needle valve sticking
Carburettor jets blocked (fuel contaminated)
Other fuel system fault (see Chapter 3)

Engine cuts out – other causes
Serious overheating
Major mechanical failure (eg camshaft drive)

Engine overheats

Ignition (no-charge) warning light illuminated
Slack or broken drivebelt – retension or renew (Chapter 2)

Ignition warning light not illuminated
Coolant loss due to internal or external leakage (see Chapter 2)
Thermostat defective
Low oil level
Brakes binding
Radiator clogged externally or internally

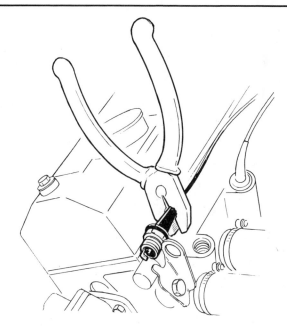

Crank engine and check for spark. Note use of insulated tool to hold plug lead

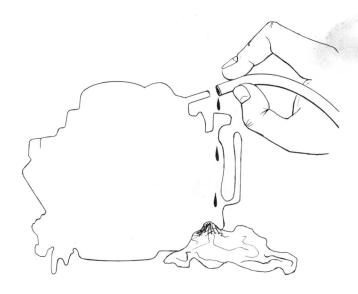

Remove pipe from carburettor and check for fuel delivery

Engine waterways clogged
Ignition timing incorrect or automatic advance malfunctioning
Mixture too weak

Note: *Do not add cold water to an overheated engine or damage may result*

Low engine oil pressure

Gauge reads low or warning light illuminated with engine running
Oil level low or incorrect grade
Defective gauge or sender unit

Wire to sender unit earthed
Engine overheating
Oil filter clogged or bypass valve defective
Oil pressure relief valve defective
Oil pick-up strainer clogged
Oil pump worn or mountings loose
Worn main or big-end bearings

Note: *Low oil pressure in a high-mileage engine at tickover is not necessarily a cause for concern. Sudden pressure loss at speed is far more significant. In any event, check the gauge or warning light sender before condemning the engine.*

Engine noises

Pre-ignition (pinking) on acceleration

Incorrect grade of fuel
Ignition timing incorrect
Distributor faulty or worn
Worn or maladjusted carburettor
Excessive carbon build-up in engine

Whistling or wheezing noises

Leaking vacuum hose
Leaking carburettor or manifold gasket
Blowing head gasket

Tapping or rattling

Incorrect valve clearances
Worn valve gear
Worn timing chain or belt
Broken piston ring (ticking noise)

Knocking or thumping

Unintentional mechanical contact (eg fan blades)
Worn fanbelt
Peripheral component fault (generator, water pump etc)
Worn big-end bearings (regular heavy knocking, perhaps less under load)
Worn main bearings (rumbling and knocking, perhaps worsening under load)
Piston slap (most noticeable when cold)

Chapter 1 Engine

Contents

Specifications

General

Engine type	Four cylinder, in line, ohc, water cooled, transverse mounting
Engine type reference:	
Early models:	
XL3	304 Saloon and Estate
XL3S	304 Saloon S, Convertible and Coupe models
Later models:	
XK5	GL Estate
XL5	GL Saloon, SL Estate
XL5S	SLS Saloon
Bore:	
XL3 models	76.0 mm (2.99 in)
XK5 models	78.0 mm (3.071 in)
XL5 models and XL5S models	78.0 mm (3.071 in)
Stroke:	
XL3 models	71.0 mm (2.80 in)
XK5 models	59.0 mm (2.32 in)
XL5 and XL5S models	67.5 mm (2.657 in)
Cubic capacity:	
XL3 models	1288 cc
XK5 models	1127 cc
XL5 models	1290 cc
Compression ratio (all models)	8.8 : 1
Location of number 1 cylinder	At clutch end of block
Firing order	1-3-4-2

XL3 and XL3S engines

Engine specifications known to be different from the XL5/XK series engines

Valve clearances (cold):	
Inlet	0.10 mm (0.004 in)
Exhaust	0.25 mm (0.009 in)
Liner protrusion	0.190 to 0.260 mm (0.007 to 0.010 in)
Liner protrusion – all four ideal	0.210 mm (0.008 in)
Liner gaskets available:	
Blue code	0.065 mm (0.0025 in)
White code	0.085 mm (0.0033 in)
Red code	0.102 mm (0.0040 in)
Yellow code	0.130 mm (0.0051 in)
Liners parallel to within 0.04 mm (0.0015 in)	Block to top face
Crankshaft endfloat (maximum)	0.07 to 0.23 mm (0.002 to 0.009 in)
Crankshaft thrust washer thicknesses available	2.30 mm (0.090 in) 2.40 mm (0.094 in) 2.45 (0.096 in) 2.50 mm (0.098 in)
Drive pinion endfloat	0.25 to 0.40 mm (0.0098 to 0.0157 in)
Drive pinion thrust washers – available thicknesses	0.07 mm (0.002 in) 0.15 mm (0.005 in) 0.20 mm (0.007 in) 0.25 mm (0.009 in) 0.50 mm (0.019 in)
Oil pump inner/outer rotor thickness	26.077 to 26.059 mm (1.026 to 1.025 in)

XK5, XL5 and XL5S engines

Cylinder head

Type	Pressure die-cast aluminium alloy, bi-spherical combustion chambers, offset valves, taper seats for spark plugs and five bearings for camshaft
Camshaft bearing diameters:	
1 (clutch end)	40.1 to 40.139 mm (1.5787 to 1.5803 in)
2	40.5 to 40.539 mm (1.5945 to 1.5960 in)
3	40.9 to 40.939 mm (1.6102 to 1.6118 in)
4	41.3 to 41.339 mm (1.6260 to 1.6276 in)
5 (timing end)	41.7 to 41.739 mm (1.6417 to 1.6433 in)
Maximum distortion or out-of-flat on joint face	0.05 mm (0.002 in)

Valves

Head diameter:	
Inlet	39.5 mm (1.5551 in)
Exhaust	32.5 mm (1.2795 in)
Seat angle:	
Inlet	120° to 120° 25'
Exhaust	90° to 90° 25'
Stem diameter:	
Inlet:	
Bottom	7.97 to 7.98 mm (0.3138 to 0.3142 in)
Top	7.98 to 7.99 mm (0.3142 to 0.3146 in)
Exhaust:	
XL5 – Bottom	7.95 to 7.96 mm (0.3130 to 0.3134 in)
XL5 – Top	7.97 to 7.98 mm (0.3138 to 0.3142 in)
Valve seat width:	
Inlet	2.3 mm (0.0906 in)
Exhaust	2.8 mm (0.1102 in)

Valve springs

Type	Single coil spring
Free length (approx):	
XK5 engine	46.2 mm (1.818 in)
XL5 and XL5S engines	47.2 mm (1.858 in)
Height:	
Valve open (XK5 engine)	30.0 at 77 kg load (1.18 in at 169.7 lbs load)
Valve open (XK5 and XL5S engine)	32.3 mm at 54.9 to 57.9 kg load (1.2678 in at 121.0 to 127.6 lbs load)
Valve closed (XK5 engine)	41 mm at 26kg load (1.61 in at 57.3 lbs load)
Valve closed (XL5 and XL5S engine)	40.0 mm at 23.8 to 27.4 kg load (1.5748 in) at 52.5 to 60.4 lbs load)
Fitting direction:	
XK5	Immaterial
XL5 and XL5S	Joined spiral towards head
Valve rocker adjustment (engine cold):	
Inlet	0.10 mm (0.0039 in)
Exhaust	0.25 mm (0.0098 in)

Camshaft

Camshaft drive	Chain and sprockets
Camshaft bearings	5, plain, unlined, in cylinder head
Endfloat	0.04 to 0.15 mm (0.001 to 0.005 in)
Side-play	0.05 to 0.11 mm (0.002 to 0.004 in)
Maximum outer bearing ovality allowable	0.02 mm (0.0007 in)
Valve opening:	
XK5 engine	6.235 mm (0.249 in)
XL5 and XL5 engine	4.972 mm (0.194 in)

Cylinder block

Type and material	Cylinder block integral with top half of crankcase, pressure die-cast in aluminium alloy with cast iron bearing blocks for crankshaft

Liners

Length, overall	133 mm (5.236 in)
Identification	1 to 4 lines on upper edge
Bore:	
1 line	78.0 to 78.01 mm (3.0709 to 3.0713 in)
2 lines	78.01 to 78.02 mm (3.0713 to 3.0717 in)
3 lines	78.02 to 78.03 mm (3.0717 to 3.0720 in)
4 lines	78.03 to 78.04 mm (3.0720 to 3.0724 in)
Liner protrusion on assembly:	
Relative to cylinder block joint face	0.14 to 0.21 mm with 0.21 mm as ideal (0.005 to 0.0083 in with 0.008 in as ideal)
Relative to adjacent liner(s)	0.04 mm (0.0016 in) max
Maximum out-of-squareness	0.02 mm (0.0008 in)
Liner gasket thicknesses:	
Blue	0.087 mm (0.0034 in)
White	0.102 mm (0.0040 in)
Red	0.122 mm (0.0048 in)
Yellow	0.147 mm (0.0058 in)

Pistons

Type	Aluminium alloy with two compression and one oil control ring. Gudgeon pin free to rotate in piston – press fit in connecting rod.
Identification	Letter A, B, C or D and number 1, 2 or 3 on piston crown
Diameter:	
A	77.914 to 77.924 mm (3.0674 to 3.0678 in)
B	77.924 to 77.934 mm (3.0678 to 3.0682 in)
C	77.934 to 77.944 mm (3.0682 to 3.0686 in)
D	77.944 to 77.964 mm (3.0686 to 3.0694 in)

Note: A grade A diameter piston must be used in a liner with 1 line marked, grade B in a liner with 2 lines and so on

Gudgeon pin bore diameter:	
Piston marking 1 pin mark blue	20.515 to 20.512 mm (0.8076 to 0.8075 in)
Piston marking 2 pin mark white	20.512 to 20.509 mm (0.8075 to 0.8074 in)
Piston marking 3 pin mark red	20.509 to 20.506 mm (0.8074 to 0.8073 in)
Piston ring thicknesses:	
Upper compression	1.75 mm (0.0688 in)
Lower compression	2.0 mm (0.0787 in)
Oil scraper	4.011 mm (0.1579 in)
Gudgeon pin:	
Length	68 mm (2.6772 in)
Diameter grades:	
Blue	20.500 to 20.497 mm (0.8071 to 0.8070 in)
White	20.497 to 20.494 mm (0.8070 to 0.8069 in)
Red	20.494 to 20.491 mm (0.8069 to 0.8067 in)

Note: *A blue grade pin must be used in a piston marked 1, white grade in 2 and red grade in 3*

Connecting rods

Type	H section, steel forging with no bush fitted in small end
Length between centres	132.7 mm (5.2244 in)
Big-end bearing thickness:	
Standard	1.814 to 1.820 mm (0.0714 to 0.0716 in)
Overhaul 0.30 mm (0.0118 in)	1.964 to 1.970 mm (0.0773 to 0.0775 in)
Big-end bearing diameter:	
Standard	44.991 to 44.980 mm (1.7712 to 1.7708 in)
Overhaul 0.30 mm (0.0118 in)	44.691 to 44.680 mm (1.7594 to 1.7590 in)

Small-end bearing diameter	20.465 to 20.478 mm (0.8057 to 0.8062 in)
Maximum permissible weight difference in set of 4 connecting rods ...	3g (0.1058 oz)

Crankshaft and main bearings

Number of bearings	5
Main journal diameter:	
New	53.027 to 53.046 mm (2.0877 to 2.0884 in)
Regrind 0.30 mm (0.0118 in)	52.727 to 52.746 mm (2.0759 to 2.0766 in)
Crankpin diameter:	
New	44.991 to 44.980 mm (1.7713 to 1.7709 in)
Regrind 0.30 mm (0.0118 in)	44.691 to 44.680 mm (1.7595 to 1.7591 in)
Crankpin throw:	
XK5	59.0 mm (2.322 in)
XL5 and XL5S	67.5 mm (2.657 in)
Crankpins and journals – maximum allowable ovality	0.007 mm (0.00027 in)
Bearing to journal tolerance	0.012 to 0.062 mm (0.0004 to 0.002 in)
Crankpin to con-rods tolerance	0.024 to 0.062 mm (0.0009 to 0.002 in)
Crankshaft endfloat	0.07 to 0.27 mm (0.0028 to 0.0106 in)
Thrust washers:	
Material:	
Series 1 engines	Steel backed, tin/aluminium/lead alloy faced
Series 2 engines	Steel backed, aluminium/lead alloy faced
Number fitted:	
Series 1 engines	2, in cylinder block, No 2 bearing
Series 2 engines	2, in cylinder block, No 2 bearing, and 2 on No 2 bearing cap
Thicknesses available	2.30, 2.40. 2.45 and 2.50 mm (0.0906, 0.0949, 0.0965 and 0.0984 in)

Note: *Series 1 thrust washers can be fitted to Series 2 engines but the reverse is not permissible*

Main bearing thickness XK5, XL5 and XL5S engines – early models:	
New	1.876 to 1.882 mm (0.0738 to 0.0740 in)
Repair	2.176 to 2.182 mm (0.0856 to 0.0859 in)
XK5, XL5 and XL5S engines	From serial number 4 031 501
Main bearing thickness:	
New	1.874 to 1.880 mm (0.0738 to 0.0740 in)
Repair	2.024 to 2.030 mm (0.0797 to 0.0799 in)
Bearing cap shells	Plain
Cylinder block shells	Grooved

Lubrication system

Type	Wet sump – pressure and spray
Oil filter:	
Type	Full flow, renewable cartridge
Make	Purflux LS 176 or DBA FC 114
System capacity	4.5 litres (7.9 pints)
Oil pump type	Eccentric bi-motor
Oil pressure	4 bars (58 lbf/in^2)
Low pressure warning	0.6 bars (8.7 lbf/in^2)
Oil pump inner and outer rotor thicknesses	29.977 to 29.959 mm (1.180 to 1.179 in)

Torque wrench settings
XL3 and XL3S engines

	lbf ft	kgf m
Crankshaft sludge trap plugs	29.0	4.0
Crankshaft sprocket and gear nut	65.0	9.0
Main bearing cap nuts	38.0	5.25
Big-end cap nuts	29.0	4.0
Oil passage cover bolts	9.0	1.25
Cylinder head bolts:		
Stage 1	29.0	4.0
Stage 11	40.0	5.5
Engine mountings:		
Upper left intermediate support (generator bracket)	14.5	2.0
Upper left intermediate support (head/block)	23.5	3.25
Wing valance reinforcement	14.5	2.0
Flexible block nut	23.5	3.25
Timing case bolts	11.0	1.5
Rocker cover bolts	5.5	0.75
Spark plugs	18.0	2.5
Clutch housing bolts	9.0	1.25
Clutch flywheel bolts	18.0	2.5
Clutch housing cover bolts	7.25	1.0
Pulley bolt on crankshaft	47.0	6.5

XL5, XL5S and XK5 engines

Cylinder head bolts:		
Stage 1	32.5	4.5
Stage 11	40.0	5.5
Camshaft sprocket bolts	14.5	2.0
Timing case bolts – refer to Section 38 of this Chapter		
Main bearing cap bolts	38.0	5.25
Big-end bearing cap nuts	27.1	3.75
Sump filter gauze bolts	4.3	0.6
Sump cover bolts	7.2	1.0
Sump drain plug	19.9	2.75
Crankshaft sprocket and gear bolt	79.6	11.0
Timing chain tensioner blade pivot	9.4	1.3
Timing chain tensioner bolts	4.3	0.6
Oil gallery cover plate bolts	9.0	1.25
Exhaust manifold nuts	10.8	1.5
Gear selection rod front bolt	13.0	1.75
Starter motor bolts	25.3	3.5
Crankshaft pulley bolt	65.1	9.0
Spark plugs	13.0	1.75
Engine to gearbox bolts	9.4	1.3
Clutch housing bolts	9.0	1.25
Water pump bolts	9.0	1.25
Fan belt jockey pulley nut	29.0	4.0
Adjuster/pulley support bolts	13.0	1.75

1 General description

The engine fitted to all Peugeot 304 models throughout its production period is a four cylinder, in-line, single overhead camshaft, water cooled power unit, mounted transversely and tilted forwards 20° to allow a lower body line. Early models were fitted with the 1288cc XL3 or XL5 series engine. Later models were fitted with the 1290cc XL5 or XL5S engine. One other engine type was fitted to the pre-1979 GL Estate model and this was the 1127cc XK5 engine.

Although certain modifications and/or alternative minor design variations have been made throughout the years, the basic engine design has remained the same on all models.

A manual gearbox is bolted to the bottom of the engine and uses a common oil system. The final drive to the roadwheels is via a differential unit on the front of the gearbox. Drive to the gearbox is via conventional clutch on the left-hand side of the engine, through an input pinion free-running on the crankshaft and located between the clutch and the engine block (photos).

All the major casings and housing are manufactured from pressure die-cast aluminium alloy. The cylinder block has removable wet cylinder liners which are centrifugally cast from special iron alloy and the main bearing caps are made of cast iron. The cylinder head is bi-spherical squish effect combustion chambers each having one exhaust valve, one inlet valve, and a taper seated spark plug location. Single springs are fitted to the valves which are operated by rockers each incorporating an adjustable screw and locknut for valve clearance setting.

The aluminium alloy pistons are fitted with three rings, two compression and one 'perfect circle' scraper. The pistons are assembled to the forged steel connecting rods by a gudgeon pin which is a force fit in the connecting rod small-end.

The crankshaft is carried in five main bearings and has a polygon taper (with three faces) at the left-hand end on which the clutch and flywheel assembly is mounted. The other end is keyed to drive the camshaft chain sprocket and also a shaft by which the oil pump, fuel pump and distributor are driven. A twin pulley is bolted to the clutch end of the crankshaft to drive the coolant pump/fan assembly and the alternator via separate drivebelts.

Because of the unusual layout of the engine and transmission systems, extra care and attention are necessary during maintenance and overhaul procedures which, in many instances, differ from more conventional systems.

Read through the various Sections concerned before tackling any job, to analyse the instructions and so that any snags or possible difficulties can be noted in advance. Because the sub-assembly castings are made from aluminium alloy, it is of utmost importance that, where specified, all fastenings are tightened to the correct torque and, in some instances, in the correct sequence.

You will probably be aware that accessibility can be very difficult, especially for the distributor, fuel pump and starter motor. This difficulty arises principally as a result of the move on right-hand drive cars of the brake master cylinder from the left to the right side of the bulkhead. Frequently, work involves the disturbance of unrelated components or assemblies. However, quite a lot of work can be done with the power unit installed, but this often requires the use of special tools.

XL5 engine models produced from serial numbers 304 DOI 4 181 349 and 304 TOI 4 181 230, (from August 1979)

The above mentioned models differ from the earlier engine types in that they have a three point engine mounting system instead of the four point system previously used. Some information was available concerning these differences at the time of writing, but the engine/transmission removal, refitting and associated details mainly

1.2a The XL5 engine and transmission assembly viewed from its front face showing:

1	Cylinder head and cam/rocker cover	4	Differential housing
2	Exhaust manifold	5	Clutch housing
3	Cooling fan	6	Engine mounting bracket – (left-hand side)

1.2b The XL5 engine and transmission assembly viewed from its rear
face showing positions of:

1   Transmission   4   Carburettor and inlet manifold
2   Timing case   5   Starter motor
3   Engine mounting bracket
    (right-hand side)

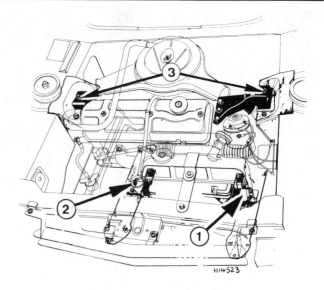

Fig. 1.1 The engine mounting locations (Sec 4)

1   Lower left-hand side   3   Upper left and right-hand
2   Lower right-hand side   sides

concern the four point mounting system more commonly used. In view
of this, when working on a three point mounting system model, ignore
the four point mounting, or at least the upper mounting references.
The other differences directly concerned with the three point mounting
engine models are as follows:

(a) *Front wing valance and front frame*
(b) *Gearbox cover*
(c) *Clutch type and housing*
(d) *Exhaust downpipe*
(e) *Radiator, mountings and filler cap (also cooling fan and
      thermostat)*
(f) *Air filter inlet hot air case on exhaust manifold (instead of
      attached to downpipe sleeve)*
(g) *Gearchange controls*
(h) *Electrical wiring harness*
(j) *Cylinder head*
(k) *Starter ring gear teeth*

In most instances, the items mentioned are not directly interchangeable between the three and four point mounting engine types,
but your Peugeot dealer will be able to advise you.

2   Major operations possible with engine installed

The following operations are possible with the engine in the car:

(a)* *Removal and refitting of the clutch unit*
(b)* *Removal and refitting of the input pinion and oil seals*
(c)* *Removal and refitting of the cylinder head*
(d) *Removal and refitting of the timing case*
(e) *Removal of the engine mountings*
*These tasks can only be achieved with the use of special Peugeot
tools.*

3   Major operations requiring engine removal

The engine must be removed for the following operations:

(a) *Removal and refitting of the transmission unit*
(b) *Removal and refitting of the crankshaft and main bearings*
(c) *Removal and refitting of the piston and connecting rod
      assemblies*
(d) *Renewal of the big-end bearings*

4   Engine and transmission unit – removal

1   The engine and transmission unit must be removed as a complete
assembly and cannot be separated until removed. The combined
weight of the two components is not great due to the extensive use of
aluminium alloy, but certain operations are awkward and care must be
taken not to damage adjacent components in the engine
compartment, especially during removal, as space is limited in which
to manoeuvre the assembly out. It therefore pays to have an assistant
on hand whenever possible.
2   To disconnect the driveshafts from the final drive, the
manufacturer recommends that the front suspension arm each side be
detached from the chassis pivot points. However, it was found that
with the engine hanging free on the hoist, the driveshafts could be
detached at the transmission end, without disturbing the front
suspension each side. A 1977 GL Estate was used for the exercise and
it might be necessary on other models to disconnect the suspension
arms although this is doubtful. It is worth trying to remove the engine
and transmission assembly before disturbing the suspension. If unsuc-
cessful, refer to Chapter 9 and detach the suspension arms and extract
the driveshafts each side from the differential housing.
3   Position the car with the engine under the lifting tackle location
and make sure that there is sufficient room around the car to work
comfortably. With a mobile hoist the engine assembly can obviously
be wheeled away after removal, but if the hoist location is fixed then
ensure that there is room for the car to be moved back after lifting the
engine out.
4   Chock the rear wheels and apply the handbrake.
5   Raise and support the bonnet. Mark the position of the hinge
brackets on the bonnet so that they can be reassembled in the same
position. Support the bonnet and remove the retaining bolts in the
hinge brackets and support stud. Lift the bonnet clear and remove it to
a safe place.
6   Disconnect and remove the battery as described in Chapter 10.
7   Remove the retaining screws and lift out the front grille.
8   Remove the two battery tray retaining nuts and lift out the tray
(photo).
9   Refer to Chapter 2 and drain the cooling system. Also drain the
engine oil and refit the plug (photo).
10 Refer to Chapter 2 and remove the radiator.
11 Refer to Chapter 3 and remove the air cleaner and air intake.
12 Disconnect the hoses from the engine such as the brake servo
hose on the manifold, heater hoses and so on. When disconnecting the
fuel feed hose, plug it temporarily to prevent fuel loss and dirt ingress.

4.8 Remove the battery tray

4.9 Sump drain plug

4.14 Earth lead to timing case connection

4.23 Lower engine mounting attachment to subframe

4.27 Remove each engine mounting nut from the wing valance mountings

13 Detach the HT leads from the spark plugs, remove the distributor cap and remove the assembly from the engine.

14 Take careful note of their positions and disconnect the following electrical connections:

    (a) *Coolant temperature sender*
    (b) *Oil pressure switch*
    (c) *Coil*
    (d) *Radiator temperature sender (fan switch)*
    (e) *Starter solenoid*
    (f) *Earth wire from top of timing case (photo)*
    (g) *Reversing light switch*

15 Don't disconnect the electrical wires on the alternator but remove the alternator, referring to Chapter 10 if necessary, and swing it to one side away from the engine. Similarly, leave the voltage regulator connections attached but unbolt it from the inside wall of the left-hand front wheel arch and swing it out of the engine to provide more room to move the engine when it is free.

16 Disconnect the throttle cable and the choke cable from the carburettor.

17 Unbolt and detach the fuel pump from its location at the rear of the engine on the right-hand side. You will find that access to the pump retaining bolts is improved by reaching through the aperture on the inner wing panel adjacent to the pump.

18 Note the position of the distributor and make adjacent alignment marks between its body and an adjoining component, then loosen off the distributor clamp screw and rotate the distributor so that its automatic advance/retard diaphragm hose nozzle will be clear of the brake master cylinder when the engine is lifted out. The diaphragm markings made enable the distributor to be repositoned for correct timing on reassembly.

19 Disconnect the clutch control cable or on earlier models unbolt the clutch slave cylinder (leaving the hydraulic line attached) and move the cylinder out of the way.

20 Disconnect the gearchange linkage connection balljoints by prising them free at the balljoints.

21 Jack up the front of the car and support it on axle stands positioned under the front subframe assembly; alternatively put ramps under the front wheels.

22 Remove the front section of the exhaust pipe from the engine assembly.

23 Remove the lower engine mounting nut from each side on the inner subframe (photo).

24 Now working inside the car, slide the seat on one side fully forward. Then reach underneath at the rear and unscrew the seat retaining nuts each side (inside each runner) and lift out the seat.

25 Fold back the carpet each side of the transmission tunnel cover and remove the cover retaining screw each side. Lift the cover clear and over the gear lever.

26 Unbolt and detach the gear selector lever mechanism from the floor mounting, lift it and pull the selector rod and lever assembly rearwards as far as is possible. This prevents the selector rod linkage balljoints from fouling the engine/ transmission when lifting them clear.

27 Unscrew and detach the engine mounting nut to the inner wing panel on each side (photo).

28 Connect the lifting sling to the two lugs on the cylinder head, but before lifting make a check to ensure that all of the engine and associated fittings are detached. Where possible fold wires, cables and hoses back out of the way.

29 Lift the engine enough to clear the bottom mounting and at the same time pull it forwards so as to keep the rear edge of the transmission case clear of the steering mechanism.

30 Loosen the locknut, remove the retaining screw and pull the speedometer drive cable out of its location in the transmission unit.

31 Move one of the front wheels on to full steering lock to retract its driveshaft. Then by gently lifting and manoeuvring the engine forward and over to the opposite side, disconnect that shaft from the final

4.31 Lifting the engine out of the car

4.32 Support driveshafts with suspended
wire (arrowed) if car is to be moved

drive. This needs care as there is very little room in which to move the
assembly and it is easy to damage something if it is allowed to swing
out of control. With care the shaft can be extracted and then the other
driveshaft can be withdrawn in a similar manner. Rest the two shafts
on the subframe and carefully lift the engine unit out of the car (photo).
You may find that you need to remove the engine oil filter to allow
extra room for manoeuvering the engine clear.

32 Once the engine/transmission unit is clear wheel the car back if
necessary so that the engine can be lowered, but before moving the
vehicle, support the driveshaft each side with wire as shown (photo).

33 Once the engine is clear of the car it can be lowered and removed
to the area where it can be cleaned down and dismantled.

7 Don't throw away the old gaskets as it sometimes happens that an
immediate replacement is not available and the old gasket is then
useful as a template. Hang up the old gaskets as they are removed on
a suitable hook or nail.

8 If the engine and transmission units are to be separated you will
have to first remove the clutch assembly (see Chapter 5) and then the
timing case.

9 A supply of wooden blocks of varying sizes will be useful in
supporting the assembly as it is being worked on.

10 Whenever possible refit nuts, bolts, and washers finger tight from
wherever they were removed as this helps avoid later loss or muddle.
If they cannot be refitted, lay them out in such a fashion that it is clear
from where they came. Make sketches or notes if you think you may
forget the position of washers etc.

---

5 Engine dismantling – general

1 A good size clean work area will be required, preferably on a
bench. Before moving the engine and transmission assembly to the
work area it should be cleaned to remove road dirt, oil and grease.

2 During the dismantling process care should be taken to avoid
contaminating the exposed internal parts with dirt. Although
everything will be cleaned separately before reassembly, road dirt or
grit can cause damage to parts during dismantling and could also
affect inspection and checks.

3 A good proprietary grease solvent will make the job of
engine/transmission cleaning much easier but if this is not available
use paraffin. With a solvent the usual procedure is to apply it to the
contaminated surfaces and, after a suitable soaking period has
elapsed, to wash it off with a jet of water. Where the grease or oil and
dirt mixture is encrusted the solvent should be worked in using a stiff
brush.

4 After rinsing off the solvent and dirt, wipe down the exterior of the
assembly and then, only when it is clean and dry, the dismantling
process can be started.

5 As the unit is stripped, the individual parts should be examined
before being washed in a bath of paraffin and wiped dry. The
examination need only be cursory at this stage but it is sometimes
helpful as the cleaning procedure might wash away useful evidence of
running conditions. Avoid immersing parts with internal oil passages,
such as the crankshaft and the timing case, in paraffin. To clean such
parts use a paraffin-damped rag and clean out the oilways with wire.
If an air supply is available the oilways can be blown through to clear
them.

6 The re-use of old gaskets or old oil seals is a false economy and
can lead to fuel, oil or coolant leaks, if nothing worse. To avoid the
possibility of such problems, always use new gaskets throughout.

---

6 Engine dismantling – ancillary items

1 Irrespective of whether you are going to dismantle the engine
completely and rebuild it, or are simply going to exchange it for a new
or reconditioned unit, the ancillary components will have to be
removed.

2 The only possible method of determining the exact condition of
the engine and assessing the extent of reconditioning required is to
dismantle it completely. If, having done this, it is decided that a
reconditioned short block is needed then the unit can be loosely
reassembled, but check that a replacement is available first.

3 Refer to the relevant Chapters, if necessary, and remove the
following components or assemblies:

(a) *Distributor (Chapter 4)*
(b) *Fuel pump and operating plunger (Chapter 3)*
(c) *Carburettor (Chapter 3)*
(d) *Inlet and exhaust manifolds (Chapter 3)*
(e) *Coolant pump and fan assembly (Chapter 2)*
(f) *Starter motor (Chapter 10)*
(g) *Coil, diagnostic socket and TDC sensor complete with con-
     necting harness, where applicable (Chapter 4)*
(h) *Coolant temperature sender (Chapter 2)*
(i) *Oil pressure sender*
(k) *Thermostat and housing (Chapter 2)*
(l) *Oil filter and dipstick tube*
(m) *Clutch assembly (Chapter 5)*

4 If the engine is to be exchanged, check what ancillary items are
included in the exchange unit. Make sure that the old engine is cleaned
before being exchanged.

7.3 Cylinder head removal (engine in car) –
remove items shown:

1	Battery leads	4	Cam/rocker cover
2	Drain cooling system and disconnect hoses	5	Engine mounting each side (upper only)
3	Remove air filter and ducting – detach carburettor controls	6	Alternator or dynamo

7 Cylinder head – removal with engine in position

1 When the cylinder head is being removed there is a risk of disturbing the wet liners in their locations. Because of this certain checks are necessary to confirm that the liners are correctly located. If it is found that they are not within permissible limits, new gaskets will have to be fitted between the liners and the cylinder block. *This job will entail removal of the engine/transmission unit from the car and the virtual complete dismantling of the unit on the bench.* It can be seen that removing the cylinder head on this engine, when installed, should only be undertaken if full facilities are available to remove and dismantle the engine – even though they may not be required. Alternatively, be prepared to have the car towed to your Peugeot agent if the liner gaskets have to be renewed.

2 First drain the cooling system, referring to Chapter 2 for details if necessary.

3 Disconnect the battery cables and remove the battery from the car. Remove the air cleaner and air intake, referring to Chapter 3 for details. Pull the ignition leads off the spark plugs, unclip the distributor cap, disconnect the HT lead from the coil and remove the cap and leads from the engine (photo).

4 Remove the retaining screws and lift clear the rocker cover.

5 Detach the carburettor/fuel pump supply pipe and also the coolant hoses to the carburettor and inlet manifold.

6 Disconnect the choke and accelerator cables from the carburettor.

7 Disconnect the heater hoses and coolant hoses from the cylinder head.

8 Detach the generator from its mountings but leaving its wires attached, lay it on top of the inner wing panel out of the way.

9 Remove the distributor, referring to Chapter 4 if necessary.

10 Detach the wires from the engine oil pressure switch and also the coolant temperature switch. Another lead to be detached is the earth lead to the cylinder head.

11 Unbolt and detach the exhaust downpipe from the manifold flange.

12 Before removing the upper engine mounting brackets each side you will need to support the engine/transmission assembly. To do this either position a suitable jack under the differential housing or position a couple of steel packing blocks (10 x 25 x 75 mm) between the gearcase and frame, and a wood block (220 x 40 x 15 mm) between the frame and the cylinder block.

13 Detach and remove the inlet manifold leaving the carburettor attached (unless this has to be removed), referring to Chapter 3.

Fig. 1.2 Packing block locations between gearbox and frame (1) (Sec 7)

Fig. 1.3 Wood block location between frame and cylinder block (Sec 7)

Fig. 1.4 Peugeot special tool number 80 140 used to retain the camshaft sprocket (Sec 7)

1 A new locking plate fitted before using	2 The pad of the tool bolted to the sprocket

Fig. 1.5 Retain cylinder head nuts in position with modelling clay where indicated (Sec 7)

14   Unscrew the exhaust manifold retaining nuts and withdraw the manifold.

15   On XL3 and XL3S series engines it is now necessary to remove the timing case, release the timing chain tension and remove the camshaft sprocket and chain. Refer to Section 8 for details.

16   On XL5, XL5S and XK5 series engines it is possible to remove the cylinder head leaving the timing case and chain in position. You will require the use of Peugeot special tool number 8.0140 with which to support and simultaneously withdraw the camshaft sprocket (with chain), away from the camshaft. This will enable the cylinder head to be removed. Should the special tool not be available you will have to remove the timing case and remove the camshaft sprocket and chain as described in Section 8. If using the special tool, proceed as given in the following paragraphs 17 to 20 inclusive.

17   Remove the earthing bolt in the top front hole in the timing case and remove the two bolts in the top rear holes.

18   Bend back the lips of the locking plate behind the three bolts retaining the camshaft timing sprocket. Turn the engine to get No 2 piston at the top of the compression stroke (No 3 cylinder on valve overlap, ie both valves open).

19   Put a piece of clean, fluff-free cloth in the timing case below the three sprocket securing bolts to avoid the danger of dropping something down the timing case. Restrain the sprocket from turning and undo the three bolts; remove the bolts and the old locking plate but don't disturb the sprocket.

20   Put a new locking plate on the pad of the sprocket retaining tool, (Peugeot part number 8.0140) and undo the thumbscrew in the tool. Put the tool over the wall of the timing case and, with the pad and locking plate against the sprocket, tighten the two bolts to hold the sprocket. Withdraw the piece of rag from the timing case and hand tighten the thumbscrew to hold the tool onto the timing case. Carefully slide the sprocket off the end of the camshaft.

21   Position a piece of modelling clay or similar compound under the front left-hand cylinder head nuts to keep them in position when the bolts are removed.

22   Following the tightening sequence in reverse, (see Section 33 paragraph 6), progressively loosen the 10 cylinder head bolts; as they are loosened, the rocker shaft assembly will lift under the influence of the valve springs. Remove the bolts and the rocket shaft assembly.

23   Remove the cylinder head. If it appears to be stuck insert two bars into cylinder head bolt holes, taking care not to damage the head, and rock it free of the block. Don't, on any account, hammer on the cylinder head as it can be damaged very easily. Fit temporary restraining straps made of strip material to the block to keep the cylinder liners in position, secure them with bolts and nuts in the cylinder head bolt holes.

24   Carefully cut and remove the upper, exposed portion of the timing case gasket level with the face of the cylinder block.

8   Timing case, chain and sprockets – removal

1   If the engine is removed from the vehicle, proceed from paragraph 3. If the engine is in position in the vehicle, first disconnect/remove the following items:

     (a)   Disconnect the battery, remove the battery and its tray
     (b)   Drain the engine oil
     (c)   Remove the air cleaner unit
     (d)   Remove the distributor (Chapter 4)
     (e)   Remove the fuel pump (Chapter 3)
     (f)   In earlier models remove the coil from the inner right-hand wing panel
     (g)   Remove the rocker cover

2   Before removing the right-hand upper engine mounting support bracket, position a suitable block spacer between the lower engine support and the gearbox. The spacer block dimensions need to be about 10 x 25 x 75 mm.

3   Unbolt and remove the upper mounting bracket.

4   The timing case lower retaining bolts can now be unscrewed and removed. As they are withdrawn note their sizes and positions and detach the earth lead (if the engine is still in position in vehicle). The timing case bolt sizes and locations are shown for the XL5, XL5S and XK5 engines.

5   Carefully remove the timing case. If it is stuck, gently break the joint by tapping with a soft-faced hammer, but don't use excessive force as the light alloy casting can be easily damaged. Remove the old gasket.

6   Clean off all traces of old gasket and any sealer, but don't use emery cloth or hard metallic scrapers. The mating surfaces must be free from all traces of scoring, burrs, impact dents and other damage. If the oil filter is not removed from the timing case it need not be renewed, unless of course it is due for renewal with an oil change. However, if it is removed a new one must be fitted on reassembly.

7   Before removing the timing chain it should be mentioned that if the cylinder head is not being removed, but the crankshaft is to be rotated after the chain is removed, there is a danger of a piston contacting the valve gear. The same applies if the camshaft is rotated after the chain is removed and any pistons are at the TDC position. To safeguard against this possibility, position the crankshaft as you would for retiming, that is with the sprocket timing mark on the horizontal. For the XL3 series engines this is to the right of centre whilst on the XK5 and XL5 series engines this is to the left of the centre. When the crankshaft is set in this position the pistons are all positioned at the half way point of travel within their cylinder bores.

8   Unscrew and remove the bolt from the timing end of the crankshaft. On XK5 and XL5 series engines, lock the crankshaft if necessary by inserting an 8 mm (0.315 in) dia rod in the hole just above the crankshaft and engaging the rod with the slot milled in the

8.8 Inserting crankshaft alignment rod (XK5 and XL5 engines) – with timing gear dismantled and engine removed

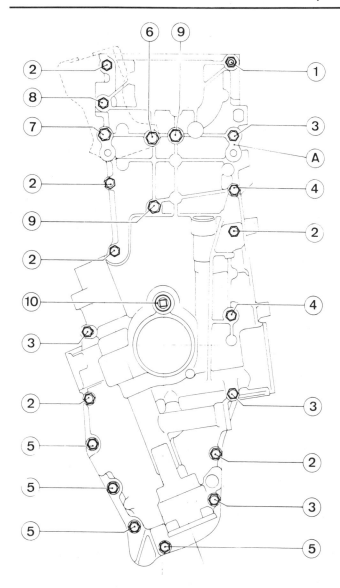

Fig. 1.6 The timing case securing bolts (XK5, XL5 and XL5S engines) giving the locations, sizes and tightening torque requirements (Sec 8)

1	Earth bolt
2	M7 100 x 51.5 bolts (6 off) with spring washers
3*	M7 100 x 80 bolts (4 off) with spring washers
4	M7 100 x 95 bolts (2 off) with spring washers
5	M7 100 x 25 bolts (4 off) with spring washers
6	M8 125 x 30 bolt with Blocfor washer
7	M8 125 x 85 bolt with Blocfor washer
8	M7 100 x 85 bolt with Blocfor washer
9	M8 125 x 30 bolts (2 off) with copper washers
10	TDC hole plug with 16 mm metallised plastic washer.

*Where boss thickness A is 57.5 mm thick use an M7 100 x 75 bolt at this point

Bolt torque wrench settings:	lbf ft	kgf m
Bolts 1, 2, 3, 4, 5 and 8	10.8	1.5
Bolts 6, 7 and 9	12.6	1.75
Plug 10	19.8	2.75

XL3 and XL3S engines

The timing cases on the XL3 and XL3S series engines are of similar design but the bolt sizes in some instances may differ, few details being available at the time of writing. Therefore note the bolt sizes and their locations as they are removed. The torque wrench setting for all bolts of these engine types is given as 11 lbf ft (1.5 kgf m)

Fig. 1.7 The seal plug bolt location on the XL3 engine timing chain tensioner. Also note the chain timing mark links (arrowed) are positioned opposite the respective sprocket reference marks (Sec 8)

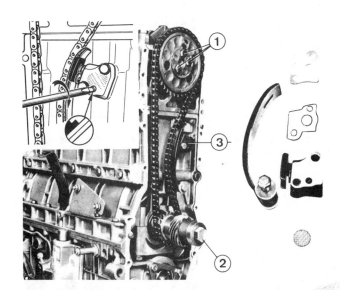

Fig. 1.8 Timing chain tensioner unit 3 of the XK5 and XL5/XL5S models. Inset shows tensioner release method (Sec 8)

web. (Pistons 2 and 3 are at TDC when the rod is engaged). Remove the locking rod (photo).

9   Unlock the chain tensioner to release the tension from the timing chain. On earlier models you will have to first remove the seal plug bolt and then insert a 3mm Allen key into the piston recess and turn it anti-clockwise to release the shoe loading on the chain. On later models the tensioner is released by inserting a screwdriver into the adjuster on the outer face and turning it clockwise as shown. The tensioner will be neutralised.

10   Undo the tensioner unit retaining bolts and remove the tensioner.

11 Undo the bolt at the bottom of the chain rubbing plate and remove the plate from the block (later models only).
12 Remove the fine mesh filter from the tensioner location on the block.
13 Remove the timing chain from the crankshaft and camshaft timing sprockets.
14 Slide the sprocket, wormwheel and spacers off the crankshaft, noting the order in which they were assembled and also the way round each was fitted.
15 Bend back the locktabs on the three bolts retaining the camshaft sprocket then remove the bolts, the lockplate and sprocket. The lockplate must be renewed when reassembling.

9 Cylinder head – removal with engine on bench

1   Support the engine with wooden blocks and then, referring to Section 33, progressively loosen the ten cylinder head bolts in the reverse sequence to that for tightening. As the bolts are undone the rocker assembly will lift off the head due to the pressure of the valve springs and cams. Remove the bolts and retrieve the nuts from the webs in the block.
2   Lift the rocker assembly off the cylinder head.
3   Remove the cylinder head from the block. If necessary insert a couple of rods in bolt holes in the head and rock the head off the block. Don't hammer the head to free it and don't insert a wedge such as a screwdriver to lever the head off – this will damage the joint faces.
4   Fit a restraining strap, or straps, to the block to keep the cylinder liners in position if it is not intended to proceed with further dismantling. The strap(s) should be bolted to the block utilising the cylinder head bolt holes and can be made up from any available strip material, requiring only bolt holes to be drilled, spaced to suit the holes in the block. Remove any burrs before fitting to avoid damaging the head joint face.

10 Clutch and housing – removal

1   The clutch can be removed with the engine installed in the car or with the engine/transmission on the bench. Refer to Chapter 5 for details of the procedure and special tools required, disregarding references to the engine being in the car if appropriate.

11 Engine and transmission – separation

1   With the timing mechanism and the clutch and housing removed, only the bolts in the front and rear joint flanges hold the engine and transmission together.
2   Position the assembly under a hoist, or the hoist over the assembly if possible, and progressively loosen the bolts in the two joint flanges. Take the weight on the hoist and remove the bolts. Lift the engine assembly off the transmission unit and lower it onto the workbench.

12 Pistons, connecting rods, and crankshaft – removal

1   The pistons, connecting rods and crankshaft can only be removed from the engine with the engine removed from the car and with the timing case, clutch, transmission and cylinder head removed from the engine.
2   Inspect the big-end assemblies and ensure that the connecting rods and caps are marked to identify their location and orientation. If necessary use a file or centre punch, applied lightly, to mark them.
3   Turn the crankshaft to position the pistons at top and bottom dead centres and, on the bottom dead centre assemblies, undo the nuts holding the bearing caps. Work on one assembly at a time and, after removing the nuts, remove the bearing cap and bearing shell. You may have to prise the cap and shell off, but be careful not to damage them as they may be fit for re-use. If you intend to remove the liners the liner and piston assembly can be removed together complete from the block after first removing the restrainer and rocking the liner to ease it out of the bottom joint. Alternatively, keep the liner held in position and, using a hammer shaft, push the piston and connecting rod up out

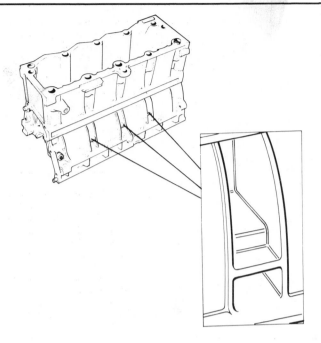

Fig. 1.9 The later cylinder blocks have the main bearing cap bolt holes sealed from serial number 3 928 630 and shorter bolts are fitted (Sec 12)

of the liner. Temporarily refit the bearing shell, bearing cap and nuts to the connecting rod, observing correct orientation. Watch out for the upper half bearing shell sticking to the crankshaft – if it does, remove it and replace it in the connecting rod to keep it safe.
4   Repeat the piston removal procedure on the remaining assemblies.
5   Note the piston crowns are marked to show which liner they fit and also which way round they fit. If necessary, make your own marks to be sure that you can refit everything in its original position. It is important to fit the piston correctly on reassembly as the gudgeon pin bore is slightly off centre.
6   Don't attempt to separate the piston from its connecting rod. Not only is it necessary to renew the piston is this is done but a heating process involving the use of a special jig is essential for reassembly. Your Peugeot agent should be consulted if you have to fit new pistons, gudgeon pins or connecting rods.
7   Note that the five caps for the crankshaft main bearings are numbered 1 to 5 on the timing side face. Undo the ten bolts retaining the caps. On models prior to serial number 3 928 630 (March 1977), the main bearing cap bolts are secured by nuts on the oil channel side. Retrieve these nuts as the bolts are removed. On engine from that serial number, the main bearing cap bolts on that side fit into blind holes and do not have nuts. This modification was to prevent oil leakage past the bolt threads.
8   Remove the main bearing caps, keeping the plain half bearing shells with their relative caps.
9   Lift the crankshaft out of the upper half bearings. These shells are grooved and they should be removed and stored with their relative lower shells and bearing caps. Remove the two split thrust washers from the No 2 bearing, noting that their grooved faces are towards the crankshaft web, mark them so that they can be reassembled correctly, but on the bearing face. Later models have two split thrust washers in addition in the bearing cap.

13 Piston rings – removal

1   To remove the piston rings, slide them carefully over the top of the piston, taking care not to scratch the aluminium alloy. Never slide them off the bottom of the piston skirt. It is very easy to break the iron piston rings if they are pulled off roughly so this operation should be

done with extreme caution. It is useful to employ three strips of thin metal or feeler gauges to act as guides to assist the rings to pass over the empty grooves and to prevent them from dropping in.

2   Lift one end of the piston ring to be removed out of its groove and insert the end of the feeler gauge under it.

3   Turn the feeler gauge slowly round the piston and as the ring comes out its groove apply slight upward pressure to that it rests in the land above. It can then be eased off the piston.

14 Camshaft – removal

1   If the engine is installed in the car the cylinder head will have to be removed before it is possible to remove the camshaft. If the engine is on the bench the timing case and mechanism will need removing and the top end will need dismantling as far as the removal of the rocker shaft assembly and, as the head will not be retained, temporary bolts should be fitted while the camshaft is removed. Alternatively the camshaft can be removed after the head has been removed from the engine.

2   With the rocker assembly and timing sprocket removed, undo the camshaft retaining plate bolt and remove the bolt and plate.

3   Carefully slide the camshaft out of its bearings in the cylinder head towards the timing end. Take special care not to damage the bearing surfaces with the sharp edges on the cam profiles.

15 Lubrication system – description

A pressure feed system of lubrication is fitted, with oil being circulated round the engine by a pump which draws oil from the sump below the transmission unit.

The high output rotary pump is located in the bottom of the timing case and it is driven by a shaft and skew gear off the crankshaft. Oil is drawn through a strainer in the sump and delivered to a filter cartridge mounted on the front of the timing case. A relief valve operates to prevent excessive pressure.

On leaving the cartridge filter the oil is ducted by a gallery to the crankshaft main bearings and by an external pipe to the transmission bearings. An internal duct conducts oil up to the camshaft and it is distributed to the camshaft bearings and rocker mechanism through the hollow rocker shaft. The big-end bearings are supplied with oil through drillings in the crankshaft.

After lubricating the bearing surfaces to which it is ducted the oil leaks into the engine interior where, as spray or mist, it lubricates the other bearing surfaces such as cylinder walls, small-ends, gears and so on. The oil then drains down into the sump to repeat the cycle.

A pressure switch located in the filter outlet duct will light the oil pressure warning light in the instrument panel if the pressure falls below 8.7 lbf/in^2 (0.6 bars) with the ignition switched on. In the event of the cartridge filter bcoming clogged a safety bypass valve located in the filter mounting will open to prevent oil starvation. Unfiltered oil is then supplied to the bearings.

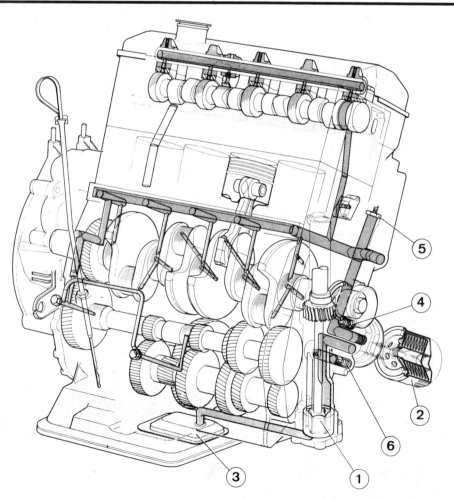

Fig. 1.10 The engine and transmission lubrication system (Sec 15)

1	Oil pump	3	Sump strainer screen	5	Oil pressure sender switch
2	Oil filter cartridge	4	Safety by-pass valve	6	Oil pressure relief valve

16 Oil filter – removal and refitting

1 A full-flow type oil filter is fitted to the front of the timing case on the right-hand side of the engine.
2 This is a renewable cartridge type filter which screws directly on to a threaded spigot in the timing case (photo).
3 Before unscrewing the oil filter cartridge, locate a suitable receptable underneath in which to catch any oil spillage. The best tool to undo the cartridge is a strap or chain spanner but a large hose clip (of the worm screw variety), or two small ones joined together, when tightened round the case will provide a good purchase by which to unscrew the filter.
4 Before fitting the new filter ensure that the securing thread is correct as two types have been used, being either 18 x 150 mm or $\frac{3}{4}$ in BSF.
5 Wipe the filter location on the timing case clean and lubricate the new cartridge seal with clean oil before fitting it to the cartridge. Fit the cartridge to its spigot and hand tighten only until the mating surfaces meet. Then give the cartridge a further $\frac{3}{4}$ turn to correctly tighten it.
6 When possible run the engine and check for leaks; then stop the engine and top up the oil to the full mark on the dipstick.

17 Cylinder head – dismantling, inspection and renovation

1 Having removed the cylinder head, place it onto a clean workbench or work area where it can be dismantled and examined. Remember that it is made of light alloy and must be treated carefully to avoid damage.
2 Remove each valve and spring assembly using a valve spring compressor. Extract the split collets from between the spring retaining cup washer and the valve stem.
3 Progressively release the tension of the compressor until it can be removed, the spring and retainer withdrawn, and the valve extracted from the guide. Remove the old seals from the guides.
4 As the valves are removed keep them in order by inserting them in a piece of cardboard having suitable holes punched in it, numbered 1 to 8. Keep the spring, retainer and split collets together with their original valve.
5 Wash the cylinder head clean in paraffin and carefully scrape away the carbon build-up in the combustion chambers and exhaust ports. Use a scraper which will not damage the surfaces to be cleaned and be especially careful with the cylinder head joint face. Dry the head thoroughly after cleaning.
6 Wash the valves, springs, retainers and collets in paraffin and scrape off all deposits on the valves. The heads can be cleaned with emery cloth but don't use this on the bearing surfaces or the stems. Wipe all the parts clean and dry after washing.
7 After cleaning the cylinder head examine it for cracks or damage. In particular inspect the valve seat areas for signs of hairline cracks, pitting or burning. Check the head mating surfaces for distortion and flatness using an accurate straight-edge and feeler gauges. The

maximum permissible distortion or out-of-flat is 0.05 mm (0.002 in). Minor bruises can be carefully blended out but retain the original flatness. Note that resurfacing of the cylinder head on the Peugeot 304 engine is strictly forbidden.
8 Minor surface wear and pitting of the valve seats can probably be rectified when the valves are reground. Serious wear, ridges or burnt areas should be shown to your Peugeot dealer or a competent automotive engineer who will advise you on the action necessary.
9 Carefully inspect the valves, in particular the exhaust valves. Check that the stems are not bent or bowed and that no wear ridges are visible. The valve seat faces must be in reasonable condition and if they have covered a high mileage they will probably need to be resurfaced on a valve grinding machine. This work can be done by your Peugeot agent or a suitably equipped garage. If the valves have been refaced previously they will probably need renewal if their seat faces are in poor condition.
10 Insert each valve into its respective guide and check for wear. Worn valve guides and/or stems allow oil to be drawn past the inlet valve stem causing a smoky (blue-white) exhaust and high oil consumption, while exhaust gas leakage past the exhaust valve stems can overheat the guides and stems causing sticking valves and heavy carbon deposits.
11 If the valve guides need renewing this will have to be done by your Peugeot agent as they are an interference fit in the head and specialist equipment is necessary.
12 Assuming that the valves and seats are in reasonable condition, or that new valves are being fitted, they must be ground in using valve grinding paste to produce a gastight joint when the valves are closed.
13 The carborundum paste used for this job can be obtained in a double-ended tin with coarse paste at one and fine at the other. The coarse paste is used only if the condition of the valve face and seat needs it but, if used, regrinding must be done afterwards using the fine paste. The fine paste is always used to get the correct finish. A suction tool will be needed to rotate and lift the valve during the grinding process. To grind in a valve, first smear a trace of paste onto the seat face and fit the suction tool to the valve head. Fit the valve to its guide and with a semi-rotary motion grind the valve face onto its seat, lifting and repositioning the valve occasionally to redistribute the grinding paste. When a dull matt continous line has been produced on both the valve seat and the valve then the paste can be wiped off. If coarse paste was used repeat using the fine grinding paste. A light spring fitted under the valve head to hold the head up when the pressure of the grinding tool is released will help speed up the job. If a continuous matt seat cannot be achieved by grinding, or if it is apparent that the valve seat shows signs of excessive grinding or ridges are visible, it probably means that the seat needs refacing or, in extreme cases, renewing altogether. In either case your Peugeot agent should be consulted as specialist equipment is necessary.
14 Consideration should be given to renewing all the valve springs at this stage. However, if they meet the Specifications regarding free length and compressed heights they can be refitted. Obviously any broken springs must be renewed together with any that show distortion or other signs of distress.
15 Before starting reassembly, clean the cylinder head thoroughly free of all traces of grinding paste. Be very meticulous over this

16.2 Oil filter location on timing case

17.15a Fit a new valve stem seal and ...

17.15b ... then fit the valve

17.15c Fit the spring seat washer and ...

17.15d ... then fit the spring and spring retainer, followed by ...

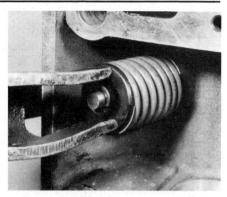

17.15e ... the split collets (note spring compressor)

17.16a Insert the camshaft into position ...

17.16b ... and locate its retaining plate

because any trace left in will be spread through the engine and lead to very expensive repair bills. Fit new oil seals to the valve guides, then lubricate the valve stems and guides with clean engine oil and refit the valves following the reverse of the removal procedure. Make sure that original parts are fitted to their original locations. Note that the valve springs have a closed soil at one end and an open coil at the other; the closed coil should be fitted towards the cylinder head on assembly (photos).

16 After fitting the valve, springs, etc the camshaft can be fitted. Make sure that it is clean and that the bearing surfaces are freely lubricated with clean engine oil. Take great care not to damage the bearings as the shaft is slid home and secure it with the retaining plate, bolt and lockwasher. Cover the assembly to keep it clean until required for fitting to the engine (photos).

18 Crankshaft – examination and renovation

1 Carefully examine the crankpin and main journal bearing surfaces for signs of scoring or scratches and check the ovality of each bearing surface. Use a micrometer to measure the diameter of each bearing in turn at a number of positions. The discrepancy between the various measurements on a single bearing surface indicates the degree of wear and if a journal or pin is more than the specified maximum ovality the shaft will have to be reground. Where there are scores, grooves or scratches don't bother to measure the bearing surfaces as regrinding will be necessary in any case.

2 Crankshaft regrinding will have to be done by your Peugeot agent or by a specialist workshop. The regrind will remove 0.30 mm (0.0118 in) from the diameter of each journal and crankpin and of course new, undersize bearing shells will be needed.

3 If the crankshaft is found to be in good condition and regrinding is not required, new bearing shells of the original size should be fitted on reassembly.

4 Check before reassembly that the crankshaft oilways are clean, particularly if the shaft has been reground. Blow through with a high pressure air line and then pump engine oil through until it emerges from each journal oil hole in turn in a clean condition. To clean out a severely blocked oilway on XL3 series engines you will have to remove the four sludge trap plugs and then when cleaned through, refit the plugs tightening to the specified torque wrench setting. Punch mark the plugs on completion to stake them for security. Use Peugeot special key number 0.0131 for plug removal/refitting if available. On XL5, XL5S and XK5 engines, the crankshaft oilways are drilled diagonally and there are no sludge trap holes.

Fig. 1.11 Removing the sludge trap plugs on the XL3/XL3S engines (Sec 18)

19 Big-end and main bearings – examination and renovation

1   The bearing surface on the bearing shells is highly polished when new but becomes a matt grey after use; there should be no sign of pitting, ridging, grooving or picking up. Even if the bearing shells appear to be in good condition it is still worthwhile renewing them if you have gone to the trouble of removing the crankshaft, particularly if the engine has had extensive use. Of course renewal is essential if there is any sign of damage or if the crankshaft has been reground.

2   If you have found the crankshaft to be in good condition and intend only to fit new bearing shells, check whether or not the crankshaft has been reground before. This will be indicated by the bearing shells that were fitted; the new set should have the same part number as those removed during dismantling.

3   The big-end bearings are subject to wear as a greater rate than the crankshaft main bearings. Big-end failure is accompanied by a knocking from the crankcase and a slight drop in oil pressure. Main bearing failure is accompanied by vibration which can be quite severe as the engine speed is increased. At the outset of either of these conditions the engine should be switched off as any further running will only make matters worse very quickly.

20 Cylinder liner bores – examination and renovation

1   The liner bores may be examined for wear either in or out of the engine block; the cylinder head must, of course, be removed in either case. If the liners are still in the block the retaining strap(s) should be kept in place where possible to avoid having to relocate the liners in their beds. However if the engine is dismantled to the point of piston removal it is better to remove the liners for inspection.

2   The top edge of each liner carries a marking of one to four lines indicating the size grade of the bore. The grade is an average of the diameters measured at six points and is used to match the liner to the piston which is similarly graded but which is marked with a letter. The four grades of piston are identified by the letters A to D inclusive and a grade A piston must be used in a liner with a grade mark on one line. Similarly a grade B piston must be used in a liner with a grade mark of two lines and so on. The grade sizes of the liners and pistons are listed in the Specifications.

3   The liner bores must be examined for taper, ovality, scoring and scratches. Start by inspecting the top of the bores. If they are worn, a slight ridge will be found on the piston thrust side. This marks the top limit of the piston ring travel. You will probably have a good indication of the bore wear prior to dismantling the engine or removing the cylinder head. Excessive oil consumption accompanied by blue exhaust smoke is a sure sign of worn liner bores and piston rings.

4   Measure the bore diameter just under the ridge with an internal micrometer and compare it with the diameter at the bottom of the bore which is much less prone to wear. Also make comparative measurements of the liner diameter parallel with the gudgeon pin and at right-angles to it to determine the extent of ovality. Taper and ovality will decrease from the top of the liner down to the bore. If a micrometer is not available comparative measurements can be made with a set of feeler gauges and a pair of internal calipers but considerable care is needed to get good results.

5   As a general guide it may be assumed that any variations more than 0.010 inch (0.25 mm) indicate that the liners should be renewed. Provided that all variations are less than this it is likely that the fitting of new rings to the pistons will rectify excessive piston-to-bore clearance. If the liner has a top ridge a special stepped piston ring can be fitted which will clear the ridge. Alternatively the ridge can be removed by stoning with a carborundum stone. Where new liners are fitted, new pistons and rings will also be required.

21 Cylinder liner protrusion – checking and adjusting

1   The protrusion of the cylinder liners when assembled to the block must be within prescribed limits so that a gastight seal can be achieved when the head is bolted on. One liner protruding too much or not enough will, despite the cylinder head gasket, make it impossible to secure a gas or watertight joint.

2   First check the squareness of each liner in the block. This is done using a dial test indicator (clock gauge) based on the cylinder head

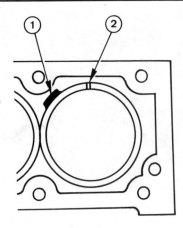

Fig. 1.12 Cylinder liner identity tag 1 in relation to the liner marks 2 when fitted into cylinder block (Sec 21)

mating face on the cylinder block. Gauge the top face of the liner at four equi-spaced points to measure parallelity of the liner face with the block face. The faces must be parallel to each other within a limit of 0.02 mm (0.0008 in) for XL5 and XK5 series engines or 0.04 mm (0.0015 in) for the XL3 series engines. Repeat the check on all four liners.

3   Next check the protrusion of each liner above the face of the block. This is most easily checked with an accurate straight-edge and a set of feeler gauges. Lay the straight-edge across the liner in a fore and aft direction (right-angles to the crankshaft) and measure the gap between the straight-edge and the block face. If this check is being done after fitting new liner gaskets, press down on the liner to compress the gasket when using the feeler gauges. Measure the front and back clearances; they should be within the limits given in the Specifications. Repeat the check on the other three cylinders. It is permissible to tap all around the top of a liner after new gaskets have been fitted so as to seat it firmly. The check must be repeated after doing this.

4   Finally check the difference in height between adjacent liners. Use the dial test indicator to measure the difference in height, if any, between adjacent liners at a point on each lying along the centre axis parallel with the crankshaft on the top face. Each difference in level must not exceed the maximum specified.

5   The three separate checks of squareness, protrusion and height difference are sequential and each must be correct before proceeding to the next. If, for example, the first check shows a liner to be out of square beyond the permissible limit the cause must be found and eliminated. It could be due to a gauging error so check the measuring equipment for cleanliness and accuracy. It could also be due to a distorted liner (if you are doing a check with the engine installed this is more likely) or there could be foreign matter between the liner and the block (more likely if you are doing the check on reassembly after complete dismantling).

6   If the checks reveal a discrepancy on an installed engine it will be necessary to renew the liner gaskets or even one or more liners. In either case the engine/transmission unit will have to be removed for dismantling.

7   When inserting the respective liners into position the gasket colour identity tabs must be located as shown to avoid the possibility of the tabs overlapping when fitting the adjacent liners.

8   Once the checks have shown the liners to be within limits of protrusion and squareness reassembling can continue or, if appropriate, temporary retainer straps should be fitted to hold them in position. *Don't turn the crankshaft if the liners are not restrained from movement.* Cover the exposed engine internal parts if there is likely to be a delay before completing reassembly.

22 Connecting rods, piston and piston rings – examination and renovation

1   With the piston and connecting rod assemblies removed from the liners, give them a thorough cleaning using paraffin. Scrape the carbon deposit off the piston heads but avoid damaging them. Remove the old

rings carefully, keeping them in their assembled sequence and orientation. Clean out the ring grooves in the piston using an old hacksaw blade or a piece of broken ring, taking care not to score or widen the grooves. Protect your fingers if using a piece of piston ring – the edges can be sharp.

2   The top ring groove is likely to have worn the most. After the groove has been cleaned out put the top ring into the groove and check the fit with a feeler gauge.

3   Examine each piston carefully for wear or damage; especially look for hair cracks around each gudgeon pin area.

4   If any of the pistons are obviously badly worn, cracked, burnt or otherwise defective, new ones must be fitted. A badly worn top ring groove in an otherwise satisfactory piston can be machined out to take a thicker ring. If necessary, this can be a stepped ring having a step on its outer face to clear the ridge in the liner resulting from previous use. New pistons must be matched by grade with their liners (see the previous Section). Removal from and assembly to the connecting rods will have to be done by your Peugeot agent as the gudgeon pin is an interference fit in the rod little end.

5   Providing that the engine has not seized or suffered any other serious damage, the connecting rods should require no attention other than cleaning and a check for obvious defects. If damage has occurred or there is evidence of irregular wear in the pistons, liners or bearings it is advisable to have the connecting rod alignment checked. This requires specialist tools and should be left to your Peugeot agent or a suitably equipped engineering workshop.

6   Before fitting new rings to the pistons each should have the gap checked. Peugeot supply the rings pre-gapped but, if there is any doubt, insert a ring halfway down the liner bore, making sure that it is

22.8 The rings fitted to the piston

square in the liner, and measure the end gap with feeler gauges. A gap of between 0.010 and 0.040 in (0.254 and 1.016 mm) will be satisfactory.

7   When fitting new pistons and rings to new liners the ring gaps can be measured, if required, at the top of the bore as the bore will not now taper.

8   Fit the three-piece scraper ring to the piston first, followed by the middle, compression, rings. When fitted, arrange the scraper ring gaps and the expansion ring split as shown. Check if the compression rings are TOP marked and fit them accordingly, (to the piston crown). When fitted arrange the compression ring gaps so that they are not in line. Fit the rings in the reverse way they were removed, but exercise care as the two top ones are very brittle and easily broken (photo).

23 Timing chain and sprockets – examination and renovation

1   Examine the teeth of both sprockets for wear. Each tooth on a sprocket is an inverted V-shape and wear becomes apparent when one side of the tooth appears more concave in shape than the other. When badly worn the teeth become hook-shaped and the sprockets must be renewed.

2   If the sprockets need renewing then the chain will have worn as well and should be renewed. If the sprockets are satisfactory examine the chain and look for play between the links. When the chain is held horizontally with the link pins vertical it should not bend appreciably – the greater the amount of bending in this position the more the chain is worn. A chain is a relatively cheap item and it is well worthwhile fitting a new one if you have dismantled the engine.

3   Check the condition of the chain tensioner blade for grooving by the timing chain; if this is pronounced renew the blade. It is recommended that the tensioner unit is not dismantled as reassembly is difficult.

24 Camshaft and rocker assembly – examination and renovation

1   The camshaft lobes should be examined for signs of flats or scoring or any other form of wear and damage. At the same time the rocker arms should be examined, particularly on the faces which bear on the cam lobes, for signs of wear. If the case-hardened faces of the rocker arms or the surfaces of the cam lobes have been penetrated it will be quite obvious as there will be a darker, rough pitted appearance to the surface in question. In such cases the parts concerned must be renewed. Where the cam or rocker arm surfaces are still bright and clean, although showing slight signs of wear, they are best left alone. Any attempt to reface either will only result in the case-hardened surface being reduced in thickness with the possibility of subsequent rapid and extreme wear.

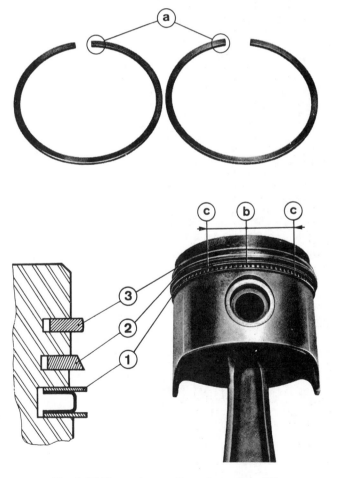

Fig. 1.13 Piston rings to fit as shown (Sec 22)

(a)   Ring marks to face upwards (2 marked)
(b)   Expansion ring split to be over gudgeon pin axis
(c)   Ring splits of oil scraper 1 to be 20 to 50 mm apart

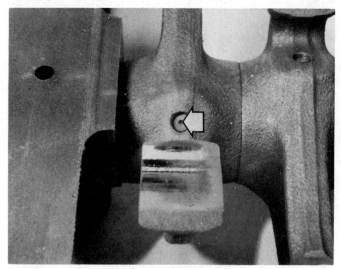

24.6 Check that the oil jet (arrowed) in each rocker arm is clear

2   The camshaft bearing journals should be in good condition and show little signs of wear as they are relatively free from stress.

3   If the bearing surfaces are found to be discoloured, or wear is evident, it is possible that the camshaft is not running true and, in this case, it will have to be renewed. For an accurate check get your Peugeot agent to inspect both the camshaft and the cylinder head.

4   The rocker assembly can be dismantled after removing the setscrew in the mounting block furthest from the timing sprocket end. When removing the various components from the shaft, take careful note of the sequence in which they are removed. Note the differences between the mounting blocks. Keep the components in order as they are removed for cleaning and inspection.

5   Check the rocker shaft for signs of wear, and check it for straightness by rolling it on a flat surface. It is unlikely to be bent but if this is the case it must be carefully straightened, if possible, or renewed. The shaft surface should be free of wear ridges caused by the rocker arms. Inspect the oil feed holes and clear them out if blocked.

6   Check each rocker arm for bearing wear by sliding it on to an unworn part of the shaft. Inspect the oil jet (photo) and make sure that it is clear. Inspect the end of the valve clearance adjusting screw for signs of cracks or serious wear that may have penetrated the case-hardening. If present the screw must be renewed.

7   Reassemble the rocker assembly in the reverse order to dismantling. Lubricate all bearing surfaces with clean engine oil, except the rocker pads which should have Molykote applied when installed on the cylinder head, and make sure that all components are the right way round and in the correct sequence.

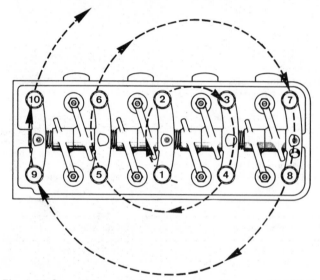

Fig. 1.14 General layout of the rocker assembly on the XL3/XL3S engines

Note the bolt loosening/tightening sequence which is the same for all models (Sec 24)

25 Starter ring gear – examination and renovation

1   Examine the starter ring gear on the flywheel for signs of obvious damage such as worn, chipped or broken gear teeth. If several of the teeth are broken or missing or the front edges of all teeth are obviously badly worn then it would be advisable to fit a new gear ring. The ring is shrunk onto the flywheel after being heated and, apart from the friction plate, it is the only renewable part in the flywheel/clutch assembly. The assembly is balanced on production and must otherwise be renewed complete when defective.

2   Renewing the ring gear is a job best left to a suitably equipped garage or workshop as the difficulty of heating the gear without overdoing it and thereby adversely affecting its hard wearing properties is usually beyond the ability of the average home mechanic. However, the procedure is straightforward given the right facilities.

3   The old ring gear can be removed by cutting a slot between two gear teeth, using a hacksaw, and then splitting it with a cold chisel. Note that one side of the gear teeth has a lead for the starter pinion and the ring must be fitted the right way round.

4   To fit a new ring gear requires it to be heated to about 200°C (say 400°F) but no more. Ideally this should be done in a temperature controlled oil bath (don't use a naked flame), but a makeshift method

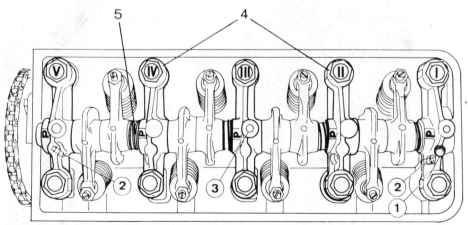

Fig. 1.15 Rocker shaft bearing blocks identification (Sec 24)

1   Screw seating on block I
2   Locating dowels on blocks I and V
3   Tapped hole for rocker cover bolt in block III

4   Blocks II and IV are identical
5   Letter P on all blocks must be towards sprocket

can be adopted using a blowlamp or welding torch if either is available. Polish four equally spaced areas on the gear ring upper face and support the ring on suitable heat resisting material such as firebricks. Apply heat evenly all round the ring until the polished areas start to turn a light yellow colour. This colour is an oxide film which gives some indication of temperature. The important thing is to heat the ring evenly and not to exceed the specified temperature.

5   When the ring is hot enough, fit it to the flywheel and tap it into position all round its periphery – get it on the right way round! Let it cool down naturally without quenching.

26 Oil pump – examination and renovation

1   The oil pump is located in the bottom of the timing case and it is driven by a shaft from a skew gear on the crankshaft. It is an eccentric rotor type pump and access can be gained by a cover bolted on the bottom of the pump housing.

2   Undo the four bolts retaining the cover and remove the cover and its gasket. The rotors can then be withdrawn as the inner rotor has a sliding keyway to mate with the key in the shaft. Wash the rotors in paraffin and wipe dry with fluff-free rag. Clean the pump housing with a paraffin-damped rag and wipe dry with fluff-free rag.

3   Inspect the pump rotors and housing for damage, scores or obvious signs of wear. Normally this type of pump has a long life but wear will eventually occur resulting in reduced output. If the components are defective or the pump output is suspect after prolonged use

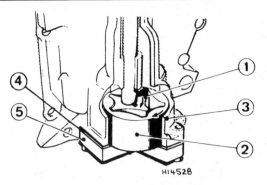

Fig. 1.16 The oil pump (Sec 26)

1   Inner rotor
2   Outer rotor
3   Timing case
4   Pump cover gasket
5   Pump cover

a new pair of matched rotors should be fitted but, as wear is also likely to have occurred in the pump housing on an old engine, a new timing case might be required, in addition, to effect a complete cure.

4   Reassembly is the reverse of the removal procedure, but lubricate the moving parts liberally with clean engine oil and use a new cover gasket (photos).

26.4a Fit the key to the driveshaft keyway

26.4b Locate the outer rotor followed by ...

26.4c ... the inner rotor and finally ...

26.4d ... the cover with a new gasket

27 Inlet and exhaust manifolds – examination

1   The inlet manifold is conencted to the cylinder head by four short lengths of flexible housing and it is worth renewing these when overhauling the engine. The hose clips must be in good condition; if in doubt, renew them to avoid the possibility of weak mixture problems. Check the carburettor mating face for flatness and freedom from damage. Finally flush the coolant passages in the manifold with clean water.

2   Examine the exhaust manifold for cracks and obvious damage. Use a straight-edge to check the faces mating with the cylinder head for flatness and lack of distortion. If there should be any sign of pitting or distortion in the mating faces it might be possible to have the defects removed by refacing at a suitably equipped workshop but if this is not possible, or if the problem is too severe for this remedy, a new manifold will be needed. Any accumulations of carbon in the exhaust manifold can be removed using a flexible wire brush or a scraper.

28 Engine mountings – inspection

1   The engine mounting rubbers are often ignored simply because they do not normally present any problems. If they show signs of deterioration due to oil impregnation, heat or simply age, they should be renewed. Mountings that have lost their resilience and are unable to resist shock will result in engine/transmission vibration and will increase the risk of failure in other components and cause fatigue for the driver and passengers (photo).

29 Engine reassembly – general

1   In the course of reassembling the engine, one or two basic principles must be observed to ensure a long, trouble free life.

2   Paramount is the need for absolute cleanliness. The working area, the engine components, the tools and hands of those working on the engine must be completely free of grime, grit and any other foreign matter. One speck of carborundum dust, or a small piece of swarf for instance, can ruin a bearing very quickly and undo all your efforts.

3   Always use new gaskets, locking tabs, seals, self-locking nuts etc. It is pointless to spend considerable time and money overhauling an engine only to have it fail as a result of, say, a defective re-used circlip. If necessary delay the rebuilding.

4   Don't rush the job. Anyone, however skilled and experienced, can make a mistake if he is trying to beat the clock.

5   Check that all nuts and bolts are clean and in good condition and, ideally, renew all spring washers, tab washers and similar locking devices as a matter of course.

6   In addition to most of the tools used during dismantling you will need a supply of clean engine oil, clean fluff-free cloths (domestic kitchen paper is a good alternative) and a torque wrench.

7   The torque wrench is really essential for this engine and, if you haven't got one borrow or hire one. The need arises because so much of the engine and transmission is made of light alloy which, although it has the advantage of low weight, is easily distorted by abnormal loads. The various fastenings must be torque loaded, where specified, to avoid such distortion while being tight enough to perform their intended task. Cracked or distorted casings are expensive to renew, so beware.

30 Engine – preparation for reassembly

1   Assuming that the engine has been completely stripped for overhaul and that the block is now bare, before any reassembly takes place it must be thoroughly cleaned both inside and out. If it has not already been removed, undo the five bolts retaining the oil gallery cover along the side of the block, remove the cover and discard the old gasket. Also remove the O-ring located on the spigot in the block/transmission face at the clutch end.

28.1 Check the engine mounting rubbers

2   The easiest way to clean the block is to immerse it in a garage's cleaning tank and leave it to soak before getting to work on it with a stiff brush and a selection of scrapers and probes. Clean out all the crevices but be careful not to scratch mating faces. Sediment collects round the liner settings so check for this and clean it out.

3   Hose down the block with a garden hose and if an air supply is available use it to blow off surplus liquid. Dry and thoroughly clean the block with lint-free rags.

4   Oilways should be cleaned out using a thin bottle-brush, pipe cleaners and similar implements. Again, blow them through with compressed air if a supply is available. Squirt clean engine oil through to check that the oilways are clear.

31 Crankshaft – refitting

1   Ensure that the crankcase/cylinder block is thoroughly clean, if necessary refer to the previous Section. Position the casing with the cylinder head joint face downwards on the bench.

2   Install the five bearing upper half shells in their locations after wiping the locations clean and dry. These shells have an oil groove (as opposed to the half shells in the caps which are plain) and the locating tongues should be fitted snugly in their slots in the case. If you are reusing the original bearings make sure that they are fitted in their original locations. After installation oil the shells freely with clean engine oil (photo).

3   Fit the half thrust washers in the No 2 bearing block with their bronze face grooves facing towards the crankshaft (photo).

4   Check that the crankshaft is perfectly clean and carefully lower it into the main bearings in the case (photos).

5   Check that each main bearing cap is clean and fit the plain lower half bearing shells (photo). Again if the original shells are being refitted make sure that each is in its correct cap. On later XL5 and XK5 engines another two half thrust washers must be fitted to the No 2 main bearing cap, again with the grooves facing the crankshaft.

6   Check that all the main bearing cap locating spigots are present in the case. Oil the bearings then fit the caps to their respective bearings – each cap is numbered, No 1 being at the clutch end (photos).

7   Fit new plain washers to the ten cap retaining bolts. If the crankcase has bolt holes that are not blind, ie the hole goes right through, apply thread locking compound to the bolt threads. If the bolt holes are blind do not use thread locking compound. Fit the bolts and tighten them to the specified torque (photo).

8   The crankshaft endfloat must now be checked. In fact this check could be done before fitting the bearing caps on XL5 and XK5 engines which have 2 half thrust washers in the case only. On the later engines, 4 half thrust washers are fitted and all should be in position

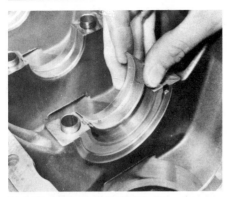

31.2 Fit the crankshaft upper half bearing shells (grooved)

31.3 Locate a half thrust washer

31.4a Fit the crankshaft

31.4b Note the milled slot in the crankshaft web (XL5 engine) which is used for setting the TDC accurately

31.5 Locate the plain lower half bearing shells to the bearing caps

31.6a Lubricate the moving parts, in this case the main bearings on assembly

31.6b Fitting the No 2 main bearing cap – with thrust washer on the later Series II (XL5 and XK5) engine

31.7 Tightening the main bearing cap bolts with a torque wrench

31.8 Measure crankshaft endfloat using a feeler gauge

to check the endfloat. Push the crankshaft axially in one direction to its limit and using feeler gauges measure the clearance between the thrust washers and the crankshaft face (photo). The endfloat should be within the tolerance quoted in the Specifications. If it is not, new thrust washers should be selected from the range available which will produce the correct endfloat. Note that the washers must all be the same thickness on the engine. After adjusting the endfloat, or if it is found to be within tolerance, rotate the crankshaft and make sure that it turns smoothly without binding and without tight spots.

32 Pistons, connecting rods and liners – refitting

1   First the liners must be fitted to the block and checks made to

ensure that each liner is square. Liner protrusion above the cylinder head joint face and protrusion relative to the adjacent liner(s) must be within tolerance.

2   Turn the cylinder block upright and make sure that the seat for each liner is meticulously clean. This is very important because the slightest trace of dirt here could cause eventual cylinder head gasket leaks. Where original liners are being re-used they must locate in their original positions and the marks made during dismantling should be used for this purpose. Check that each liner is clean and that its bottom joint face is perfectly free of any old joint material, dirt, etc.

3   Insert the liners into their locations without base gaskets and, preferably using a dial test indicator (clock gauge), measure the protrusion of each liner relative to the cylinder block top face. Make four measurements on each liner at 90° intervals and note the readings. In the absence of a dial test indicator, a straight-edge and

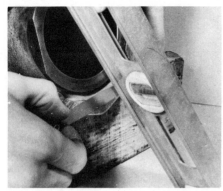

32.3a Use a straight edge and feeler gauge to check each liner protrusion ...

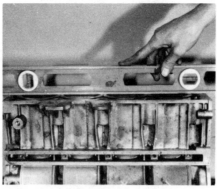

32.3b ... and the relative protrusional difference of adjacent liners

32.8a Fitting a big-end upper half bearing shell

32.8b Inserting a piston into a liner using a ring compressor

32.9 Ensure that the liner gasket is fitted carefully with its inner lugs in the liner groove

32.10 Inserting a piston and liner assembly into the block

32.11a A piece of steel bar being used as a liner retaining strap

32.11b Locate a big-end bearing cap, then ...

32.11c ... fit and torque tighten the retaining nuts

feeler gauges can be used, but care is needed to produce accurate results (photos).

4   Study the protrusion readings obtained for each liner. All four readings should be identical on each liner; if they vary by more than the specified amount on the same liner, the liner is not squarely located.

5   Select the appropriate gasket for each liner which will produce the specified protrusion without exceeding the maximum relative liner difference. One gasket only must be fitted to each liner. Where difficulty arises check that there is no dirt between the liner and the block and that your measuring equipment is accurate. New liners can be exchanged with others in the block. If the required result still cannot be obtained it is possible that the liners are distorted and you should have them professionally checked.

6   Fit the selected gasket to each liner, assemble the liners into the block and make a check of the protrusions and squareness again to confirm that all is well. Refer to Section 21 if necessary. This repeat

check is worth doing as a leaking cylinder head gasket can prove to be an expensive fault.

7   Where the original pistons are being used, identify them with their liners using the marks made during dismantling. Before fitting each piston to its liner the ring gaps must be positioned correctly. The expander in the bottom composite scraper should have the gap located directly over the axis of the gudgeon pin and the gaps in the thin scraper rings should be within 20 to 50 mm (0.79 to 1.96 in) to each side of the expander gap. The tapered face compression ring gap and the top, curved face compression ring gaps should be located at 120° on opposite sides away from the expander gap. Lubricate the rings and pistons with clean engine oil.

8   Fit the upper half shells to the big-ends after wiping their locations clean and dry (photo). Lubricate each liner bore with clean engine oil and, using a suitable ring compressing tool, insert the piston and connecting rod into the liner (photo).

9   Ensure that the liner gasket inner lugs are engaged in the liner

groove (photo) and position the gasket so that when the liner is fitted the colour identification tab is located as shown, to avoid the possibility of the tabs overlapping when fitting the adjacent liners.

10 Make sure that the liner gasket is snugly fitted and insert the liner into the block guiding the connecting rod onto the crankpin (photos). Make sure also that the liner is fitted the right way round in the block and the piston is the right way round in the liner. Previously used components should have the marks made during dismantling correctly aligned. Mark new liners to identify their location.

11 When all the liner and piston assemblies are fitted, install the liner retaining strap(s) to keep them in position while the big-end caps are being fitted (photo). Wipe each cap clean and dry and fit the lower half bearing shells. Identify each cap with its correct connecting rod and, after well lubricating the crankpin and bearing shells with clean engine oil, fit the caps (photo). Make sure that the locating tabs on the bearing shells butt each other on the same side. Fit and tighten the cap retaining nuts to the specified torque (photo).

12 Check that the crankshaft is still free to rotate without tight spots.

33 Cylinder head – refitting with engine on bench

1   Assuming that the cylinder head assembly has been overhauled as described in Section 17 and the cylinder block assembled to the stage reached in the last Section, temporarily fit the timing sprocket and key to the crankshaft and turn the crankshaft so that the marked tooth on the sprocket is aligned with the left-hand (right-hand for XL3 series) joint faces of the adjacent main bearing cap and cylinder block. This will position all the pistons at mid-stroke. Remember not to turn the crankshaft after fitting the cylinder head until after the timing chain has been fitted otherwise damage might result from the pistons contacting the valve heads.

2   Remove the liner retaining strap(s) and make sure that the cylinder block mating face is thoroughly clean and that the cylinder head centering dowel is in position at the rear corner at the timing case end. Check for any burrs or other accidental damage in the face and then position a new gasket on the head. Do not use any jointing compound.

3   Give the cylinder head a last check for cleanliness and lack of damage to the joint face and then lower the head carefully onto the cylinder head gasket on the block. Turn the crankshaft so that its drive end is positioned as shown.

4   Give the rocker assembly a check to see that all is well and spray the rocker arm cam pads with Molykote 321 R or a suitable alternative (photo). Lower the assembly on to the cylinder head, engaging the locating dowels in the two end bearing blocks in their holes in the head (photo).

5   Temporarily fit the timing cover into position without its gasket and secure it with a couple of bolts. This is to ensure that the head gasket is correctly positioned when tightening the cylinder head bolts.

Fig. 1.17 Crankshaft timing mark to be positioned as shown for the XK5, XL5 and XL5S engines (Sec 33)

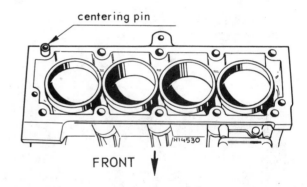

Fig. 1.18 Ensure that the centering pin is in position (Sec 33)

33.4a Spray the rocker pad with Molykote before ...

33.4b ... lowering the rocker assembly onto the cylinder head

33.6 Tightening the cylinder head bolts

Fig. 1.19 On the XL5, XL5S and XK5 engines position the camshaft as shown (Sec 33)

6   Oil the threads of the ten cylinder head bolts and also under their heads. Fit the bolts and nuts but don't use any washers. Following the sequence shown, tighten the bolts to the Stage 1 torque quoted in the Specifications (photo). Then go round again in the same sequence tightening to the Stage 2 torque. This procedure is the same for all engine types, but note the following.

7   In June 1980, Peugeot introduced an increased torque for the cylinder head bolts and, at the same time, a modified camshaft and stronger cylinder head bolts. *It is absolutely forbidden to use the higher torque on earlier engines* unless the new camshaft and new bolts are fitted in place of the originals. The camshafts can be identified by a coloured paint dab adjacent to the centre bearing journal and the bolts by numbers on the heads of the bolts as follows:

	Old	New
XL5 (118) camshaft	Green	Blue
XK5 (127) camshaft	None	Pink

The early cylinder head bolts are identified by the 8.8 mark on their head face whilst the later type bolts are marked 10.9.

8   When the cylinder head bolts are tightened down, remove the timing case.

34 Cylinder head – refitting with engine in vehicle

1   Make sure that all mating faces are clean, that the cylinder liner protrusion and squareness checks have been done with satisfactory results and that a new cylinder head gasket, a new timing case gasket, a new rocker cover gasket and new exhaust manifold gaskets etc are available.

2   If the timing case has been removed proceed as in Section 33 to refit the cylinder head. When the cylinder head is refitted, reassemble the timing chain and sprocket assemblies as given in Section 34 or 35 and then refit the timing case as given in Section 38, after which proceed as from paragraph 20 in this Section.

3   On the XL5/XL5S and XK5 series engines where the timing case has been left in position and Peugeot special tool number 8.0140 has been used to support the camshaft sprocket and chain assembly proceed as follows.

4   Measure a distance of 125 mm (4.92 in) from the top of the new timing case gasket down each side and cut off the top portion using a razor blade to get a clean cut. Stick this new gasket to the timing caseexposed face (the gasket will extend above the timing case), using jointing compound and fill the two unused holes at the bottom of the gasket.

5   Lightly lubricate the walls of the 4 liners using clean engine oil and, if necessary and if liner retaining straps are fitted, turn the crankshaft to position Nos 2 and 3 pistons at TDC (top of compression stroke No 2). In this position check that the distributor rotor arm is pointing out towards the right wing – if not rotate the crankshaft a full revolution – and align the timing marks on the pulley and timing plate (see Chapter 4 if in doubt).

6   Remove the liner retainer straps and clean off any excess jointing compoint in the corners between the timing case face and the cylinder head face.

7   Wipe the mating faces of the cylinder head and block clean and fit a new, dry cylinder head gasket to the block.

8   Clean the threads on the cylinder head bolts and in the nuts. Oil the bolt threads and under the bolt heads.

9   Turn the camshaft to the position shown which is the position when both valves are open on number 3 cylinder, piston at TDC. If this is not done there may be trouble with valves contacting pistons, and it will be impossible to fit the camshaft sprocket.

10   Wipe the rocker arm faces clean and lightly spray them with Molykote 321 R or equivalent.

11   Carefully lower the cylinder head into position on the block and then fit the rocker assembly into position on the cylinder head. Fit the cylinder head bolts and nuts but leave them untightened for the moment.

13   Refit the upper timing case bolts in the order shown, tightening them initially to 3 to 4 lbf ft (0.5 kgf m): they will need to be fully tightened after the cylinder head bolts are tightened down to their correct torque.

14   Follow the sequence shown in the figure and tighten the cylinder head bolts. Two stages of tightening are necessary. Go right round all bolts and tighten to the Stage 1 torque quoted in the Specifications and then go round again tightening to the Stage 2 specified torque.

15   The bolts in the timing case can now be fully tightened to the specified torque, as can the four bolts securing the engine mounting bracket.

16   Push a piece of fluff-free rag into the timing case under the sprocket holding tool to prevent anything falling down into the case. Fit one sprocket retaining bolt to the hole not covered by the special tool (but don't tighten it yet) and locate the sprocket on the camshaft; the sprocket should fit without having to force it. Remove the piece of rag and check that the timing chain is properly located on the tensioner rubbing plate and then put the rag back into place.

17   Undo the two bolts in the sprocket holding tool, remove the bolts and the special tool. Then fit the remaining two bolts in the camshaft sprocket and tighten all three bolts to the specified torque. Bend up the locking plate to lock each bolt and then remove the piece of rag from the timing case.

18   The timing chain tension must now be checked. A long hooked tool is required; this could be made up from a piece of strong fence wire or similar. The procedure is to reach down into the timing case with the tool and hook it into the fifth free link below the sprocket in the rear leg of the chain (the front leg runs down onto the tensioner rubbing plate). Exert a strong pull on the hook to deflect the chain.

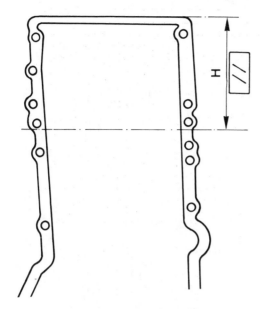

Fig. 1.20 Cut off new timing case gasket at point H (Sec 34)

H = 125 mm

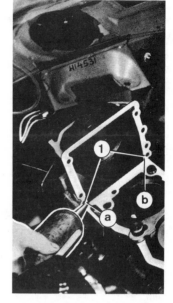

Fig. 1.21 Apply jointing compound to each corner (a and b) and to the unused holes 1 (Sec 34)

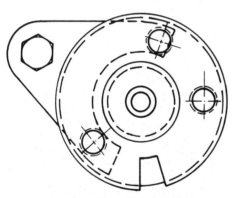

Fig. 1.22 Align the camshaft in this position before refitting the cylinder head (Sec 34)

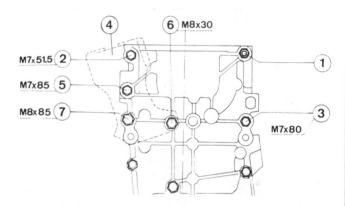

Fig. 1.23 Upper timing case bolt sizes and tightening sequence (Sec 34)

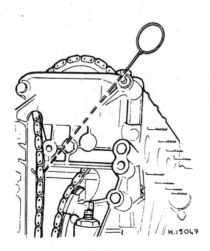

Fig. 1.24 Check the timing chain tension (Sec 34)

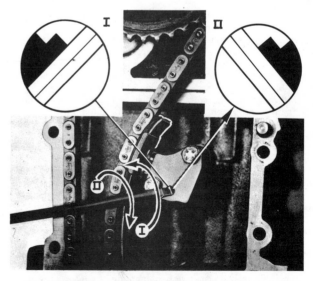

Fig. 1.25 Timing chain tensioner release/adjustment – XL5/XL5S/XK5 engines (Sec 34)

When released the stretch of chain should remain untensioned. If this is not so, the timing case will have to be removed (refer to Section 8) and the tensioner slackened off as given in Section 36.

19 Carefully cut off the surplus part of the timing case gasket flush with the rocker cover mounting face.

20 Adjust the inlet and exhaust valve clearances; refer to Section 39 for this procedure.

21 Refitting of all the removed components now follows. It is broadly a reversal of the removal procedure but take note of the following points:

(a) *Tighten fasteners to the correct torque according to the list in the Specifications*

(b) *Fit new gaskets to the exhaust manifold and check that the crimped side of the gasket is against the manifold not the cylinder head*

(c) *Make a thorough check that no loose articles are left on the rocker mechanism before refitting the rocker cover, especially check that the piece of rag is removed from the timing case. Fit a new gasket to the cover*

(d) *Refill the cooling system and check the engine oil level before starting the engine*

22 After starting the engine, check for leaks and then run it until the electro-magnetic fan engages. Stop the engine and when it is cool top up the cooling system.

23 After the engine has been allowed to cool for at least two hours the cylinder head bolts must be retightened. First remove the rocker cover and, following the sequence in the figure, slacken the first bolt and then retighten it to the Stage 2 specified torque. Then slacken the second bolt and retighten it, and so on until all bolts have been separately retightened.

24 Following the retightening of the cylinder head bolts the inlet and exhaust valve clearances must be reset.

25 Finally, after the car has travelled between 1000 and 1500 miles (1500 and 2500 km), the cylinder head bolts must again be slackened and retightened and the valve clearances again reset.

35 Timing sprockets and chain (XL3 series engine) – reassembly

1 Check that the crankshaft position has been kept so that when fitted, the timing sprocket mark will be at 90° (on the horizontal line to the right). Check that the keyways are clean and then insert the keys.

2 Slide the drive sprocket into position on the crankshaft so that it butts against the shoulder. Ensure that the keyway is in line when fitting, and assemble the sprocket with its timing mark facing outwards.

3 Now slide the oil pump pinion into position in a similar manner, locate the new lockwasher and securing nut. Tighten the nut to the specified torque setting and then peen over the lockwasher to secure. When tightening ensure that the crankshaft does not turn.

4 Turn the crankshaft and set it at the position shown with the two threaded holes that are closer together positioned upwards with the lower hole about 15° from the engine centre line.

5 If dismantled, reassemble the chain tensioner unit by fitting the shoe, spring and piston, and locking them by turning the Allen screw clockwise (3 mm Allen key). Fit the unit to the cylinder block, tighten the retaining bolts to their specified torque setting and peen over the lockwasher tabs to secure. When fitted check that the tensioner shoe slides freely in its bore.

6 Locate the camshaft sprocket into the timing chain so that the sprocket timing reference mark is between the two copper plated links of the chain. Holding the camshaft sprocket in this position, fit the chain into position so that it is engaged on the crankshaft sprocket with the single copper plated link aligned with the pinion timing reference mark.

7 Fit the camshaft sprocket to the camshaft and using a new lockwasher, insert the retaining bolts. Tighten them to the specified torque setting and bend over the lockwasher tabs to secure.

8 The chain tensioner can now be actuated by inserting the 3 mm Allen key and turning it clockwise. When the chain is tensioned, remove the Allen key and refit the seal bolt with its tab washer. Bend the tab washer over the bolt head to secure.

Fig. 1.26 Position the camshaft as shown for correct timing setting when refitting the camshaft sprocket and chain – XL3 and XL3S engines (Sec 35)

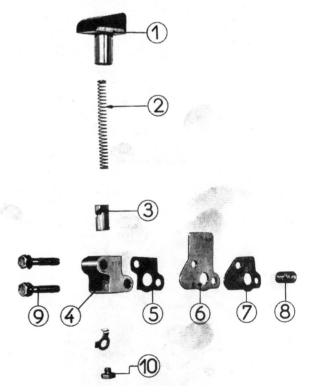

Fig. 1.27 The chain tensioner components – XL3/XL3S engine (Sec 35)

1	Shoe	7	Plate gasket
2	Spring	8	Filter
3	Piston	9	Retaining bolts
4	Body	10	Adjuster seal bolt and
5	Gasket		tab washer
6	Backing plate		

36.2 The marked tooth should be aligned with the mating face joint

36.4a Fit the camshaft sprocket, then ...

36.4b ... tighten the bolts and ...

36.4c ... bend up the lock washer. Note the marked tooth at the 9 o'clock position

36 Timing sprockets and chain (XK5 and XL5 series engines) – reassembly

1 Make sure that the keyways in the end of the crankshaft are clean and fit the keys.

2 Assemble the sprocket, teeth towards the block, followed by the skew gear and spacer. Then fit the retaining bolts and washer but do not tighten yet. The marked sprocket tooth should be aligned with the main bearing cap/cylinder block mating faces if the crankshaft was positioned as described in Section 33, paragraph 1 (photo).

3 Assemble the chain tensioner rubbing plate pivot bolt, spacer and washers as shown in the figure and coat the bolt thread with thread locking compound. Fit the assembly to the block and tighten the bolt to its specified torque. Check that the plate moves freely.

4 Fit the camshaft sprocket to the shaft (photo), then fit the locking plate and the three retaining bolts. Tighten the bolts to the specified torque and bend up the locking plate to lock the bolts (photo). Align the marked sprocket teeth at the nine o'clock position when looking at the sprocket (photo).

5 The timing chain has three links marked white to facilitate correct valve timing. If these are not visible mark the links by first putting a mark on an outer link plate as a starting point. Count off 16 outer link plates, including the one just marked, and mark the 16th and 17th

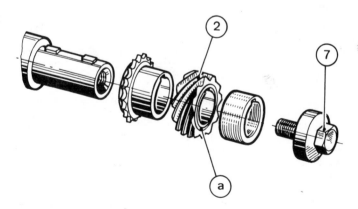

Fig. 1.28 Reassemble the crankshaft drive components ensuring that groove (a) in pinion face 2 is towards the securing bolt 7 end (Sec 36)

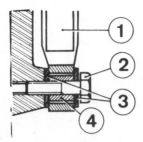

Fig. 1.29 Sequence of assembly of tension plate pivot (Sec 36)

1   *Chain tensioner rubbing plate*   3   *Washers*
2   *Pivot bolt*   4   *Spacer*

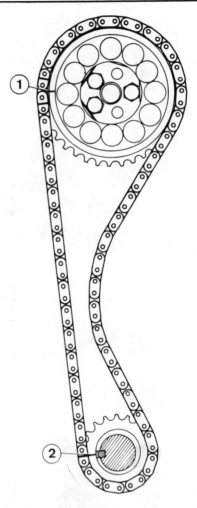

links. Fit the chain to the sprockets with the single marked link aligned with the marked tooth on the crankshaft sprocket and the twin marked links each side of the mark on the camshaft sprocket. If necessary slightly adjust the camshaft position to fit the chain.

6   Refit the chain tensioner filter in its recess in the block. Check that the tensioner shoe is locked in the retracted position and assemble the two retaining bolts and locking washers, the joint gasket and the spacer plate to the tensioner. Fit the tensioner to the block and tighten the two bolts to their specified torque. Arm the tensioner by turning the lock ratchet in a clockwise direction and allow the tensioner to automatically take up the chain tension; don't assist the action of the tensioner (photos).

7   The crankshaft sprocket retaining bolt can now be tightened to the specified torque. Lock the crankshaft if necessary as described in Section 8, paragraph 8.

37 Engine and transmission – reassembly

1   Refer to Chapter 6, Section 7 and reassemble the transmission unit to the engine.
2   If the transmission unit has not been dismantled it is advisable to remove the bottom cover plate and then remove the oil pump suction filter gauze, retained by three bolts. Clean the filter gauze thoroughly in paraffin and, if available, dry with compressed air. Refit the filter gauze using a new rubber seal and tighten the three bolts to the specified torque. Then refit the bottom cover using a new gasket and tighten the thirteen bolts to the specified torque. This additional chore is well worth while, ensuring that any sludge or particles trapped in the filter gauze or sump will not be circulated around the rebuilt engine.

38 Timing case – reassembly and refitting

1   Fit the combined skew gear and fuel pump cam into its location in the timing case, slide the driveshaft into position and engage the drive dogs (photo). Lubricate the mechanism with clean engine oil.
2   Reassemble the oil pump components, referring to Section 26 for details if necessary.
3   Check that the oil pressure relief valve, spring and cap are perfectly clean, lubricate them with clean engine oil and fit them to their location adjacent to the filter mounting (photos), using a new sealing washer.
4   Fit the oil pressure sender to its location using a new sealing washer (photo).
5   Refitting of the timing case for the XK5 and XL5 series engines differ from that for the XL3 series engines. Therefore now proceed as described in paragraphs 6 to 14 inclusive or paragraphs 15 to 20 inclusive for your engine type, then paragraphs 21 and 22 for both types.

XK5 and XL5 series engines
6   Fit the distributor clamp plate and secure it with the single retaining bolt and lockwasher.
7   Install a new O-ring on the oil transfer spigot in the block joint face near the chain tensioner plate (photo).

Fig. 1.30 Assembling the timing chain to the sprockets (Sec 36)

1   *Camshaft sprocket timing mark*
2   *Crankshaft sprocket timing mark*

Fig. 1.31 The crankshaft TDC positioning rod in position – Peugeot tool number given (Sec 38)

36.6a Fit the chain tensioner oil filter

36.6b The tensioner shoe in the retracted position. Note the position of the lock ratchet

36.6c After fitting the tensioner ...

36.6d ... arm it by turning the lock ratchet clockwise

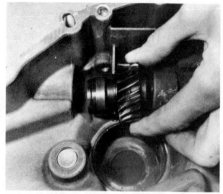

38.1a Fit the skew gear to the timing case and ...

38.1b ... slide the driveshaft into position...

38.1c .. ensuring that the drive dogs are engaged

38.3a Fit the oil pressure relief valve and spring, then ...

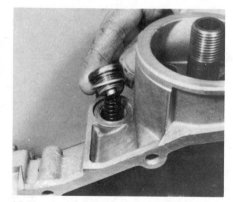

38.3b ... locate the retaining cup using a new seal washer

38.4 The oil pressure sender being fitted

38.7 New O-ring fitted to the oil transfer spigot

38.8 Fit a new timing case joint gasket

38.10 The distributor drive dog slot (arrowed) before fitting the timing case

38.11a Locate the timing case into position

38.11b The distributor drive dog slot orientation after fitting the timing case

8   Position a new timing case joint gasket on the block face using sealing compound to hold it in position (photo).
9   Using a spanner on the crankshaft pulley bolt, turn the engine to position No 2 piston at TDC on the compression stroke. To do this an alignment rod is required. It should be 8 mm (0.315 in) diameter and at least 100 mm (4 in) long. Make sure that the rod is clean and insert it in the hole just above the crankshaft in the block wall. Turn the crankshaft until No 2 piston is approaching TDC on compression (ie with No 3 cylinder valves both open) and gently press the rod in against the crankshaft counterweight web. At TDC the rod will enter a slot milled in the web and will prevent further rotation. Rock the crankshaft carefully in both directions to make sure that the rod is in fact in the slot. When satisfactory, remove the rod and take care not to turn the crankshaft until after assembly is completed.
10   The distributor drive in the timing case must now be aligned so that, when assembled, the distributor is in the correct relationship with the crankshaft to permit accurate ignition timing. Looking down on the drive it will be seen that a horizontal slot divides the drive into unequal parts. Turn the drive so that the smaller part is on the outside of the drive housing and the slot is in an east-west alignment, that is, parallel wth the crankshaft axis (photo).
11   Carefully refit the timing case to the engine. As the driveshaft wheel meshes with the worm on the crankshaft the shaft will turn slightly. If the mesh is correct it will have moved the slot in the drive

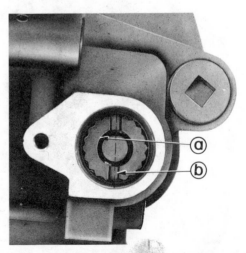

Fig. 1.32 Distributor driveshaft position before fitting timing case – XL3/XL3S engines, with groove (b) parallel to mating face – (a) indicates smaller side (Sec 38)

38.12 Tighten the timing case bolts to their specified torque setting

38.14 Trim off the surplus part of the joint gasket

Fig. 1.33 Distributor driveshaft position after refitting timing case (Sec 38)

slightly clockwise as shown (photo). If the drive slot is in any other position, remove the timing case and make another attempt at aligning the driveshaft so that, on assembly, it finishes up in the correct position.

12 Fit the retaining bolts in their correct positions, referring to the figure if necessary, but don't tighten any until they are all located. Then they can be tightened to the specified torques (photo).

13 Refit the engine mounting bracket and flexible mounting. Where the timing case bolts do not locate in the joint flange they should have thread sealer applied to their threads. Tighten all engine mounting bolts to the specified torque.

14 When fitted, carefully trim off the surplus part of the joint gasket which protrudes above the rocker cover face (photo).

XL3 series engine

15 Turn the crankshaft to position the number 4 piston at top dead centre, (end of exhaust stroke – start of inlet).

16 Locate a new O-ring seal into position on the oilway. Smear it with oil before fitting.

17 Now position the distributor drive shaft as shown in the figure, so that when looking down on the drive, the horizontal engagement slot is positioned as shown with the small section side to the mating face of the timing cover, and the slot aligned with it.

18 The timing case and its new gasket can now be relocated onto the mating face of the cylinder block. As the case is fitted the distributor shaft will rotate one tooth in a clockwise direction caused by engagement with the helical cut of the drive and driven pinion teeth. When the case is fully located against the block the distributor drive engagement slot will be positioned as shown in the figure. When fitted in this position, the distributor will be in correct relationship with the crankshaft and valve timing to permit correct ignition timing. If the engagement slot is not positioned as shown, remove the timing case and reposition the driveshaft to give the correct alignment.

19 Locate the casing retaining bolts with their washers into their respective positions and tighten them to the specified torque wrench settings.

20 When fitted, carefully trim off the surplus part of the joint gasket protruding above the rocker cover face.

21 Refit the distributor, referring to Chapter 4 for detailed instructions.

22 The rest of the reassembly follows the reverse of the removal procedure. Don't forget to refit the safety stop plate at the right-hand track control arm, and tighten the pivot bolt nut to its specified torque. When all is reassembled replenish the sump with the engine oil, run the engine and adjust the ignition timing as described in Chapter 4. If necessary adjust the idling speed as described in Chapter 3.

39 Valve rocker clearances – checking and adjusting

1 This operation is the same whether carried out with the engine installed or on the bench. If installed it must only be done when the engine is cold. The importance of correct rocker arm clearances cannot be overstressed as they vitally affect the performance of the engine. If the clearances are too big, engine efficiency is reduced as the valves open too late and close too early. On the other hand inadequate clearances may prevent the valves closing when the engine is warmed up, resulting in burnt valve seats and possible warping.

2 As well as during the routine specified services, checking and setting the valve clearances must always be carried out after removing and refitting the cylinder head and also whenever the cylinder head bolts are retightened following overhaul.

3 During adjustments the engine can be progressively turned over to the position required by either jacking up a front wheel so that it is clear of the ground, then with 4th gear selected turn the wheel as required. The second and easiest method is to use an extension socket applied through the aperture of the left-hand wing valance and fitting onto the crankshaft pulley bolt. For this method the gearbox should be in neutral.

4 If the engine is installed, remove the air cleaner and the rocker cover.

5 It is important that the clearance is set only when the rocker of the valve being adjusted rests on the heel of the cam, that is directly opposite the peak of the cam. This can be ensured by carrying out the

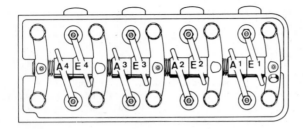

Fig. 1.34 Valve rocker clearance check sequence – XL3/XL3S engine type shown although XL5/XL5S and XK5 are checked in the same sequence (Sec 39)

Valves fully open	Adjust the rockers	
A1	E3	A4
A3	E4	A2
A4	E2	A1
A2	E1	A3

adjustments in the following sequence, which also avoids turning the engine more than necessary:

Valve fully open	Adjust valve numbers
1 exhaust	3 inlet and 4 exhaust
3 exhaust	4 inlet and 2 exhaust
4 exhaust	2 inlet and 1 exhaust
2 exhaust	1 inlet and 3 exhaust

The correct clearances are listed in the Specifications. The engine can be turned with a spanner on the pulley retaining bolt; removal of the plugs will make the job easier. Exhaust valves are at the front of the engine (when installed in the car), inlet valves at the rear.

6   Set the clearances by positioning a valve fully open and inserting a feeler gauge in the gap between the tappet and valve stem of the appropriate valve. Loosen the locknut with a spanner and turn the adjuster screw with a screwdriver (photo). Adjust the screw so that the feeler gauge slides in the gap with a slight drag. Tighten the locknut, recheck the clearance and readjust if necessary. Repeat until all clearances have been set.

7   Check that the rocker cover seal is in good condition, renewing it if in doubt, and refit the cover. Fit new sealing washers under the retaining bolts and tighten the bolts. Refit the air cleaner on an installed engine (photos).

39.6 Adjusting the valve clearances

39.7a Check the rocker cover seal and ...

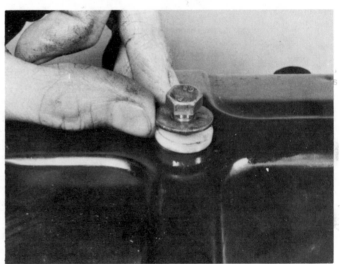

39.7b ... fit the cover to the cylinder head ...

39.7c ... using new seal washers under the bolt heads

41.2 Refit the oil gallery plate

40 Input pinion and clutch assembly – refitting

To refit the input pinion and clutch assembly refer to Chapter 5 Sections 10 and 9.

41 Engine reassembly – final stages

1 Having reassembled the major engine components, the various ancillary components and minor fittings can be re-installed. It is best to reassemble as much as possible before installing the engine/transmission in the car. If you elect to defer refitting some components until after installation be certain that it is in fact possible to refit them then.
2 Use a new gasket and, after checking that all is perfectly clean, refit the oil gallery cover plate (photo). Tighten the five bolts to the specified torque with new copper washers under their heads.
3 Refit the following components, referring to other Chapters if necessary:

(a) Thermostat (Chapter 2)
(b) Coolant pump and fan (Chapter 2)
(c) Exhaust manifold and damper
(d) Fuel pump (Chapter 3)
(e) Starter (Chapter 10)
(f) Distributor and coil (Chapter 4)

Leave the inlet manifold and carburettor until the engine is installed as it will then be easier to get to the gearchange mechanism and the fuel pump inlet to reconnect then. Fit the pump outlet pipe now if not already fitted.
4 Finally check the complete engine/transmission unit to make sure that nothing is missing unless it is being deliberately deferred until after the unit is installed.

42 Engine and transmission unit refitting – general

1 Before refitting the power unit give the bay a good clean out. A thick poultice of dirt and oil tends to accumulate round the bottom end which should be removed with a proprietary solvent and washed off. Make a general inspection for frayed and damaged wires, corrosion, cracks and so on. If appropriate, touch up the underbody protection wherever required in the engine bay. Make sure that the driveshaft splined ends are clean and lubricated with clean engine oil.
2 Although it is feasible for the engine unit to be refitted by one person using a suitable hoist, it is much easier for two people to work together so that the upper and lower parts of the assembly can be attended to whilst the unit is being manoeuvred into position, especially in view of the limited accessibility.
3 Check that new seals have been fitted to the differential final drives and that the space between the two lips in each seal has been filled with grease. See Chapter 6 for details.

43 Engine and transmission unit – refitting

1 Generally speaking the installation of the engine/transmission unit is the reverse of the removal procedure. First check that the lifting arrangements and sling are adequate for the job and securely attached to the lifting lugs on the engine.
2 Before lowering check that all loose wires, hoses and components in the engine bay are moved back out of the way. Apply a few drops of thread locking compound in the hole in the gear selector cover which accommodates the vertical bolt in the front end of the gear selection rod. Unscrew the threaded stud and locknut in the speedometer drive adaptor to permit entry of the speedometer drive cable end fitting.
3 Carefully lower the assembly into the bay. Keep the assembly moving slightly to confirm that it is not caught up as it is being lowered, and manoeuvre it over to one side of the bay. As soon as the unit is low enough engage the first driveshaft in the final drive, taking great care not to damage the oil seal in the drive. Move the engine assembly over towards the engaged shaft and turn the other front wheel outwards at the front to provide more room. Engage the second driveshaft. It might help in cases of difficulty to rock the car slightly and thereby alter the relationship between the shaft and final drive to permit engagement. Again be very careful not to damage the oil seal in the drive.
4 After engaging both shafts, fit the speedometer cable end fitting in the drive adaptor. Fit the retaining screw and locknut, tightening them both in that order.
5 Refit the oil level dipstick guide tube.
6 Move the assembly and lower it slowly to position the transmission rear edge under the steering box and locate the bottom right-hand mounting (photo) and left-hand mounting.
7 If they have not yet been fitted, install the two upper mounting brackets on the engine and lower the engine into final position. Fit and tighten all upper mounting nuts and bolts to the specified torque (see photo 4.27). Fit and tighten the lower mounting bolts to the specified torque. Unhook and remove the lifting tackle.
8 Clean the thread on the gear selection rod front bolt and lubricate the balljoint fittings with the specified grease. Reconnect the balljoints and fit the bolt, tightening it to the specified torque (photo). To assist

43.3 Engaging the left-hand drive shaft

43.6 The bottom right-hand mounting assembly

43.8 Reconnect the gearchange linkages

in this operation, get an assistant to support and move as necessary the main selector rod within the car, whilst you locate the balljoint to the gearbox linkage and engage the retaining clip to secure the joint.

9   If the starter motor is not already fitted refer to Chapter 10 for details and refit it. Reconnect the electrical connections and tighten the nuts.

10 Refer to Chapter 5 and refit the clutch control cable, adjusting it as described. On hydraulically operated clutch models, refit the operating cylinder onto the clutch housing and reocnnect the coil spring to the lever.

11 Refit the fuel pump and reconnect its feed hose. Also refit the ignition coil at this stage if it has been removed.

12 Reconnect the electrical connections to the coil and distributor.

13 Fit the inlet manifold and carburettor, making sure that all eight hose clips are in good condition and done up tightly. Fit the manifold support bracket, tightening the bolt in the engine/transmission joint face to its specified torque. Reconnect the coolant hoses to the carburettors and to the inlet manifold. Reconnect the fuel supply pipe and the vacuum advance pipe to the carburettor and the brake servo pipe to the manifold.

14 Refer to Chapter 10 and refit the generator then tension the drivebelt. Refit the voltage controller to its location on the left wheel bay wall.

15 Refer to Chapter 3 and refit the exhaust system piping. Make sure that there is a suitable clearance between the pipe and the rear subframe behind the sump.

16 Refer to Chapter 2 and refit the radiator. It would be worthwhile fitting new coolant hoses to and from the radiator if the originals have seen much service.

17 Refitting the battery tray and battery, but don't reconnect it yet.

18 Refit the front grille.

19 Reconnect the remaining coolant hoses and after a check to make sure that the system is complete, refill the system with new antifreeze mixture. Refer to Chapter 2 for details.

20 Reconnect the electrical harness connectors and any loose wires that remain. Make sure that the distributor rotor is fitted, then fit the cap and ignition harness. Fit a set of new spark plugs after checking their gaps and connect the ignition leads. Note that the plugs must be tightened to the correct torque on this engine as explained in Chapter 4.

21 Refer to Chapter 3 and reconnect the choke and accelerator controls. Leave the air filter until after the engine has been given its initial run.

22 Refill the sump with the correct grade of engine oil up to the full mark on the dipstick.

23 Go carefully round the engine to make sure that all reconnections have been made. Especially check that the electrical earth connections are made, the drivebelts are correctly tensioned, the carburettor controls are connected and that there are no apparent oil or coolant leaks. Remove all loose tools, rags, etc.

24 Reconnect the battery leads and check the operation of the electrical circuits.

25 If the suspension was disconnected to remove the engine/transmission unit, refer to Chapter 9 and reconnect it.

26 The engine is now ready for its initial run which is dealt with in the next Section.

44 Engine – initial start-up after overhaul

1   Make sure that the battery is fully charged, that fuel is in the tank and that coolant and lubricants are topped up.

2   It will require several revolutions of the engine on the starter motor to pump fuel up to the carburettor and fill it.

3   As soon as the engine fires and runs, keep it going at a fast tickover only (no faster) and bring it up to normal working temperature as indicated by the fan engaging.

4   As the engine warms up there will be unusual smells and perhaps some smoke as parts get hot and burn off oil deposits. Examine all systems closely for signs of leaks of coolant, oil or fuel. In addition check the exhaust manifold and connections in the exhaust system for leaks as these usually settle down after being heated and vibrated. When the engine is stopped these connections will need retightening.

5   If necessary a temporary adjustment of the carburettor idle setting can be made but final adjustment will be needed later with the air intake cleaner fitted.

6   When satisfactory running is achieved with no leaks, no tell-tale warning lights alight and no abnormal indications, exercise the accelerator and run the engine over its speed range but don't race it unnecessarily.

7   Stop the engine and check again for leaks. When cool enough, retighten the exhaust pipe connections and manifold nuts.

8   Allow at least two hours for the engine to cool down and then remove the rocker cover and retighten the cylinder head bolts as explained in Section 34, paragraph 21. Following this reset the valve clearances as explained in Section 39. Refit the rocker cover and fit the air cleaner as described in Chapter 3. Retighten the crankshaft pulley bolt to its specified torque. Refit the bonnet using the marks made on the hinges to ensure a good fit. Top up the oil and coolant to the full levels if required.

9   Restart the engine and, if necessary, trim the carburettor idle setting. Road test the car to check that the timing is correct and that the engine is giving the necessary smoothness and power. Don't race the engine – if new bearings and/or pistons have been fitted treat it as new and run it in at reduced speed, avoiding harsh acceleration, and using the gearbox to avoid loading the engine at low rpm.

10 After the car has travelled between 1000 and 1500 miles (1500 and 2500 km) the cylinder head bolts must again be retightened and the valve clearances reset.

45 Fault diagnosis – engine

Symptom	Reason(s)
Engine fails to start when starter switch operated	Battery discharged Battery connections loose or corroded Starter connection, or engine or battery earth straps, loose or broken Starter motor or solenoid fault (see Chapter 10) Ignition/starter switch fault Major mechanical failure (seizure)
Starter motor turns engine slowly	Battery discharged Battery connections loose or corroded Starter connections, or engine or battery earth straps, loose Incorrect grade of oil in use Starter motor fault (see Chapter 10)
Starter motor turns engine normally but engine fails to start	HT leads damp ot dirty Contact breaker points fouled or incorrectly gapped Spark plugs fouled or incorrectly gapped Loose or broken ignition connection Other ignition fault (see Chapter 4) Fuel tank empty, or pump defective Excessive/insufficient choke Choke linkage incorrectly adjusted Air cleaner clogged Carburettor jet(s) blocked Other fuel system fault (see Chapter 3) Valve clearances incorrect Incorrect timing (after rebuild) Poor compression
Engine fires but will not run	Loose ignition connection or internal fracture in wire Air leak at inlet manifold or carburettor joint face Fuel pump defective Other fuel system fault (see Chapter 3)
Engine idles erratically	Carburettor maladjustment or blockage (see Chapter 3) Ignition timing incorrect (see Chapter 4) Valve clearances incorrect Air leak at inlet manifold or carburettor joint face Air cleaner element clogged Uneven compression due to wear or leakage Worn distributor Worn timing components or valve gear

Chapter 2 Cooling system

Contents

Specifications

General
System type	Pressurised thermo syphon assisted by fan and pump
System capacity	5.8 litres (10.2 pints) or 6.7 litres (11.8 pints) if fitted with expansion tank

Radiator
Type	Plain or corrugated tin
Cap pressure rating:	
All early models	0.28 bars (4.06 lbf/in^2)
*Models from August 1979	0.8 bar (11.6 lbf/in^2)

*Radiator cap identification number is 800 in place of 280

Thermostat
Type	Wax capsule or bellows
Location	Cylinder head – clutch end
Opening temperature:	
Non accessible type thermostat	
Reference 1717	75°C (167°F)
Reference 2115	78°C (171°F)
Reference 3553	88°C (190°F)
Accessible type – electromagnetic fan equipped engines	
Reference V4856 (Calorstat) or 104006 (Thompson)	75°C (167°F)
Accessible type – conventional fan equipped engines	
Reference V4868 (Calorstat) or 104006 (Thompson)	78°C (171°F)
Accessible type – cold climate type with expansion tank	
Reference V4863 (Calorstat) or 104002 (Thompson)	88°C (190°F)
Accessible type – cold climate type without expansion tank	
Reference V4965 (Calorstat) or 104002 (Thompson)	88°C (190°F)
Late models from August 1978 on	82°C (180°F)

Coolant pump
Pump type .... Centrifugal impeller
Drive .... By V belt (adjustable from crankshaft pulley)

Electro-magnetic cooling fan
Armature to electro-magnet clearance .... 0.30 mm (0.011 in)
Electro-magnetic winding current at 12 volts .... 0.7 to 0.9 amps

Fan belt tension adjustment
Alternator equipped models .... 101.5 to 102 mm (3.99 to 4.01 in)
Dynamo equipped models .... 102 to 102.5 mm (4.01 to 4.03 in)

Torque wrench settings

	lbf ft	kgf m
Jockey pulley M7 bolts	9.4	1.3
Lower jockey pulley pivot bolt	39.7	5.5
Temperature sender (taper seat – no sealing washer)	20.0	2.75

1 General description

The cooling system is of the pump-assisted syphon type and is pressurised by means of a pressure valve filler cap. The main components of the system are the radiator, the coolant pump, the thermostat, the cooling fan (conventional or electro-magnetic), the heater and the various connecting hoses. The Coupe and Convertible models also have an expansion tank, and in this instance the system pressure cap is fitted to this rather than the radiator. The system operates as follows.

Cold coolant from the bottom of the radiator is pumped into the coolant passages of the engine cylinder block and cylinder head. Heat from the combustion chambers and moving parts of the engine is absorbed by the coolant which is then directed to the upper section of the radiator. The passage of air through the radiator (due to the action of the cooling fan, when engaged, and to the forward movement of the car) cools the coolant as it passes down through the radiator matrix and the cycle is then repeated.

To accelerate the warming-up process when starting the engine, and thereafter to maintain the correct operating temperature, a thermostat is fitted in the coolant outlet from the engine to the radiator top hose. When the coolant is cold the thermostat is closed and circulation is limited to the engine coolant passages by means of a bypass route. As coolant temperature rises, the thermostat opens to allow coolant to flow through the radiator.

The system is pressurised to raise the boiling point of the coolant. This allows the engine to achieve its most efficient operating temperature as well as reducing the amount of coolant needed. It also brings the risk of scalding if the cap is removed whilst the system is pressurised.

Hot coolant is tapped from the system to supply the heater matrix for car interior heater and also to supply heat to the carburettor and inlet manifold to improve fuel vaporisation. Some models are fitted with a conventional fan whilst others are fitted with an electro-magnetic type fan in which the fan pulley incorporates an electro-magnetic drive which is only energised when the coolant is hot. By this means the fan is only driven when it is really needed, with a consequent reduction in noise and power consumption.

2 Cooling system – draining

1   If the engine coolant is known to be in good clean condition and contains the correct ratio of antifreeze to water, it can be used again. Obtain a clean container of suitable capacity and position it under the radiator drain tap.

2   Set the heater control to hot.

3   On models fitted with an expansion tank, remove the pressurised filler cap from the tank. On other models remove the radiator filler cap. If the engine is cold, remove the pressurised filler cap by turning the cap anti-clockwise. If the engine is hot, then turn the filler cap very slightly until pressure in the system has had time to be released. Use a rag over the cap to protect your hand from escaping steam. If, with the engine very hot, the cap is released suddenly, the drop in pressure can result in the water boiling. With the pressure released the cap can be removed.

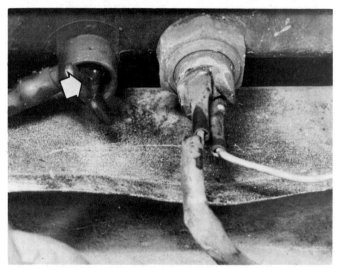

2.4 The radiator drain tap (arrowed). The fan thermo switch is to the right (where fitted)

4   Open the drain tap, located at the front bottom face of the radiator (photo).

5   When the coolant has finished draining, probe the drain cock with a piece of wire to dislodge any particles of rust or sediment which may cause blockage.

6   Remember that, without dismantling, it is impossible to drain the system dry as some coolant will be retained in the heater matrix. If there is no antifreeze in the system, frost damage is still possible in winter even though the system is 'drained'.

7   If you intend to re-use the coolant, cover it to prevent dust or other contaminants from affecting it.

3 Cooling system – flushing

1   Every two years the cooling system should be drained, thoroughly flushed and refilled with fresh coolant. This is necessary because sediment, rust and scale will have accumulated in the system and, if not removed, could lead to overheating. In addition, the corrosion inhibitors in the antifreeze fluid deteriorate with time and, to restore protection, the antifreeze mixture must be periodically renewed. The procedure is covered in Section 12 but it is convenient to combine the two operations.

2   Drain the system as described in the previous Section and remove the drain tap from the radiator. Cover the engine and all electrical circuits with a sheet of plastic to stop water getting on them, as you are bound to cause some splashing. Insert a hose in the radiator filler neck and flush the system with fresh water for ten to fifteen minutes.

3   In extreme cases of sediment formation it may be necessary to use a proprietary chemical cleaner and/or to reverse flush the system. In

the latter case disconnect the bottom hose from the radiator and remove the thermostat (Section 6). Direct the hose into the thermostat housing so that water is forced through the engine coolant passages and out of the bottom hose. To reverse flush the radiator it is advisable to remove it as described in Section 5 and invert it whilst flushing.

4   Flushing should be continued until the water runs clear and you are satisfied that the system is clean; then close the drain tap and refit any components which were removed.

4   Cooling system – filling

1   Check the condition and security of all cooling system hoses and connections, and ensure that the drain tap is firmly closed and that the heater temperature control is in the 'hot' position.
2   Fill the system slowly, using the antifreeze mixture, until the level approaches the radiator filler neck. Refit the radiator filler cap on expansion tank models and continue filling through the expansion tank. Carefully compress the top and bottom hoses with the hand to remove any air locks from the system, then continue filling until the level is within 2 in (50 mm) of the bottom of the filler neck in the radiator or to the maximum mark indicated on the expansion tank.
3   Firmly refit the filler cap and then start the engine and let it idle until the coolant is just warm. At this stage accelerate the engine several times to a fast speed to help move any air locks, then switch it off.
4   Carefully remove the filler cap and top up the coolant level as described in paragraph 2, then refit the cap.
5   If the original antifreeze is being re-used, remember that topping it up with plain water will dilute the mixture and weaken its properties; therefore it is best to use an antifreeze mixture for topping up.
6   Finally run the engine again and check the system for any leaks.

5   Radiator – removal, inspection, cleaning and refitting

1   Drain the cooling system as described in Section 2.
2   Loosen the clips securing the top and bottom hoses to the radiator and carefully ease the hoses off the connecting tubes. Detach the expansion tank connecting hose (where applicable) in a similar fashion.
3   Disconnect the electrical leads from the fan thermal switch located at the bottom front of the radiator.
4   Undo and remove the two bottom securing nuts in the radiator brackets and retrieve the rubber mounting washers. Undo the top securing bolt and carefully remove the radiator (photos).
5   Radiator repairs are best left to a specialist as without the relevant equipment it is quite easy to make matters worse, although minor repairs can be tackled with a proprietary compound. The radiator matrix, header and bottom tanks should be thoroughly examined for signs of damage, deterioration and leakage; very often a rusty sediment will have been deposited where a leak has occurred.
6   After inspection, the radiator should be flushed as described in Section 3 and the matrix and exterior cleaned of dirt and dead flies wth a strong jet of water.
7   Refitting the radiator is a reversal of the removal procedure but the following additional points should be noted:

   (a) Examine and renew any clips, hoses and rubber mounting washers which have deteriorated (photo)
   (b) Refill the cooling system as described in Section 4
   (c) Peugeot have fitted several radiator types over the years of production of the 304 and therefore if renewing, ensure that the replacement is suitable for your particular model

6   Thermostat – removal and refitting

1   The function of the thermostat is to enable the engine to reach its most efficient operating temperature in the shortest time, and this is accomplished by restricting the circulation of coolant to the engine during warming up; after reaching the operating temperature the thermostat opens and allows the coolant to circulate through the radiator.
2   A faulty thermostat can cause overheating or slow engine warm-up as well as affecting performance of the heater.
3   One of three types of thermostat will be fitted. In all cases the

5.4a Detach the thermal switch wires (1) and remove the lower mounting nuts (2)

5.4b Disconnect the radiator upper mounting support bolt

5.7a Renew the rubber mounting washers if necessary

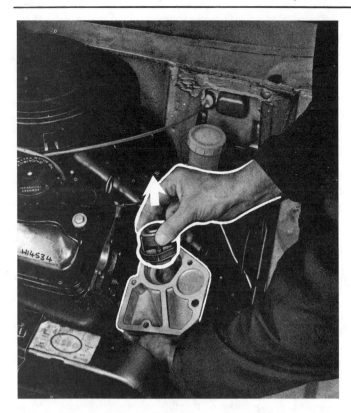

Fig. 2.1 Extracting the thermostat from the alternator bracket (Sec 6)

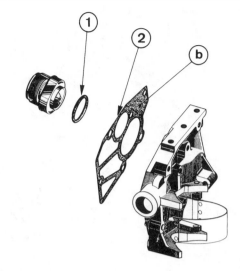

Fig. 2.2 Smear gasket (1) with oil before assembling. Check that gasket (2) has tab shown (b) (Sec 6)

Fig. 2.3 Thermostat removal (Type 11) (Sec 6)

thermostat is to be found at the clutch end of the cylinder head. The three types are removed and tested as follows. Refer to Type I, II or III as applicable for your model, having first drained off sufficient coolant to allow the thermostat removal, see Section 2. To test the thermostat refer to Section 7.

Type I (Internal thermostat)

4   Disconnect and remove the alternator referring to Chapter 10 if necessary for details.

5   Position a chock between the engine and subframe for support but do not raise the engine. Now detach and remove the upper left-hand engine mounting for access to the thermostat.

6   Unbolt and remove the alternator mounting bracket from the cylinder head end face, then extract the thermostat from it.

7   Clean the old gasket from the cylinder head/alternator bracket faces and then fit a new gasket and seal washers. It should be noted that there are two gasket types available and the 304 model has the gasket with tab (b) shown in the illustration.

8   Refitting of the thermostat and associated components is otherwise a reversal of the removal process. When the alternator is refitted and the drivebelt tensioned, top up the cooling system and then run the engine up to its normal operating temperature to check for any signs of coolant leaks. Don't forget to remove the wooden chock.

Type II (External thermostat)

9   Wrap a piece of polythene or suitable covering over the alternator to protect it from possible coolant spillage.

10   Unscrew and remove the thermostat housing to mounting bracket bolts and then withdraw the housing by pulling on the hose. Extract the thermostat from its recess in the bracket.

11   Clean off the housing to bracket mounting faces before reassembly and use new rubber seal rings each side of the thermostat. Ensure that the thermostat is inserted and positioned with the bleed notch facing upwards.

12   On reassembly, top up the coolant level, run the engine up to its normal operating temperature and check for leaks.

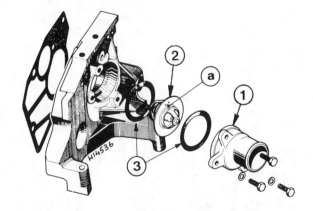

Fig. 2.4 Type II external thermostat and housing components (Sec 6)

1	Housing (outer)	3	Seal washers
2	Thermostat	(a)	Bleed notch to be positioned uppermost

6.13 Location of third type thermostat – access is not good when engine is in vehicle. Note that the housing hose connector pipe is angled towards the inlet manifold

6.16a Locate rubber seal washer and thermostat ...

6.16b ... followed by second washer and housing

Type III (Later models)

13 This thermostat is removable externally, but its access is obscured by the engine mounting on that side which is directly over the top of it (photo). Having partially drained off the coolant, detach and remove the intake ducting from the air cleaner unit.

14 Place a piece of polythene or rag over the alternator to protect it from coolant spillage then unscrew and remove the thermostat housing securing bolts to allow the housing to be withdrawn. You will find access restricted and may find it necessary to detach the coolant hose from the housing. Possibly the engine mounting itself may have to be removed. If this is the case place a chock between the subframe and engine for support.

15 Once the housing is removed extract the thermostat from its location in the cylinder head for testing or renewal.

16 Clean off the sealant faces prior to reassembly. Locate a new rubber washer seal each side of the thermostat as it is fitted (photos) and ensure that the bleed notch is uppermost.

17 Refitting is otherwise the reversal of the removal procedure. Refill the cooling system on completion, run the engine up to its normal operating temperature and check for any signs of leaks. Remove the wooden chock.

7 Thermostat – testing

1 If the cooling system thermostat is suspected of being defective, the only way to test it is to remove it as described in the previous Section. The testing procedure is the same for all thermostat types.

2 To test whether the thermostat is serviceable suspend it by a piece of string in a pan of water. Do not let the thermostat touch the pan. Heat the water. Use a similarly suspended thermometer to check the operating temperatures of the thermostat with reference to the information given in the Specifications. If the thermostat is faulty it must be renewed.

8 Coolant pump – removal, inspection and refitting

1 An impeller-type pump is located behind the radiator fan. The pump case is bolted to the front of the cylinder block by four bolts. The seal between the pump case and the cylinder block is a rubber O-ring fitted into a square recess. The pump is belt-driven from a pulley on the crankshaft. The belt is made to change direction from a 90° on two jockey pulleys, one of which is adjustable to permit adjustment of the belt tension.

2 Before removing the coolant pump, disconnect the battery earth lead. Refer to Section 2 and drain the cooling system. Refer to Section 5 and remove the radiator.

3 On models fitted with a conventional cooling fan, unscrew and remove the three fan to pump hub retaining bolts (with washers).

4 On models fitted with an electro-magnetic fan clutch unit, undo the three nuts securing the fan to the electro-magnetic clutch and remove the fan assembly. Do not disturb the three adjusting studs. Release the wire clip retaining the electrical brush in its housing on the magnetic clutch and carefully remove the brush, ensuring that it is not damaged (photo).

5 Slacken the belt tension adjuster on the lower jockey puller bracket and slacken the pulley pivot nut and bolt. Remove the drivebelt (photo).

6 Undo and remove the bolts securing the pump case to the cylinder block. Carefully remove the pump from the block; you might need to use a wooden lever to free the pump. Remove the old O-ring seal from the groove in the cylinder block.

7 Once the pump is on the bench, clean the exterior thoroughly. Undo the bolts securing the front half of the pump to the rear half and separate the two halves. Clean off all traces of the old gasket and sealer from the two halves and also clean the interior passages and the impeller.

8 Check the pump spindle for smooth rotation in its bearing and for freedom from sideways play. A small amount of endplay may be tolerated but if it is excessive and if there is an appreciable amount of sideways play the bearing is worn and the pump will need renewing.

9 Check that the fan hub revolves freely on its bearings on the pump spindle. Only a small degree of play is tolerable here. On models with

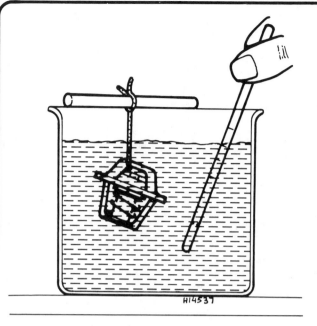

8.5 The water pump belt tensioner

Fig. 2.5 Thermostat test method (Sec 7)

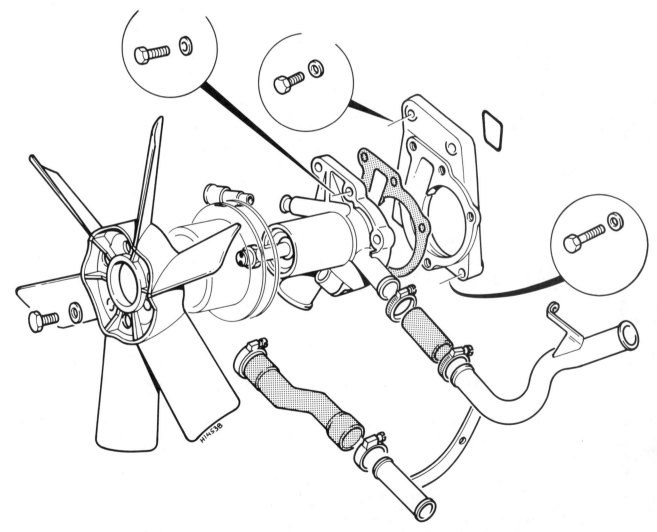

Fig. 2.6 Coolant pump and fan (conventional type) assembly components (Sec 8)

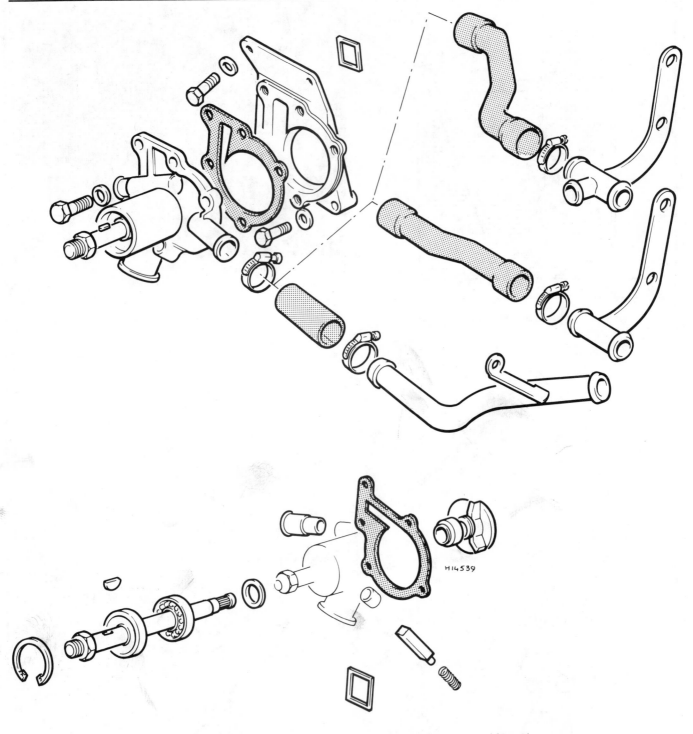

Fig. 2.7 Coolant pump unit components (electro-magnetic fan type) (Sec 8)

an electro-magnetic fan clutch unit, the gap between the fan hub and the pump pulley is adjustable and should be checked and, if necessary, adjusted as explained in Section 9.

10 The electro-magnet in the fan clutch should also be checked as explained in Section 9.

11 Reassembling and refitting the coolant pump, hub and fan assembly are essentially the reverse of the removal and dismantling sequences. Use a new gasket and sealer when reassembling the pump and a new O-ring in the cylinder block groove when refitting the pump. If wished, the pump case may be fitted to the block first, followed by the body of the pump (photos).

12 Retension the drivebelt on completion as described in Section 10.

9 Electro-magnetic fan clutch – checking and adjustment

1 The electro-magnetic fan clutch ensures that the fan is only driven when the temperature of the coolant is high enough to require assisted airflow through the radiator – when the car is moving slowly in traffic on a hot day, for example. A temperature switch in the bottom of the radiator closes when the coolant is hot, and electric current is directed to the clutch magnetic coil by a carbon brush located behind the fan. The clutch being part of the coolant pump, is always rotating when the engine is running. When energised, the fan is driven to assist radiator airflow. When de-energised, the fan spins freely if the car is in motion.

8.11a Locate a new O-ring seal into the block groove ...

8.11b ... then fit the pump case

8.11c Use a new gasket when fitting the pump

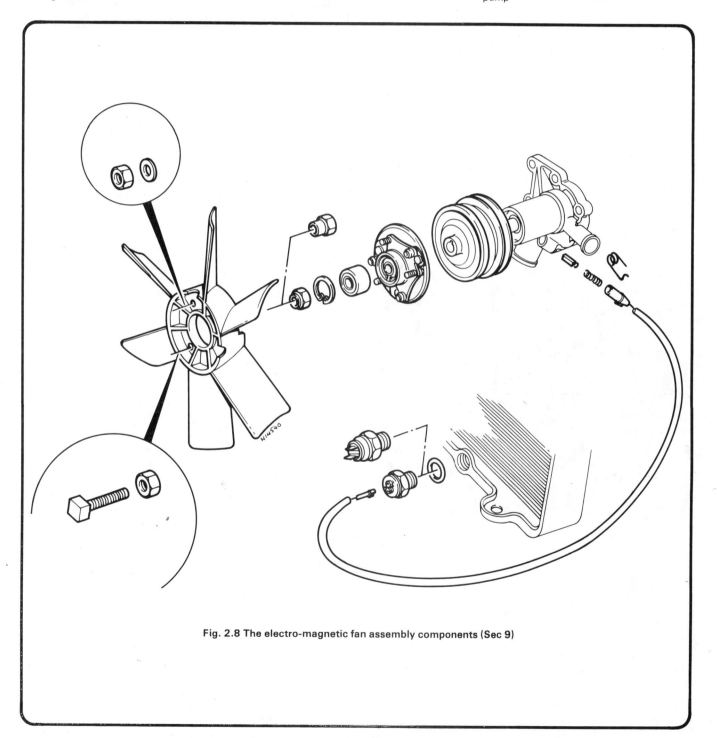

Fig. 2.8 The electro-magnetic fan assembly components (Sec 9)

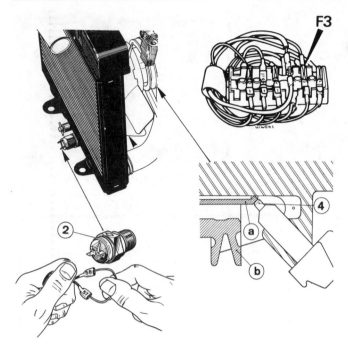

Fig. 2.9 Items to be checked in the event of the electro-magnetic fan malfunctioning (Sec 9)

F3   Fuse No 3
2   Switch wires (57 and 58)
4   The brush, collector ring (a) and pulley (b)

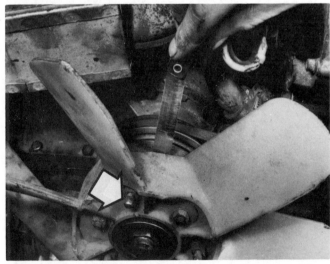

9.5 Measuring the fan to clutch clearance. Arrow indicates one of the three adjusting studs

2   To check the operation of the fan clutch, disconnect the electrical leads from the radiator temperature switch and, with the ignition switched on, short out the two connectors in the lead with a piece of wire. You should hear the electro-magnet click as the connectors are short-circuited.

3   If there is no noise of the electric-magnetic clutch being energised, first check condition of fuse number 3. If this is in order, examine the contact brush. Release the wire clip retaining the brush and carefully remove the brush from its housing. Examine for wear or contamination with dirt, grease etc, and check that it moves easily in its housing. Reassemble the brush and check that it is in contact with the collector ring on the clutch body.

4   To check the winding of the electro-magnet in the fan pulley, connect a 12 volt battery and ammeter in series with the clutch but to avoid dismantling put the carbon brush back in the holder temporarily and connect the lead from the positive terminal of the battery to the brush. **Do not** attempt to push a wire or prod through the brush holder direct onto the slip ring. You may scratch or burn it. Compare the ammeter reading with those listed in the Specifications. A high reading indicates a partial or complete short-circuit whilst a lower or zero reading denotes a break in the winding. In either case, or if the collector ring is scratched or damaged, the electro-magnet/pulley assembly will need renewing.

5   The gap between the fan assembly and the electro-magnet/pulley assembly is critical for the correct operation of the clutch. With the ignition switched off, that is with the clutch de-energised, measure the gap, using feeler gauges, at three points adjacent to the three adjusting studs in the fan. Compare the gap with that listed in the Specifications. To adjust the gap, loosen the locknut and turn the adjusting stud in or out as required. Tighten the locknut before rechecking the gap and repeat the procedure on the other two adjusting studs.

6   The coolant temperature switch is a simple thermal switch which closes two contacts at a given temperature and opens them on cooling. If you have a thermometer you can check its operation by first connecting a 12V bulb to the switch in place of the lead to the electro-magnetic clutch and to earth. Run the engine and monitor the temperature of the coolant in the radiator with the thermometer noting when the light comes on and when it goes out. It should cut in at between 84 to 90° and cut out between 68 to 82°C. A more accurate test could be made by immersing the threaded part of the switch in water with a lamp wired in series with a 12V battery and checking the light operation with a thermometer in the water as it is heated. However, this procedure would entail removal of the switch from the radiator which in turn would require the system to be drained.

10 Drivebelt – tension adjustment

1   Correct tensioning of the drivebelt will ensure that it has a long life. If the belt is loose, pump and fan functioning will be adversely affected and if it is too tight it will cause unnecessary bearing wear. Either way the belt itself will suffer.

2   On some models the generator is also driven by the fan belt. On later models the alternator drive is by a separate belt driven by the outer track of the crankshaft pulley. Photo 11.3 illustrates the later type.

3   The drivebelt is tensioned by adjusting the position of the lower of the two jockey wheels on the later models. If you are reassembling the engine the water pump drivebelt must always be fitted before the alternator drivebelt.

4   To tension the drivebelt first ensure that the lower jockey pulley pivot pin nut and pin are slightly loosened, that the belt is snugly fitted on all four pulleys, and that maximum twist is 90° on each leg between pulleys. With the belt slack make two marks on the belt 100 mm apart (work in metric units for this adjustment). Tighten the lower jockey pulley adjusting bolt to tension the belt so that the marks open up to 101.5 to 102 mm (on alternator equipped models) or 102 to 102.5 mm for dynamo equipped models. Alternatively, tighten the adjuster until the belt has 0.5 in (13 mm) play when deflected by thumb pressure at a point mid-way between pulleys. Tighten the jockey pulley pivot pin and nut to the specified torque.

5   If you have fitted a new belt and tensioned it, run the engine briefly and then readjust the tension. Check the tension again after about 500 miles (800 km) as some belts tend to stretch initially.

6   For the procedure for tensioning the alternator drivebelt on later models refer to Chapter 10, Section 13.

11 Drivebelt – removal and refitting

1   If the driveshaft is worn, frayed or unduly stretched it should be renewed. However, the most common reason for renewing a belt is that the original has broken, and it is therefore advisable to carry a replacement in the car for such an occurrence. The same reasoning applies to the alternator drivebelt on later models.

2   To remove the water pump drive belt on later models first refer to

11.3 View showing the water pump drivebelt arrangement on later models with the alternator and its drivebelt removed

12.4 The temperature gauge sender unit

Section 10 and remove the alternator drivebelt and then proceed as follows.

3   Loosen off the lower jockey pulley pivot pin nut then screw back the adjuster bolt in the pulley bracket (photo) sufficiently to enable the belt to be disengaged from the jockey pulley(s) and generator.

4   Slip the belt out of the crankshaft and pump pulleys and lift it over the fan blades, turning the fan to help removal of the belt.

5   Fit a new belt on the pulleys and make sure that the maximum twist is 90° between pulleys. Tension the belt as described in the previous Section.

6   Refer to Chapter 10 for the procedure for changing the alternator drivebelt.

12 Antifreeze mixture

1   In weather conditions where the ambient temperature is likely to drop below freezing point it is essential to use an antifreeze solution in the cooling system; if the coolant is allowed to freeze in the engine or radiator, serious damage can result which could be very expensive to repair. A further consideration is the need for anti-corrosive protection especially in modern alloy engines. As approved antifreeze fluids containing anti-corrosive additives are available it is recommended that antifreeze mixture is used all the year round for double protection.

2   Peugeot recommend that a 40% mixture of antifreeze and clean (preferably rain) water is used in the 304. The system holds a total of 10.2 pints (5.8 litres) and to mix a 40% solution, 4.1 pints (2.3 litres) of antifreeze will be needed.

3   Before filling with fresh antifreeze mixture, drain and flush the system as described in Sections 2 and 3. The easiest way to make the mixture is to put two or three pints of water into the system, add the correct amount of antifreeze and top up with water. Follow the full filling procedure described in Section 4.

4   Antifreeze mixture can remain in the system for up to two years

when it should then be renewed. It is a sensible precaution to have the strength of the mixture checked periodically, especially at the onset of winter, and adjusted as required. Special antifreeze hydrometers are now available in motor accessory shops and are simple to use, following the maker's instructions. Alternatively your local garage will make the check for you.

5   Renew any hoses or clips whose condition is doubtful before adding fresh antifreeze mixture to the system.

13 Temperature gauge and sender unit – testing, removal and refitting

1   If the temperature gauge is faulty and gives an incorrect reading, either the sender unit, the gauge, the wiring or the connections are responsible.

2   First check that all the wiring and connections are clean, sound and secure. The sender unit and the gauge cannot be repaired by the home mechanic, and therefore they must be renewed if proved faulty.

3   The wiring can be checked by connecting a substitute wire from the sender unit direct to the temperature gauge, running the engine (make sure no loose wires foul the fan) and observing the result. Alternatively, a test lamp or electrical multi-meter can be used to check the continuity of the wires.

4   A suspect sender unit is best checked by substituting a new unit. The sender unit is located just in front of the thermostat housing at the top left-hand side of the cylinder block. Before removing it, partially drain the system as described in Section 2, then disconnect the supply lead and unscrew the unit (photo).

5   Refit the new sender unit using a reversal of the removal procedure, and then refill the cooling system as described in Section 4.

6   Details of removing and refitting the temperature gauge are contained in Chapter 10.

Fault diagnosis overleaf

14 Fault diagnosis – cooling system

Symptom	Reason(s)
Overheating (check gauge for accuracy)	Low coolant level (due to leakage or neglect) Broken or slipping pump drivebelt Engine oil level low or incorrect grade Thermostat defective Fan clutch not operating correctly Coolant pump defective Internal or external clogging of radiator matrix Internal clogging of engine waterways Radiator pressure cap defective New engine not yet run-in (drive more slowly!) Brakes binding (see Chapter 8) Ignition timing retarded or automatic advance defective (see Chapter 4) Mixture too weak (see Chapter 3) Cylinder head gasket blown Cylinder head or liner(s) distorted or cracked
Overcooling (check gauge for accuracy)	Defective thermostat Fan clutch not operating correctly
External leakage	Overfilling (loss due to expansion) Loose or perished hoses Leaking coolant pump or thermostat gaskets Defective pressure cap Coolant pump seals defective Radiator matrix damaged Heater matrix damaged
Internal leakage	Blown head gasket (steam in exhaust and/or combustion gases in coolant) Head or liner(s) cracked or warped Inlet manifold cracked

Chapter 3 Fuel and exhaust systems

Contents

Specifications

Air cleaner
Type .... Oil bath type or dry disposable element type

Fuel pump
Type .... Mechanical engine-driven pushrod operated

Fuel tank
Type and location .... Flat tank under rear floor
Capacity .... 9.2 gal (42 litres)

Fuel grade
All models .... Super grade 4-star petrol (97 RON)

Carburettor types fitted:
XL3 engine .... Solex 34 PBISA3 or Solex 34 PBISA4
XL3S engine .... Solex 35 EEISA
XK5 engine .... Solex 34 PBISA5 (PEU 102)
XL5 engine .... Solex 34 PBISA5 (PEU 110)
XL5S engine .... Solex 32/35 TCICA (PEU 103)

Carburettor specifications

	PBISA3	PBISA4	PBISA5(XK5)	PBISA5(XL5)
Venturi	26	26	26	26
Main jet	140	*132.5	130 ± 2.5	132 ± 2.5
Correction jet	180	150	140 ± 10	160 ± 10
Emulsion tube	E2	E24	S01	S01
Idle jet	55	55	44 ± 5	43 ± 5
Bleed (air) orifice	220	180	180	180
Accelerator pump injector	45	40	45	45
Pump stroke/butterfly opening	6.5	6.5	6.0 ± 0.5	6.0 ± 0.5
Mixture jet	–	E40	–	–
Needle jet	1.5	1.5	1.5	1.5
Float weight (g)	5.7	5.7	5.7	5.7
Uniform CO jet	–	–	30	30
Uniform CO air orifice	–	–	180	180
Normal idle position (NIP)	–	–	40'	40'
Throttle positive opening (OP)	–	–	12°40'	13°

* Main jet from 1972 (PEU 82 carburettor)   130 to 135

	35 EEISA
Main jet	122.5
Venturi	24
Correction jet	120
Emulsion tube	ND
Idle jet	50
Bleed (air) orifice	80
Bleed (below choke)	200
Bypass (slot)	0.6 x 6
Accelerator pump injector	35
Pump movement for butterfly opening	Cam
Needle valve	1.8
Float weight (g)	6.2

	32/35 TCICA	
	1st barrel	2nd barrel
Venturi	24	24
Main jet	117.5	120
Correction jet	140	160
Emulsion tube	SO8	S1 P1
Idle jet	51	50
idle air orifice	125	50
Accelerator pump injector	40	–
Pump stroke (full) for throttle opening	Cam No 4	–
Uniform jet (CO)	100 ± 10	–
Needle valve	1.5	1.5
Float weight (g)	7.2	7.2
Throttle normal idle position	30'	45'

Idling speed ...... 900 ± 50 rpm

1 General description

The fuel system on the Peugeot 304 model range is conventional in layout and operation. The fuel tank is located at the rear underneath the luggage compartment. Fuel is drawn from the tank by a mechanical diaphragm operated pump located on the engine timing case beneath the distributor. The pump is operated by a pushrod activated by an eccentric cam on the oil pump/distributor driveshaft. The fuel pump incorporates a mesh filter.

One of six types of Solex carburettor are fitted, depending on the engine model, being of either single or twin choke downdraught design. The carburettor body is warmed by hot coolant tapped from the engine cooling system. A Mesh type filter is fitted to the carburettor fuel inlet connection.

Depending on model and year of manufacture, the carburettor air filter will be an oiled element type, an oil bath air filter type or a renewable dry element type.

On some models the air intake temperature is controllable by means of a flap valve near the exhaust manifold within the intake ducting. This is manually controlled and is really designed for seasonal adjustment. Some models have an automatic temperature control unit within the filter body itself.

2 Air filter element – removal and refitting

1   Several types of air filter element have been fitted to the Peugeot 304. On earlier models an oiled element type filter was used whilst later models have a dry element filter, which is in fact made of oil moistened porous material.
2   As air is drawn into the carburettor, dust and dirt adhere to the element which progressively becomes contaminated and must eventually be renewed. Under severe conditions in dusty atmospheres renewal must be more frequent than normal. The maker recommends that normal renewal should be at the following intervals:

Oiled element filter (neoprene mesh) – 12 500 miles (20 000 km)
Oiled element filter (formed polyurethane) – 12 500 miles (20 000 km)
Dry element filter – 18 500 miles (30 000 km)

3   When operating in severe dusty conditions these renewal mileages should be halved.

Fig. 3.1 The oil bath air filter location (for certain countries only) (Sec 2)

4   In addition to the above renewal intervals, the oil bath type element should be removed, washed in fuel and its container also cleaned out. When dried the element should then be soaked in engine oil and the container topped up with the required amount of clean engine oil to the level mark in the container, the amount of oil required for this are about 0.44 pint (250 cm³). The element and top cover are then refitted. The intervals at which this task should be carried out being 4500 miles (7500 km).
5   To remove the filter element on the oil bath type prise free the retaining clips and lift the top cover away sufficiently to enable the element to be lifted out of the container.
6   On the dry element type filter the element is removed by unscrewing the top cover retaining nuts and lifting the cover clear taking care not to stress the hose connection and, where applicable, the automatic pre-heat control.

2.10 Insert element and refit the top cover

2.11 Air filter unit removal from carburettor

7 Withdraw the old element and wipe clean the inside of the container and cover using a fluff-free rag.

8 On the oil bath type element top up the oil level in the container (see paragraph 4) and insert the new (or cleaned) oiled and drained element.

9 The dry type element is simply located in position in the container, but with both types ensure that the element is seated correctly.

10 Refit the top cover and make secure with its clips of nut(s) (photo).

11 To remove the element container, first remove the element as described previously and then unscrew the container unit to carburettor or external bracket fastenings whichever is used. Detach the hose connections and unhook the intake pipe spring (if one is fitted). Lift the container unit clear.

12 Refit in the reverse order of removal ensuring all connections are secure on completion.

3 Air cleaner – inlet preheat device

1 The air cleaner unit is fitted with either a manually operated or automatically operated inlet preheat device depending on model. This system operates by drawing hot air from around the exhaust manifold. This hot air assists in increasing the carburettor's efficiency when the

Fig. 3.2 Manual setting lever for summer/winter air intake to air cleaner (Sec 3)

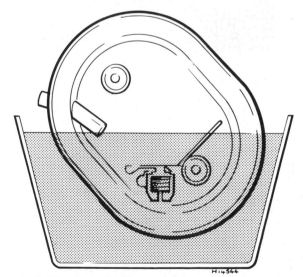

Fig. 3.3 Immerse the filter container as shown into water preheated to specified temperature to test operation of thermal unit (Sec 3)

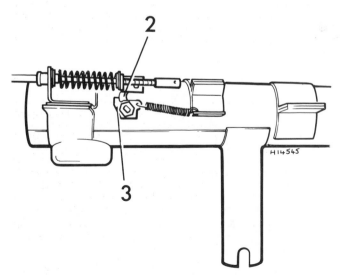

Fig. 3.4 Levers 2 and 3 should contact after specified period (Sec 3)

engine is cold and the ambient air temperature is below 10°C (50°F).

2   With the manual setting type the valve lever on the air intake tube should be set to 'HIVER' (winter) at temperatures below 10°C (50°F) or to 'ETE' (summer) when the ambient temperature rises above this figure.

3   With the automatic type preheat control system a temperature sensing device is fitted into the air cleaner unit container and this opens or closes, as required, the hot air distributor flap in the air intake.

4   The preheat sensor device can be tested for operation by removing the air filter and extracting its element, then immersing the container, as shown, into water at 15°C (60°F) so that the thermal unit is submerged. After being submerged for a period of five minutes the distribution flap should close the hot air intake, shown by the levers being in contact.

5   If necessary adjustment can be made by altering the cable stop setting to provide the correct movement.

4   Fuel pump – removal, servicing and refitting

1   The fuel pump is located at the right-hand rear corner of the engine, mounted on the timing case. Access is diffucult because, on right-hand drive cars, the brake servo and master cylinder are mounted directly over the distributor which itself is located over the fuel pump (photo). The pump has an inlet and an outlet hose connection and it is secured to the timing case by two bolts. More than one type of pump has been fitted by the makers on these models but they all operate on the usual lever-actuated diaphragm principle. Although routine filter cleaning should present few problems, make sure that a servicing kit is available before completely dismantling a pump; it may be necessary to fit a new pump if the installed one is giving trouble and no servicing spares are obtainable.

2   To remove the pump, disconnect the inlet and outlet hoses and temporarily plug them to prevent loss of fuel or ingress of dirt. Unscrew the two retaining bolts and carefully lift the pump clear from the timing case. Remove the old gasket.

3   On the type of pump shown in the photographs the top cover is retained by two screws. Other models of pump may have a different number of screws. Remove the cover retaining screws and note that they have sealing washers under their heads. Remove the cover and the gasket underneath. The filter will be seen in the pump body (photo).

4   Take the filter and wash it in clean fuel (photo). Don't use any cloth or tissue for filter cleaning, let the filter dry in air. Clean out the pump bowl with fuel; you may find some sediment in the bottom which must be removed. Again don't use rags for cleaning.

5   Further dismantling may not be possible on some types of pump. Even if it is, it should only be attempted if you have a repair kit. First mark the top and bottom halves of the pump for reassembly and then progressively loosen and remove the screws holding the two halves together. The diaphragm is connected to the operating mechanism beneath, and details will vary with different pumps. Note the sequence of assembly so that reassembly can be achieved in the same order.

6   Renew all defective parts; the kit will contain a variety of seals or gaskets which should be fitted in place of the originals regardless of the fact that they may appear fit for further use.

7   Reassembly is the reverse of the dismantling sequence. Make sure that the upper and lower halves of the pump body are aligned and tighten the joint screws progressively and diagonally. Don't overtighten the top cover screws.

8   Before refitting the pump check that the operating plunger is in position in the timing case and use a new gasket which must be of the same thickness as the original. Tighten the two securing bolts to the specified torque and make sure that the fuel hoses are connected to their correct pump connections (photo).

5   Fuel pump – testing

1   If the performance of the fuel pump is in doubt, first examine for fuel leaks and check that the fuel line connections are all sound.

2   Disconnect the fuel hose at the carburettor inlet connection and

4.1 Fuel pump removal/fitting and access point is through the aperture in the right-hand wheel arch valance

4.3 Remove the top cover

4.4a Extract the fuel filter for cleaning

4.4b Clean out the pump bowl

4.8 Use new gasket and check that operating plunger is in position when refitting

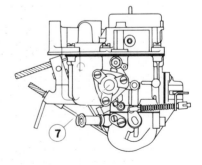

Fig. 3.5 The Solex 34 PBISA4 carburettor showing location of the enrichment device fitted to certain models (Sec 6)

disconnect the high tension lead from the coil. Ensure that the tank contains fuel.

3   Direct the fuel feed hose into a suitable container and have an assistant operate the starter to crank the engine. A good spurt of fuel should be delivered on every second revolution of the engine. If not, check that the hose is not blocked. If that is clear the pump will need removal for examination of renewal.

6   Carburettors – general description

1   Over the years of production of the Peugeot 304, six types of Solex carburettor have been fitted. The carburettor type is stamped on an identification plate attached to the carburettor.

2   All carburettors are of downdraught design, the 34 PBISA series Solex being a single barrel type, whilst the 35 EEISA and 32/35 TCICA Solex models are twin choke types. The twin choke carburettors are only fitted to the XL3S and XL5Sseries engines.

3   All carburettors are relatively conventional in design and incorporate the following features:

(a)   a cold start system
(b)   an idling circuit
(c)   a uniform CO circuit
(d)   a progression circuit
(e)   a main circuit
(f)   a diaphragm type accelerator pump

4   Operation of the carburettors follows conventional practice. Fuel enters through a mesh filter and fills a chamber to a level which is controlled by a float operated valve.

5   During normal engine running above idling, the depression generated in the venturi draws fuel through a main jet to an emulsifying tube located in the venturi where the air/fuel mixture is admitted to the main air stream. A conventional butterfly valve throttle controls the flow of the mixture.

6   At idling, due to inadequate depression at the venturi, an air/fuel mixture is delivered to the edge of the almost closed throttle butterfly where a greater depression exists. Mixture and volume control screws are provided to adjust the engine idling speed.

7   On the twin choke (or compound) carburettor types, the primary barrel is designed to regulate the full mixture supply during the low and medium engine speed ranges, whilst the secondary barrel becomes operational only during high engine speeds or under full load conditions. The secondary barrel circuit is operated mechanically by interconnecting levers on the 35 EEISA carburettor. On the 32/35 TCICA model it is controlled automatically by means of a depression diaphragm (vacuum capsule) reacting in accordance with the vacuum being created within the throttle barrels.

8   The 32/35 TCICA incorporates an Econostat device in the secondary barrel which supplies fuel to an outlet above the venturi where, with an open throttle, the depression is large enough to cause the fuel to enter the airstream. At lower engine speeds with the throttle nearer the closed position this depression diminishes and no fuel flows. In this way the engine receives a weaker mixture at low engine speeds. Such a mixture at high engine speeds would cause overheating and possibly mechanical damage.

9   The choke flap incorporates a poppet valve which is lightly sprung closed. When the engine is being turned on the starter the poppet remains closed, accentuating the choke effect and thereby assisting starting. As soon as the engine is running the poppet opens to reduce the choke effect.

10   The diaphragm type accelerator pump ejects fuel directly into the venturi on each occasion that the throttle is opened. The pump recharges itself when the throttle is closed. This additional fuel helps to produce smooth acceleration as otherwise there would be a momentary weakening of the air/fuel mixture entering the engine due to the inertia of the fuel.

11   Reverting to the single barrel carburettor types, it should be noted that two types of 34 PBISA carburettors have been used according to the engine ignition distributor type. If the engine has an M43 type distributor the carburettor will incorporate a vacuum advance control, but if an M70 distributor is fitted there is no vacuum advance control and in addition the carburettor will be fitted with an enrichment device.

7   Carburettor – maintenance

1   Before blaming the carburettor for any shortcomings in engine performance, remember that there is no reason why the carburettor should lose tune and in fact what usually happens is that, as the engine gets older and less efficient, more or less fruitless attempts are made to restore performance by interfering with the carburettor. In those parts of the world where exhaust emission is regulated by law it is inadvisable and may be illegal to alter carburettor settings without monitoring exhaust emission levels using special equipment.

2   The ultimate cause of most carburettor problems is wear in moving parts or dirt in the jets. The Solex carburettor has no continuously moving parts except for the float and the throttle spindle which makes it a very reliable device so long as dirt does not get in. A drop of oil on the various linkages and flap spindle will ensure that they last for years without trouble; in consequence carburettor overhaul should be no more frequent than major engine overhaul.

3   Routine carburettor maintenance consists only of periodic cleaning of the float chamber and jets and an occasional look at the small gauze filters fitted in the fuel inlet connection and on the accelerator pump inlet valve. These tasks can be undertaken with the carburettor installed on the engine. The jets can be identified and located by reference to the relevant illustrations. The gauze filters are also shown.

4   Before separating the top of the carburettor from the bottom, give the outside a good clean using paraffin or a proprietary cleaner and a stiff brush, afterwards drying with clean rag. It is well worth taking this extra trouble to reduce the risk of dirt getting into the carburettor. Take care when separating the top cover not to damage the gasket or a new one will have to be fitted on reassembly. This is always advisable.

5   The following special precautions should also be observed when cleaning or overhauling carburettors:

(a)   35 EEISA carburettor: Do not alter the settings of the butterfly stop screw or the butterfly partial opening screw when the choke flap is open
(b)   32/35 TCICA carburettor: Do not alter the setting of the by-pass screw. This is pre-set during manufacture
(c)   After removing the jets clean them by washing in clean fuel and blowing air through them. Never use a piece of wire as the jet calibration can be easily altered.

6   The float can be removed after taking out the hinge pin. The float needle valve can then be unscrewed and washed in fuel. Clean any dirt out of the float chamber using clean fuel but don't use rag for drying. The fuel inlet filter gauze and the accelerator pump inlet valve gauze should both be washed in clean fuel and dried in air, again don't use rag to dry them.

7   Check the float level before refitting the top cover. For further checks and adjustments, refer to the relevant Section concerned for your carburettor type (photo).

7.7 Carburettor type is given on a data tab (arrowed)

Fig. 3.6 The Solex 35 EEISA carburettor idle speed screw (Z) and mixture screw (W) positions depending on model (Sec 8)

Chapter 3 Fuel and exhaust systems

8.4 The volume or idle speed setting screw of the 34 PBISA 5 (PEU 102) carburettor

8.5 The mixture screw adjustment (34 PBISA 5 carburettor)

8 Carburettor – adjustments

1   Generally speaking unless the carburettor is obviously out of tune or is malfunctioning it is not advisable to tamper with it. In any case the only running adjustment that can be made is to the idling.

2   Correct adjustment can only be achieved provided that the engine is in generally good condition. The valve clearances must be correct and the ignition system must be in good condition and adjusted correctly.

3   An independent tachometer is necessary to make accurate adjustment and it should be connected to the engine in accordance with the maker's instructions. The air filter must be fitted. Run the engine until warmed (as indicated by the engagement of the cooling fan where applicable).

4   If local regulations preclude adjustment other than the volume control screw, adjust the idling speed to that listed in the Specifications (photo).

5   Where it is not illegal to adjust on both the volume and the mixture screws, first adjust the volume control screw over the accelerator pump link (photo) to obtain the specified idling speed plus 50 rpm, giving 950 rpm. On the XL5S model increase the idle speed to 980 rpm (32/35 TCICA carburettor).

6   If fitted remove the tamperproof plug from the mixture screw and then turn this screw, either way, to achieve the maximum rpm at that throttle setting. Repeat the adjustments on the volume control screw and then the mixture screw until the maximum speed achieved, after adjusting the mixture screw, is 50 rpm above the specified idling speed. When this point is reached tighten the mixture screw slightly to reduce the idling speed to that specified.

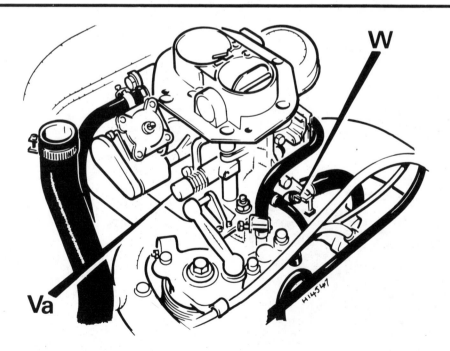

Fig. 3.7 The Solex 32/35 TCICA carburettor adjustment screws (Sec 8)

Va   – Idle speed (volume) screw   *W   – Mixture screw*

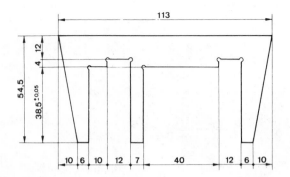

Fig. 3.8 Details of float level setting gauge for the Solex
34 PBISA5 carburettor – dimensions in mm (Sec 9)

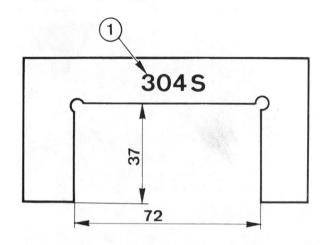

Fig. 3.9 Details of float level setting gauge for the Solex
35 EEISA carburettor – dimensions in mm (Sec 9)

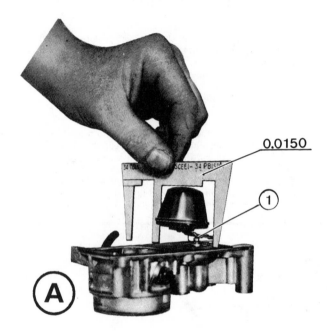

0,0150

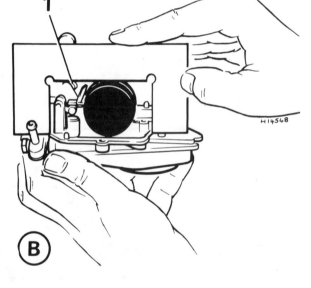

Fig. 3.10 Using the float level setting gauge (Sec 9)

A 34 PBISA5 carburettor
B 35 EEISA carburettor
C 32/35 TCICA carburettor
(1) indicates adjustment point

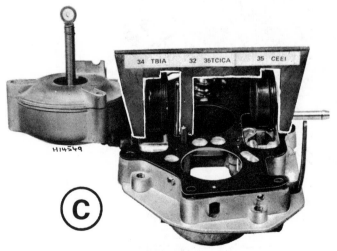

Fig. 3.11 Float level adjustment on the 32/35 TCICA carburettor is on arm tab indicated (Sec 9)

10.3 Detach the fuel and vacuum hoses

10.9 Reconnect the coolant hoses

9 Carburettor – float level adjustment

1   The float level should be checked before reassembling the carburettor after routine maintenance or when the level adjustment may be in doubt. Flooding of a carburettor is nearly always due to dirt in the needle valve or a punctured float. However, incorrect level adjustment can also be the culprit even though it is unlikely.

2   Incorrect fuel level in the carburettor will drastically affect engine performance and it is essential to maintain the correct level. This is easily done by adjusting the float which controls the needle valve. A special gauge is necessary but one can be made from scrap material quite simply by the home mechanic. The carburettor top cover must be removed for this adjustment.

3   To make the gauge that you require for your particular model of carburettor, refer to the figures and cut one out to the shape and exact size shown. It can be made from thin sheet metal or plastic. Material is not important, but accuracy in size is critical so take care on this.

4   Apply the gauge to the inverted top of the carburettor, making sure that the sealing gasket is in position. The flaot should just contact the gauge with the needle valve closed. As the Solex 35 EEISA carburettor hold the gauge so that it rests on the outer sealing surfaces of the cover as shown. In this position the smaller diameter section of the float should just be in contact with the gauge (needle valve shut).

5   If adjustment is necessary, proceed as follows:

   (a) Solex 32/35 TCICA and 34 PBISA carburettors: bend the float arm tab

   (b) Solex 35 EEISA: bend the float arm bracket. Do this carefully and then recheck the adjustment with the gauge.

10 Carburettor – removal and refitting

1   Carburettor removal requires either partial draining of the cooling system or the clamping of the two coolant hoses connected to the carburettor to prevent loss of coolant. Refer to Chapter 2 for coolant draining procedures.

2   Remove the air cleaner unit referring to Section 2 if necessary.

3   Loosen the fuel feed hose connection and pull the hose off the carburettor inlet union. Temporarily plug the hose to prevent fuel loss and dirt ingress (photo).

4   Pull free the vacuum advance pipe which leads to the distributor from its carburettor connection.

5   Undo the choke cable retainer and disconnect the cable from the carburettor control lever.

6   Disconnect the throttle cable from the spring-loaded drum and the bracket on the carburettor.

7   Undo and remove the nuts securing the carburettor to the intake manifold and lift the carburettor off. Retrieve the old joint gasket and put a piece of cloth over the aperture in the manifold to prevent anything from falling in accidentally whilst the carburettor is removed.

8   Refitting the carburettor is the reverse of the removal procedure. Remove all traces of the old gasket and use a new one on installation. After fitting the carburettor reconnect the choke and throttle controls, Make sure that the choke is correctly adjusted. When the control is pushed fully in, the flap should be fully open and there should be a small amount of possible additional movement on the control knob.

9   After reconnecting the two coolant hoses remove the clamps if these were used and in any case top up the cooling system (photo).

10 Adjust the idle speed on completion as described in Section 8.

11 Solex 34 PBISA carburettor – dismantling, reassembly and adjustment

1   The carburettor should not normally need to be dismantled except for cleaning and checking the float level.

2   If the carburettor is to be dismantled, remember that it is a relatively delicate instrument and therefore requires careful handling.

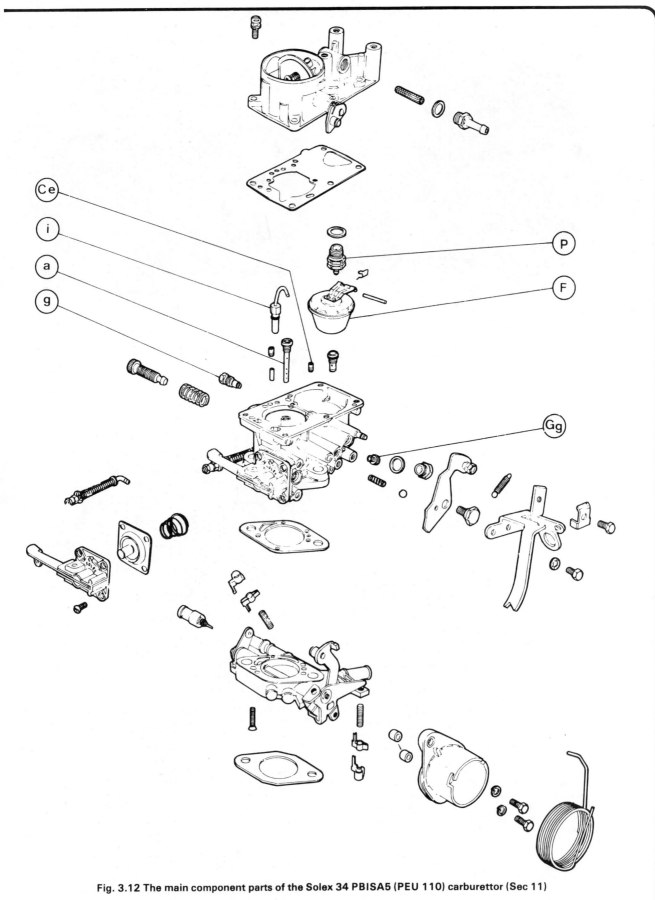

Fig. 3.12 The main component parts of the Solex 34 PBISA5 (PEU 110) carburettor (Sec 11)

Gg	Main jet	g	Idling jet	P	Needle valve	Ce	Econostat orifice
a	Corrector jet	i	Pump in injector	F	Float		

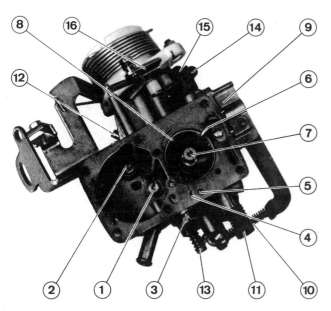

Fig. 3.13 Float body components – 34 PBISA5 carburettor (Sec 11)

Fig. 3.14 Upper body components – 34 PBISA5 carburettor (Sec 11)

1 Main jet	10 Connecting rod (accelerator pump/throttle)
2 Accelerator pump inlet valve	11 Pilot screw (idle speed adjuster)
3 Idle jet	12 Vacuum hose to distributor union
4 Idle air orifice	13 Mixture screw
5 Constant CO jet	14 Throttle stop screw
6 Accelerator pump injector	15 Screw - throttle closure adjustment
7 Correction jet	16 Choke control lever
8 Removable venturi	
9 Accelerator pump	

17 Inlet union
18 Choke
19 Needle valve

20 Constant CO orifice
21 Choke control lever

Use the correct tools for the job and do not interchange jets or clean them out with wire or any similar item which could damage them and interfere with their calibration.

3 Before dismantling the carburettor or any part of it, first clean the outside and prepare a clean work area. When taking anything mechanical apart, and this applies particularly to such components as carburettors, it is always sound policy to make sure that the individual parts are put back exactly where they came from, and even the same way round if it is possible to do otherwise, even though they may appear to be interchangeable. To help in this procedure mark or label items, put small parts in boxes or tins so that they don't get mixed up, and lay parts out in order of assembly on clean paper.

4 Identify the relevant illustrations for the carburettor being dismantled. Remove the top of the carburettor by undoing the retaining screws and separating the cover from the lower part. The float can be removed by pushing out the hinge pin and then the needle valve assembly can be unscrewed from the cover. Unscrew the fuel inlet connection and remove the gauze filter. Examine the filter for particles of foreign matter.

5 Remove the accelerator pump operating rod and then remove the cover by progressively undoing the four retaining screws, restraining it against the action of the spring under the diaphragm. Examine the diaphragm for splits or damage.

6 Remove the accelerator pump inlet valve cover located in the bottom of the float chamber, taking care not to lose the ball valve. Examine the filter for contamination.

7 Unscrew and remove the jets, checking them for dirt or blockage. Observe the caution mentioned in paragraph 2.

8 It should not be necessary to interfere with any adjusting screws but, if this is necessary, count the number of turns required to remove the screw so that it can be refitted in approximately the same position.

9 Do not disturb the choke flap and throttle butterfly valves or spindles. Their actuating mechanisms are external and normally require no attention unless excessively worn. If the spindles are worn

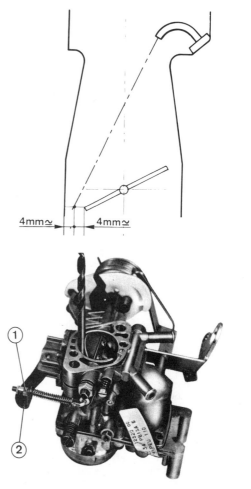

Fig. 3.15 34 PBISA5 carburettor – accelerator pump stroke check method and adjuster nut (1) and lever (2) (Sec 11)

in the carburettor body then serious consideration should be given to renewing the complete carburettor. Such wear is an indication that the carburettor is due for renewal and it would be false economy to refit the original instrument. Air leaks around worn spindles make it impossible to tune the carburettor correctly and poor performance and impaired economy will inevitably result.

10 The respective chambers, passages and jet seats can be brush cleaned using clean fuel and they should then be blown dry, if an air supply is available, or allowed to dry naturally. Don't use rag or cloth. Clean and blow through the jets in a similar manner.

11 Reassembly is the reverse of the dismantling procedure. Whenever possible use new washers, gaskets, or seals wherever fitted. During reassembly check and adjust the float level as described in Section 9, and set the accelerator pump stroke and injector as given below.

Accelerator pump stroke and injector check/adjustment

12 After disturbance of the accelerator pump linkage, or if the performance of the pump is suspect, the pump stroke and the injector seating should be checked. Any adjustment found necessary can easily be made. The carburettor must be removed for this check.

13 The pump stroke is set by using a gauge to position the throttle butterfly and then adjusting the pump linkage. The gauge can be of an appropriate size twist drill, but the shank must be in good condition. See the Specifications for the diameter required.

14 To make the check the carburettor must be inverted. Loosen the nut on the pump linkage rod between the throttle lever and the pump operating arm. Open the throttle and insert the drill shank between the edge of the flap and the intake bore. Lightly hold the flap in this position, turn the adjusting nut (or screw) until it just contacts the pump operating arm and then tighten the locknut. Check the adjustment and then remove the drill from the carburettor barrel.

15 Fuel from the accelerator pump is delivered by an inverted U-tube nozzle in the carburettor bore. The setting of the nozzle should be checked and adjusted whenever the accelerator pump performance is suspect.

16 The carburettor should not be installed for this check as neat fuel would be injected into the manifold. For this reason position a suitable receptacle under the carburettor and, with the fuel hose connected, fill the float chamber. Open the throttle manually and observe the pattern of fuel spray as it is ejected into the carburettor bore. It should be midway between the edge of the throttle and the barrel wall when the throttle is open about 8 mm (0.315 in).

17 If correction is necessary, gently bend the injection nozzle to obtain the required direction of spray. Recheck after adjustment.

12 Solex 35 EEISA carburettor – dismantling, reassembly and adjustment

1 The main components of this carburettor are shown in the figure. The dismantling, cleaning and inspection procedures are similar to those given in Section 11 for the Solex 34 PBISA carburettor.

2 Whenever this carburettor is being overheated, it is important that the following items are not removed or their settings altered.

   (a) Butterfly stop screw
   (b) Butterfly partial opening (choke flaps open) setting screw
   (c) The correction jets

3 Before refitting the top cover assembly, check the float level setting as given in Section 9.

4 Use a new top cover gasket when reassembling.

5 When the carburettor is refitted to the car, check the adjustment of the butterfly partial opening settings before refitting the air cleaner unit. Then check the accelerator pump setting. The details of these checks are given below.

Butterfly partial opening check (under choke)

6 Pull out the choke control knob and then push the vacuum capsule operating rod to give partial choke flap opening. Using a suitable gauge rod of 2 to 3 mm diameter (a drill shank is ideal), insert it between the primary barrel and the butterfly flap as shown. Should adjustment be necessary to correct this clearance, loosen off the choke cable to lever nut and move the lever. Then retighten the cable securing nut. Withdraw the gauge and refit the air cleaner unit.

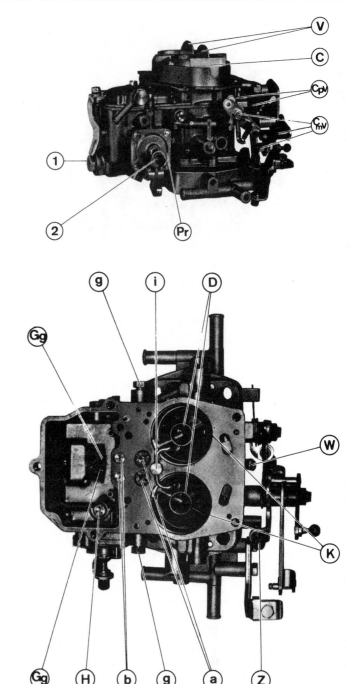

Fig. 3.16 The Solex 35 EEISA carburettor showing the main component locations (Sec 12)

1	Float bowl plug (access for main jets)	W	Mixture screw
		a	Correction jets (fixed)
2	Accelerator pump plunger adjustment screw	b	Bleed jets (fixed)
		D	Sprayers
C	Choke flaps	g	Idle jets
CmV	Manual choke control	Gg	Main jets
CpV	Pneumatic choke control	H	Acceleration pump valve
Pr	Accelerator pump	i	Dual injector (accelerator
V	Choke flaps		pump)
Z	Idle running stop screw	K	Choke tubes

Accelerator pump adjustment

7   Before making this check, run the engine up to its normal operating temperature and ensure that the idle speed is as specified, then turn the engine off.

8   Check that the choke is fully released (flaps open). Then with the pump level in contact with the throttle spindle cam, loosen off the adjuster screw to give a suitable clearance between it and the accelerator pump plunger. Operate the plunger and check that it returns fully to the stop and then retighten the adjuster screw so that it just contacts the plunger.

13 Solex 32/35 TCICA carburettor – dismantling, reassembly and adjustment

1   Dismantling procedures are similar to those given for the 34

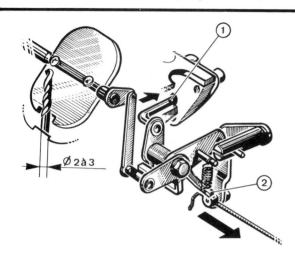

Fig. 3.17 Solex 35 EEISA carburettor – partial butterfly opening check (Sec 12)

1   *Vacuum capsule rod*   2   *Adjustment lever*

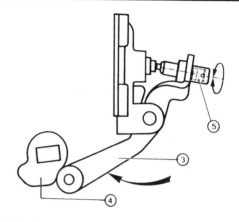

Fig. 3.18 Solex 35 EEISA carburettor – acceleration pump adjustment (Sec 12)

3   *Lever*   5   *Adjustment screw*
4   *Cam*

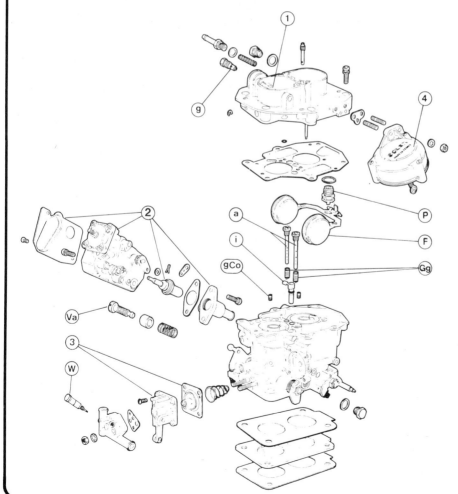

Fig. 3.19 Solex 32/35 TCICA carburettor components (Sec 13)

1   *Choke flap*
2   *Automatic cold start device*
3   *Accelerator pump*
4   *Vacuum capsule (2nd barrel operation)*
(g)   *Idling jet*
(a)   *1st and 2nd barrel correction jet*
Gg   *1st and 2nd barrel main jet*
i   *Accelerator pump injector*
Va   *Volume (idle speed) control screw*
W   *Mixture screw*
F   *Float*
P   *Needle valve*
gCo   *Uniform CO jet*

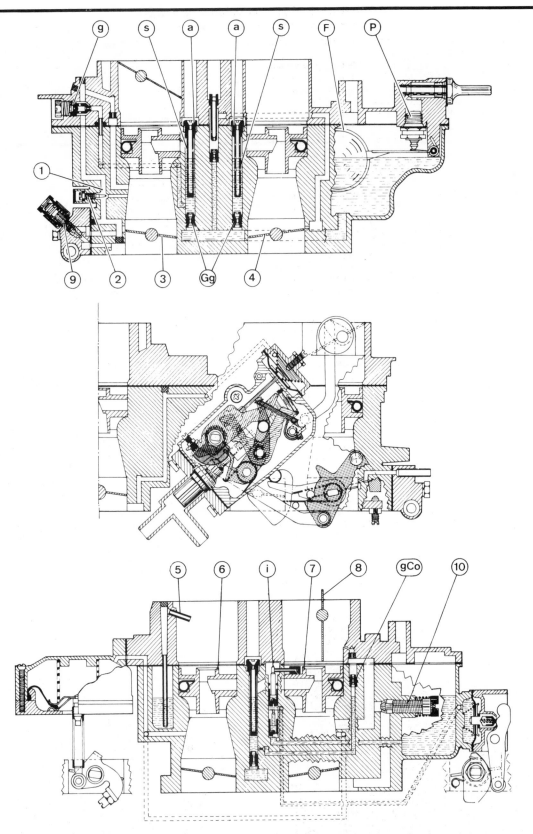

Fig. 3.20 Solex 32/35 TCICA carburettor – sectional views showing locations of main components
(Sec 13)

1	Bypass	6	1st barrel venturi	10	Volume (idle) control screw	g	Idle jet
2	Bypass screw	7	2nd barrel venturi	Gg	Main jets	gCo	Uniform CO jet
3	1st (primary) barrel throttle	8	Choke flap	a	Correction jets	P	Needle valve
4	2nd (secondary) barrel throttle	9	Mixture control screw	s	Emulsion tubes	F	Float
5	Econostat						

PBISA carburettors in Section 11. Do not remove or alter the bypass screw, the position of which is shown.

2   Where a tamperproof plug is fitted to the throttle stop screw it can be removed by simply gripping with suitable pliers and pulling free. The mixture screw tamperproof plug can be removed in a similar manner, but you will have to break the head of the plug first.

3   It is not advisable to dismantle the automatic cold start device any more than is essential. If necessary the wax expansion capsule can be renewed by removing the end cover and gasket. Renew the gasket on assembly.

4   Before refitting the top cover assembly, check the float level setting as described in Section 9, the same gauge tool and procedure being necessary.

5   Reassemble in the reverse order using new gaskets for the pre-heat union, capsule and upper cover. Also fit a new progression circuit O-ring.

6   Before fitting the carburettor checks should be made on the primary and secondary throttle valve angles in their normal idling position. This requires the use of specialised equipment and should therefore be entrusted to your Peugeot dealer as the settings are quite critical. On refitting the carburettor refer to Section 14 and make the necessary adjustments and checks given in that Section before refitting the air filter unit.

14 Solex 32/35 TCICA carburettor – adjustments with carburettor fitted

1   Three checks/adjustments are possible on this carburettor with it fitted and these are:

(a) Idle mixture adjustment
(b) Choke opening (on starting)
(c) Positive opening

To check the idle adjustment, refer to Section 8 for details.

Choke opening check/adjustments

2   To check the operation and adjustment of the choke opening after starting you will need Peugeot special gauge tool number 8-0143. If this is available proceed as follows.

3   Start the engine and run it up until its normal operating temperature is reached. Then remove the air filter unit and the cold start operating device cover plate.

4   With the engine running, locate the gauge (8.0143) as shown so that the gauge hole is over the pivoting roller and with the gauge pivoted so that it abuts the casing. In this position the choke flap

Fig. 3.21 Solex 32/35 TCICA carburettor – choke opening adjustment (Sec 14)

1   Locknut   2   Adjustment screw

Fig. 3.22(a) Solex 32/35 TCICA carburettor – positive opening adjustment (Sec 14)

1   Adjuster screw   X = 2 mm clearance

Fig. 3.22(b) Special gauge (8.0143) location (Sec 14)

Fig. 3.22(c) Detach spring (inset) and pushdown on lever (3) (Sec 14)

should allow a 5 mm gauge rod (drill shank) to pass down between itself and the carburettor inner wall.

5   If adjustment is necessary, loosen off the adjuster screw locknut and adjust the screw accordingly, then retighten the locknut.

Positive opening check/adjustment

6   This check/adjustment also requires the use of Peugeot special gauge tool number 8.0143, and a tachometer.

7   If not already checked, first inspect the choke opening as described previously to ensure that it is correct, then proceed as follows.

8   Check the choke assembly pivot roller position with the engine running and the cover plate removed. Measure the clearance between pointer 'X' which should be 2 mm (0.07 in), Should adjustment be necessary to achieve this clearance, insert a screwdriver and adjust the screw outlined (1).

9   Now locate the gauge (8.0143) on the cold start casing as shown and then tighten the screw to the point where the roller is registered with the gauge notch. Remove the gauge.

10 With the pivoting roller adjustment correct the positive opening can be set. Unhook and remove the coil spring and then pull down the lever as shown so that it abuts the roller. In this position the engine speed should be 3800 rpm ($\pm$ 50 rpm) with the fan inoperative. If adjustment to achieve this engine speed, tighten the positive opening stop screw to increase, or loosen to reduce the engine speed. Blip the

accelerator and recheck this adjustment, then refit the coil spring, the cover plate and air cleaner unit to complete.

Idle speed

The idle speed adjustment screw can be adjusted when the engine is at its normal operating temperature to give the specified idle speed.

---

15 Accelerator cable – removal and refitting

1   Undo the nut and bolt clamping the inner cable of the accelerator control to the spring-loaded drum on the carburettor, remove the cable from the groove on the drum and pull the cable and its outer protective sheath from the anchor point on the carburettor bracket.

2   Working inside the car, detach the cable end fitting from the end of the accelerator foot pedal. Withdraw the cable assembly from the car by pulling it into the passenger compartment, at the same time feeding it through the bulkhead grommet.

3   Before fitting a new cable assembly lubricate the inner cable with engine oil.

4   Refitting an accelerator cable assembly is the reverse of the removal procedure. Before tightening the inner cable clamp bolt check that the inner cable is correctly located in the groove on the spring-loaded drum (photo). Tighten the clamp bolt and nut and check that the throttle is fully closed with the foot pedal free. If necessary readjust the inner cable in the clamp bolt and nut.

Fig. 3.23 Idle speed adjustment screw on the 32/35 TCICA carburettor (Va) (Sec 14)

15.4 Accelerator cable must locate in groove (arrowed)

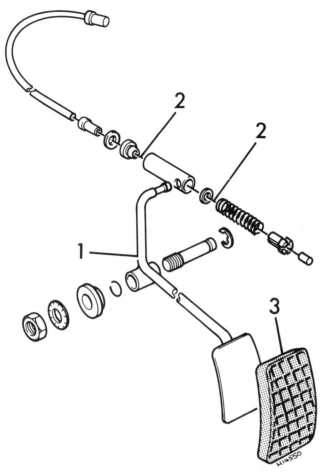

Fig. 3.24 The accelerator cable and pedal attachment components (Sec 15)

1   Pedal assembly and pivot   3   Pedal rubber
2   Cable assembly

16.1 Inner cable securing bolt (arrowed)

17.2a Fuel tank gauge transmitter unit location

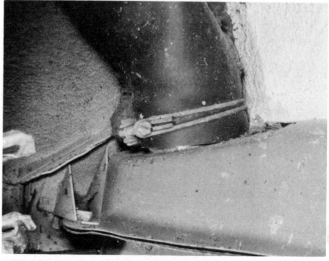

17.2b Filler hose to tank connection

16 Choke cable – removal and refitting

1   Loosen the clamp bolt securing the inner cable in the choke flap operating link (photo).
2   Loosen the bolt securing the clamp plate which holds the outer sheath on the carburettor bracket. Detach the inner cable and outer sheath from the carburettor.
3   Working inside the car, remove the knob from the choke control cable and undo the control retaining nut. Push the control through the facia and then disconnect the choke warning light cable from the switch on the control.
4   Pull the control assembly into the car, working it through the rubber grommet in the bulkhead.
5   Refitting the choke control is the reverse of the removal procedure. When fitted, with the air cleaner removed, check that the choke is fully open when the control knob is pushed home and closed when the knob is pulled. Check that the warning light is on when the choke is pulled.

17 Fuel tank – general

1   The fuel tank is located under the car floor between the rear wheels.
2   If it is necessary to remove the tank, first drain or siphon out as much fuel as possible. Access to the fuel feed and the fuel gauge transmitter is gained by removing the plastic cap in the boot floor. Disconnect all connections referring to the photos for details and, after

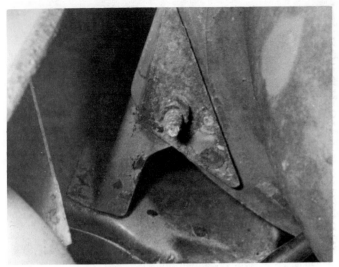

17.2c Petrol tank secured at rear by nuts and bolts ...

17.2d ... and at the front by bolts at each corner

18.2a The exhaust manifold down pipe coupling with the exhaust damper to the left. Note the hot air duct take off ...

18.2b ... which fits as shown ...

removing the tank attachment bolts, manoeuvre it off its support ledges and remove it from the car (photos).

3   Don't attempt to repair a tank unless it is completely empty of fuel and fuel fumes. This can only satisfactorily be achieved by steam cleaning and it is best to leave this sort of repair to a specialist.

4   On refitting the fuel tank, refill it and then check it and its connections for any signs of leaks.

18 Exhaust system – general

1   A conventional type of exhaust system is fitted to all models although it may differ according to model and year of production.

2   A couple of items which are perhaps slightly unusual in the system are the exhaust damper unit which is mounted to the underside of the manifold and the main manifold downpipe which has a fitting which enables hot air to be ducted to the air cleaner (photos). No additional maintenance is required on these items.

3   Maintenance is limited to checking for gas leaks and repair by renewal. Whilst temporary repairs can be made with proprietary materials such as tape or paste, the only satisfactory repair is renewal of the system, or part system if the fault is limited to one area.

18.2c ... locating with the intake ducting at the top end

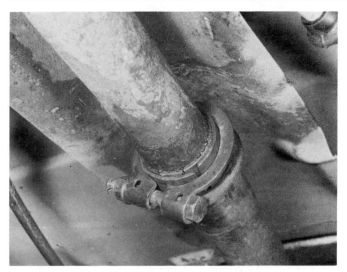

18.3a Check the system joints ...

18.3b ... and location straps for security and condition

However when one part of the system requires renewal it often follows that the whole lot is best renewed.

4   When removing the old system don't waste a lot of time trying to undo rusted and seized bolts. Cut them off. New ones will be required in any case if they are that bad.

5   When fitting the new system use an exhaust joint sealant when assembling pipe sections to ensure that the respective joints are free from leaks. Get the system into position but don't tighten anything up until everything is properly located. After checking that all is well you can then tighten the securing bolts or nuts. If the flexible hangers are breaking up or otherwise deteriorated they must be renewed, otherwise the system will vibrate leading to leaks or even fractures.

Fault diagnosis overleaf

19 Fault diagnosis – fuel and exhaust systems

Unsatisfactory engine performance and excessive fuel consumption are not necessarily the fault of the fuel or carburettor. In fact they more commonly occur as a result of ignition and timing faults. Before acting on the following it is necessary to check the ignition system first. Even though a fault may lie in the fuel system it will be difficult to trace unless the ignition is correct. The faults below, therefore, assume that this has been attended to first (where applicable).

Symptom	Reasons
Excessive fuel consumption	Excessive use of throttle Short journeys (engine not warming up) Leakage Air cleaner blocked Choke control maladjusted Incorrect use of choke control Carburettor float level incorrect or needle valve defective Carburettor badly worn Excessive carbon build-up in cylinder head Engine badly worn
Difficult starting when cold	Choke control maladjusted Carburettor float level incorrect Air leaks at inlet manifold or carburettor
Difficult starting when hot	Air cleaner blocked Choke control maladjusted Carburettor float level incorrect or needle valve defective Vapour lock in fuel line (especially in hot weather or at high altitude)
Backfiring in exhaust system	Air leaks in manifold(s) or exhaust system Weak mixture Incorret valve clearances or burnt exhaust valve(s) Inocrrect valve timing (after rebuilding) Incorrect ignition timing or other ignition fault
Spitting back in carburettor	Incorrect valve clearances or burnt inlet valve(s) Weak mixture Incorrect valve timing (after rebuild) Incorrect ignition timing or other ignition fault
Insufficient fuel delivery	Tank empty Fuel tank vent pipe blocked Fuel line blocked Leak on suction side of pump (air bubbles in delivered fuel) Pump defective or filter blocked Carburettor inlet union filter blocked

Chapter 4 Ignition

Contents

Specifications

Type .... 12 volt, negative earth, coil and contact breaker type distributor

Firing order 1-3-4-2

Distributor
XL3 engine with Solex 34 PBISA3 carburettor .... Ducellier M43
XL3 engine with Solex 34 PBISA4 carburettor .... Ducellier M70
XL3S engine with Solex EEISA carburettor .... Ducellier M75
XK5 engine .... Ducellier M90 or Paris-Rhone DA4 ES5
XL5 engine .... Ducellier M89 or Paris-Rhone DA4 ES4
XL5S engine .... Ducellier M91 or Paris-Rhone DA4 ES6
Distributor drive .... Skew gear from crankshaft and off-set dogs in driveshaft
Ignition advance .... Centrifugal and vacuum control
Contact breaker gap .... 0.015 in (0.40 mm)
Dwell angle .... 57° ± 2°
Percentage dwell .... 63% ± 3%

Static advance
Engine with M43 distributor .... 12° BTDC
Engine with M70 or M75 distributor .... 5° BTDC
All XK5, XL5 and XL5S engines .... 8° BTDC

Spark plugs
Type:
    XL3 engine .... Champion N7
                                        AC 41/2 XLS
                                         Marchal 34/5HS
    XL3S engine .... Champion N6Y
                                           Marchal 34/5HS
    XK5, XL5 and XL5S engines .... Champion BN9Y
                                           AL 42 LTS
                                           Bosch WA 200T 30

Electrode gap .... 0.024 in (0.6 mm)

Torque wrench settings

	lbf ft	kgf m
Spark plugs	13.0	1.75

1 General description

In order that the engine may run correctly it is necessary for an electrical spark to ignite the fuel/air mixture in the combustion chamber at exactly the right moment in relation to engine speed and load.

Basically the ignition system functions as follows. Low tension voltage from the battery is fed to the ignition coil, where it is converted into high tension voltage. The high tension voltage is powerful enough to jump the spark plug gap in the cylinder many times a second under high compression pressure, providing that the ignition system is in good working order and that all adjustments are correct.

The ignition system comprises two individual circuits known as the low tension (LT) circuit and the high tension (HT) circuit.

The low tension circuit (sometimes known as the primary circuit) comprises the battery, lead to ignition switch, lead to the low tension or primary coil windings and the lead from the low tension coil windings to the contact breaker points and condenser in the distributor.

The high tension circuit (sometimes known as the secondary circuit) comprises the high tension or secondary coil winding, the heavily insulated ignition lead from the centre of the coil to the centre of the distributor cap, the rotor arm, the spark plug leads and the spark plugs.

The complete ignition system operation is as follows:

Low tension voltage from the battery is changed within the ignition coil to high tension voltage by the opening and closing of the contact breaker points in the low tension circuit. High tension voltage is then fed, via a contact in the centre of the distributor cap, to the rotor arm of the distributor. The rotor arm revolves inside the distributor cap, and each time it comes in line with one of the four metal segments in the cap, these being connected to the spark plug leads, the opening and closing of the contact breaker points causes the high tension voltage to build up, jump the gap from the rotor arm to the appropriate metal segment and so via the spark plug lead, to the spark plug where it finally jumps the gap between the two spark plug electrodes, one being earthed.

The ignition timing is advanced and retarded automatically to ensure the spark occurs at just the right instant for the particular load at the prevailing engine speed.

The ignition advance is controlled both mechanically and on most models, by a vacuum-operated system. The mechanical governor mechanism comprises two weights which move out under centrifugal force from the central distributor shaft as the engine speed rises. As they move outwards they rotate the cam relative to the distributor shaft, and so advance the spark. The weights are held in position by two light springs, and it is the tension of these springs which is largely responsible for correct spark advancement.

The vacuum control comprises a diaphragm, one side of which is connected, via a small bore tube, to the carburettor, and the other side to the contact breaker plate. Depression in the induction manifold and carburettor, which varies with engine speed and throttle opening, causes the diaphragm to move so moving the contact breaker plate and advancing or retarding the spark.

From August 1979 onwards, all models were fitted with a diagnostic socket. This device is designed to enable Peugeot mechanics using specialised equipment, to pinpoint any problem within the ignition system. Unfortunately without the necessary equipment, the diagnostic socket is of little use to the home mechanic.

2 Contact breaker points – initial adjustment

1 To adjust the contact breaker points accurately, the use of a dwell meter is required and this is explained in the next Section. As many owners will not possess a dwell meter the following paragraphs describe adjusting the points with a feeler gauge. This will enable the car to be taken to a garage where the points can be accurately set with a dwell meter. Even if you have a dwell meter you will need to make an initial check/adjustment of the contact breaker gap clearance before checking the dwell angle. Where the contact breaker points have been removed, for servicing or renewal, they will have to be reset to the specified clearance before you can tune with the meter.

2 First prise the distributor cap retaining clips away and lift the cap

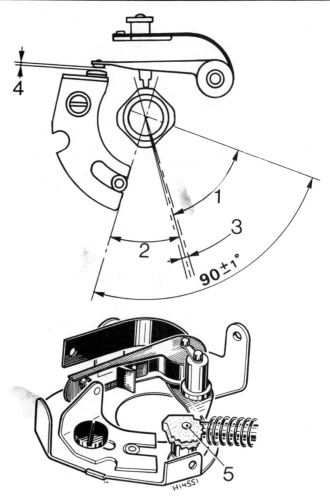

Fig. 4.1 Contact breaker points and dwell angle settings on the earlier distributor

1 Dwell angle
2 Opening angle
3 Tolerance angle
4 Specified points gap

5 Toothed quadrant on early models with vacuum advance

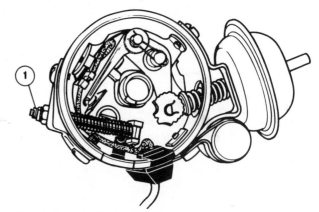

Fig. 4.2 Contact breaker adjustment on the later Ducellier type distributor – turn nut 1 (Sec 2)

from the distributor. Clean the cap thoroughly with a clean dry cloth and check that the segments are not excessively burnt. Examine the cap closely for cracks. Burnt segments or cracks in the cap will require the cap to be renewed.

3 Check that the carbon brush in the roof of the cap moves in and out freely by depressing it once or twice and check that the brush is not broken or chipped.

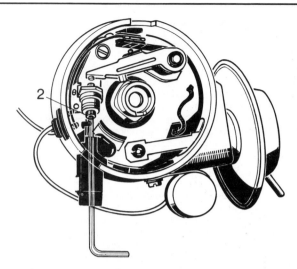

Fig. 4.3 Contact breaker adjustment on the later type Paris-Rhone distributor – use a 3 mm Allen key in the fixed contact recess 2 (Sec 2)

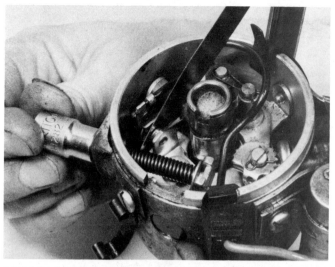

2.10 Adjusting the contact breaker gap – later model Ducellier distributor

4   Carefully lift the rotor arm off the cam and clean it with a clean dry cloth. Excessive burning of the brass distributor arm or cracks in the rotor moulding will require the rotor to be renewed.

5   Using a small screwdriver carefully prise the contact points open and examine them closely. If they are rough, pitted, worn or dirty it will be necessary to remove them for servicing or renewal as described in Section 4.

6   Assuming that the points are satisfactory, turn the crankshaft in the normal direction of rotation using a spanner on the pulley bolt, until the moving contact heel is positioned on the highest point of one of the cam lobes.

7   Using feeler gauges of the correct thickness (see Specifications) check the contact breaker gap. The feelers should slide between the points with a slight drag but without forcing the points wider apart. Take care not to contaminate the point faces with oil from the feeler gauge.

8   If adjustment is required, proceed according to the type of distributor as follows.

9   On early models the adjustment is made by loosening off the fixed point locking screw and then prising the plate in the direction required to reduce or enlarge as required the clearance. On retightening the screw, recheck the points clearance in case tightening the screw has altered the setting.

Later models – Ducellier
10   Use a 7 mm open-ended or box spanner on the adjusting nut protruding from the side of the distributor and turn to obtain the correct gap (photo).

Later models – Paris-Rhone
11   Insert a 3 mm Allen key in the hole in the plastic plug protruding from the side of the distributor and engage it with the recess in the fixed contact. Turn to obtain the correct gap.

12   After adjustment, turn the crankshaft until the heel of the moving contact is on the peak of the next cam lobe and check the gap again. Repeat on the other two lobes. Any variation indicates that the distributor spindle is bent and, if excessive, it must be renewed.

13   Refit the rotor arm and distributor cap and make sure that the clips are secure.

3   Dwell angle – adjustment

1   The dwell angle is the number of degrees that the cam rotates whilst the contact points are closed and this angle is measured with a dwell meter. The contact points are adjusted so that the dwell angle corresponds with the maker's specifications; a large gap produces a small dwell angle and vice versa.

2   To adjust the dwell angle a dwell meter is required and you should follow the instructions supplied with the meter. Note especially how to read the meter for a 4-cylinder engine as many meters can be used on 4, 6 or 8-cylinder engines. Also check that the meter can be used on negative earth circuits.

3   The procedure is broadly as follows. If necessary set the meter to zero. This is only possible if the meter has an adjusting screw on the needle pivot. Connect the red lead to the coil ignition switch connection and the black lead to earth. Disconnect the LT lead between the coil and the distributor. Get an assistant to turn the ignition key and crank the engine for a few seconds while you read the meter. Turn the adjusting screw on the meter until the needle is set according to the maker's instructions and the meter is then ready for use.

4   After setting the meter remove the black lead from its earth connection and connect it to the LT lead between the coil and the distributor which was disconnected to zero the meter. Again get your assistant to crank the engine while you read the dwell angle on the meter. Compare your reading with that quoted in the Specifications.

5   If the reading is wrong you will have to adjust the contact breaker points gap as described in the previous Section. Remember that to reduce the dwell angle you must increase the gap and vice versa.

6   After adjusting the points recheck the dwell angle and when you are satisfied that it is correct, disconnect the meter and reconnect the LT lead between the coil and the distributor.

4   Contact breaker points – removal, servicing and refitting

1   If the contact breaker points are excessively burnt or pitted they must be removed for refacing or renewal.

2   To remove the points unclip the distributor cap and lift it away, then pull the rotor arm off the central cam.

Early models
Prise free the retaining clip from the terminal posts and remove it together with the washer. Lift out the moving contact (with spring blade) and detach the condenser lead from the distributor body and spade terminal. Now remove the fixed contact retaining screw together with the washers and lift the contact from the distributor.

Later model Ducellier
3   Unscrew the adjuster nut. Remove the two screws and then remove the adjustment stud together with its spring. Slide the plastic plug and LT wire out of the slot in the distributor case and prise out the retaining lug next to it with a small screwdriver. Remove the retaining screw and lift out the fixed contact. Carefully remove the spring clip and withdraw the moving contact.

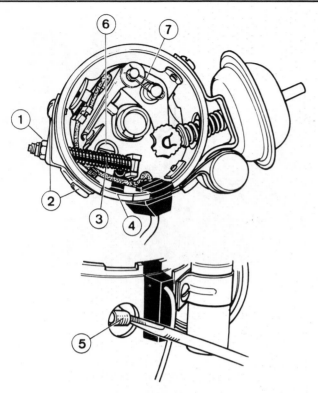

Fig. 4.4 Renewal of Ducellier contact breaker points on later models (Sec 4)

1 Adjuster nut	5 Retaining lug
2 Screws	6 Retaining screw
3 Adjustment stud	7 Spring clip
4 Plastic plug	

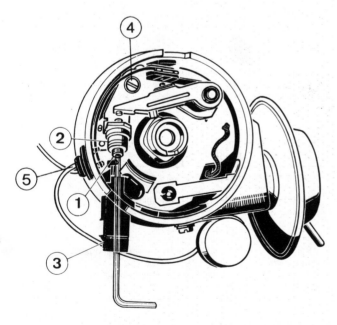

Fig. 4.5 Renewal of the Paris-Rhone contact breaker points on later models (Sec 4)

1 Adjustable contact	4 Retaining screw
2 Contact carrier	5 Spring clip
3 Plastic capsule	

Later model Paris-Rhone

4   Remove the retaining screw. Unfasten the spring clip by sliding it up and remove the contact breaker assembly.

All models

5   Dress the face of each contact squarely on an oilstone, or with a special equalising file available from accessory shops, until all traces of pips and craters have been removed. After repeated dressing of the contact points, the tungsten tips will be reduced to the base metal and it will then be necessary to fit new points.

6   Refitting the contact breaker points is a reversal of the removal procedure, but the following additional information should be noted:

    (a) *Clean the points, even if they are new, with methylated spirit before assembly*

    (b) *Lightly lubricate the moving contact pivot and the cam lobes with petroleum jelly*

    (c) *When refitting the Paris-Rhone adjustable contact, make sure that it is centred in relation to its carrier*

    (d) *Take care to reassemble all washers in the same sequence as originally installed; if necessary make written notes during dismantling to avoid mistakes*

    (e) *Adjust the contact points gap as described in Section 2 and check the dwell angle as described in Section 3*

5   Condenser – removal, testing and refitting

1   The condenser acts as a 'buffer' in the low tension circuit of the ignition system by absorbing the surges of current which are produced by the contact breaker points opening and closing. This greatly reduces the arcing at the points, and its action also assists in the rapid collapse of the magnetic field set up by the primary winding within the coil. Failure of the condenser will reduce the spark plug voltage in the high tension circuit, and if difficulty in starting the engine is experienced accompanied by 'missing' under load, the fault may well be in the condenser.

2   To remove the condenser, first unclip the distributor cap and remove it, then lift the rotor arm off the central cam.

Ducellier model

3   Disconnect the condenser lead by pulling its terminal from the socket. Undo the condenser retaining screw and remove the condenser (photo).

Paris-Rhone model

4   Disconnect the LT cable from the distributor at the coil terminal and disconnect the spring clip. Undo the screw holding the insulating block retaining plate, remove the plate and withdraw the insulating block from the distributor case. Undo the condenser retaining screw, taking care not to lose the distributor cap clip, and remove the condenser and leads assembly.

5.3 Removing the condenser (Ducellier distributor)

5 Without the use of specialist equipment the only way of diagnosing a faulty condenser is to renew it and note if there is any improvement. However, a simple test is to separate the points by hand with the ignition switched on; if this action is accompanied by a strong blue flash across the points, condenser failure is indicated (a weak flash is normal).

6 Refitting the condenser is a reversal of the removal procedure but tighten the retaining screw(s) securely.

6 Distributor – lubrication

1 Periodically the distributor should be lightly lubricated. Smear a little petroleum jelly or high melting-point grease on the lobes of the distributor cam to provide lubrication for the contact point heel.

2 Remove the rotor arm and apply two drops of engine oil into the cam recess. Apply a small drop of oil to the moving contact pivot.

3 Apply two or three drops of oil through the aperture between the baseplate and cam spindle to lubricate the governor weights.

4 Great care must be taken not to use too much lubricant and all surplus should be wiped up. Excessive oil or petroleum jelly may contaminate the contact points and cause ignition failure.

7 Distributor – removal and refitting

1 Although the removal and refitting sequence of the distributor is similar for all models, the timing setting differs according to engine and distributor type. The early XL3 and XL3S models are timed with the number 1 cylinder at TDC. Later XL3 and XL3S models are fitted with a timing plate marked with 0° to 12° graduations and as with the XK5, XL5 and XL5S variants, they are timed with the number 2 cylinder at TDC/ The XK5, XL5 and XL5S engine types differ in that they have a timing plate with 0° to 8° graduation marks.

2 On all models the distributor is fitted at the right-hand rear corner of the engine.

3 Removal and refitting of the distributor will disturb the ignition timing and you must be sure of what you are doing if problems are to be avoided. With an installed engine it is best carefully to note the exact position of the rotor arm before removing the distributor, marking the position of the distributor relative to the timing case and then making sure that the crankshaft is not turned after removing the distributor. It is then a simple matter to refit the distributor in its original position. If you cannot avoid moving the crankshaft while the distributor is removed, or if you are in the process of reassembling the engine or its timing mechanism after overhaul, then you will have to time the distributor from scratch on assembly.

4 Identify the spark plug leads so that they can be refitted to their original plugs, then carefully pull them off the plug terminals. Disconnect the HT lead from the coil and then unclip and remove the distributor cap and leads assembly.

5 Disconnect the coil-to-distributor LT lead at the coil terminal.

6 Disconnect the vacuum pipe from the vacuum capsule (where applicable).

7 Turn the crankshaft with a spanner on the pulley bolt until the distributor rotor arm approaches the point where it faces the number 1 or number 2 (paragraph 1 refers) segment in the distributor cap. The pulley notch should be aligned with the timing mark on the timing plate (photo).

8 Mark the distributor body and the timing case so that you can eventually refit the distributor in the same position, then unscrew and remove the single bolt and spring washer. Do not loosen the clamp bolt in the mounting plate.

9 Carefully lift the distributor up and out of the timing case.

10 To refit the distributor where the crankshaft and timing mechanism have not been disturbed, first check that the notch in the crankshaft pulley does still line up with the timing plate notch.

11 Turn the distributor spindle until the rotor arm is in alignment with the number 1 or 2 (as applicable) segment in the distributor cap. Check the dogs on the driving end of the distributor spindle for alignment with the off-centre slot in the engine drive; if all is well they should be in the same relative position. Insert the distributor and engage the drive dogs with their slot. Turn the distributor case – only very slight movement should be necessary – and align the marks made before removal. Fit and tighten the clamp plate retaining bolt and washer and finally check that the rotor arm is still aligned with the No 1 or 2 segment in the cap.

12 If the timing has been disturbed as a result of other work, a few extra precautions are necessary on assembly to ensure that the ignition timing can be accurately set.

13 The crankshaft must first be turned to the correct timing position but this is complicated on XL3 models with a 0° to 12° timing plate and all XK5, XL5 and XL5S models, by the fact that there are two notches in the crankshaft pulley rear flange at 180° to each other. In fact these are used to check any variation between the ignition timing of all four cylinders using a stroboscopic lamp with the engine running. The ignition is timed on No 2 cylinder and, to identify which of the two notches to use, first turn the crankshaft in the normal direction of rotation (clockwise looking at the pulley face) until No 2 cylinder is rising on the compression stroke. This can be recognised by removing the valve rocker cover and watching for both valves of No 2 cylinder to be closed, ie with clearance on both rockers. At this point one of the notches on the pulley will be approaching the timing plate. Turn the crankshaft until that notch aligns with the first notch in the timing plate. Check that No 2 cylinder is still on compression stroke.

14 On the early XL3 engine, fitted with the Ducellier M43 distributor, the crankshaft position can be set as described in Section 10 using an 8 mm rod inserted through the timing hole in the clutch housing.

15 On the XL3 and XL3S engines fitted with the Ducellier M70 or M75 distributor the crankshaft position is set as described in Section 10 paragraphs 14 and 16.

16 The distributor can now be fitted by following the procedure in

7.7 Pulley notch in line with TDC notch on timing plate – XK5 engine

7.11 Refitting the Ducellier M90 distributor to the XK5 engine

DUCELLIER

PARIS-RHONE

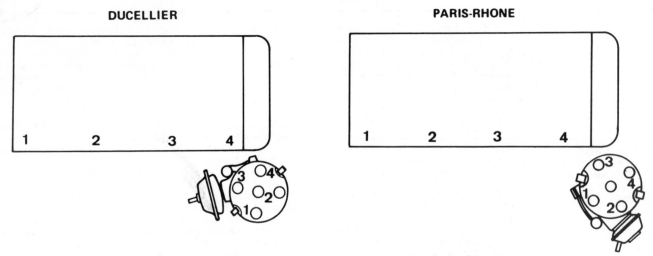

Fig. 4.6 The positions of the plug HT leads in the two distributors (Sec 7)

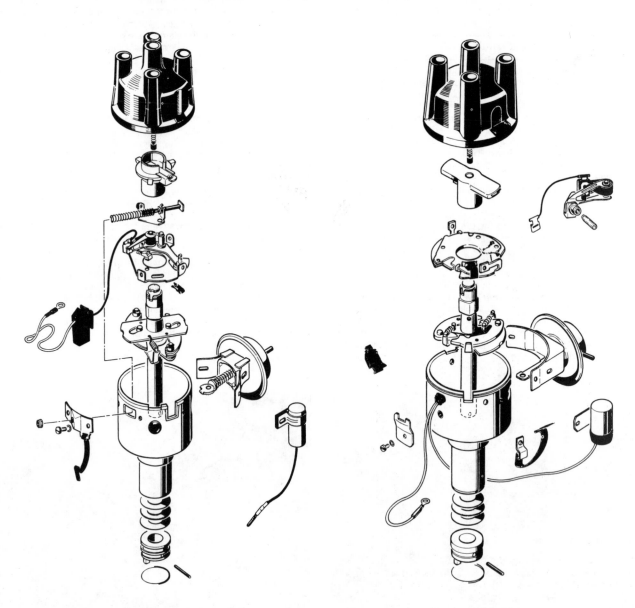

Fig. 4.7 Exploded view of the Ducellier distributor (typical) fitted with a vacuum advance capsule (Sec 8)

Fig. 4.8 Exploded view of the Paris-Rhone distributor (typical) (Sec 8)

paragraph 11, desregarding references to alignment marks if these are not applicable.

17 After refitting the distributor check the ignition timing as described in Section 10, then tighten the clamp bolt and clamp plate retaining bolt. Refit the distributor cap and reconnect the spark plug leads and LT lead. Reconnect the HT lead to the coil and refit the vacuum pipe to the vacuum capsule (where applicable).

8 Distributor – overhaul

1 It has been found from practical experience that overhauling a distributor is not worthwhile even if all parts are available. The usual items needing attention are such parts as the distributor cap, rotor arm, contact breaker points and condenser. After these have been considered, there is not a great deal left to wear except the shaft assembly, bush and automatic advance system. If one of these parts is worn then it is reasonable to assume the remainder are, so all in all it is best to obtain a guaranteed service exchange unit which could work out cheaper than purchasing a complete set of individual parts. For the more ambitious, exploded views of the two main types of distributor fitted to the Peugeot 304 are given. No problems should arise in stripping and rebuilding provided that the exact location of each part, however small, is noted.

2 The assembly sequence of the Ducellier distributor is shown (photos).

8.2a Check that the counterweight mechanism is clean, lightly oil then ...

8.2b ... fit the base plate and ...

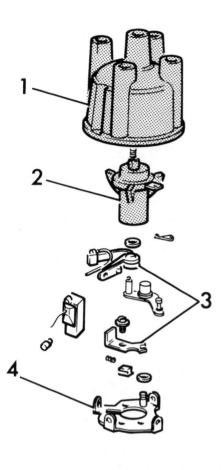

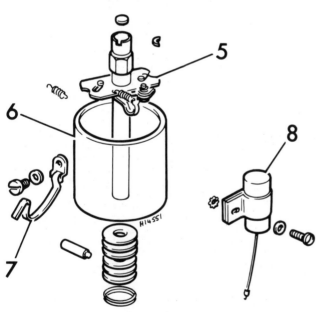

Fig. 4.9 Exploded view of the Ducellier M70 and M75 distributor types fitted to earlier variants fitted with the XL3 and XL3S engines (Sec 8)

1 Cap	5 Advance weight assembly
2 Rotor	6 Body
3 Contact breaker assembly	7 Cap retaining clip
4 Baseplate	8 Condenser

8.2c ... the insulated block

8.2d Secure the baseplate with a screw through the spring clip

8.2e Connect the vacuum advance mechanism and ...

8.2f ... secure with a screw through clip and into baseplate

8.2g Make sure that the adjusting star wheel is aligned as before dismantling

8.2h Fit adjuster bracket to baseplate with stepped screw and wavy washer

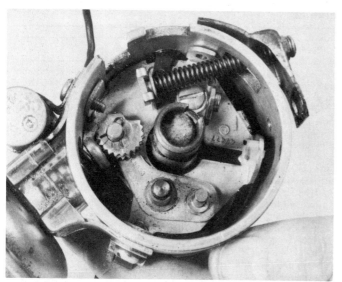

8.2j Connect and secure adjuster

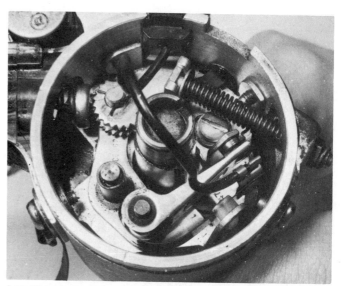

8.2k Fit contact moving point and lead with spring in insulated block ...

8.2l ... and secure with hairpin clip and insulated washer

8.2m Fit the plastic plug to the body

8.2n Fit the LT leads and block

9.3 Remove the plug (arrowed) in the timing case

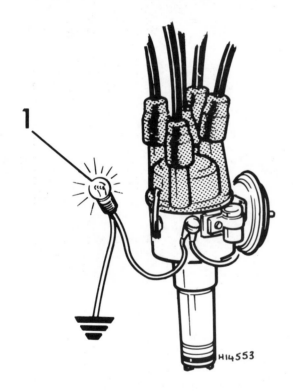

Fig. 4.10 Test lamp connection for static ignition timing (Sec 10)

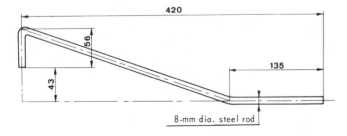

Fig. 4.11 Profile and dimensions of 8 mm diameter rod required to locate in clutch mechanism notch (dimensions in mm) on XL3 engine with M43 Ducellier distributor (Sec 10)

9 Timing plate – checking and adjusting

This operation is applicable to the following engines only: XL3 and XL3S engines fitted with a 0° to 12° timing plate and all XK5, XL5 and XL5S engines.

1   The ignition timing plate is bolted to the clutch housing adjacent to the crankcase pulley. After initial installation and adjustment a dab of paint is applied as a seal. If the plate has been moved during overhaul or on renewal of the clutch housing, or if you suspect the accuracy of setting, it can be checked and adjusted as follows.

2   An alignment tool is provided by Peugeot as a special tool but you can easily make one from a piece of rod 8 mm (0.315 in) diameter and about 130 mm (5 in) long.

3   Remove the plug in the timing case just above the cover over the end of the crankshaft (photo). Turn the crankshaft using a spanner on the pulley bolt to line up one of the notches in the pulley flange with the second notch in the timing plate, rotating the pulley in a clockwise direction looking at the pulley face. Push the rod partly into the timing case hole and rock the crankshaft slightly. If you are lucky the rod will enter a slot in the crankshaft web and lock the crankshaft in the TDC position for Nos 2 and 3 positions. If you are not lucky you will be 180° out so turn the crankshaft half a rev and try again aligning the other pulley notch with the timing plate. Do not lose the rod inside the timing case hole!

4   With the crankshaft locked in the TDC position you can now examine the timing plate for accuracy. If the pulley notch is not aligned precisely with the 'O' gradation, slacken the retaining bolt slightly, reposition the plate accurately and tighten the bolt. When you are satisfied, clean off the old paint mark and apply a new one.

5   Remove the alignment rod and refit the blanking plug.

10 Ignition timing

1   After servicing the contact breaker or the distributor, or whenever the ignition timing has been disturbed or is suspect, the timing must be checked and if necessary adjusted. Correct ignition timing is vital for efficient engine operation. There are two ways of checking the timing, statically (with the engine at rest) or, and this method is more accurate, dynamically (with the engine running).

Static timing – XL3 engine with the Ducellier M43 distributor

2   To check the static timing on this engine you will need a 12 volt test lamp and this must be connected between the distributor LT lead and earth. Remove the distributor cap or the coil HT lead so that the engine cannot fire.

3   You will also require a suitable length of cranked 8 mm diameter rod with which to insert through the 8 mm hole in the clutch housing so that when the engine is turned over (use a spanner on the crankshaft pulley bolt to do this), the rod contacts the periphery of the flywheel. Switch on the ignition and then turn the engine over by hand in its normal direction of rotation to the point where the rod engages with the timing notch in the clutch unit. At this point the timing lamp should light up.

4   If the lamp lights too early or too late, loosen the distributor clamp bolt and rotate the distributor slightly so that the lamp is just lit. Retighten the clamp bolt. Withdraw the rod, turn the crankshaft over again and recheck that the lamp lights when the rod drops into the timing notch, then remove the rod. Switch off the ignition, detach the test light and refit the distributor cap or coil HT lead.

Static timing – other models

5   Connect a 12 volt test lamp between the distributor LT lead and earth. Remove the distributor cap or the coil HT lead so that the engine cannot fire.

6   Switch on the ignition and use a spanner on the crankshaft pulley bolt to turn the crankshaft in the normal direction of rotation. The test lamp should light every time that one of the crankshaft pulley notches comes into line with the first notch on the timing plate.

7   If the lamp lights too early or too late, align the timing notches and slacken the distributor clamp bolt (photo). Rotate the distributor slightly so that the lamp is just lit. Tighten the clamp bolt, rotate the crankshaft further and check again.

10.7 Loosen off the distributor clamp bolt to adjust the timing setting

8   When satisfied that the timing is correct, switch off the ignition, disconnect the test lamp and refit the distributor cap or coil HT lead.

Dynamic timing
9   Dynamic timing can only be checked using a stroboscopic timing light and an engine tachometer.
10   Run the engine up to its normal operating temperature and then reduce the idle speed to 800 rpm by gradually loosening off the idle speed setting screw on the carburettor (see Chapter 3). Switch off the engine. The idle speed must be reduced since at greater engine speeds the centrifugal advance mechanism in the distributor will become operational.
11   Disconnect and plug the distributor vacuum pipe. Connect the stroboscopic timing light in accordance with the manufacturer's instructions and then proceed as follows for your engine type.

XL3 engine fitted with the Ducellier M43 distributor
12   Start the engine and allow it to idle at 800 rpm then shine the timing light into the 8 mm hole in the clutch housing. If the timing is correct the notch in the clutch unit periphery will be fully visible through the hole as shown. Should adjustment be required loosen off the distributor clamp bolt and rotate the distributor so that the full notch is shown, then retighten the distributor clamp bolt and recheck.
13   On completion readjust the engine idle speed to 900 rpm.

XL3 and XL3S engines fitted with the Ducellier M70 or M75 distributor – timing plate marked 0° to 20° and crankshaft pulley having one timing mark
14   On these models (pre March 1972), the location of the timing plate is as shown. Because of its location the dynamic timing is made by aiming the stroboscope at the circular timing mark on the flywheel and this is viewed through the second of the two holes in the clutch housing.
15   Where the original type 200 DE or TS190 type clutch has been renewed, you may find that this marking has not been made. It is stamped into the flywheel when the new clutch unit (which includes the flywheel) is fitted. To check this turn the crankshaft over by hand using a spanner on the pulley bolt, in its normal direction of rotation, whilst inserting a suitable length of 7 mm diameter rod down through the housing hole. When the rod is felt to engage with the notch in the flywheel continue rotation to take up the play.
16   The circular timing mark should now be visible through the second (8 mm diameter) hole in the housing. If it is not, you will need to make up a suitable hardened punch to the dimensions shown, with which to punch mark the flywheel for timing. This position corresponds to a crankshaft position of TDC for numbers 1 and 4 pistons. If the distributor has been removed, this is its correct fitting position for retiming, the distributor fitting orientation being as shown.

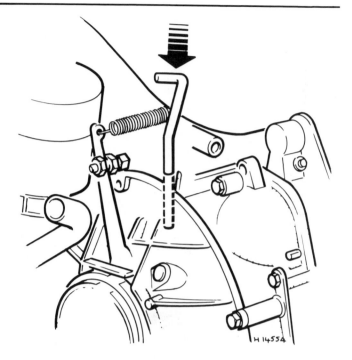

Fig. 4.12 8 mm timing rod location through clutch housing (Sec 10)

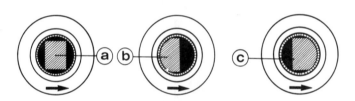

Fig. 4.13 Stroboscopic timing check on the XL3 series engine – fitted with the Ducellier M43 distributor (Sec 10)

(a)   Adjustment correct   *(c)   Too far retarded*
(b)   Too far advanced

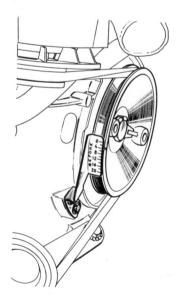

Fig. 4.14 Timing plate on pre-March 1972 models (Sec 10)

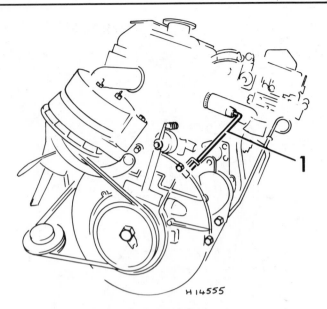

Fig. 4.15 7 mm diameter rod is passed through hole (1) for initial flywheel setting when making timing mark on pre-March 1972 models (Sec 10)

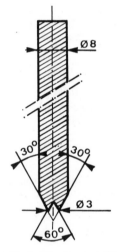

Fig. 4.16 Timing mark punch (Sec 10)

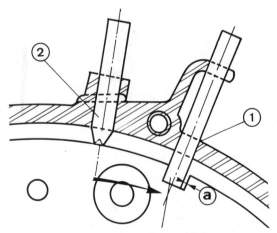

Fig. 4.17 Sectional view to show exact timing mark position (Sec 10)

1	7 mm rod	(a)	Take up any play before
2	8 mm rod		making timing mark

17 The dynamic timing check can now be made as described in paragraphs 9 to 13 inclusive, but aim the stroboscope at the timing mark made through the 8 mm hole and not the notch through the 7 mm hole. Adjust (if necessary) the distributor setting, to centralise the timing mark through the viewing hole as shown. Reset the engine idle speed to 900 rpm on completion.

XL3 and XL3S engines with timing plate marked 0° to 12° – pulley with two notches and all XK5, XL5 and XL5 S engines (marked 0° to 8°)

18 Although procedures relating to the timing plates and the static timing differ, those for the dynamic timing check and adjustment on the XL3(S) and the XK5, XL5(S) models are the same.
19 Proceed as given in paragraphs 9 to 11 inclusive then as follows.
20 Clean the timing plate and the crankshaft pulley rim and then mark the two pulley notches and the appropriate timing plate notch for your model (5° to 8° as applicable). Use white chalk or quick drying paint. Typist's correction fluid is ideal.
21 Start the engine and run it at 800 rpm then shine the timing light onto the timing plate. If the distributor timing is correct the two pulley notches will appear as one and be aligned with the appropriate timing mark on the plate.
22 Should adjustment be required to achieve the required visual alignment, loosen off the distributor clamp bolt and turn it slightly in the required direction. When the timing is correct retighten the clamp bolt.
23 Disconnect the timing light and reset the engine idle speed to 900 rpm.

All models

24 If difficulty is experienced in obtaining the correct dynamic timing it is quite possible that the distributor is excessively worn or possibly defective. This can only be positively checked by distributor removal and inspection, but before resorting to this a basic check can be made on the centrifugal and vacuum advance mechanisms. It is not possible for the home mechanic to check the operation of the centrifugal and vacuum advance mechanisms with any accuracy. However, under the stroboscope the timing marks should be seen to advance as the engine speed is increased to a fast idle; the advance should increase if the vacuum pipe is reconnected, (where fitted).

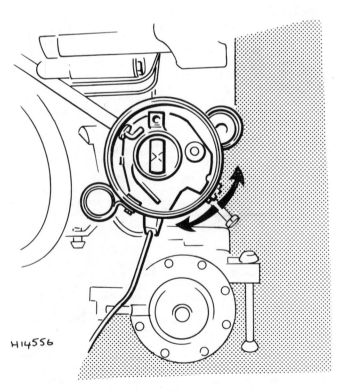

Fig. 4.18 Fitted position of distributor when crankshaft set at TDC on numbers 1 and 4 cylinders – pre-March 1972 models (Sec 10)

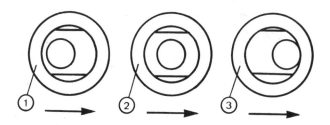

Fig. 4.19 Stroboscopic timing check for XL3 and XL3S series
engines (Sec 10) fitted with the Ducellier M70 or M75 distributor.
Timing mark to be as shown in (2)

(1) Too far advanced   *(3) Too far retarded*

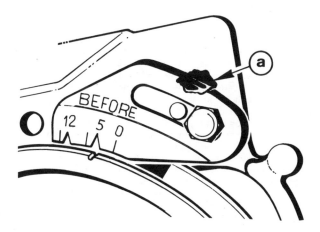

Fig. 4.20 The 0° to 12° timing plate fitted to XL3 and XL3S
engines fitted with a Ducellier M70 or M75 distributor. 'a' is to
indicate preset plate adjustment position (Sec 10)

Fig. 4.21 XL5/XL5S and MK5 engines have a 0° to 8° timing plate
(Sec 10)

a – 0°   *b – 8° BTDC*

11 Spark plugs and HT leads

1 The correct functioning of the spark plugs is vital for the correct
running and efficiency of the engine.

2 At the intervals specified in Routine Maintenance the plugs should
be removed, examined, cleaned, and if worn excessively, renewed. The
condition of the spark plugs will also tell much about the overall
condition of the engine.

3 If the insulator nose of the spark plug is clean and white, with no
deposits, this is indicative of a weak mixture, or too hot a plug (a hot
plug transfers heat away from the electrode slowly — a cold plug
transfers it away quickly).

4 If the top and insulator nose are covered with hard black looking
deposits, then this is indicative that the mixture is too rich. Should the
plug be black and oily, then it is likely that the engine is fairly worn, as
well as the mixture being too rich.

5 If the insulator nose is covered with light tan to greyish brown
deposits then the mixture is correct and it is likely that the engine is in
good condition.

6 If there any traces of long brown tapering stains on the outside of
the white portion of the plug, then the plug will have to be renewed,
as this shows that there is a faulty joint between the plug body and the
insulator, and compression is being lost.

7 Plugs should ideally be cleaned by a sand blasting machine, which
will free them from carbon more thoroughly than cleaning by hand.
The machine will also test the condition of the plugs under
compression. Any plug that fails to spark at the recommended
pressure should be renewed.

8 The spark plug gap is of considerable importance, as, if it is too
large or too small, the size of the spark and its efficiency will be
seriously impaired. The spark plug gap should be set to the figure given
in the Specifications at the beginning of this Chapter.

9 To set it, measure the gap with a feeler gauge, and then bend
open, or close, the **outer** plug electrode until the correct gap is
achieved. The centre electrode should **never** be bent as this may crack
the insulation and cause plug failure if nothing worse.

10 Details of the approved types of spark plug are listed in the
Specifications. These plugs all have a tapered seat to mate with taper
faces in the cylinder head and they must *not* have plug washers fitted
on installation. Furthermore, as they fit into a light alloy head they
must not be overtightened. Ideally they should be tightened to the
specified torque using a torque wrench with a long plug socket, or
using the special spark plug spanner supplied with the vehicle. This
should be retained on the bulkhead by clips as shown when not in use
(photo).

11 Make sure that the plug taper seats and the cylinder head mating
faces are thoroughly clean when fitting the plugs. The plug leads from
the distributor must be fitted to the correct plugs.

12 The plug leads require no routine maintenance other than being

11.10 The special spark plug spanner supplied with your Peugeot

kept clean and dry and being wiped over regularly with a clean dry cloth. When removing the plugs for servicing or renewal, remove the leads from the distributor cap, one at a time to avoid confusion, and make sure that no water has penetrated the connections. Remove any corrosion from the lead end fittings and wipe the distributor cap lead location clean before refitting each lead.

13 Apart from routine wear and tear, plugs suffer a slow fall off in performance and it is good practice to renew them at alternate routine servicings in order to maintain optimum engine performance. When fitting new plugs keep the old ones and, after having them cleaned, you can carry them in the car for emergency use or for when you want to have the fitted plugs cleaned.

12 Fault diagnosis – ignition system

1   By far the majority of breakdown and running troubles are caused by faults in the ignition system in the low tension or high tension circuit. There are two main symptons indicating ignition faults. Either the engine will not start or fire, or the engine is difficult to start and misfires. If it is a regular misfire, ie the engine is only running on two or three cylinders, the fault is almost sure to be in the secondary, or high tension, circuit. If the misfiring is intermittent, the fault could be in either the high or low tension circuits. If the car stops suddenly, or will not start at all, it is likely that the fault is in the low tension circuit. Loss of power and overheating, apart from faulty carburation settings, are normally due to faults in the distributor or incorrect ignition timing.

Engine turns but will not start

2   If the engine fails to start and the car was running normally when it was last used, first check that there is fuel in the petrol tank. If the engine turns over normally on the starter motor and the battery is evidently well charged, then the fault may be in either the high or low tension circuits. First check the HT circuit.

3   One of the commonest reasons for bad starting is wet or damp spark plug leads and distributor. Remove the distributor cap. If condensation is visible internally, dry the cap with a rag and wipe over the leads. Refit the cap.

4   If the engine still fails to start, check that current is reaching the plugs, by disconnecting each plug lead in turn at the spark plug end, and holding the end of the cable about $\frac{3}{16}$ inch (5 mm) away from the cylinder block. Hold the lead with insulating material – a rubber glove, a dry cloth or insulated pliers – to avoid electric shocks. Have an assistant spin the engine on the starter motor.

5   Sparking between the end of the cable and the block should be fairly strong with a regular blue spark. If current is reaching the plugs, then remove them and clean and regap them to the specified gap. The engine should now start.

6   If there is no spark at the plug leads, take off the HT lead from the centre of the distributor cap and hold it to the block as before. Spin the engine on the starter once more. A rapid succession of blue sparks between the end of the lead and the block indicates that the coil is in order and that the distributor cap is cracked, the rotor arm faulty or the carbon brush in the top of the distributor cap is not making good contact with the spring on the rotor arm.

7   If there are no sparks from the end of the lead from the coil, check the connections at the coil end of the lead. If it is in order, start checking the low tension circuit. First clean and gap the contact breaker points as described in Section 2 and check again for a spark from the coil HT lead. If there is still no spark, carry on with the checks below.

8   Use a 12 volt voltmeter or a 12 volt bulb and two lengths of wire. With the ignition switch on and the points open test between the low tension wire to the coil (it is marked +) and earth. No reading indicates a break in the supply from the ignition switch. Check the connections at the switch to see if any are loose. Refit them and the engine should run. A reading shows a faulty coil or condenser or broken lead between the coil and the distributor.

9   Take the condenser wire off the points assembly and with the points open, test between the moving point and earth. If there now is a reading, then the fault is in the condenser. Fit a new one and the fault is cleared.

10 With no reading from the moving point to earth, take a reading between earth and the negative (-) terminal of the coil. A reading here indicates a broken wire which must be renewed between the coil and distributor. No reading confirms that the coil has failed and must be renewed. Remember to connect the condenser wire to the points assembly. For these tests it is sufficient to separate the contact breaker points with a piece of paper.

Engine misfires

11 If the engine misfires regularly, run it at a fast idling speed. Pull off each of the plug caps in turn and listen to the note of the engine. Hold the plug cap in a dry cloth or with a rubber glove as additional protection against a shock from the HT supply.

12 No difference in engine running will be noticed when the lead from the defective circuit is removed. Removing the lead from one of the good cylinders will accentuate the misfire.

13 Remove the plug lead from the end of the defective plug and hold it about $\frac{3}{16}$ inch (5 mm) away from the block. Restart the engine. If the sparking is fairly strong and regular, the fault must lie in the spark plug.

14 The plug may be loose, the insulation may be cracked, or the points may have been burnt away, giving too wide a gap for the spark to jump. Worse still, one of the points may have broken off. Either renew the plug, or clean it, reset the gap, and then test it.

15 If there is no spark at the end of the plug lead, or if it is weak or intermittent, check the ignition lead from the distributor to the plug. If the insulation is cracked or perished, renew the lead. Check the connections at the distributor cap.

16 If there is still no spark, examine the distributor cap carefully for tracking. This can be recognised by a very thin black line running between two of more electrodes, or between an electrode and some other part of the distributor. These lines are paths which now conduct electricity across the cap, thus letting it run to earth. The only answer is a new distributor cap.

17 Apart from the ignition timing being incorrect, other causes of misfiring have already been dealt with under the section dealing with the failure of the engine to start. To recap, these are that:

   (a) The coil may be faulty giving an intermediate misfire
   (b) There may be a damaged wire or loose connection in the low tension circuit
   (c) The condenser may be short circuiting
   (d) There may be a mechanical fault in the distributor (broken driving spindle or contact breaker spring)

18 If the ignition timing is too far retarded, it should be noted that the engine will tend to overheat, and there will be a quite noticeable drop in power. If the engine is overheating and the power is down, and the ignition timing is correct, then the carburettor should be checked, as it is likely that this is where the fault lies.

Measuring plug gap. A feeler gauge of the correct size (see ignition system specifications) should have a slight 'drag' when slid between the electrodes. Adjust gap if necessary

Adjusting plug gap. The plug gap is adjusted by bending the earth electrode inwards, or outwards, as necessary until the correct clearance is obtained. Note the use of the correct tool

Normal. Grey-brown deposits, lightly coated core nose. Gap increasing by around 0.001 in (0.025 mm) per 1000 miles (1600 km). Plugs ideally suited to engine, and engine in good condition

Carbon fouling. Dry, black, sooty deposits. Will cause weak spark and eventually misfire. Fault: over-rich fuel mixture. Check: carburettor mixture settings, float level and jet sizes; choke operation and cleanliness of air filter. Plugs can be re-used after cleaning

Oil fouling. Wet, oily deposits. Will cause weak spark and eventually misfire. Fault: worn bores/piston rings or valve guides; sometimes occurs (temporarily) during running-in period. Plugs can be re-used after thorough cleaning

Overheating. Electrodes have glazed appearance, core nose very white – few deposits. Fault: plug overheating. Check: plug value, ignition timing, fuel octane rating (too low) and fuel mixture (too weak). Discard plugs and cure fault immediately

Electrode damage. Electrodes burned away; core nose has burned, glazed appearance. Fault: pre-ignition. Check: as for 'Overheating' but may be more severe. Discard plugs and remedy fault before piston or valve damage occurs

Split core nose (may appear initially as a crack). Damage is self-evident, but cracks will only show after cleaning. Fault: pre-ignition or wrong gap-setting technique. Check: ignition timing, cooling system, fuel octane rating (too low) and fuel mixture (too weak). Discard plugs, rectify fault immediately

Chapter 5 Clutch

Contents

Specifications

Type .... Single dry plate, diaphragm spring
Actuation .... Hydraulic or cable
Clutch unit types – according to year and model:
    Ferodo 200 DE .... Clutch disc outer diameter 200 mm (7.8 in)
    Verto 200 DE .... Clutch disc outer diameter 190 or 200 mm (7.4 or 7.8 in)
    Luk TS 190 .... Clutch disc outer diameter 190 mm (7.4 in)
    Luk T 190 .... Clutch disc outer diameter 190 mm (7.4 in)
    Luk TS 200 .... Clutch disc outer diameter 200 mm (7.8 in)
Note: *Some clutch types are interchangeable – check with your Peugeot dealer for advice on interchangeability, which is dependent on input pinion with 60° entry chamfer and oil deflector*

Adjustment data
Clutch fork minimum travel (at tips):
    Cable operation .... 25 mm (0.984 in)
    Hydraulic operation .... 10 mm (0.394 in)
Clutch pedal free play:
    Cable operation .... 10 mm (0.394 in)
    Hydraulic operation .... 5 mm (0.196 in)
Clutch pedal travel (less free play)
    Cable operation .... 135 mm (5.315 in)
    Hydraulic operation .... 135 mm (5.315 in)

Overhaul data
Clutch housing gasket face permissible distortion:
    Between two points more than 100 mm apart .... 0.10 mm (0.004 in) maximum
    Between two points less than 100 mm apart .... 0.05 mm (0.002 in) maximum
Drive pinion endfloat .... 0.25 to 0.40 mm (0.010 to 0.016 in)
Endfloat adjusting shim sizes .... 0.07, 0.15, 0.20, 0.25 and 0.50 mm (0.003, 0.006, 0.008, 0.010 and 0.017 in)

Torque wrench settings

	lbf ft	kgf m
Clutch outer case bolts	7.2	1.0
Clutch cover to engine bolts	9.0	1.25
Crankshaft pulley bolt:		
Early XL3 engines (nut with tab washer)	47.0	6.5
Late XL3/XL3S, XL5/XL5S and XK5 engines	65.0	9.0
Clutch pressure plate to flywheel bolts:		
Early XL3 engine types	7.2	1.0
Late XL3/XL3S, XL5/XL5S and XK5 engines	18.0	2.5

1 General description

The clutch is a single dry plate diaphragm type located at the left-hand end of the engine. The complete assembly is bolted to the rear face of the flywheel.

The clutch disc or driven plate is splined to the input pinion of the gearbox train and is free to move between the faces of the flywheel and the pressure plate. The double friction lining on the outer portion of the disc is attached to the inner splined hub by means of six coil spring dampers which cushion the initial take-up of the drive.

The input pinion is located on the crankshaft from which it is separated by a double row needle bearing. The clutch assembly is located outboard of the input pinion gear teeth which mesh with the gearbox primary shaft. Although oil sealing arrangements are more complicated, this arrangement allows the clutch to be removed or serviced without interfering with the geartrain.

The clutch mechanism is mounted on the end of the crankshaft to which it is mated by a polygon taper – one which has three faces to transmit the drive positively. A special tool is essential to separate the clutch from the crankshaft.

The pressure plate is actuated by a release bearing which slides on a locating sleeve and depresses the diaphragm centre fingers; this causes the annular plate to move away from the driven plate friction linings and drive from the clutch assembly to the input pinion ceases.

On earlier models the release arm/bearing is actuated by hydraulic means, an operating cylinder being attached to the clutch housing and its hydraulic fluid being drawn from the master cylinder.

On later models the release bearing is moved by the release arm which is actuated by a cable and spring return. The cable is connected at its other end to the clutch pedal.

On depressing the clutch pedal the operating cylinder or cable, moving the release arm causes the release bearing to bear on the diaphragm fingers. The periphery of the diaphragm lifts the pressure plate away from the driven plate which can then remain motionless while the clutch assembly spins round it. In this state no drive is transmitted by the input pinion to the gearbox.

On releasing the clutch pedal the reverse operations take place and, when the drive plate is squeezed between the pressure plate and the flywheel, drive is transmitted through the input pinion to the gearbox.

2 Clutch – adjustment

1 The makers recommend that the free play is checked every 10 000 miles (15 000 km) but it would be worthwhile making this check more frequently as it doesn't involve much work.

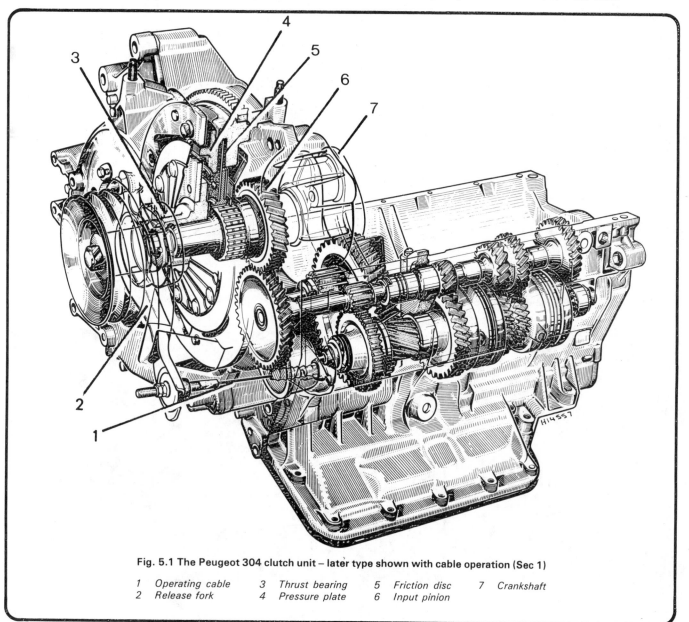

Fig. 5.1 The Peugeot 304 clutch unit – later type shown with cable operation (Sec 1)

1 Operating cable	3 Thrust bearing	5 Friction disc	7 Crankshaft
2 Release fork	4 Pressure plate	6 Input pinion	

2   First check the pedal travel by measuring the distance through which it can be depressed from the normal up position to fully down. The minimum distance is given in the Specifications. With the clutch pedal in the normal up position, lift it upwards and measure the distance through which it moves, that is the amount of free play. The minimum distance is again given in the Specifications.

Hydraulic control adjustment

3   On models fitted with hydraulic clutch control, the thrust pad is in continuous contact with the diaphragm, and the return spring pulls the pedal to the upper limit of its free play. Should adjustment be necessary, loosen off the pedal adjuster locknut and adjust the free

play to the required amount shown at point 'X'. This in turn will provide an equivalent clearance between the operating rod and piston in the clutch operating cylinder at 'a' (photo).

4   Retighten the adjuster locknut and then fully operate the clutch. With the clutch pedal fully returned, recheck the pedal free play.

5   Should the free play specified be difficult to obtain, it is quite possible that the hydraulic control system may be at fault or simply need bleeding in which case refer to Section 4.

Cable control adjustment

6   On models fitted with a cable control for the clutch (from 1978 on), the control pedal and cable are retained under tension by the coil spring which pulls the pedal downwards.

7   Adjustment, if required, is made at the engine end of the cable where the end fitting connects with the release arm (photo). Loosen the locknut on the threaded end fitting and turn the adjoining nut to obtain the required adjustment. Operate the foot pedal several times and then recheck the pedal travel and free play. If necessary, readjust; when the correct adjustment is achieved tighten the end fitting locknut. When using a spanner on the locknut or the adjusting nut, prevent the end fitting from turning with a spanner on the flats at its inner end. On completion recheck the clutch pedal operation. Also check that a small clearance exists between the pedal arm and its stop where the pedal is pulled up from rest position (photo).

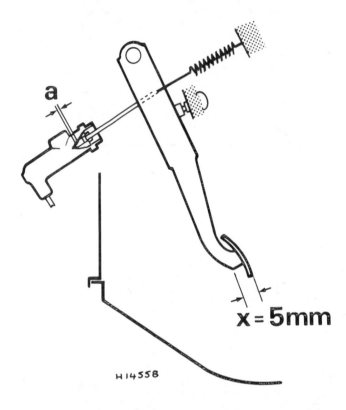

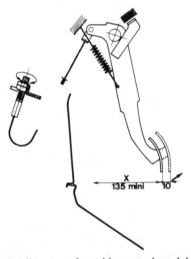

Fig. 5.2 Clutch adjustment for hydraulic control models (Sec 2). Distance 'X' to equal 5 mm – pedal free play

Fig. 5.3 Clutch adjustment for cable control models. Dimensions shown are in mm (Sec 2)

2.3 Adjusting the clutch on the early models with hydraulic actuation

2.7 The clutch cable adjustable end fitting

3 Clutch cable – removal and refitting

Note: *Once a clutch cable has been removed it must not be refitted; a new cable must be used. It is not permissible to grease a cable as this is done on manufacture using a special grease which will not mix with the usual commercially available greases.*

1 Jack up the front of the car and support it on ramps or axle stands. Apply the handbrake.

2 Loosen the locknut and undo the adjusting nut on the engine end of the clutch cable. The clutch bearing release arm in which the cable end fitting fits is slotted and the cable, together with its washers and nuts, can be slid out of the release arm and the stop bracket.

3 Working inside the car, remove the carpet and sound proofing in the vicinity of the clutch pedal to gain access to the pedal and its mounting.

4 Unhook the return spring from the pedal and unscrew and remove the pivot nut and bolt. Disconnect the cable end fitting from the special arm.

5 To disconnect the cable outer sheath from the bulkhead, turn the cable sheath end fitting through 90° after prising the locating pip in the flange or its hole. By turning the end fitting, two retaining lugs are brought into alignment with clearance slots and the cable assembly

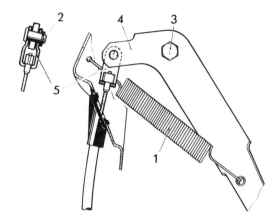

Fig. 5.4 The clutch pedal and cable attachment (Sec 3)

1	Return spring	4	Pedal arm
2	Cable fitting pivot	5	Cable end fitting
3	Pedal pivot		

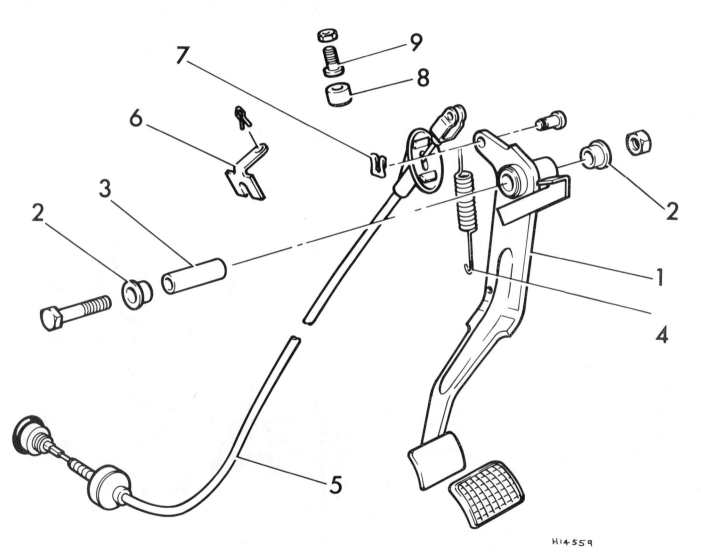

H14559

Fig. 5.5 The clutch pedal and cable components (Sec 3)

1	Pedal	4	Spring	7	Clip
2	Bush	5	Clutch control cable	8	Buffer
3	Spacing tube	6	Casing retainer	9	Screw

can then be pulled forward into the engine bay. Remove the cable from the car (photo).

6   Refitting a new cable is essentially the reverse of the removal procedure, but the following points should be noted:

   (a)   *On assembly, grease the clutch pedal pivot and the cable end fitting on the pedal using a general purpose grease. Do not grease the cable in its outer sheath*

   (b)   *Fit a new Nyloc nut to the pedal pivot bolt and tighten to the specified torque*

   (c)   *Reassemble the rubber washers, metal washers, and nuts on the cable engine end fitting in the same sequence as originally fitted. Lightly grease the domed adjusting nut where it contacts the bearing release arm using a general purpose grease*

   (d)   *On completion, adjust the clutch control as described in Section 2*

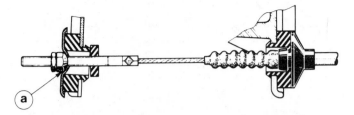

Fig. 5.6 Assembly details of the cable fittings at the engine end (Sec 3)

a   Apply general purpose grease at this point only

4   Hydraulic system – bleeding

1   The need for bleeding the cylinders and fluid line arises when air gets into the system, because of a joint or seal leaking or when any part of the system is being dismantled. Air also gets into the system if the level in the fluid reservoir becomes too low. Bleeding is the process of excluding air from the system.

2   Make sure the reservoir is filled and obtain a piece of $\frac{3}{16}$ in (4.76 mm) bore diameter rubber tube about 2 to 3 feet long and a clean glass jar. A small quantity of fresh clean hydraulic fluid is also necessary.

3   Detach the cap (if fitted) on the bleed nipple at the clutch slave cylinder and clean up the nipple and surrounding area. Unscrew the nipple $\frac{3}{4}$ turn and fit the tube over it. Put about $\frac{1}{2}$ in (13 mm) of fluid in the jar and put the other end of the pipe in it. The jar can be placed on the ground under the car.

4   The clutch pedal should then be depressed quickly and released slowly until no more air bubbles from the pipe. Quick pedal action carries the air along rather than leaving it behind. Keep the reservoir topped-up.

5   When the air bubbles stop, tighten the nipple at the end of a down stroke.

6   Check the operation of the clutch is satisfactory. Even though there may be no exterior leaks it is possible that the movement of the pushrod from the clutch cylinder is inadequate because fluid is leaking internally past the seals in the master cylinder. If this is the case, it is best to renew all seals in both cylinders.

7   Always use clean hydraulic fluid which has been stored in an airtight container and has remained unshaken for the preceding 24 hours.

5   Slave (operating) cylinder – removal, overhaul and reassembly

1   The clutch system hydraulic fluid is drawn from the hydraulic fluid reservoir mounted on top of the brake master cylinder. Because of this, whenever any work is to be undertaken on the clutch slave cylinder or master cylinder, it is advisable to seal the reservoir to minimise the fluid leakage from disconnected items. To do this, clean and remove the hydraulic reservoir filler cap, then stretch a suitable piece of clean polythene over the filler neck and refit the cap.

2   Disconnect the return spring from the cylinder mounting to release fork (photo).

3   Unscrew and remove the hydraulic hose connection to the slave cylinder and plug it to prevent the ingress of dirt and possible leakage (photo).

4   Unscrew the retaining bolts and lift the slave cylinder from the top of the clutch housing.

5   Peel back the dust cover and remove the circlip.

6   Eject the internal components of the slave cylinder either by tapping the end of the unit on a piece of wood or by applying air pressure from a tyre pump at the fluid hose connection.

7   Wash all components in clean hydraulic fluid or methylated spirit. Discard the seals and examine the piston and cylinder bore surfaces for scoring or bright areas. Where these are evident, renew the complete assembly. Obtain a repair kit and examine all the items

3.5 Cable sheath attachment at bulkhead

5.2 Clutch slave cylinder showing return spring and securing bolts to the clutch housing

supplied for damage, particularly the seals for cuts or deterioration in storage.

8   Commence reassembling by dipping the new seals in clean hydraulic fluid and fitting them to the piston, using the fingers only to manipulate them.

9   Use all the new items supplied in the repair kit and reassemble in reverse order to dismantling, lubricating each component in clean hydraulic fluid before it is fitted into the cylinder bore.

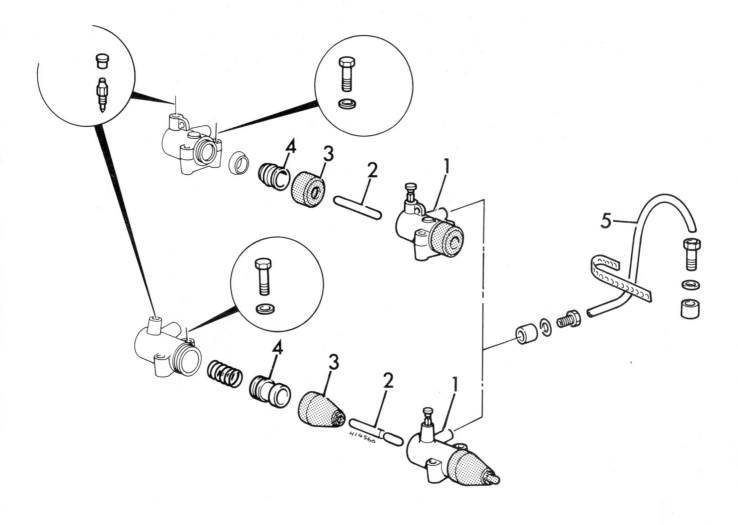

Fig. 5.7 Clutch slave cylinder types fitted showing exploded view of components (Sec 5)

1	*Body*	3	*Protection boot*	5	*Tube assembly*
2	*Pushrod*	4	*Piston and seal assembly*		

10 When all the internal components have been installed, fit a new circlip and the new rubber dust cover supplied with the repair kit.

11 Refit the slave cylinder to the clutch housing, reconnect the fluid supply pipe, the operating pushrod to the clutch release lever and the return spring.

12 Bleed the hydraulic system, as described in Section 4.

13 Adjust the operating rod nut, as described in Section 2.

6 Master cylinder – removal, overhaul and reassembly

1 Refer to the previous Section and proceed as given in paragraph 1.

2 Access to the clutch master cylinder, which is bolted to the bulkhead directly in line with the clutch pedal, is not very good and you may wish to remove the air filter unit to improve access to it. Refer to Chapter 3 for details on the air filter unit removal and refitment (photo).

3 Unscrew and disconnect the hydraulic feed pipe at its master cylinder connection from the reservoir and also detach the feed pipe to the slave cylinder. Plug both of these pipes to prevent the ingress of dirt and leakage.

4 Unscrew and remove the two bolts which secure the master cylinder to the engine rear bulkhead and then withdraw the cylinder. Wipe clean any hydraulic fluid spillage from paintwork and/or fittings.

6.2 Clutch master cylinder location

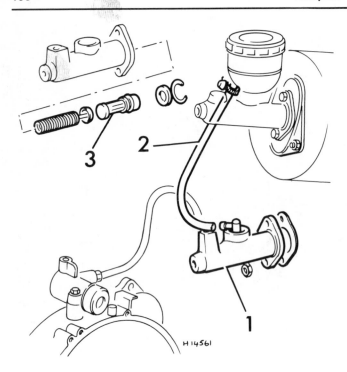

Fig. 5.8 Clutch master cylinder and piston assembly components (Sec 6)

1 Body	3 Piston and seal assembly
2 Rubber feed tube	

5   Remove the gasket from the master cylinder flange face.

6   Clean off the master cylinder externally before dismantling.

7   Extract the retaining snap-ring from its groove within the end of the cylinder body and then eject the internal cylinder components by either tapping the end of the cylinder with a piece of wood or by applying air pressure through the outlet connection to the slave cylinder whilst blanking or plugging off the inlet connector.

8   Clean all components in clean hydraulic fluid or methylated spirit. Examine the internal surfaces of the master cylinder for scoring or bright areas; also the surface of the piston. Where these are apparent, renew the complete master cylinder assembly.

9   Discard all rubber seals, making sketches if necessary before removing them from the piston so that the new seals will be fitted with their lips and chamfers the correct way round.

10   Obtain a repair kit and examine all the items supplied for damage, particularly the seals for cuts or deterioration.

11   Commence reassembling by dipping the new seals in clean hydraulic fluid and fitting them to the piston, using only the fingers to manipulate them into their grooves. Ensure that they are correctly located with regard to the counter as originally fitted.

12   Use all the new items supplied in the repair kit and reassemble in the reverse order to dismantling, lubricating each component in clean hydraulic fluid before it is fitted into the master cylinder.

13   When all the internal components have been installed, fit a new snap-ring into position to retain the assembly in the cylinder and then locate a new flange gasket into position.

14   Ensure that the pushrod is clean then refit the master cylinder into position on the bulkhead.

15   Unplug and reconnect the hydraulic feed and supply hoses, then top up the master cylinder reservoir and bleed the system as given in Section 4.

16   On completion, refit the air cleaner unit (if removed) and then check the clutch adjustment as given in Section 2.

7   Clutch – removal

1   Removing the clutch assembly from the crankshaft requires the use of special tools. Removal with the engine in the car is virtually impossible without the use of special Peugeot tools, dependent on clutch type. Of these, the most essential tool is the clutch hub puller which is needed to free the clutch from the tapered end of the crankshaft; even with the engine removed from the car, separation is unlikely using a standard universal puller. In our workshop when the engine was removed we had to fabricate further attachments to achieve the necessary concentric pulling action required to withdraw the assembly from the shaft. With the engine in the car, access is very restricted and this method would not therefore be possible. In this instance, unless you can borrow or hire the special tools listed, it would be advisable to entrust the work to a Peugeot dealer (photos).

2   If the clutch is to be removed with the engine out of the car, proceed as from paragraph 15 or 16.

3   Disconnect the battery earth lead (photo).

4   Drain the cooling system and remove the radiator as given in Chapter 2.

5   Remove the air cleaner unit and the intake ducting.

6   Loosen off the alternator and/or fan belt tensioner and disengage the belt(s) from the crankshaft pulley and the tensioner. Unbolt the tensioner bracket from the clutch housing, and place the tensioner out of the way.

7   Unbolt and remove the dynamo/alternator and also the regulator unit, leaving their wires attached, place them out of the way.

8   If the pinion seals are likely to be renewed which is advisable, drain the engine oil and when refitting the drain plug use a new sealing washer and tighten the plug to the specified torque setting.

9   Position a jack under the left-hand side of the sump and raise to support the engine. A piece of wood fitted between the jack and sump will protect the sump from being damaged.

10   Unbolt and remove the engine mounting at the top on the left-hand side.

11   Detach the heater hose from the water pump.

12   Unbolt and withdraw the starter motor.

13   On hydraulic clutch control models, detach the return spring from the release fork. If the drive pinion and oil seals are to be removed, detach the hydraulic operating cylinder but leave the hose attached. Place the cylinder out of the way.

7.1a The minimum special tools required for clutch removal – engine in situ

7.1b Special clutch removal tool in position (puller No 8.0206A)

7.3 Detach battery leads (1), drain cooling system (2) and remove the air cleaner unit and intake ducting (3)

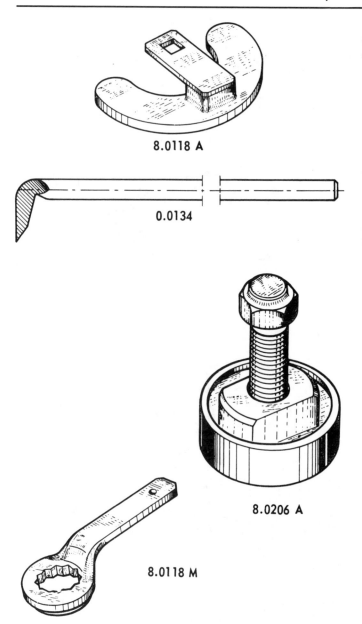

8.0118 A

0.0134

8.0206 A

8.0118 M

Fig. 5.9 Peugeot special tools for clutch removal/refitting on the early XL3/XL3S models (Sec 7)

8.0118A – Jaw for crankshaft rotation
0.0134   – Pulley bolt lock tool
8.0118M – Pulley bolt wrench
8.0206A – Clutch hub puller

14 On cable controlled clutch models, detach the cable from the operating lever (release arm).

15 On early type XL3/XL3S engine models (timed on cylinders 1 and 4 – see Chapter 4 for details), locate the special tool No 8.0118A and rotate the crankshaft so that the lock tab of the pulley bolt points downwards for convenience. Then prise the tab free from the bolt head, engaging the hooked end of special tool 0.0134 onto the tab and driving it downwards to release the tab. Now unscrew and remove the pulley screw using special tool No 8.0118M and extension bar whilst holding the crankshaft in position with tool No. 8.0118A. Withdraw the crankshaft pulley and where fitted the backing spring. The clutch housing cover bolts can now be unscrewed (note their lengths and positions) and the cover, complete with the clutch release mechanism and bearing, removed.

16 On later XL3/XL3S engines (timed on cylinders 2 or 3) and on

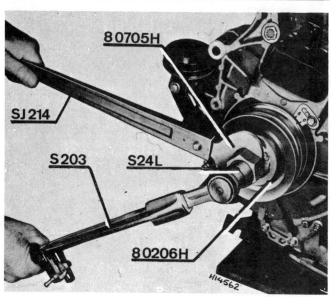

Fig. 5.10 Peugeot special tools for clutch removal and refitting on late XL3/XL3S models and XL5/XL5S/XK5 models (Sec 7)

Fig. 5.11 Using special tool No 0.0134 to release the pulley bolt washer locktab on the XL3/XL3S early models (Sec 7)

7.16a Crankshaft pulley bolt removal (XK5 engine shown) with rod inserted through the release arm aperture to jam flywheel

7.16b With pulley bolt loosened, remove bolt and pulley

7.16c Remove clutch cover bolts and withdraw cover

7.18a Universal puller used for clutch removal. Note split ring (1) and suitable socket acting as a spacer – also prevents damage to crankshaft end-face

XL5/XL5S and XK5 engine types where the engine is in the vehicle, place the car in gear and firmly apply the handbrake. This should enable you to unscrew and remove the crankshaft pulley retaining bolt without the need of using the special pulley retaining tool No 8.0206 H2. If the engine is removed you may be able to join the flywheel with a suitable bar through the release arm housing. This will prevent the crankshaft from turning whilst removing the pulley bolt, but take care not to damage the aluminium housing. Failing this method, you will need to use the Peugeot special tool (No 8.0206 H2) to restrain the crankshaft from turning and enabling the pulley bolt to be loosened off and removed (photos). Withdraw and remove the pulley. The clutch housing cover bolts can now be removed. Note their lengths and positions, then withdraw the cover complete with release arm assembly and the water pump drivebelt corner pulley unit (photo), also the release bearing.

17 On XL3 and XL3S models, align the clutch mechanism notch (in cover) with the 8 mm pin hole in the clutch housing.

18 As previously mentioned, to withdraw the clutch unit, Peugeot special tool No 8 0206 A will be required if the engine is in position. If removed a substantial universal puller and flanged plate will be required. If using the special tool the two half collars locate in the groove on the clutch spigot and they are retained by the sleeve. This removal method is illustrated. Since this tool may not be available you can improvise by using a universal puller of the type shown in photo 7.18a located over a split ring fitted into the clutch hub grease (photo

7.18b Split ring location

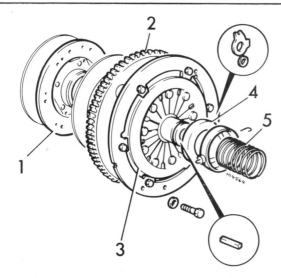

Fig. 5.12 Early type clutch assembly (with backing spring) (Sec 7)

1 Friction disc
2 Flywheel
3 Diaphragm spring assembly
4 Ball bearing race
5 Thrust spring

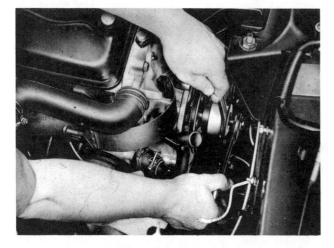

Fig. 5.13 Clutch removal using the special puller No 8.0206A on the XL3/XL3S engine (Sec 7)

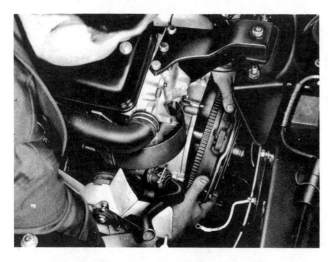

Fig. 5.14 Once freed from the crankshaft the clutch unit complete with flywheel can be lifted out (Sec 7)

7.18b). This arrangement is necessary in order to apply the necessary concentric pressure required for clutch withdrawal. The split ring shown was fabricated from two 14 mm exhaust clamps cut and ground to suit.

19 Whichever method is used, a considerable withdrawal pressure may well be required and possibly you will have to judiciously tap the flywheel with a soft head mallet through the starter motor aperture in the clutch housing.

20 When the assembly is released from the crankshaft extract it from the housing and withdraw it.

8 Clutch – dismantling, inspection and assembly

1 Before dismantling the clutch assembly it should be noted that the unit parts are balanced and therefore only the clutch driven disc and starter ring gear may be renewed separately. To ensure the correct reassembly, mark a reference line on the ring gear support in alignment with the notch in the clutch cover.

2 Progressively loosen off the six bolts securing the pressure plate mechanism to the flywheel/ring gear support and remove the bolts and washers. Lift the pressure plate clear.

3 Prior to extracting the clutch driven disc take a note of which way round it is fitted. This is most important since numerous clutch types have been fitted to the Peugeot 304 over its years of production and the central hub orientation will vary according to type. If the driven disc is fitted the wrong way round this will be apparent when reassembly is complete. The clutch will not operate.

4 Remove the three coil springs from the location dowels of the flywheel.

5 The clutch disc (driven plate) should be examined for wear or deterioration of the friction linings and the six damper springs. If the linings have worn to within 0.04 in (1.0 mm) of the rivet heads, or if they are contaminated with oil, the disc must be renewed. The cause of any oil contamination must be determined and rectified. The likelihood is that oil will have leaked past a defective seal in the inner half case or in the input pinion bore, see Section 9.

6 Examine the machined faces of the clutch pressure plate and the flywheel. These should be bright and smooth although occasional shallow scores are acceptable. If the disc linings have worn excessively it is possible that the rivet heads have worn grooves in the machined faces. It is useless fitting a new disc to an assembly with scored faces hoping that the defect will be cured. Slip, juddering and rapid wear will soon occur requiring very early renewal. Where scoring is present it might be possible to have it machined out by an engineering works but more likely new parts will be required.

Fig. 5.15 Make reference line (a) adjacent to notch in cover (1) (Sec 8)

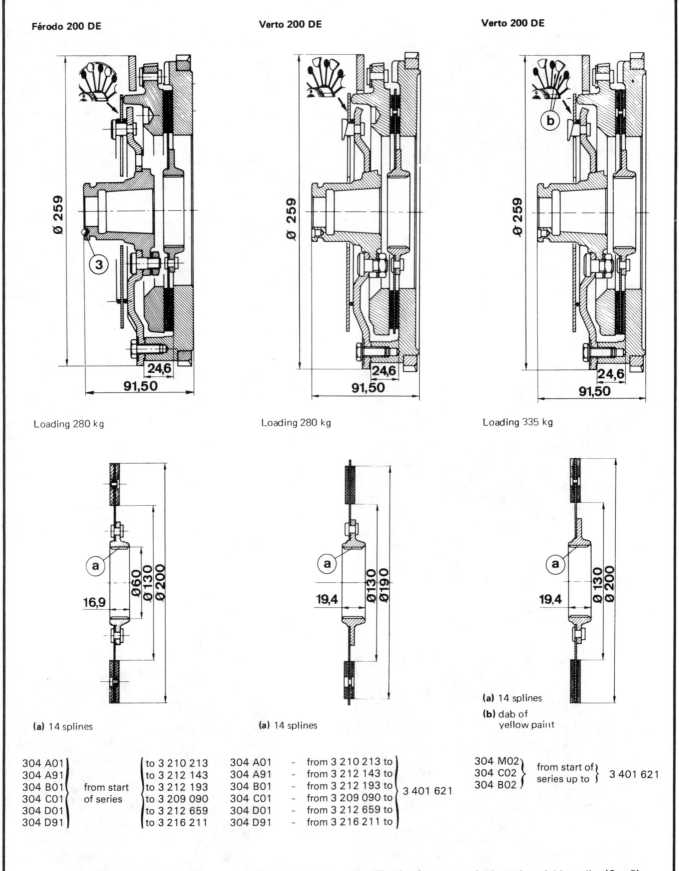

Férodo 200 DE | Verto 200 DE | Verto 200 DE

Loading 280 kg | Loading 280 kg | Loading 335 kg

(a) 14 splines | (a) 14 splines | (a) 14 splines
| | (b) dab of yellow paint

304 A01		to 3 210 213	304 A01	– from 3 210 213 to		304 M02	from start of	
304 A91		to 3 212 143	304 A91	– from 3 212 143 to		304 C02	series up to	3 401 621
304 B01	from start	to 3 212 193	304 B01	– from 3 212 193 to	3 401 621	304 B02		
304 C01	of series	to 3 209 090	304 C01	– from 3 209 090 to				
304 D01		to 3 212 659	304 D01	– from 3 212 659 to				
304 D91		to 3 216 211	304 D91	– from 3 216 211 to				

Fig. 5.16 Clutch unit types fitted – cross section views to show identification features and orientation of driven disc (Sec 8)

Verto 200 DE　　　　　　　**Verto 200 DE**　　　　　　　**Verto 200 DE**

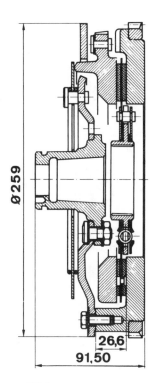

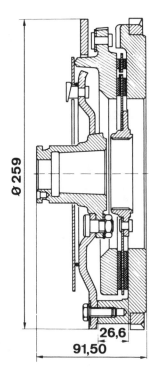

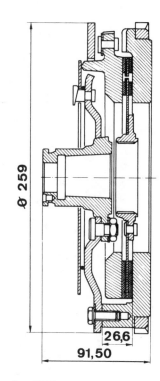

Loading 335 kg　　　　　Loading 335 kg　　　　　Loading 335 kg

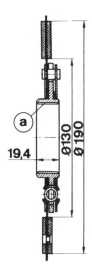

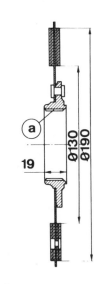

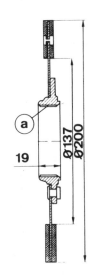

(a) 14 splines　　　　　　**(a)** 14 splines　　　　　　**(a)** 14 splines

304 M01 ⎫ from 3 401 622 to 3 507 147　　304 M01 ⎫ from 3 507 148 to 3 706 955　　304 M01 ⎫ from 3 706 956 to 3 713 955
304 D01 ⎭　　　　　　　　　　　　　304 D01 ⎭　　　　　　　　　　　　　304 D01 ⎭

304 M02 ⎫　　　　　　　　⎧ B 694 265
304 C02 ⎬ from 3 401 622 to ⎨ end of series
304 B02 ⎭　　　　　　　　⎩ end of series

Check dimensions against old clutch unit to ensure correct replacement. Note that the early types Ferodo 200 DE and Luk TS190 units are fitted with a roll pin for pulley drive (3)

Verto 200 DE

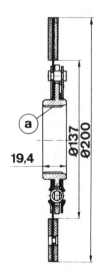

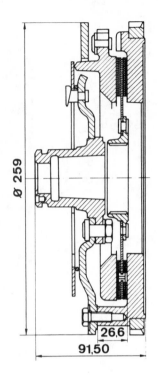

Loading 335 kg

(a) 14 splines

304 M02 - from 3 694 266 to 3 709 971

Verto 200 DE

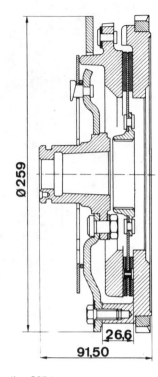

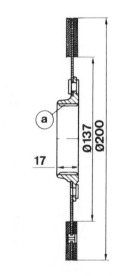

Loading 335 kg

(a) 14 splines

304 M01} from 3 713 956 to 3 753 500
304 D01}

Verto 200 DE

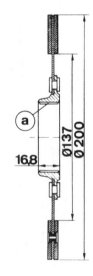

Loading 335 kg

(a) 14 splines

304 M01} from 3 753 501
304 D01}

Check dimensions against old clutch unit to ensure correct replacement. Note that the early types Ferodo 200 DE and Luk TS190 units are fitted with a roll pin for pulley drive (3) (continued)

Luk TS 190

Luk T 190

Luk T 190

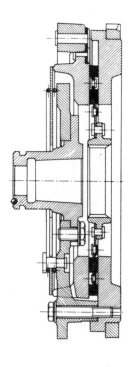

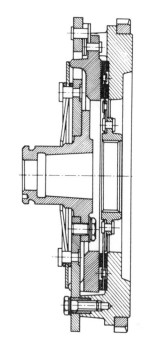

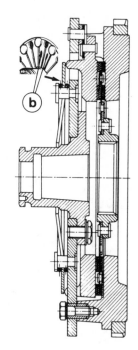

Loading 290 kg

Loading 310 kg

Loading 310 kg

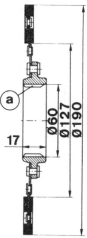

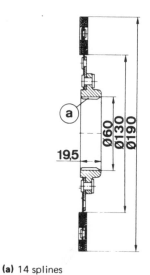

Ø60 Ø127 Ø190

17

Ø60 Ø130 Ø190

19,5

Ø60 Ø130 Ø190

19,5

(a) 14 splines

(a) 14 splines

(a) 14 splines
(b) dap yellow paint

304 A01		
304 B01		
304 C01	since start	to April 1970
304 D01	of series	
304 D91		
304 A91		

304 A01 – from 3227 387 to 3401 621
304 B01 – from 3228 534 to end of series
304 C01 – from 3228 785 ⎫ to 3401 621
304 D01 – from 3229 246 ⎭
304 A91 – from 3227 896 ⎫ to end of series
304 D91 – from 3242 094 ⎭

304 C01		to end of series
304 D01	from 3 401 622	to 3 713 955
304 M01		to 3 713 955
304 M02		
304 C02	from 3 298 001 to 3 401 622	
304 B02		

Check dimensions against old clutch unit to ensure correct replacement. Note that the early types Ferodo 200 DE and Luk TS190 units are fitted with a roll pin for pulley drive (3) (continued)

Luk T 190

Luk T 190

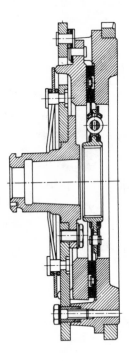

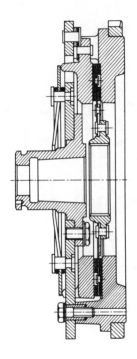

Loading 310 kg

Loading 310 kg

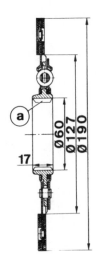

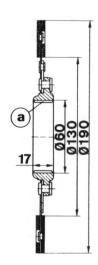

(a) 14 splines

(a) 14 splines

304 M01 ⎫
304 D01 ⎭ from 3 713 956

304 M02 - from 3 709 972

Check dimensions against old clutch unit to ensure correct replacement. Note that the early types Ferodo 200 DE and Luk TS190 units are fitted with a roll pin for pulley drive (3) (continued)

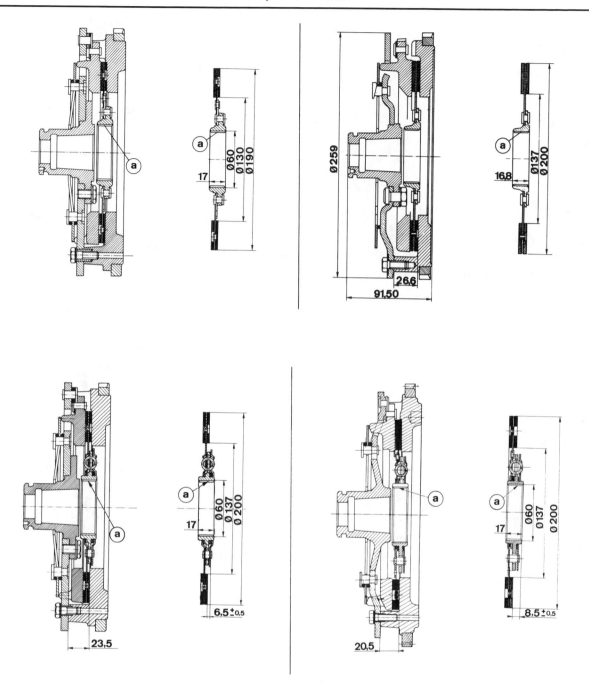

Fig. 5.17 Clutch unit types fitted from 1979 on. Cross section view for identification and driven disc orientation (Sec 8)

(a) = 28 splines

7   If only light scoring is present on the machined faces and the assembly appears otherwise fit for use, rub the faces over lightly with emery cloth and clean them thoroughly with methylated spirit. Take care not to contaminate the cleaned surfaces with oily finger marks.

8   Dismantling of the pressure plate is not practicable for the home mechanic. If defects are found in either the pressure plate assembly or in the flywheel they must both be renewed as a matched pair. These parts are balanced together during manufacture and it is not permissible to renew one without the other.

9   Examine the gear teeth on the starter ring which is shrunk onto the flywheel. Look for localised wear as it is not uncommon for wear to be concentrated in one segment of the periphery. The starter ring can be changed as an independent part but this work is best left to a suitably equipped garage or engineering works (see Chapter 1).

10 The clutch release thrust bearing which slides on the pressure plate spigot should be checked for wear by spinning it and observing whether there is any excessive wear or harshness present. Considering the amount of work involved in gaining access to the release bearing, it is prudent to renew the bearing, especially if a new clutch disc (driven plate) has been fitted.

8.11a Place flywheel face down ...

8.11b ... and then locate the clutch disc on it

8.12 Relocate the coil springs

8.13 Refit the pressure plate

11 Reassemble the clutch assembly by first placing the flywheel face down on the bench. Locate the clutch disc on the face ensuring that it is fitted the correct way round, (as noted during removal) (photos).
12 Check that the two diametrically opposed locating dowels are in position in the flywheel and position the three springs in their locations. Place the pressure plate down on the flywheel, checking that the three springs enter their locations on the pressure plate. Also ensure that the ring gear support/clutch cover marks are aligned (photo).
13 Locate the six retaining bolts. New bolts must always be fitted on reassembly together with new wavy washers, but do not tighten at this stage as the clutch disc must be centralised on the crankshaft first (photo).
14 Although it is not really part of the clutch, examine the input pinion on the crankshaft, particularly the splines which mate with the clutch disc for wear or corrosion. These can lead to the fault of clutch spin. Removal and refitting of the input pinion are covered in Section 10.

9 Clutch – refitting

1 When refitting a clutch assembly which has been dismantled, it is necessary to centralise the clutch disc during a trial fit. If the assembly has not been dismantled, ignore intervening paragraphs and proceed

as given in paragraphs 7 to 10 for early type XL3/XL3S engines or from paragraph 16 for later type XL3/XL3S engines and XL5/XL5S and XK5 engines.
2 First ensure that the protruding polygon end of the crankshaft on which the clutch is located is perfectly clean then spray it with a coating of Molykote 321, but take care not to spray the drive pinion oil seal.
3 On the earlier models check that the crankshaft is positioned with its reference dimple, in the end face aligned with the top of the cylinder block at the TDC position of cylinders 1 and 4.
4 The clutch unit can now be refitted to the crankshaft. Position it so that timing notch on the outer circumference of the clutch mechanism cover is aligned with the timing pin hole of the clutch housing (just to the right of the slave cylinder). Turn the clutch back and forth just enough to ensure that the clutch disc is fully engaged on the pinion.
5 Temporarily refit the crankshaft pulley and tighten its retaining bolt to the point where the clutch is fully engaged. The six clutch mechanism cover retaining bolts can now be tightened to their specified torque setting.
6 Unbolt and remove the crankshaft pulley.
7 Smear some multi-purpose grease into the groove of the clutch hub groove, then locate the thrust bearing and if fitted a thrust spring. If a new thrust bearing is to be used, ensure that it is identical to the one it replaces since four types have been fitted. If you have been

Fig. 5.18 Crankshaft, flywheel and clutch refitting positions on the early XL3/XL3S engine types (Sec 9)

(a)   Notch in clutch cover
(b)   Reference dimple in crankshaft end face
(c)   Pulley location pin
(d)   Hub groove must be greased

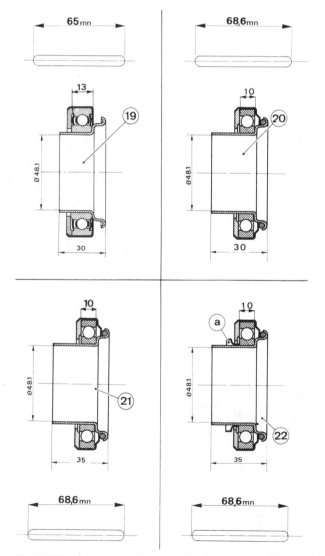

Fig. 5.20 Ball thrust bearing identification features. When renewing thrust bearing (19) the slave cylinder thrust rod of 68.6 mm in length must also be renewed (Sec 9)

Fig. 5.19 Clutch refitting on the earlier models using Peugeot special tools (Sec 9)

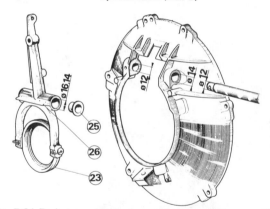

Fig. 5.21 Early type clutch cover and release arm assembly, (dimensions in mm) (Sec 9)

(25) Bush   (23) Bearing
(26) Fork

supplied with a bearing whch doesn't compare with the old one, check its suitability for use with your clutch type before assembling. Your Peugeot dealer should be able to advise you on this as possibly the original is no longer available.

8   The clutch housing cover can now be refitted. If the release arm was removed during dismantling relocate this into the housing. Ensure that correct replacement parts are being fitted if renewing any items.

9   Locate the clutch housing cover into position ensuring that the flat section of the release fork backing flange faces the thrust bearing. Fit and tighten the clutch cover bolts to their specified torque setting.

10   Relocate the crankshaft pulley together with the thrust spring, where applicable, which engages onto a shoulder on the inner face of the pulley. Models not having a thrust spring are fitted with a different pulley. Fit the pulley retaining bolt using a new tab washer and tighten to the specified torque setting. Then bend up the tab washer to secure the bolt. Note that the threads of the bolt should be oiled prior to fitment. If available use Peugeot special tool No 8.0118M together with No 8.0118A (reaction jaw) to prevent the crankshaft from turning when tightening the pulley bolt.

9.11a Remove the deflector plate circlip ...

9.11b ... and withdraw the plate

9.12 Temporarily fit the pulley ...

9.13 ... then tighten the clutch bolts to the specified torque

9.16 After refitting the oil deflector, relocate the clutch unit

9.17a Load the clutch spigot groove with grease and ...

9.17b ... then locate the release bearing

9.18a Grease the release arm ball pivot ...

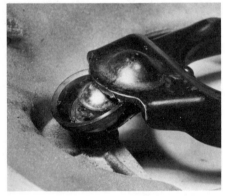
9.18b ... and locate the arm over the ball

9.20a Fit the crankshaft pulley and ...

9.20b ... then tighten its retaining bolt

Late XL3, XL3S models and XL5, XL5S and XK5 models

11 The oil deflector plate on the input pinion must be removed prior to the clutch disc centering operation. Use a pair of circlip pliers to open the circlip on the pinion, remove the circlip and the oil deflector plate. Remove the old O-ring behind the plate (photo).

12 Check that the six assembly bolts in the clutch mechanism are loose and offer the assembly up to the crankshaft, aligning the pin in the end of the clutch spigot with the mark on the end of the crankshaft. Push the assembly home and, with luck, it will go on. If not, the clutch disc needs slight realignment so remove the assembly, move the disc slightly and have another attempt. When it is home check that the clutch pin is still aligned with the mark on the crankshaft and temporarily fit the crankshaft pulley and bolt but only lightly nip the bolt – remember that the assembly has got to come off again (photo).

13 Progressively and evenly tighten the six clutch assembly bolts to the specified torque (photo).

14 Remove the clutch mechanism, if necessary using the special extractor to which reference is made in Section 7. Fit a new O-ring to the input pinion and fit the oil deflector so that its outer periphery is dished in towards the engine. Refit the retaining circlip, pressing the deflector in against the O-ring seal.

15 Thoroughly clean the tapered polygon seating for the clutch on the crankshaft and give it a light spray of Molykote 321 or equivalent, including the splines on the input pinion. Make sure that the Molykote does not come into contact with oil seals or their contacting surfaces.

16 Refit the clutch mechanism, after cleaning the mating faces in the

bore, and align the pin on the clutch spigot with the crankshaft mark – at this stage just push the clutch into position (photo).

17 Load the groove in the clutch spigot with a good general purpose grease but don't overfill it, and then fit the clutch release thrust bearing (photos).

18 Lightly spray the working surfaces of the clutch release arm with Molykte 321 or equivalent and apply a little graphited grease to the ball pivot in the outer half case. Fit the release arm in the case, making sure that the spring clips fit under the rubber cup (photos).

19 Fit the clutch case and tighten the attachment bolts to the specified torque.

20 Clean and oil the threads on the crankshaft pulley bolt and fit the pulley, making sure that the pin on the clutch spigot is located in its hole in the pulley rear face. Tighten the pulley bolt to the specified torque, using the special tool 8.0206 HZ to restrain the crankshaft from turning if necessary (photos).

21 The remainder of the clutch refitting details are dependent on whether the engine is in the vehicle or not. If the engine has been removed then the refitting details will have been covered in Chapter 1, Section 43. If the engine is in the vehicle proceed as follows.

22 Refit the starter motor using new washers under the bolt heads and tighten the three bolts to the specified torque.

23 Refit the engine mounting bracket at the left-hand end of the engine, tighten the nuts to the specified torque, then remove the wedge from between the engine and subframe underneath and lower the jack.

24 Reconnect the clutch cable or slave cylinder as applicable to the release arm and initially adjust the clutch referring to Section 2.

25 If removed, refit the adjustable jockey pulleys for the cooling fan/water pump drivebelt, then refer to Chapters 2 and/or 10 as applicable. Refit the generator and locate the drivebelt(s) and adjust the tension.

26 Reconnect the voltage regulator to its location on the left-hand wheel valance and reconnect the wiring (if disconnected).

27 Refit the radiator and top up the cooling system as given in Chapter 2.

28 Refit the air cleaner unit and intake ducting referring to Chapter 3 if necessary.

29 Refit any remaining components that may have been disconnected or removed in the reverse sequence to removal. On completion, start the engine and run it gently up to its normal operating temperature. Operate the clutch a few times then switch off the engine and check the clutch adjustment.

30 On later XL3/XL3S, XL5/XL5S and XK5 engine types, loosen the crankshaft pulley bolt and retighten it to its specified torque. It is important not to neglect this retorquing of the pulley bolt.

31 Check the cooling system components disturbed during the operation for signs of leaks.

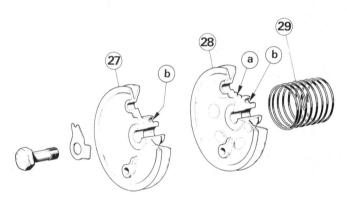

Fig. 5.22 Crankshaft pulley identification – early models (Sec 9)

(27) Pulley without shoulder at (b)
(28) Pulley with shoulder (a) for spring location and peg location (b)
(29) Thrust spring

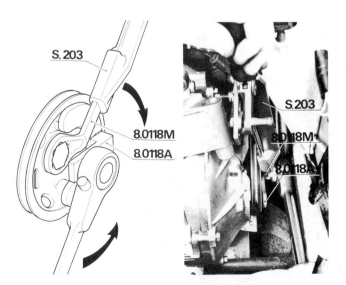

Fig. 5.23 Crankshaft pulley refitment using special tools on early models (Sec 9)

10 Drive pinion and oil seals – removal and refitting

1 Oil contamination of the clutch will most probably be caused by a defective drive pinion oil seal. Renewal of the seals is only possible after removal of the clutch unit, the procedure for which is given in Section 7. Oil contamination will necessitate cleaning the clutch unit and renewing the driven disc. The clutch dismantling and assembly details are given in Section 8.

2 Having removed the clutch unit, unscrew and remove the eight clutch housing retaining bolts from within the housing.

3 The clutch housing can now be carefully withdrawn. On early models hold the drive pinion in position on the crankshaft as the housing is withdrawn. On later models the drive pinion is withdrawn with the housing and then on removal the oil deflector, which is secured by a circlip, can be removed together with the O-ring seal. The pinion is then separated from the housing.

4 On early models withdraw the drive pinion, its thrust washer and seal from the crankshaft.

5 Cover the open end of the engine to prevent the possible ingress of dirt.

6 Remove the pinion unit and clutch housing to a cleaning area, wash in a suitable solvent and allow them to dry off for inspection. Prise free the oil seals from the clutch housing and the drive pinion.

7 If the joint between the housing and the engine has leaked oil, check the gasket face for freedom from dents or scoring. Use a

Fig. 5.24 Remove the clutch housing bolts (14) and remove the housing complete with the drive pinion (15) (early models) (Sec 10)

Fig. 5.25 Prise out the housing seal (18) and the pinion seal (19) for renewal (Sec 10)

straight-edge and feeler gauges to check the flatness of the face. The maximum acceptable distortion is listed in the Specifications.

8   Inspect the pinion unit, paying particular attention to the needle roller bearings, the splines and pinion teeth for signs of excessive wear or damage. If these are damaged, renewal is the only solution. If the drive pinion teeth are badly worn or damaged then it is probable that the driven input shaft pinion is in a similar condition. This will also require renewal (see Chapter 6).

9   If the input pinion thrust washer located on the engine block or the one in the clutch housing is worn or scored it should be renewed (photos). However it will be necessary to check, and perhaps adjust, the drive pinion endfloat in this case. Similarly, if a new drive pinion is going to be fitted, or if the clutch housing is going to be renewed, the endfloat must also be checked in these cases too. The endfloat is adjusted by shim washers located under the drive pinion thrust washer in the clutch housing.

10   To check the endfloat first locate a new clutch housing to engine gasket (dry) onto the cylinder block face, refit the drive pinion into the clutch housing and refit the housing to the engine using at least six bolts tightened to the specified torque. If you have a dial test indicator (clock gauge), mount it with the spindle button resting on the drive pinion outer face and with the spindle parallel with the crankshaft axis. Press the drive pinion in against the thrust washer on the main bearing face, set the gauge to zero and then pull the pinion forward to butt against its thrust washer in the clutch housing. Note the amount of

endfloat registered on the indicator. If you have no dial test indicator a vernier caliper with depth gauging facility can be used instead (photos). Compare your reading with the permitted tolerance quoted in the Specifications. If the endfloat is out it will be necessary to adjust the shim washers; these are available in various thicknesses as listed in the Specifications.

11   To renew the pinion thrust washer or to adjust the shim washers beneath it, lever the thrust washer out of the case. Fit the correct shim washers to achieve the specified endfloat of the drive pinion and reposition the thrust washer. When fitting the shims and washer make sure that they are perfectly clean and dry because any dirt or grit here will upset the pinion endfloat (photo).

12   Press firmly on the thrust washer and secure it with three punch marks spaced at 120° intervals to deform the housing slightly and retain the washer. Wipe the washer clean and lubricate it with clean engine oil (photo).

13   With the clutch housing engine side down on the bench and the drive pinion removed from the housing, clean the oil seal recess in the housing. Lightly grease a new seal and carefully tap it into its recess, with the lip facing in towards the engine side of the housing. Fit the seal fully into the housing (photo).

14   Clean the oil seal recess in the pinion, lightly grease a new seal and tap it into the pinion, with its lip down towards the gear end of the pinion, until it is fully home (photo).

15   The drive pinion can now be fitted to the crankshaft. First wrap

10.9a The drive pinion thrust washer (arrowed) in the engine block ...

10.9b ... and the one in the clutch housing

10.10a Fit the drive pinion and ...

10.10b ... the clutch housing to measure the pinion endfloat

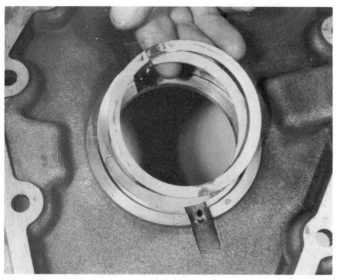

10.11 Fit the shim washers and ...

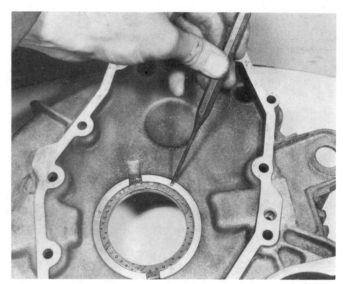

10.12 ... the securing thrust washer

10.13 Fit a new oil seal into the clutch housing and ...

10.14 ... a new oil seal to the input pinion

10.15a Wrap plastic tape over the crankshaft step and grease it before ...

10.15b ... fitting the drive pinion

10.16 Similarly wrap plastic tape onto the drive pinion and grease it before ...

10.17 ... refitting the clutch housing

10.18a Fit a new O-ring seal (later models with deflector plate) ....

10.18b ... and then remove the tape

10.19a Fit the oil deflector plate dished side inwards and ...

10.19b ... secure with retaining clip

PVC adhesive tape over the step on the crankshaft to prevent damage to the pinion internal seal lip as it is being fitted, and smear grease on the tape to assist fitting (photo). Lubricate the engine side thrust washer with clean engine oil. Grease the needle bearing and carefully fit the pinion, easing the seal lip over the greased PVC tape (photo), then remove the tape.

16 Now wrap PVC tape on the pinion to cover the splines on which the clutch disc seats and just overlap the shoulder of the bearing surface for the seal in the clutch housing. Again coat the tape with grease to aid fitting (photo). Check that all traces of old gasket are removed and fit a new gasket to the engine face. Freely lubricate the pinion and driveshaft gear teeth with clean engine oil and also lubricate the thrust washer in the clutch housing.

17 Carefully fit the clutch housing to the engine, easing the lip of the seal over the greased tape on the input pinion (photo). Fit the twelve retaining bolts using new wavy washers and tighten them to the specified torque.

18 On later models fitted with an oil deflector plate, peel back the

PVC tape on the input pinion to uncover the O-ring location, but keeping the splines covered. Fit a new O-ring seal, then remove the tape from the pinion. Fit the oil deflector plate to the input pinion with its outer periphery dished towards the engine side of the clutch housing. Press the deflector down against the O-ring seal and fit the retaining circlip, making sure that it is bedded down in its recess in the input pinion (photos).

19 Make sure that no remnants of PVC tape or grease remain on the input pinion splines or crankshaft polygon taper (photo).

20 Where the clutch housing has been renewed, transfer the timing plate from the old housing to the new one and adjust its position as described in Chapter 4.

21 Continue to reassemble the clutch, housing, and ancillary components following the procedures already described in Sections 9 and 8 and by reversing the additional dismantling procedures in this Section. Refill the cooling system and top up the engine oil before attempting to run the engine and don't omit the retorquing of the pulley bolt after the initial engine run on later models.

11 Fault diagnosis – clutch

Symptom	Reason(s)
Excessive pedal travel	Incorrect adjustment Excessive crankshaft endfloat (only on very worn engine) Hydraulic system defective (where applicable)
Clutch will not disengage	Incorrect adjustment Clutch disc rusted onto splines (only after long disuse. Depressing pedal and turning engine on starter may free) Pressure plate damaged or misaligned Drive pinion seized on crankshaft
Clutch slip (engine speed increases with no increase in road speed)	Incorrect cable adjustment (where applicable) Worn or oil contaminated friction linings Damaged or weak springs in pressure plate
Clutch judder	Engine/transmission mountings loose or worn Friction linings worn or oil contaminated Release mechanisn worn Flywheel run-out
Squeal or rumble when pedal depressed	Release bearing worn or dry Pressure plate defective

Chapter 6 Transmission

Contents

Specifications

General
Gearbox series:
    Early type (up to 1977) BB6 (402)
    Later type (from 1977) BB8 (406)
Number of gears .... Four forward, one reverse
Type of gears .... Helical, constant mesh
Synchromesh .... All forward gears

Ratios
	BB6 and BB8
1st	0.274
2nd	0.451
3rd	0.689
4th	1.014
Reverse	0.253
Input gearset	32 x 43

BB6 gearbox
Secondary shaft pinions endplay .... 0.20 to 0.35 mm (0.008 to 0.014 in)
Secondary shaft spacer thicknesses available .... 3.2, 3.6, 4.0, 4.4 and 4.8 mm (0.12, 0.14, 0.16, 0.17 and 0.19 in)
Secondary shaft 2nd gear bush to 3rd gear bush spacers available
in thickness increments of 0.05 mm from .... 2.00 to 2.90 mm (0.08 to 0.11 in)
Secondary shaft 1st gear bush to roller bearing shim thicknesses
available .... 0.15, 0.20, 0.25 and 0.50 mm (0.006, 0.008, 0.01 and 0.02 in)
Reverse gear pinion to speedometer drive worm shim thicknesses
available .... 0.15 and 0.50 mm (0.006 and 0.02 in)
2nd gear drive pinion dog to synchro cone overlap .... 1.00 mm (0.04 in)
Primary shaft snap-ring (timing gear end) - maximum allowable
outside diameter (fitted) .... 22.60 mm (0.88 in)
Reverse gear selector inner detent spring free height .... 26.15 mm (1.02 in)
Selector lever detent springs free height .... 29.50 mm (1.15 in)

BB8 gearbox
Secondary shaft endfloat (maximum) .... 0.5 mm (0.02 in)
Drive pinion clearances .... 0.20 to 0.35 mm (0.008 to 0.014 in)
1st gear bush to bearing shim thickness .... 0.75 mm (0.03 in)
2nd to 3rd gear spacer .... 2.60 mm (0.10 in)
4th pinion shim washer (early models only with 16.4 mm wide
needle roller bearing) .... 3.2 mm (0.12 in)

Torque wrench settings
BB6 gearbox

	lbf ft	kgf m
Primary shaft central bearing cap nuts (or bolts)	16.0	2.25
Primary shaft bearing retaining plate bolts	7.25	1.0
Selector housing bolts	7.25	1.0
Differential housing bolts:		
8 mm	14.5	2.0
10 mm	29.0	4.0

Differential housing end cover bolts	14.5	2.0
Oil pump strainer bolts	4.3	0.6
Transmission oil pan bolts:		
7 mm	7.25	1.0
8 mm	13.0	1.75
Sump plate side support limiting stops	23.5	3.25
Oil line union bolts	13.0	1.75
Selector change unit to bulkhead bolt nuts	7.25	1.0
Selector change unit to transmission tunnel nuts	14.5	2.0
Gear lever floor change clamp nuts	7.25	1.0

BB8 (406) gearbox - where different from BB6 type

Secondary shaft end nut	36.1	5.0
Drain plugs and core plugs	19.8	2.75
Selector return spindle	18.0	2.5
Reversing light switch	25.3	3.5

1 General description

The Peugeot 304 is fitted with a four forward speed manual gearbox mounted transversely underneath and in-line with the engine. The transmission housing is cast in aluminium alloy and, besides the gearbox, also contains the differential and final drive units. Drive to the gearbox from the engine is via an input pinion located on the crankshaft between the cylinder block and the clutch.

The gearbox has a conventional two-shaft, constant mesh layout. There are four pairs of gears, one for each forward speed. The gears on the primary shaft are fixed to the shaft, while those on the secondary shaft with which they mesh are floating, each being locked to the secondary shaft only when engaged by its synchromesh unit. The reverse idler gear is located on a separate shaft.

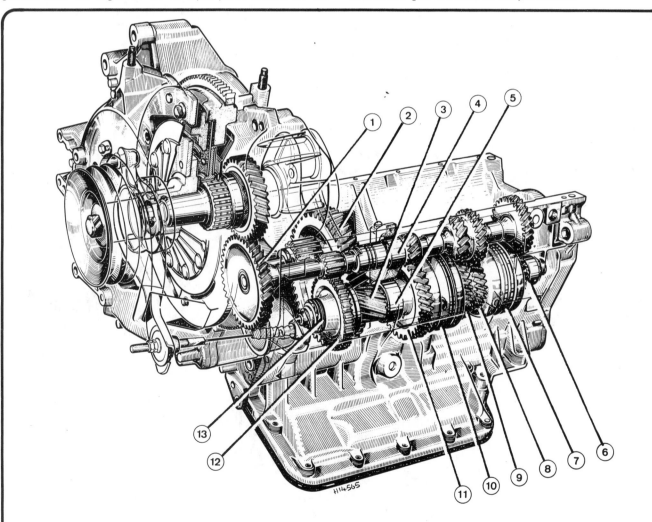

Fig. 6.1 The Peugeot 304 transmission assembly (Sec 1)

1 Input shaft	5 Secondary shaft	8 3rd gear pinion	11 1st gear pinion
2 Differential crownwheel	6 4th gear pinion	9 2nd gear pinion	12 Reverse gear pinion
3 Differential drive pinion	7 3rd/4th synchroniser	10 1st/2nd synchroniser	13 Speedometer drive worm
4 Primary shaft			

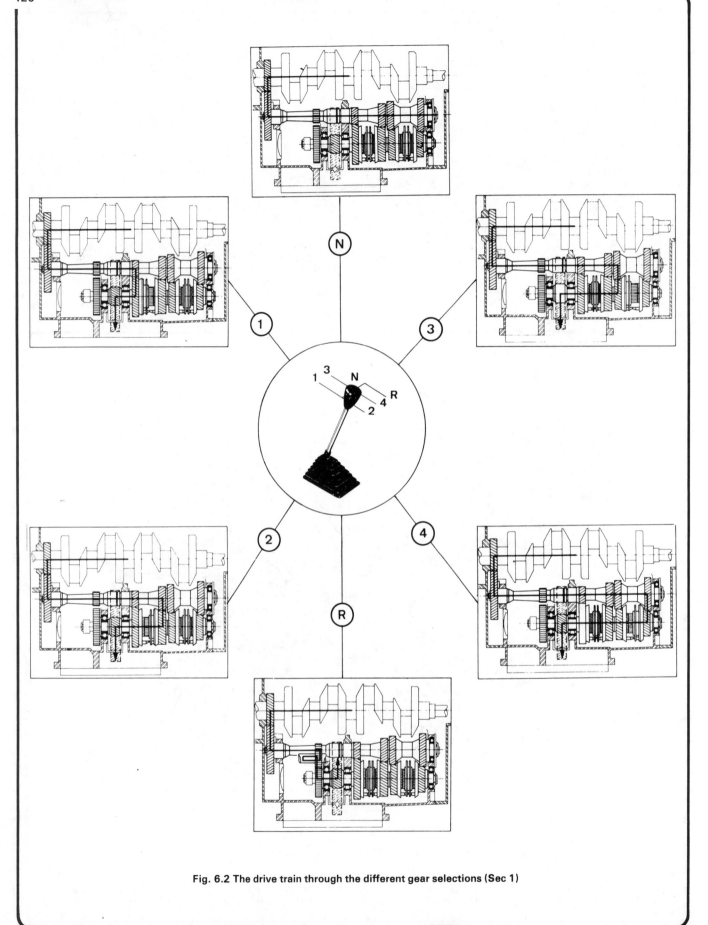

Fig. 6.2 The drive train through the different gear selections (Sec 1)

Each gear selector fork engages in a slot in the synchromesh unit; these are made to slide axially along the secondary shaft in order to engage the appropriate gear. The forks are pinned to selector shafts which are operated by levers from the manual control mechanism.

An integral gear on the secondary shaft is in constant mesh with the crownwheel gear on the differential unit which is located on the front of the gearbox. The differential incorporates the final drives and the assembly is mounted in taper roller bearings.

Although the transmission system employed is relatively simple, nevertheless a few words of warning must be stressed, before any inexperienced dismantlers start work, to make sure that they know what they are letting themselves in for.

First of all decide whether the fualt you wish to repair is worth the time and effort involved. Secondly bear in mind that, if the transmission is well worn, then the cost of the necessary component parts could well exceed the cost of an exchange factory unit and, furthermore, you will get a guaranteed job without the bother of having to do it yourself. Thirdly, if you are intent on doing it yourself, make sure that you understand how the transmission works.

Special care must be taken during all dismantling and assembly operations to ensure that the housing is not overstressed or distorted in any way. When dismantled, check the cost and availability of the parts to be renewed and compare this against the cost of a replacement unit, which may not be much more expensive and therefore would be a better proposition.

On reassembly, take careful note of the tightening procedures and torque wrench settings of the relevant nuts and bolts. This is most important to prevent overtightening, distortion and oil leakage and also to ensure smooth, trouble-free running of the unit.

In addition to the above mentioned fitting precautions, care must be taken to ensure that, where new parts are required, the correct replacements are obtained. The earlier models were fitted with the BB6 type gearbox, whilst later models have the BB8 type. The principal gearbox modifications of both types and their main differences are given in the following Section.

Finally it should be mentioned that the project vehicle used was fitted with the BB8 type gearbox and therefore the photographs shown in the dismantling, overhaul and reassembly Sections are applicable to that gearbox type. However because of the close relationship of the two gearbox types they should in many instances provide a useful guide when working on the BB6 gearbox.

2 Gearbox modification details

The same basic design of gearbox has been used throughout the years of production on the Peugeot 304. The BB8 gearbox has subsequently received further modifications. The modifications and differences between the gearbox types are given below together with a sectional diagram of each type.

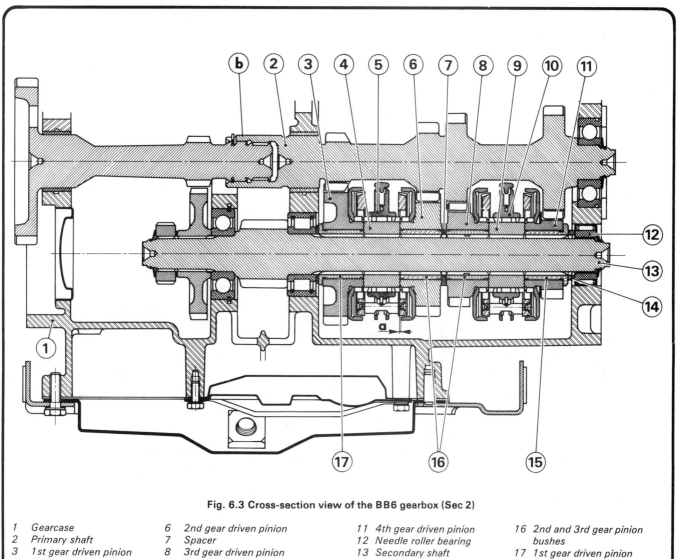

Fig. 6.3 Cross-section view of the BB6 gearbox (Sec 2)

1	Gearcase	
2	Primary shaft	
3	1st gear driven pinion	
4	1st/2nd synchro hub	
5	1st/2nd synchro	
6	2nd gear driven pinion	
7	Spacer	
8	3rd gear driven pinion	
9	3rd/4th synchro hub	
10	3rd/4th synchro	
11	4th gear driven pinion	
12	Needle roller bearing	
13	Secondary shaft	
14	Spacer	
15	4th gear pinion bush	
16	2nd and 3rd gear pinion bushes	
17	1st gear driven pinion	
b	Input shaft coupling	

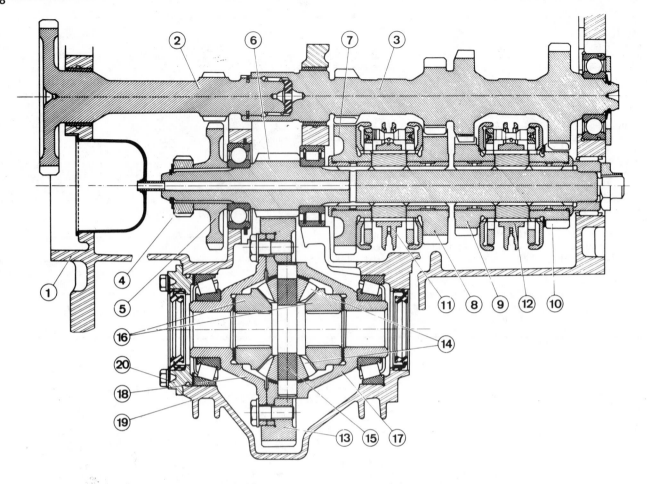

Fig. 6.4 Cross section view of the BB8 (406) gearbox (Sec 2)

1 Gearbox housing	7 1st gear driven pinion	13 Differential crownwheel	18 Differential carrier,
2 Input shaft	8 2nd gear driven pinion	14 Planet gears	LH side
3 Primary shaft	9 3rd gear driven pinion	15 Planet gear spindles	19 Differential main housing
4 Speedometer drive pinion	10 4th gear driven pinion	16 Sun gears	20 Differential side cover
5 Reverse gear pinion	11 1st/2nd synchronizer	17 Differential carrier,	
6 Crownwheel drive pinion	12 3rd/4th synchronizer	RH side	

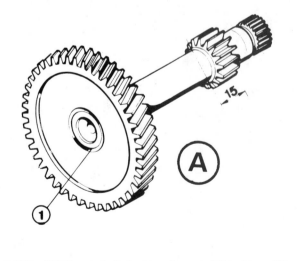

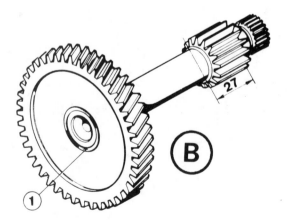

Fig. 6.5 The BB6 input shaft showing the early (A) and later (B) types fitted. Note that the XK5 engine model does not have the groove (1). Dimensions shown in mm (Sec 2)

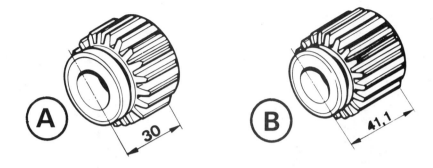

Fig. 6.6 The BB6 reverse gear idling pinion identification for the early (A) and later (B) models. Dimensions shown in mm (Sec 2)

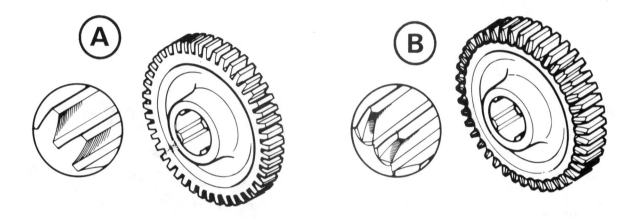

Fig. 6.7 The BB6 reverse gear driven pinion identification for the early (A) and later (B) models (Sec 2)

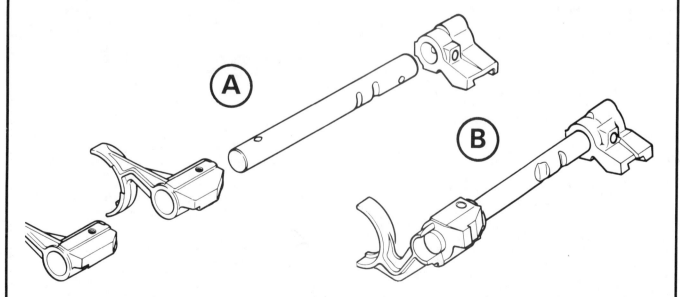

Fig. 6.8 The BB6 reverse gear selector fork identification for the early (A) and later models (B) (Sec 2)

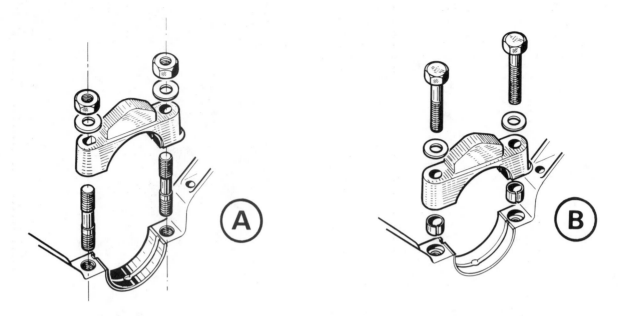

Fig. 6.9 The BB6 gearbox primary shaft bearing cap (Sec 2)

A   Early types   B   Late types

Modifications to the BB6 gearbox

1   Reverse gear train (from about August 1977).

(a) *The input shaft was modified with the reverse gear pinion having wider teeth to allow constant mesh with the idle pinion*

(b) *The reverse gear idler pinion was similarly modified to suit*

(c) *The reverse gear driven pinion also had its tooth form modified to suit for constant mesh*

(d) *The reverse gear selection fork and detent were reshaped and a revised spindle fitted*

The BB8 gearbox

2   The main differences between the earlier type BB8 gearbox and the BB6 type which it replaced are:

(a) *The primary shaft bearing cap has a twin roll pin location and is secured by two bolts instead of studs and nuts*

(b) *The secondary shaft bearing at the timing case end is smaller and is retained by a nut instead of the spring washer and circlip previously used*

(c) *The driven pinion bushes are steel (bronze used previously)*

(d) *The differential crownwheel teeth forms are different*

(e) *The differential unit planet gear spindles are cross knurled*

(f) *The differential housing on the right-hand side does not have an end cap fitted due to a smaller roller bearing being fitted*

BB8 gearbox modifications

3   Since its introduction the following modifications have been made to the BB8 type gearbox.

(a) *To provide improved lubrication to the 1st gear pinion the secondary shaft has an integral oilway. The oil is fed to it through an 'oil cup' located into the gearbox housing where the sheet metal collar was previously fitted. The 1st gear pinion has four oil holes in place of the two previously used*

(b) *The gear selector was modified in March of 1978 and now has a single link in the gearbox in place of the two links and return lever used previously. To allow this change the following items have been modified also. The gearbox cover has new shaped selection/engagement levers. The gearbox cover (and the aperture) are larger. The return spring length is reduced (99 mm in place of 129 mm). The gearchange rod length was reduced to 648 mm (was 652 mm). The selector rod remains the same*

2.3a The oil cup location in the gearbox housing of the later BB8 gearbox

4   In some instances it is possible to update the earlier type gearboxes to incorporate the modifications fitted to the later models. It may even be necessary in some cases, where the earlier type parts are no longer available. With this in mind it is obviously of utmost importance when ordering spare parts, to confirm with your Peugeot dealer exactly what parts are necessary and are interchangeable for rebuilding your particular gearbox type. Your Peugeot dealer will be able to advise you.

3   Transmission unit – removal

1   The transmission unit cannot be removed as a separate assembly from the car; the engine and transmission have to be removed first as a complete assembly. The procedure for this operation is given in Chapter 1.

2   With the engine/transmission unit removed, clean off all road dirt,

oil, grease, etc, using a proprietary engine cleaner or paraffin. Wipe the unit dry with clean rag and then remove the following ancillary components, referring to the relevant Chapters for specific procedures.

3   Unscrew and remove the gearbox-to-crankcase securing bolts.

4   Support the engine and gearbox as the last bolts are removed and carefully separate the two units. Should they stick together, carefullly lever them apart with a wooden lever.

4   Transmission unit – dismantling

1   Before proceeding with dismantling the transmission unit first read Section 1, if you have not already done so. It is assumed that the unit has already been removed from the car and separated from the engine. Don't attempt to dismantle it on the floor. The unit is not particularly heavy and you should work on it on a clean bench or table top. Later, on reassembly, you will need to renew all gaskets, but don't throw away the original gaskets as you dismantle the unit for they will act as a guide for the fitment of the new ones supplied in the gasket set. In addition to new gaskets you should also fit new lockwashers, circlips and roll pins on assembly but, again, keep the old ones as samples. If you have not already done so clean the outside of the unit of all road dirt, grease or oil and avoid contaminating the interior. Start work with clean tools, clean hands and a plentiful supply of clean rag. To simplify reassembly a methodical work routine is essential. Put parts in small containers, lay the parts out in order of assembly as they are removed, mark individual items, or make sketches as you proceed. In practice most people use a combination of these procedures.

2   First turn the unit over and remove the bolts and special washers securing the sump plate. If it has not already been removed you will first need to remove the three nuts securing the bracket for the exhaust pipe. Note that the three bolts are longer than the others and note their positions in the transmission case (photos).

3   Remove the three bolts securing the gauze oil strainer, noting the rubber seal between the screen and the case.

4   Undo the four bolts securing the oil seal retainer plate at the clutch end of the differential final drive. Mark the plate and case so that they can be reassembled correctly, and carefully remove the plate, watching out for loose shim washers as it is removed. Keep all the shims together. The O-ring seal between the plate and case, and the drive oil seal in the place, will both need renewal on assembly. On earlier models (pre serial number 3 757 510) it will also be necessary to unbolt and remove the oil seal retainer plate from the timing end of the differential final drive. Proceed as given for the opposing (clutch end) seal plate keeping the shims with the plate when removed.

5   Undo the four large and the four smaller bolts securing the differential unit to the transmission case and remove the differential housing. It may be tight, due to the locating spigot, and may require gently tapping with a soft-faced hammer to free it. The differential unit can be lifted out of its half case, but take care to keep the taper bearing outer races with their relative bearings. It is not intended to cover the dismantling and overhaul of the differential unit in this manual. If there is any fault with the assembly, or if it is excessively worn, it should be renewed complete, or referred to a Peugeot agent.

6   Remove the nut and locking screw retaining the speedometer drive and remove the drive unit.

7   On the BB8 gearbox, engage reverse gear and then carefully drive out the roll pin securing the reverse selector fork to its shaft. Hold the reverse idler pinion engaged and change to 1st gear. The input, primary and secondary shafts are now locked and the nut on the timing end of the secondary shaft can be loosened. This nut must be renewed on reassembly. Fit the new nut now and tighten it very lightly, say 3 lbf ft (about 0.5 kgf m). This is to permit endfloat and clearance checks before removal of the secondary shaft later on. The BB6 gearbox differs here only in that it has a snap-ring and spring washer at the dn of the secondary shaft instead of the nut. leave these in position for the moment to enable the endfloat checks to be made (photo).

8   Undo and remove the three bolts retaining the triangular plate which retains the primary shaft ball-bearing.

9   The bearing outer race has a groove for a special extractor and two slots are machined in the case to permit fitting the extractor claws. However, if you cannot get hold of a suitable extractor to remove the bearing it can still be removed by the following method. First remove

4.2a Remove sump noting engine mounting locations – left hand ...

4.2b ... and right-hand

4.7 Remove the pin from reverse selector fork (1), then hold reverse idler pinion in engagement (2)

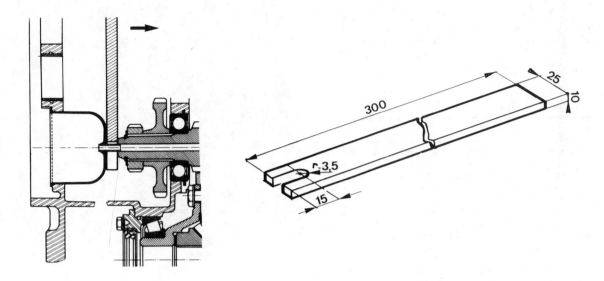

Fig. 6.10 BB8 gearbox oil collection cup removal using home made tool shown. Dimensions are in mm. Arrow shows direction of leverage (Sec 4)

the circlip and the dished washer behind it on the end of the primary shaft. Note that the outer rim of the dished washer is in contact with the ball-bearing inner race and the inner rim with the circlip. Tap the input shaft gently in towards the gear assembly and the ball-bearing on the far end of the primary shaft will be moved out slightly. Hold the bearing out with screwdriver blades in the retracting groove and have an assistant gently tap the primary shaft back into the case. Repeat the procedure, tapping first the input shaft in to move the bearing and then the primary shaft back to reposition it in the bearing inner race, and progressively you can work the bearing out of the case. Don't use excessive force and be satisfied with a little movement at a time.

10 With the bearing removed, disengage the reverse idler gear. Undo the two bolts securing the bearing cap over the primary shaft bearing in the middle of the case and remove the cap. Refit the roll pins to the case if they come out with the cap. On the BB6 gearbox it will be found that this bearing cap is located over studs and is secured by nuts.

11 Squeeze the circlip in the input and primary shaft joint and separate the two shafts. Note that there is a rubber washer in the aperture in the primary shaft on which the end of the input shaft butts when assembled. This washer must be renewed on reassembly. Remove the two shafts from the case and set the gear selectors to the neutral position.

12 On the late type BB8 gearbox an oil collecting cup is fitted in the

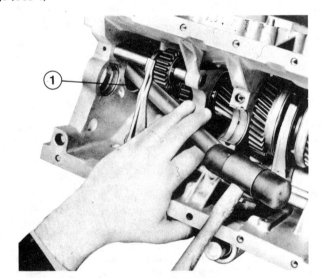

Fig. 6.11 Sheet metal seal removal method on the BB6 and early BB8 gearboxes using drift (1) (Sec 4)

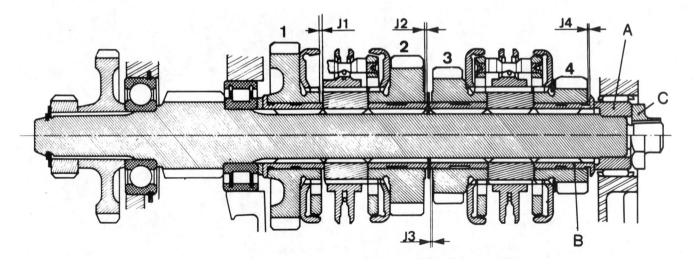

Fig. 6.12 Check the driven plate clearances, J1, J2, J3 and J4. Race A must contact bush B and nut C (Sec 4)

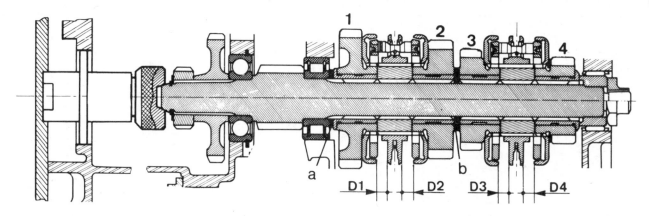

Fig. 6.13 Check the centralising of the synchronisers. Spaces D1, D2, D3 and D4 should be equal; adjustment is made on shims 'a' and/or spacer washer 'b' (Sec 4)

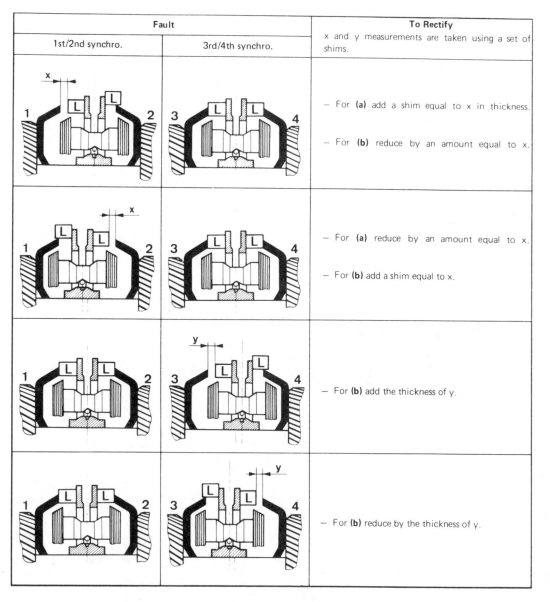

Fault		To Rectify
1st/2nd synchro.	3rd/4th synchro.	x and y measurements are taken using a set of shims.
		— For (a) add a shim equal to x in thickness. — For (b) reduce by an amount equal to x.
		— For (a) reduce by an amount equal to x. — For (b) add a shim equal to x.
		— For (b) add the thickness of y.
		— For (b) reduce by the thickness of y.

Fig. 6.14 Rectifying unequal centralising of one synchroniser (Sec 4)

x   Discrepancy on 1st/2nd synchro unit   b   Spacer washer, see Fig. 6.13
y   Discrepancy on 3rd/4th synchro unit   L   Gauging tool
a   Adjusting shims, see Fig. 6.13

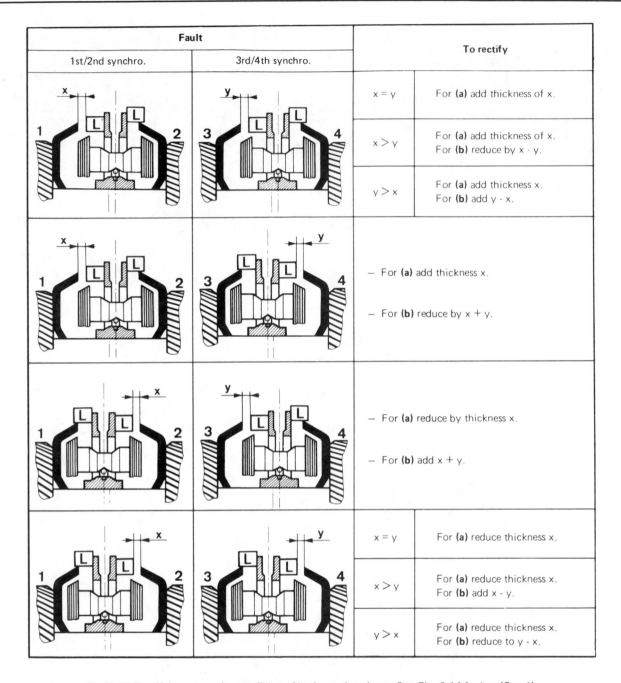

Fault		To rectify	
1st/2nd synchro.	3rd/4th synchro.		
		x = y	For (a) add thickness of x.
		x > y	For (a) add thickness of x. For (b) reduce by x - y.
		y > x	For (a) add thickness x. For (b) add y - x.
		— For (a) add thickness x. — For (b) reduce by x + y.	
		— For (a) reduce by thickness x. — For (b) add x + y.	
		x = y	For (a) reduce thickness x.
		x > y	For (a) reduce thickness x. For (b) add x - y.
		y > x	For (a) reduce thickness x. For (b) reduce to y - x.

Fig. 6.15 Rectifying unequal centralising of both synchronisers. See Fig. 6.14 for key (Sec 4)

end of the transmission case with a short connecting pipe entering the secondary shaft. This is to direct oil into the shaft to lubricate the 1st gear pinion through drilled passages. A special tool is required to remove the oil cup, but one can easily be fabricated following the details shown. Use it as shown to lever the cup out of the case.

13 Earlier gearboxes were fitted with a press-fit sheet metal seal in this housing aperture. Particular care must be taken when drifting out this seal from its housing not to damage the casing. This seal must be renewed on reassembly.

14 It is now necessary to make endfloat and clearance checks on the secondary shaft assembly to determine whether any worn parts must be renewed.

Endfloat

15 The easiest way to measure this is with a dial test indicator (clock gauge) mounted on the casing with its button resting on the end of the

secondary shaft and the spindle parallel with the shaft axle. Move the shaft to its limit in each direction axially and measure the endfloat. Alternatively a depth gauge could be used, but as the maximum permissible endfloat is only 0.5 mm (0.020 in) considerable care is needed to get an accurate assessment of the condition of the shaft ball-bearing which is what controls the endfloat. If the endfloat is found to be excessive a new bearing and a new retaining circlip must be fitted. The endfloat must then be rechecked. If it is still outside the permissible limit the gearbox housing must be renewed and obviously this would be the time to think again about renewing the complete gearbox assembly.

Clearances of driven pinions

16 Each pinion on the secondary shaft has a working clearance to permit it to rotate on the pinion bush when it is not engaged to drive the shaft. First check that the inner race of the needle bearing (at the

nut end of the shaft) is in positive contact with the 4th speed pinion bush and also that the retaining nut is in contact with the needle bearing inner race. Using feeler gauges measure the clearances J1, J2, J3 and J4 which should be between 0.2 and 0.35 mm (0.008 and 0.014 in). If the clearance is outside these limits the driven pinion bushes must be renewed.

17 The next essential check concerns the centralising of the synchronisers, but it is no use doing this until the endfloat and driven pinion clearances are within limits. However, if the gearbox housing has been renewed or if it is intended to renew the secondary shaft, selector forks, selector spindles or detent plungers, then the synchroniser centralising checks can be left until the gearbox is being reassembled.

18 When the selector forks are in the neutral position the synchroniser rings must be centred in relation to the synchroniser cones. This involves checking the distances marked D1, D2, D3 and D4 to ensure that they are equal when the parts in question are opened to the maximum. A special gauge is provided by Peugeot but the distances can easily be checked with a made-up gauge of 9 mm (0.3543 in) width for insertion in the appropriate gaps.

19 Before making the checks the secondary shaft must be lightly loaded at the speedometer drive worm end of the shaft. Again Peugeot specify the use of a special tool, shown in the illustration, but a piece of wood with a wedge can be used instead. The special tool is only hand tightened to load the shaft (to the left in the illustration) so make sure that your arrangement conforms to this. Also check that all the selector forks and shafts are in their neutral positions as registered by the shaft detent plungers.

20 Insert the gauge between each synchroniser cone and the adjacent face of the synchroniser hub but don't use force. Ideally the gauge will enter all four positions but, if it doesn't, refer to Figs. 6.14 and 6.15 where the eight possible variations are shown together with the remedial action that will be required. Adjustment is made on the shims 'a' and the spacer washer 'b' shown in the illustration. At this stage in dismantling it will be enough to note the size of the required new items and fit them on assembly. A recheck will then be required to confirm that all is well.

21 Remove the block and wedge used to load the secondary shaft, and engage 4th gear. Carefully drive out the roll pins from the 3rd/4th selector fork and the reverse idler pinion spindle. Remove the spindle and the idler pinion from the gearbox and reset the selectors to the neutral position.

22 Undo the banjo bolts securing the external oil pipe to the gearbox housing and remove the pipe, bolts and washers. Undo the four bolts securing the selector cover to the housing and carefully remove the cover, taking precautions to retain the detent balls and springs. Remove the springs and balls from the housing. Remove and discard the cover gasket.

23 Engage the reverse gear detent and rotate the selector upwards carefully. As you do this the detent ball will be ejected so be ready to prevent its loss; retrieve the spring. Drive out the roll pin connecting the detent to the reverse selector spindle and remove the detent followed by the spindle.

24 Engage 2nd gear and drive out the roll pin securing the 3rd/4th detent to its shaft. Drive out the roll pin securing the 1st/2nd selector fork to its shaft but leave the pin punch in the roll pin hole and set the fork to the neutral position. Turn the 3rd/4th selector spindle upwards a quarter of a turn to prevent the stop pin from falling out.

25 Now remove the two selector spindles, the 3rd/4th detent block, the two selector forks and the interlock plungers.

26 Remove the nut from the timing case end of the secondary shaft, (snap-ring and spring washer on the BB6 gearbox). From the other (clutch) end remove, in order, the circlip, dished washer, speedometer drive worm gear, shim, and the reverse gear driven pinion.

27 Working through the aperture normally locating the differential unit, spring open the circlip retaining the secondary shaft middle roller bearing outer race and, using a soft-faced hammer, tap the shaft towards the clutch end of the unit and remove it. Lift the synchroniser and gear assemblies out of the housing and take careful note of the washers and shims located in the assembly. Do not separate the synchronisers and hubs; these must be refitted in their original positions unless, of course, they are renewed.

28 This completes the normal dismantling of the transmission unit. Further dismantling such as the removal of the secondary shaft ball-bearing, or the removal of the input shaft bush from the transmission housing, will be dictated by the condition of parts. Do not disturb them unless there is good reason to do so. Note that, if the input shaft bush

in the housing is renewed, it is essential to have the new bush fitted by a specialist engineering shop with in-line reaming equipment as the alignment of the bush bore with the other two bearings is critical.

5 Transmission unit – inspection

1 Having removed and dismantled the transmission unit, the various components should be thoroughly washed with a suitable solvent or with petrol and paraffin, and then wiped dry. Take care not to mix components or to lose identification of where they fit and which way round they should be fitted. Don't use hand scrapers or emery cloth to clean the housing mating faces as the surface must be kept perfectly flat and undamaged.

2 Inspect the transmission housing and the differential unit housing for cracks or damage, particularly near bearings or bushes. The transmission housing, differential housing and the mainshaft centre bearing cap are all machined after assembly and none of these parts must be renewed separately.

3 Components requiring special attention will have been noted as a result of the performance of the transmission when installed in the car or will have been noted during dismantling.

4 Examine the teeth of all gears for signs of uneven or excessive wear or chipping. If you find a gear in a bad state have a close look at the gear it engages with – this may have to be renewed as well. All gears should run smoothly on their bushes or in their bearings with no sign of rocking or sloppiness.

5 A not so obvious cause of noise and trouble is bearing wear. Wash and dry the bearings thoroughly and examine them closely for signs of scoring, pitted tracks or blueing. Rotate the races and feel for smooth movement with no grittiness or abnormal noise. A new ball bearing will show no perceptible axial movement between the inner and outer races. As the bearing wears some play will be evident but if this is excessive the bearing must be renewed. After examining bearings they should be lubricated with clean engine oil to prevent corrosion, and wrapped to avoid contamination with dust and dirt. Discard the two half shell bearings of the input shaft as it is a sound proposition to fit new shells on reassembly.

6 Carefully inspect the synchromesh units for excessive wear or damage. If weak or ineffective synchromesh action has been experienced, renew the units as complete assemblies.

7 Check the selector forks for wear in the areas which contact the synchromesh units. Any wear evident should be minimal; if in doubt renew the forks.

8 Inspect the selector shafts and detents for wear which can cause imprecise gear changing, and renew where necessary.

9 All remaining components such as the speedometer gears, locking plungers, springs, balls, and so on, should be inspected for signs of wear or damage and, where necessary, renewed.

10 It is now worth reviewing the total requirements needed to restore the transmission unit to full serviceability, not forgetting the new lockwashers, circlips, roll pins, seals and gaskets. Compare the cost with that of an overhauled or good condition secondhand unit as it may be more economical to go for one of these alternatives.

6 Transmission unit – reassembly

1 All components must be spotlessly clean before reassembling the transmission unit, the work surface must be clean and you should work with clean hands. Some precision checks are necessary and you will not get accurate results unless everything is spotless. Furthermore, unless the assembled unit is free of contamination on completion, early wear, noise, a short life or even mechanical failure can result. Lubricate individual parts as they are installed with clean engine oil, particularly the bearings and moving parts.

2 Position the transmission housing on the bench and fit a new circlip in the groove in the secondary shaft ball-bearing housing (photo).

3 Fit the adjustment shims to the secondary shaft adjacent to the roller bearing inner race. The thickness of these shims will have been determined during dismantling. However, if the checks during dismantling showed that sideplay was excessive, if the shims have been lost, or if you have had to renew the driven pinion bushes, the transmission housing, the layshaft or the forks, spindles and detents,

6.2 Fit a new circlip in the secondary shaft ball bearing housing

6.3a Enter the shaft into the housing and ...

6.3b ... fit the 1st driven pinion and its bush

6.6a Fit the 3rd gear pinion and its bush to the secondary shaft

6.6b Assemble the 3rd/4th synchromesh unit ...

6.6c ... and fit it with 4th gear pinion to the shaft

6.7 Allow the circlip to contract into the outer race groove (arrowed)

6.8a Insert the two selector forks and ...

6.8b ... fit the selector spindle

6.8c An interlock plunger being fitted using a magnet

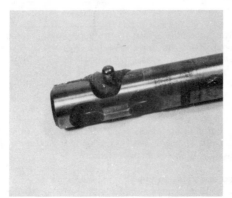
6.9a Fit the stop pin to the 3rd/4th selector spindle using grease to retain it in position

6.9b Fit the selector block as the spindle is installed

6.9c Fit new roll pins to the selector forks ..

6.9d ... and selector block

6.11a Fit the reverse gear pinion with its shallow boss towards the bearing, then ...

6.11b ... fit the speedometer drive worm wheel followed by ...

6.11c ... the dished washer with its outer rim contacting the worm wheel and ...

6.11d ... use a tube drift to secure the circlip

then shim thickness 0.75 mm (0.0295 in) should be fitted; this may need changing when the checks are done again later but it will enable a start to be made. Partly enter the shaft into the transmission housing and as it enters fit the 1st driven pinion and its bush to the shaft (photos).

4   Assemble the 1st/2nd synchromesh unit and check that the alignment marks on the hub and splined sleeve coincide. Fit the synchromesh unit to the secondary shaft. The assembly pins on the synchromesh unit are marked with three grooves and these must be positioned towards the 1st gear pinion. Then fit the 2nd gear pinion and its bush.

5   Fit the adjustment washer to the shaft next. As with the shims earlier, the thickness of the washer required will already have been determined during the checks on dismantling. However, if, for the reasons listed in paragraph 3, the size of the washer is not known, fit one that is 2.60 mm (0.1024 in) thick temporarily. Again, as for the adjustment shims, you may have to change this after doing the clearance and centring checks as stated in paragraph 16.

6   After the adjusting washer, fit the 3rd gear pinion and its bush (photo). Assemble the cones to the 3rd/4th synchromesh unit and check that the alignment marks on the hub and splined sleeve coincide (photo). Fit the synchromesh unit to the secondary shaft. The assembly pins on this unit are marked with one groove which must be positioned towards the 3rd gear pinion. Then fit the 4th gear pinion and its bush (photo).

7   Gently tap the secondary shaft assembly into the housing. As the ball-bearing approaches its circlip, hold the ring open with circlip pliers and continue to tap the assembly home. Allow the circlip to contract into its groove in the ball-bearing outer race when they are aligned (photo).

8   Insert the 1st/2nd and 3rd/4th gear selector forks into the assembly, engaging them with their respective synchromesh units (photo). Insert the 1st/2nd selector fork spindle through the hole in the 3rd/4th selector fork and position it with the interlock plunger notch on the axis of the plunger hole. Fit an interlock plunger in the hole to rest on the 1st/2nd fork selector spindle; check that it is not protruding into the 3rd/4th selector spindle hole (photos).

9   Hold the 3rd/4th selector spindle with the two flats on it upwards and fit the stop pin in its hole, using a little grease to retain it in position (photo). Fit the spindle to the housing and, at the same time, to its selector block (photo). Rotate the spindle $\frac{1}{4}$ turn towards the selector mechanism cover. Fit new roll pins to the selector fork spindles, forks and selector block (photos).

10 Fit the second interlock plunger into its hole.

11 Fit the reverse gear pinion to the secondary shaft with the shallow boss in contact with the ball-bearing inner race, then fit the speedometer drive worm wheel (photos). These are secured by a dished spring washer and circlip, but first put the dished washer in position on the shaft with its outer rim in contact with the worm wheel and check that, when the circlip is fitted, the washer will be compressed slightly. If this is not the case a shim will have to be fitted between the reverse gear pinion and the speedometer drive worm wheel to ensure that the washer is compressed. When satisfactory, put the circlip on the bevelled end of the shaft and use a tubular drift to tap it into position in its groove (photos).

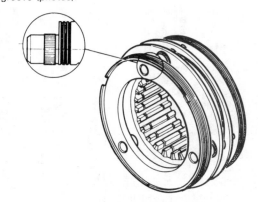

Fig. 6.16 The 1st/2nd synchroniser pins have three annular grooves (Sec 6)

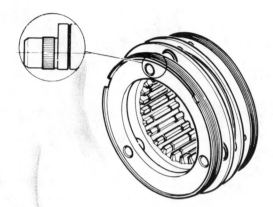

Fig. 6.17 The 3rd/4th synchroniser pins have a single annular groove (Sec 6)

12 Fit the reverse selector spindle to its bearing location in the housing with the flats towards the selector mechanism cover and fit the selector fork when at full travel (photos). If the selector block has been removed, fit it to the spindle and secure with a new roll pin.

13 Turn the spindle so that the selector block points upwards and fit the spring and ball to their location in the block (photo). Compress the spring by lowering the block and move the selector to the neutral position.

14 Fit the three springs and balls to the spindle detents and check that the locating spigot (roll pin) is in position in the face on which the selector mechanism cover beds. Fit a new gasket and fit the cover using new washers under the heads of the four retaining bolts (photos). Tighten the bolts to the specified torque. Check the operation of the four forward gear selectors – do not operate the reverse gear – and make sure that the action is smooth and positive. Leave the selectors in the neutral position.

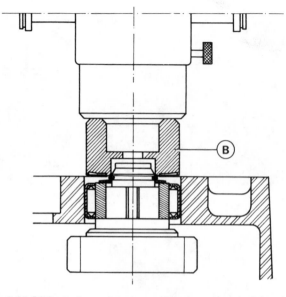

Fig. 6.18 BB6 gearbox: press home the secondary shaft bearing retaining clip (Sec 6)

BB6 gearbox

15 Stand the gearbox on its end, with the speedometer drive pinion and downwards, and position a suitable support under the end of the secondary shaft. This done, assemble the needle roller onto the top end of the secondary shaft (with its markings upwards). Then using a tube drift of suitable diameter drive or press it into position so that it abuts the 4th gear pinion bush. If pressing the bearing home do not exceed 1 ton in pressure loading. Locate a new washer and circlip into

6.12a Fit the reverse selector spindle ...

6.12b ... and the selector fork

6.13 Fit the spring and ball to the reverse selector block

6.14a Fitting of one of the three detent balls using a magnet

6.14b Fit the three springs and then ...

6.14c ... fit the selector mechanism cover

6.16a The needle bearing inner race being fitted to the secondary shaft

6.16b Using a home-made gauge to check the centering of the driven pinions

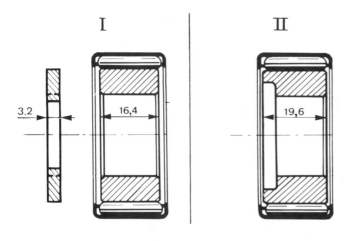

Fig. 6.19 BB8 gearbox: the two types of secondary shaft needle roller bearings fitted (dimensions in mm) (Sec 6)

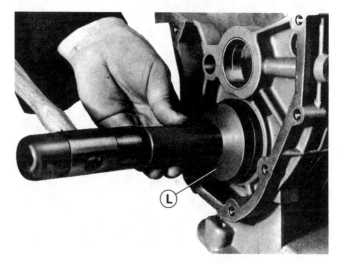

Fig. 6.20 BB6 and early type BB8 gearboxes: drifting the new sheet metal plug into position (Sec 6)

position on the end of the shaft and drift or press them home so that the circlip engages in its location groove, using a tube drift of suitable diameter. Check on fitting that the outside diameter of the fitted circlip does not exceed 22.6 mm (0.889 in). The centring of the drive pinions on the secondary shaft can now be checked or described in Section 3, paragraphs 17 to 19. Should it be necessary for further adjustments to be made, the assembly will have to be removed again and dismantled so that the appropriate shims or washers can be fitted.

BB8 gearbox

16 Fit the secondary shaft needle bearing inner race. Early models have a washer which must first be fitted, but later models have a recess counterbored in the race. This must be fitted to contact the 4th driven pinion bush (photo). Tap the race into position using a suitable tubular drift (such as a socket spanner) and fit a new retaining nut, but only tighten it lightly to (say) 3 lbf ft (about 0.5 kgf m) at this stage as the centring of the driven pinions on the secondary shaft must be checked. If, due to new parts for example, the centring check reveals the need for adjustment, the transmission assembly will have to be dismantled to have the appropriate shims and/or adjusting washer fitted to the secondary shaft assembly (photo).

17 When the centring of the pinions has been achieved satisfactorily, or if there is no need for adjustment, fit the reverse idler spindle and the idler pinion. Engage the reverse selector fork with the pinion as it

Fig. 6.21 Fitting the differential housing cover plate on the right-hand side – early models. Notches (a) to be horizontal with outlet groove as (b) as shown (Sec 6)

6.17a Fitting the reverse idler pinion and selector fork followed by ...

6.17b ... the spindle and ...

6.17c ... a new roll pin to secure it

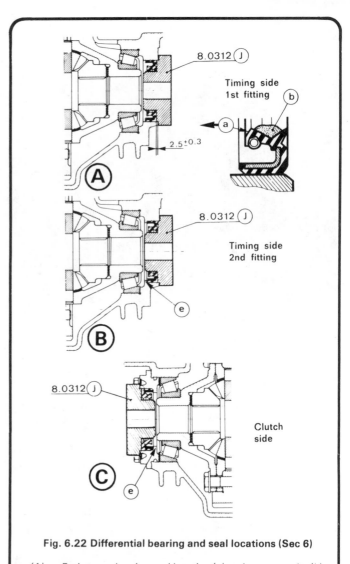

Fig. 6.22 Differential bearing and seal locations (Sec 6)

(A)   Early type showing seal location (a) and grease cavity (b)
       on the timing (right-hand side)
(B)   Later type – seal to butt against flange (e)
(C)   Left-hand side all models – seal abuts flange (e)
       8.0312(J) = Peugeot special tool

6.18 Fitting the oil collector cup

6.19 Fit the speedometer drive into position

6.20a Locate the new primary shaft bearing shells

6.20b Fit a new circlip (arrowed) to the input shaft

6.21a Fit the primary shaft

6.21b Insert input shaft through the housing and ...

6.21c ... when engaged with the primary shaft the circlip will expand into its groove

6.22a Fit bearing cap so that the D mark (arrowed) is towards the primary shaft, then ...

6.22b Tighten bolts (or nuts) to correct torque

is assembled and then fit a new roll pin to secure the spindle in the housing (photos).

General

18 On the BB6 and early BB8 gearboxes, smear sealer around the mating rim of the new sheet metal plug and carefully drift it into position in its housing. On later BB8 gearboxes, apply a light smear of sealer around the mating rim of the oil collector cup and fit it in its location in the housing. Tap it gently into position, making sure that the oil delivery spigot centres with the end of the secondary shaft (photo).

19 Fit a new O-ring to the speedometer drive assembly and smear lightly with grease. Fit the drive to the housing, meshing the worm and wheel, and align the locking screw holes. Fit the locking screw and its locknut, but do not tighten them until the power unit is installed in the car and the speedometer drive cable is fitted (photo).

20 Fit new half bearing shells to the primary shaft bearing and cap (photo). Fit a new rubber washer in the primary shaft/input shaft coupling and fit a new circlip to the input shaft (photo). Check that the half bearing locating spigots are fitted in the main housing and lubricate the half bearing shells.

21 Place the primary shaft in the housing (photo) and enter the input shaft through its plain bearing, taking care not to damage the bearing surface (photo). With the notch in the primary shaft coupling upwards, engage the input shaft in the coupling. Compress the circlip on the input shaft and push the shaft into the coupling until the circlip expands into its groove in the primary shaft (photo).

22 Fit the bearing cap with the mark D towards the primary (photo). Fit new plain washers to the two retaining bolts or nuts and tighten them to the specified torque (photo).

23 Fit the primary shaft ball-bearing to the housing and shaft, making sure that the extractor groove is towards the outside of the housing

6.23a Fit the primary shaft ball-bearing with its extractor groove outwards, then ...

6.23b ... fit the dished washer and a new circlip

6.23c Measure the circlip outside diameter to ensure that it is fully contracted

6.24a Engage 1st gear and the reverse idler pinion (both arrowed) to lock the gear train ...

6.24b ... and tighten the secondary shaft nut

6.25 Fit a new roll pin to the reverse gear selector fork and spindle

6.26 Lock the nut by compressing the skirt into the shaft flats

6.27 Fit bearing retainer plate and tighten securing bolts

6.28a Position differential unit into the half bearings and ...

6.28b ... fit the differential half housing

(photo). Tap the bearing home with a tubular drift on the inner race and make sure that it is fully seated. Fit a new dished washer and drift a new circlip over the bevelled end of the shaft. Compress the ring into the shaft groove and check that its outside diameter does not exceed 22.6 mm (0.8898 in) (photos).

BB6 gearbox

24 Engage 1st gear and also engage the reverse idler pinion in order to lock the gear train. Now tighten the secondary shaft nut to its specified torque setting.

25 Return the 1st gear to the neutral position then fit a new roll pin to the reverse gear selector fork and spindle (photo). Operate all gear selections, including reverse, and check that selection is smooth and positive both in engagement and disengagement.

BB8 gearbox

26 Lock the secondary shaft nut by compressing the skirt onto the shaft flats using a pair of self grip pliers (photo). Don't use a hammer to do this as the bearings or shaft could be damaged.

27 Fit the primary shaft ball-bearing triangular retaining plate and tighten the three bolts to the specified torque setting (photo).

Differential unit and housing – assembly and adjustment

28 Assemble the outer races to the differential taper bearings and

place the assembly in its location in the transmission housing (photo). Coat the mating faces of the differential half-housing and the transmission housing with a sealing compound and assemble them (photo). Fit the four long and four short bolts with new washers (Onduflex), and also fit new O-rings to those bolts which had them fitted on dismantling. Do not fully tighten the bolts at this stage.

29 The cover plate and bearing preload setting procedures differ according to the gearbox type. Earlier models have a cover plate and seal fitted on each side of the differential housing, whilst later models have just one cover plate fitted to the left-hand side. The right-hand side seal fits directly into the housing and abuts a shoulder within the housing aperture. In the following instructions, the accompanying photos show the later single housing fitting only.

30 Check that the oil seal(s) have been removed from the differential end cover(s) and/or right-hand housing aperture.

31 On the earlier models, fit the new seal ring and O-ring to the right-hand cover plate having first lubricated them with engine oil. Smear the bearing face with sealant and then refit the cover plate ensuring that the two notches (a) are horizontal and the outlet groove (b) is as shown, pointing to tthe top of the gearbox (gearbox is shown in inverted position). Refit and tighten the cover plate retaining bolts to the specified torque setting.

32 On later single cover models, fit the cover to the differential housing, tightening the four retaining bolts only lightly to about

6.32a Fit the end cover after removing the oilseal and ...

6.32b ... lightly tighten the securing bolts

6.33a Measuring from the cover mounting face to the outer race face and ...

6.33b ... measuring from the cover inner face to the mounting flange face

6.35a Fit selected shims and the cover (which has a new O-ring)

6.35b Tighten the short bolts in the differential housing first ...

6.35c ... followed by the long ones ...

6.35d ... and finally the cover bolts

6.36a Fit a new seal to both final drive apertures and ...

6.36b ... fill the space between the seal lips with grease

6.37a Fit a new seal to the sump screen and ...

6.37b ... then fit the screen to the bottom of the transmission unit

7 lbf ft (1 kgf m) (photos). Now lightly tighten the four smaller (8 mm dia.) bolts in the differential housing to 3 or 4 lbf ft (0.5 kgf m). When you have done this, undo the bolts in the end cover and remove the cover. Check that the outer race is bedded down on the rollers (photos).

33 On both gearbox types the differential bearing pre-load setting is now determined in the following manner. The taper bearings have to be slightly loaded when assembled and this condition is obtained by fitting shims under the end cover (left-hand end cover on early model type) so that when it is bolted down, a precise nip is achieved. To establish what size shims must be fitted, a couple of precision measurements must now be made. Use a depth gauge or a vernier gauge to measure the distance from the cover mounting face on the differential housing to the outer race face whilst lightly pressing the differential unit in (photo). Next measure the distance on the bearing cover from the face on the mounting flange to the face which would contact the outer race when assembled if it extended enough (photo). Subtract the second measurement from the first – this gives the space between the cover and bearing race. Now add 0.1 mm (0.0039 in) for early model type or 0.2 mm (0.0079 in) for late model type to that figure to give the thickness of shims which must be used to obtain the correct preloading.

34 On earlier models loosen off the right-hand cover plate retaining bolts and then tighten the housing bolts to their specified torque settings. Now retighten the right-hand cover bolts to their specified torque settings. On the left-hand side, locate the O-ring and seal ring to the cover plate. Smear the O-ring seal with oil and the cover mating surface with sealant and the shims in position, fit the cover plate with the notches positioned in the same manner as for the right-hand cover. Insert the retaining bolts and tighten them to the specified torque setting.

35 On later single cover models, fit a new greased O-ring to the cover and coat the cover mating surface with a sealing compound. Position the correct adjustment shims on the bearing outer race and fit the cover to the differential housing (photo). Use new spring washers under the bolt heads and tighten the bolts in the differential unit to the specified torque in the following sequence (photos):

(a) 8 mm dia short bolts in half-housing
(b) 10 mm dia long bolts in half-housing
(c) Cover bolts

36 Lightly grease and fit a new double lip oil seal to both apertures in the differential drives (photo). Use a suitable drift and tap the seals in gently until they bottom on the flange in the apertures. On models not having the flange in the aperture, the seal should be inserted so that it's outer face is recessed in the housing by 2.5 mm (0.098 in). Refer to the cross-section diagrams showing the seal to housing/cover fittings. Before the driveshafts are fitted on installing the power unit, the space between the two lips on each seal must be filled with grease (photo).

37 Fit a new rubber grommet to the oil sump screen (photo), and fit the screen to its location on the bottom of the transmission (photo). Tighten the three securing bolts to the specified torque.

38 Check that the mating faces of the transmission housing and sump cover are clean and undamaged. Use a new gasket and fit the sump cover (photo). When fitting the bolts use the special lockplates and refit the lower engine mountings. Fit the special nut to the lower drain spacer on the right-hand side (photo). Tighten this nut and the sump bolts to their specified torque settings. Fit a new sealing washer to the sump drain plug and tighten the plug to the specified torque.

39 The dipstick tube and the external oil pipe are best fitted after the transmission has been assembled to the engine, see the next Section for details.

7 Transmission-to-engine – reassembly

1 Refitting the transmission to the engine is a straightforward job. Fourteen bolts in total join the two assemblies in two flange joints, one on the front and one to the rear of the unit.

2 First check that the mating faces are clean and undamaged and then smear them with a jointing compound. A new O-ring seal must be fitted over the location dowel on the rear mating face corner at the clutch end. Lower the engine onto the transmission housing, guiding the two locating dowels into their spigot holes (photo).

3 Fit the coil mounting bracket to the second and third bolts from the right on the rear flange joint (photo). The manifold support bracket

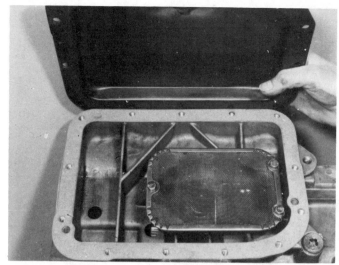

6.38 Use a new gasket and fit the sump cover

7.2 Lowering the engine onto the transmission housing

7.3 Fit the coil mounting bracket. Note that the manifold support bracket bolt has been left until engine installation (arrow)

7.5a Using a new sealing washer, fit the reversing light switch and ...

7.5b ... tighten to the correct torque

7.5c Tightening the external oil pipe banjo bolts

7.6 The dipstick can be fitted at any convenient stage of assembly

fits to the centre bolt in the rear flange joint, but it can be left until the manifold is fitted or after installation of the power unit, whichever is more convenient.

4   Fit the retaining bolts and tighten them evenly and progressively to the specified torque.

5   If the transmission unit has just been overhauled the reversing light switch can be fitted and tightened to its specified torque (photos). Fit the external oil pipe using a new joint washer on each face of the banjos – four washers together. Make sure that everything is clean before assembly and tighten the two banjo bolts to the specified torque (photo).

6   Apply thread locking compound to the dipstick tube threads and fit the tube to its location in the transmission housing. Tighten to the specified torque. If further assembly of the power unit remains to be done, eg starter assembly etc, the refitting of the dipstick tube can be left until after the other components have been fitted (photo).

7   If necessary, complete the reassembly of the power unit by reversing the dismantling sequence listed in Section 2.

8   Engine/transmission – refitting

As the transmission can only be installed in the car as part of the

assembled power unit the procedure is dealt with in Chapter 1 to which reference should be made.

9   Differential oil seals – removal and refitting

1   The differential oil seals can be renewed with the engine/transmission unit installed in the car, but the driveshafts will obviously have to be removed first. This procedure is contained in Chapter 7.

2   With the driveshafts withdrawn, lever out the old oil seals from the differential unit housing using a screwdriver. Take care not to damage the housing.

3   Clean out the seating before installing a new seal. Lightly grease the new seal to assist assembly and gently tap it into position, with the flat side outwards and using a suitable drift which will not damage the seal.

4   On late models with a shouldered flange inside the seal housing, the seal must be driven into position so that its inner face buts against the shoulder. On earlier models the seal must be driven into its housing so that when located its outer face is 2.5 mm (0.098 in) inset from the outer face of the housing.

5   Pack the space between the two lips in each seal with grease

before refitting the driveshafts. Clean the driveshafts before refitting and take great care not to damage the new seals as the shafts are being re-engaged with the differential.

10 Floor mounted gearchange – removal, overhaul and refitting

1 Two types of floor mounted gearchange linkage have been fitted, the first type being shown in Fig. 6.23 (A) was fitted up to March 1978. The second type was fitted from serial number 4 057 746 and this is shown in Fig. 6.23 (B).

2 The second type differs from the earlier type in having a shorter selection return spring (99 mm instead of 129 mm), a shorter gearchange rod (648 mm instead of 652 mm) and larger gearbox selector cover unit having a single link instead of the two and a return lever previously used.

3 The second type assembly can be fitted to the earlier type gearbox housing, but not the other way round. Should this modification be

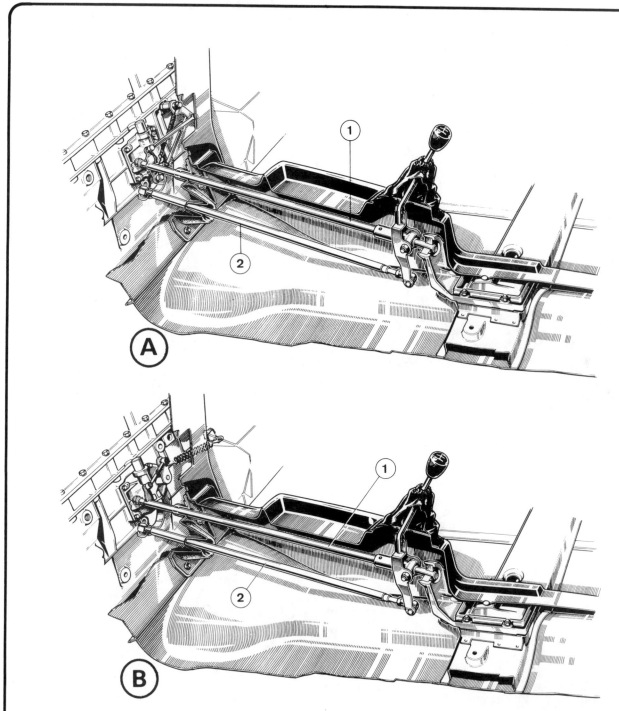

Fig. 6.23 Cutaway views showing the early (A) and late (B) type gear change linkage fitted with the BB8 gearbox (Sec 10)

| 1 Selector rod | 2 Change rod |

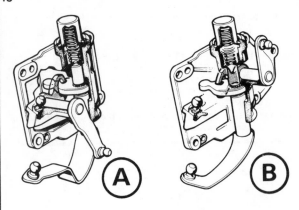

Fig. 6.24 The two gear change assembly types fitted to later models (Sec 10)

(A)   Early   (B)   Late

Fig. 6.25 Driving out the block roll pin on the early (BB6) gearbox (Sec 10)

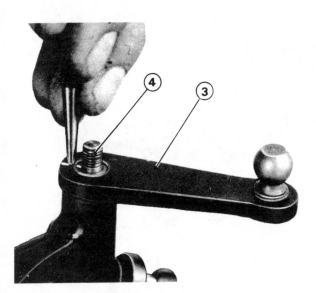

Fig. 6.26 Jack lever removal – early (BB6) type gearbox (Sec 10)

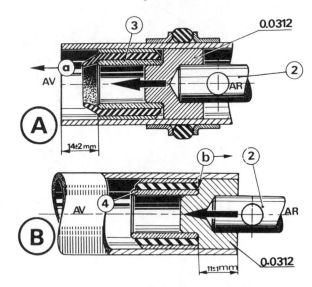

Fig. 6.27 Control rod bush renewal – early (BB6) type gearbox (Sec 10)

(A)   Front bush (3) with lip (a) to front
(B)   Rear bush (4) with smooth face (b) to rear
Note special Peugeot tool 0.0312 and drift (2)

Fig. 6.28 Jackshaft bush renewal (early BB6 gearbox) (Sec 10)

Fig. 6.29 Rubber centering ring location (early BB6 gearbox) (Sec 10)

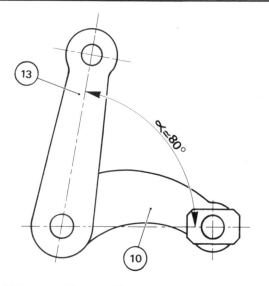

Fig. 6.30 Upper jack lever and lower jack lever showing correct fitting angle – early (BB6) gearbox (Sec 10)

required, your Peugeot dealer will be able to advise you on the parts which you require.

4   Normally the floor mounted gearchange mechanism gives no problems and overhaul consists of checking the individual components for wear and/or damage, lubricating the balljoints and pivot and renewing them if necessary. Unless there has been gross neglect, or the car has covered a high mileage or suffered damage, it is unlikely that renewal will be necessary.

5   Access to the gear lever and linkage rods assembly for checking or removal is gained after removing the central cover. To do this, remove a front seat (two bolts each side under the seat), unscrew the floor covering retaining screws and turning the cover away from the control pedals, lift it up over the gear lever to remove it.

6   The linkage assembly can then be removed by unscrewing the lever support bracket nuts (to the crossmember), removing the floor cover plate at the forward end and detaching the selector rod linkage balljoints and return spring. The assembly is then withdrawn rearwards through the aperture in the bulkhead floor (photos).

7   On earlier models the control rod is enclosed within a tubular housing and you may need to renew the control rod bushes. Before removing the gear lever, mark the location of the lever clamp plate in relation to the support. The lever can then be unbolted and lifted out. Drive out the rod to control block using a 6 mm diameter punch. Before removing the jack lever, mark its relative position to the shaft. It is secured by a snap-ring. Once dismantled the old bushes can be driven out of the tube using a suitable drift and the new bushes fitted. Locate the bushes as shown with the front bush forward lip 14 mm from the end of the tube. The rear edge of the rear bush must be

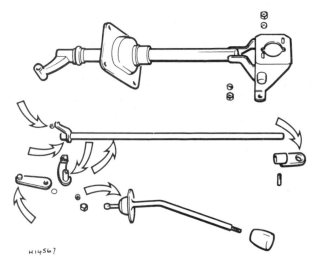

H14567

Fig. 6.31 Lubricate items indicated when reassembling the early BB6 gearbox (Sec 10)

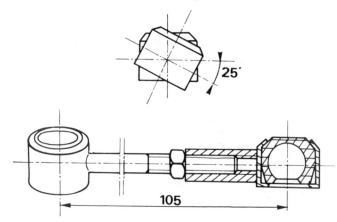

Fig. 6.32 Selector link length and angle – early models (Sec 10)

10.6a Remove the floor cover plate at the forward end of selector rods

10.6b Detach the linkages at the balljoints

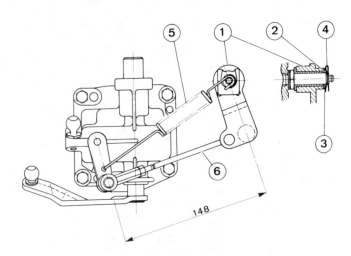

Fig. 6.33 Selector lever assembly – BB8 (406) gearbox (early type)
(Sec 10)

1	Selection lever	4	Spring clip
2	Spring washer	5	Spring
3	Plain washer	6	Rod

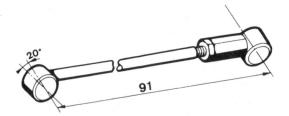

Fig. 6.34 Selection link length setting and joint angle – later type
BB8 (406) gearboxes (Sec 10)

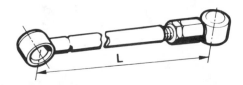

Fig. 6.35 Gear change rod length – BB8 gearbox (Sec 10)

Early $L = 652 \pm 1$ mm   Late $L = 648 \pm 1$ mm

positioned so that it is 11 mm from the rear end of the tube. Lubricate the tube to ease removal and fitting. When reassembled ensure that the control rod slides freely in the bushes. The jack shaft bushes can be renewed in a similar manner using a 12 mm diameter drift. The tube rubber centering ring at the forward end can be prised from its location groove for renewal and to ease refitting smear the ring with talcum powder. When reassembling the balljoint lever the roll pin split must face upwards. The lower jack lever is fitted with a nylon bush and this too should be renewed if necessary. When reassembled the jack levers should be positioned at the angle shown. Tighten the retaining nut to the specified torque. Don't forget to realign the lever clamp plate when refitting, and tighten the securing nuts to the same torque.
8   On all models, check the adjustment length of the rod link on reassembly. The angle of the selector link is also important on the early models. On assembly lubricate all moving joints before refitting the cover.

11 Fault diagnosis – transmission

Note: *It is sometimes difficult to decide whether it is worthwhile removing and dismantling the gearbox for a fault which may be nothing more than a minor irritant. Gearboxes which howl, or where the synchromesh can be 'beaten' by a quick gearchange, may continue to perform for a long time in this state. A worn gearbox usually needs a complete rebuild to eliminate noise because the various gears, if realigned on new bearings, will continue to howl when different wearing surfaces are presented to each other.*
The decision to overhaul therefore, must be considered with regard to time and money available, relative to the degree of noise or malfunction that the driver has to suffer.

Gearbox noisy in neutral
1   In neutral with the engine running the rotating parts are the input shaft, primary shaft, and the four gear pinions; all bearings in this train are plain bush, except at the timing case end of the primary shaft which is a ball-bearing. Noise can result from excessively worn gear

teeth or bearings and worn circlips or dished washers. Examine the gearbox for these faults and rectify by renewal.

Gearbox noisy in drive
2   In drive, in addition to the parts listed above, the other rotating parts are the secondary shaft, its two ball-bearings and one roller bearing, the differential unit and (when in reverse) the reverse idler. Examine and rectify as necessary.

Gearbox noisy in one particular gear
3   The same causes already mentioned above will result in noise in any gear or gears when selected, but the defect investigation can be concentrated on the particular train or trains in which the fault exists.

Gearbox jumps out of gear on drive or overrun
4   This is caused by worn selector forks or synchro grooves; worn synchro hubs or baulk rings; worn detent grooves in the selector shafts, or excessive endfloat on the secondary shaft. In all cases the transmission will need stripping for examination.

Ineffective synchromesh
5   The transmission will need stripping so that the synchromesh units can be examined for excessive wear. Double declutching meanwhile will result in relatively quiet changes.

Difficulty in engaging gears
6   Refer to Chapter 5 and check the clutch adjustment and operation. If the clutch is not releasing fully this will make gear engagement difficult.
7   Other causes of difficult engagement are as follows:

(a) Gearchange linkage damage or maladjusted
(b) Selector shaft interlocks and/or detents worn
(c) Needle roller bearing in crankshaft input pinion defective (see Chapter 5)

Chapter 7 Driveshafts, hubs, wheels and tyres

Contents

Specifications

Driveshafts .... Front wheel driveshafts, roller joint to wheel (outer) side, tulip joint with roller sliding motion to inner (axle) side

Driveshaft joints lubricant:
    Inner joint .... Esso Ladex HPF2 (120 g)
    Outer joint .... Esso Ladex HPF2 (240 g)

Wheel hub bearings
Front .... Twin track ball bearings
Rear .... Two taper roller bearings

Wheels
Type .... Pressed steel
Size .... Up to serial number 4 031 500 – $4\frac{1}{2}$ J14 B.3.35
After this serial number – $4\frac{1}{2}$ J14 D.3.45

Tyres
Tyre sizes and pressures in bars (lbf/in^2)

	Front	Rear
145 x 355 (145 SR 14) – Saloon	1.8 (26)	2.1 (30)
155 x 355 (155 SR 14) – Saloon	1.9 (27)	2.2 (31)
145 x 355 (145 SR 14) – Estate	1.8 26)	2.7 (39)*
155 x 355 (155 SR 14) – Estate with reinforced suspension	1.9 (27)	2.8 (40)*

*If driving for extended periods with unladen vehicle, rear tyre pressures can be lowered by up to 0.5 bar (8 lbf/in^2)

Torque wrench settings

	lbf ft	kgf m
Driveshaft/hub nut	181.0	25.0
Wheel nuts	43.0	6.0
Suspension arm pivot nuts	20.0	2.75
Anti-roll bar tie-link lower nut	9.0	1.25
Oil sump drain plug	20.0	2.75

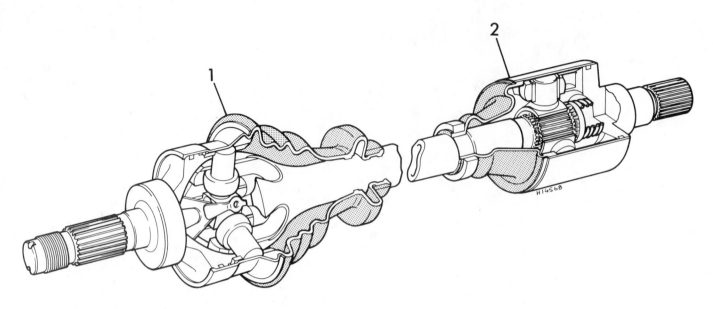

Fig. 7.1 Cutaway view of driveshaft (Sec 1)

1 Roller joint – outer   2 Tulip joint – inner

1 General description

The drive to the front wheels of the Peugeot 304 is transmitted directly from the final drive/differential unit on the front of the gearbox to the front wheel hubs by two driveshafts. Constant velocity universal joints are fitted near each end of the shafts to accommodate the steering and suspension angular movements. The inner ends of the shafts mate with the final drives with sliding splines which plunge to allow changes in length of the drives resulting from suspension and steering movements.

Little maintenance by the home mechanic is possible on the driveshafts. Even changing the rubber bellows is a specialised operation which is best entrusted to your Peugeot dealer.

The driveshafts are splined into the front wheel hubs. These run on double row ball-races located in the hub carrier at the bottom of each front shock absorber strut.

The rear wheel hubs run on conventional taper-roller bearings on stub axles in the rear trailing arms.

2 Driveshafts – removal and refitting

1 Position a suitable container under the engine oil drain plug in the sump cover, remove the plug and drain the engine oil. Clean around the plug hole, fit a new sealing washer to the plug, refit it and tighten to the specified torque. To avoid inadvertent starting of the engine before the oil is replenished, disconnect the battery earth cable.
2 Apply the handbrake and engage first gear. Position a jack under the jacking point just behind the front wheel arch. Raise and support the front of the car, then further support it with safety stands.
3 Under the car clean off all road dirt, oil and grease from the areas at both ends of the driveshaft. When the driveshaft has been removed it is important not to contaminate the exposed bearings etc with dirt. The driveshaft must now be prevented from withdrawing from the final drive/differential unit during the early removal stages. Peugeot have a special tool to do this but a makeshift arrangement can be achieved with wire around the shaft and around protruding boots of the differential case.
4 Jam the wheel hub to prevent it from turning by straddling a suitable bar diagonally across two of the wheel studs, then unscrew and remove the wheel hub retaining nut and its washer.

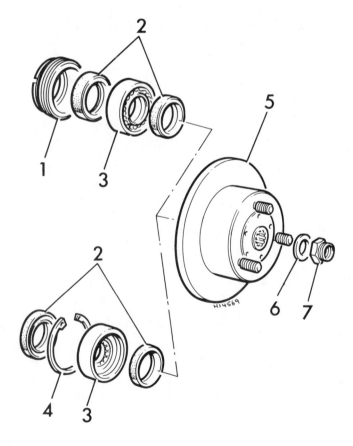

Fig. 7.2 Front wheel hub assembly components (Sec 2)

1 Locking nut	5 Hub, brake disc and wheel
2 Oil seals	studs
3 Bearing	6 Washer
4 Circlip	7 Nut

5   Detach the anti-roll bar at the suspension arm or suspension arm tie-link depending on type (See Chapter 9).
6   Unscrew and remove the suspension arm pivot bolts/nuts with washers noting how they are fitted. With the inner ends of the suspension arm free, pull the hub/steering knuckle assembly towards you. Simultaneously retain the driveshaft in the transmission, enabling the driveshaft outer connection to be withdrawn inwards and detached from the wheel hub. Take care not to damage the seal ring mating faces on the outer joint of the driveshaft as it is withdrawn.
7   Now withdraw the driveshaft from the transmission taking care not to damage the seal lips (within the differential housing) as it is extracted. Be prepared for a slight oil spillage on removal, plug housing as shown (photo).
8   If the driveshaft is to be renewed, the differential bearing cover seal ring must also be replaced as described in Chapter 6, Section 9.
9   As mentioned in Section 1, there is little that the home mechanic can do in the way of repairs or overhaul of the driveshafts or the constant velocity joints. Therefore if they are damaged or worn, repairs must be entrusted to a Peugeot dealer or new driveshafts complete with the constant velocity joints must be obtained.
10   Before refitting, check the driveshaft(s) to make sure that it is free of obvious defects. Clean the splines at both ends and, at the wheel hub end only, give the splines a thin coat of Molykote 321R or a suitable alternative anti-friction agent.
11   Lightly grease a new, double-lipped oil seal and carefully tap it into its recess in the final drive/differential unit with the side containing the spring facing into the unit. Make sure that the seal is abutting the internal shoulder in the unit case. Fill the space between the double lips with general-purpose grease. Similarly fit a new seal, of similar pattern, in the wheel hub, making sure that it abuts the bearing retaining ring. Again, fill the space between the lips with grease.
12   Carefully fit the driveshaft to the final drive/differential unit and be sure not to damage the oil seal. Prevent the shaft from disengaging by using wire, tying it back to the differential unit. Insert the driveshaft into the wheel hub, again exercising caution to avoid damaging the oil seal. Fit the thrust washer and a new nut but don't tighten it yet.
13   Relocate the suspension arm to the sub-frame pivot lugs, fitting four new Vulkollan type washers between the bushes and yokes. Lubricate the pin bolts before fitting and then fit new Nyloc nuts, but do not fully tighten them yet.
14   Refit the anti-roll bar to the suspension arm, but again do not fully tighten the fastenings yet.
15   Refit the hub washer and then fit a new hub nut, tightening to its specified torque setting. Then using a blunt punch, peen over the edges of the nut outer rim so that it is secured in the groove in the end of the shaft.
16   Refit the roadwheel and tighten the retaining nuts to the specified torque.
17   Lower the vehicle from the safety stands and jack so that it is free standing.
18   Where applicable, check that the anti-roll bar tie-link unit is correctly reassembled with the spacer in position as shown. Then locate a new Nyloc nut, but don't tighten it yet.
19   Release the handbrake and select neutral. Relax the suspension by rocking the car forwards and backwards slightly to allow the assembly to assume its normal position, then re-apply the handbrake.
20   Now tighten first the suspension arm pin nuts, then the anti-roll bar fastening(s) to their specified torque settings.
21   Replenish the engine/transmission oil and reconnect the battery lead.

2.7 Differential housing oil seal can be plugged with an old oil can cap, taped to protect the seal whilst driveshaft is removed

Fig. 7.3 Remove suspension arm pivot bolts/nuts (4 and 5) (Sec 2)

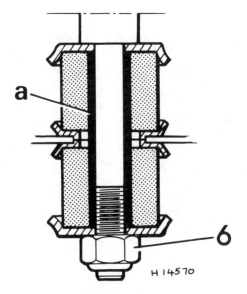

Fig. 7.4 Do not fully tighten the retaining nut until car is free standing (6). Ensure that spacer (a) is in position (Sec 2)

3   Driveshaft joints – maintenance

1   As has been stated earlier, there is little maintenance which can be done by the home mechanic on the driveshaft joints. Any attempt to dismantle them will be thwarted by the need for special equipment – particularly for reassembly.
2   In view of this it is recommended that work on the driveshafts is limited to removal, visual inspection, cleaning etc, and refitting only. Any repair or overhaul should be entrusted to a Peugeot garage.
3   Any leakage of grease from the joint protector or rubber boot must have immediate attention. Apart from the loss of the special lubricant, the risk of dirt contamination of the joint concerned demands prompt remedial action. Either take the car to a Peugeot garage or remove the shaft concerned and take that to the garage for expert attention.

4   Front wheel hub bearings – removal and refitting

1   The front hub bearings are twin track ball-races and removal for cleaning, inspection or replacement necessitates removing the wheel hub and disc brake.

2   The hub and disc unit will have to be separated from the strut assembly using a Peugeot special tool as it is not possible to use the usual sort of three or two-legged puller. As the same tool is used for extracting and inserting the bearings, as well as reassembling the hub and disc unit to the strut, it will be obvious that, either this tool must be borrowed or hired, or the job will have to be done by a Peugeot agent who will have the tool. As it is a simple matter to remove the absorber strut, and in any case removing the strut will make the job far easier, it is recommended that the strut is removed as explained in Chapter 9 and the assembly taken to the nearest Peugeot agent for servicing. The two oil seals will need renewing regardless of the condition of the bearings.

3   Reassembly is the reverse of the removal procedure. When tightening nuts and bolts, do so with the weight of the car on the suspension and tighten to the specified torque.

5.6 The oil seal in the rear wheel hub

5   Rear wheel hubs and bearings – removal and refitting

1   Each rear wheel hub runs on a pair of taper-roller bearings which must be renewed as a complete pair on a hub if the need arises.

2   To remove a rear hub, first slacken the wheel nuts of the wheel concerned. Select first gear and chock the front wheels. Jack up the rear of the car and support it on stands or substantial blocks with the wheels free. Remove the wheel nuts and the wheel, then prise off the hub cover. Undo and remove the two countersunk screws retaining the brake drum and remove the drum. If difficulty arises removing the drum, refer to Section 7, Chapter 8. Take care not to spread any brake dust in the atmosphere or, in particular, inhale it as it is a health hazard. Clean out the dust. If grease of hydraulic fluid has contaminated the brake shoes they will have to be removed, as described in Chapter 8.

3   Undo the hub retaining nut and discard it as a new one is necessary on reassembly. Remove the thrust washer from the stub axle and remove the hub. Prise out the grease seal in the back of the hub and remove the O-ring from the cover locating spigot.

4   Remove the outer and inner bearings from the hub, if they have not already been removed, and identify them so that they can be refitted to their original position if they are fit for re-use. Clean the bearings and their tracks thoroughly. Examine them for signs of wear, overheating indicated by discolouration, pitting and any other damage. New bearings should be fitted if there is any evidence of deterioration or any doubt about their condition.

5   Only remove the bearing tracks if it is intended to renew them. Carefully drift them out using suitable drifts and supports for the hub. Clean the bearing track housings before fitting new tracks. A bearing and its outer track are matched components and they must be fitted together. Don't degrease new bearings before fitting them. The best way of fitting is with a large draw bolt and two thrust plates, or suitable large socket spanners if available. Make sure that the tracks are fully bedded in their locations.

6   After fitting the outer tracks, fit the inner bearing to the hub. Fit a new oil seal, with its lip facing in towards the hub and its outer face flush with the hub rim. Wipe off all surplus grease from the outside of the hub (photo).

7   Before refitting the hub, fit the outer bearing to the cleaned stub axle and ensure that it slides on easily. If it doesn't, use some emery cloth on the axle bearing surface cautiously to obtain a free fit. Make sure that all traces of emery dust are cleaned off afterwards.

8   Try the new nut on the stub axle threads and screw it down to check that there is no abnormal resistance. If necessary deburr the grooves in the axle into which the rim of the nut will be staked.

9   When all is satisfactory fit the hub and push it on until it is properly located. Put a minimum of 80g (2.8 oz) of general-purpose grease inside the hub bore. Then fit the greased outer bearing inner race and the flat safety washer. Fit the new nut (photos).

10   Peugeot use a special tool to tighten the nut in a rather complicated procedure. A fairly accurate result can be obtained without the tool by following this suggested procedure.

5.9a After fitting the rear wheel hub ...

5.9b ... fit the outer bearing followed by ...

5.9c ... the safety washer

5.11a Tighten the nut as explained in the text to set hub bearing preload

5.11b Punch the nut skirt into the axle grooves

5.12 With a new O-ring seal in the groove of the hub, refit the grease cap/cover

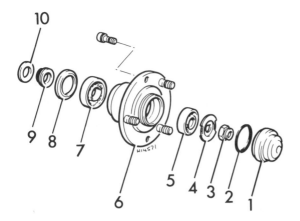

Fig. 7.5 Rear wheel hub components

1	Grease cap	6	Hub
2	O-ring	7	Inner bearing assembly
3	Nut	8	Oilseal
4	Washer	9	Spacer
5	Outer bearing assembly	10	Washer

11 Fit the brake drum and its two retaining countersunk screws. Rotate the drum and tighten the retaining nut to the initial specified torque (see Specifications). Slacken the nut off and, still rotating the drum, tighten the nut to the final specified torque. Stop rotating the drum and do not move the nut. Apply the footbrake two or three times to adjust the rear brakes (but make sure that the brake drum on the other rear wheel is fitted before doing this, if you are working on both rear wheels), and then apply the handbrake to hold the brake drum during the next stage. Carefully note the position of the nut relative to the axle and *slacken* it through 30°. This is equivalent to half a flat on the nut. Keep the nut in this position and deform the sleeve on the nut into the grooves on the axle to lock it, using a suitable punch and hammer (photos).

12 If it has not already been done, fit a new O-ring seal to the bearing cover locating spigot on the hub and refit the cover (photo). Refit the wheel, leaving the final tightening of the wheel nuts until the car is on the ground. When the car is lowered, tighten the wheel nuts to their specified torque.

6 **Wheels – general**

1 Because of the design of the suspension of the car, the strength and trueness of the roadwheels is critical, particularly at the front.

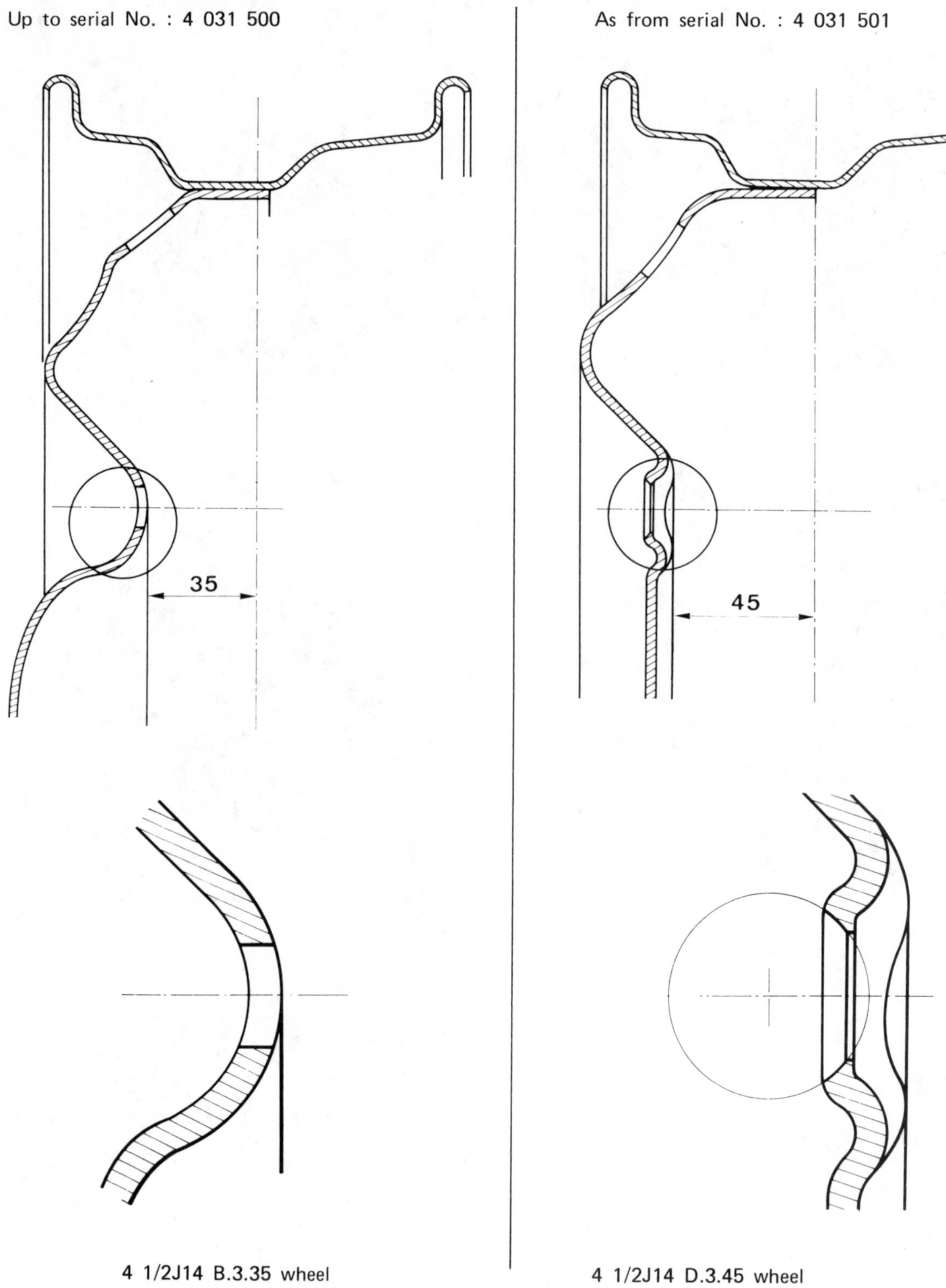

Up to serial No. : 4 031 500

As from serial No. : 4 031 501

35

45

4 1/2J14 B.3.35 wheel

4 1/2J14 D.3.45 wheel

Fig. 7.6 Sectional profiles showing the two roadwheel types fitted
(Sec 6)

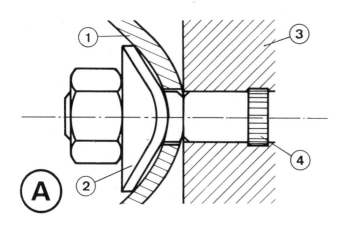
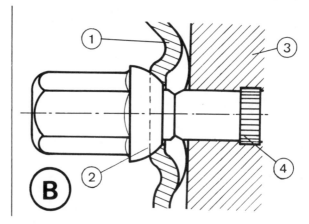

Fig. 7.7 Sectional views showing the early type 'open' roadwheel nut (A) and the later 'spherical face' cap nut (B) fitted to later type roadwheels introduced at serial number 4 031 501 (1978 models on). They are not interchangeable (Sec 6)

1 Wheel
2 Alignment plate (early) or spherical thrust face (late type)

3 Hub
4 Stub

Excessively fast wear on the wheel bearings and driveshaft joints can often be attributed to buckled and deformed wheels. Check every 5000 miles (7500 km), or when there is a sudden difference of feeling at the steering wheel, that the wheels are not buckled, dented or otherwise out of true. Check also that balance weights, where fitted, are not missing.

2 If it is suspected that the wheels are out of balance, which can often be identified by a vibration felt through the steering wheel usually at a particular speed, have your local dealer rebalance them.

3 If a wheel is badly rusted or damaged in any way do not attempt to repair it – get a replacement and be particularly cautious about secondhand wheels that may have come from a crash damaged vehicle.

4 Don't overtighten wheel nuts, for this can cause deformation of the wheel. Always check that the inner side of the wheel is free from mud and dirt since the accumulation of these can cause imbalance.

5 If renewing a roadwheel it should be noted that up to serial number 4 031 500, $4\frac{1}{2}$ J14 B.3.35 wheels were fitted. After this serial number $4\frac{1}{2}$ J14 D.3.45 roadwheels were fitted. They are not interchangeable so be sure to get the correct replacement.

7 Tyres – general

1 The recommended tyre pressures are given in the Specifications. Check tyre pressures when the tyres are cold, as after a run the pressures will increase.

2 In the same way that the condition and suitability of the wheels is critical, so it is with the tyres. Because of the long suspension travel and independent four-wheel suspension it is always best to fit radial tyres on all four wheels of these cars in order to achieve the greatest benefit. Stick to the size of tyre originally fitted to your car as any deviation could introduce unforeseen problems. Always maintain the correct tyre pressure, not forgetting the spare wheel, to achieve maximum tyre life.

3 It is recommended that wheels are balanced whenever new tyres are fitted, and re-balanced halfway through the life of the tyre to compensate for the loss of tread rubber due to wear.

4 Make a regular check of the tyre tread depth (photo) and note the tyre tread wear pattern. Any uneven wear will almost certainly be caused by incorrect tyre pressures or a defect in the suspension/steering system either caused by wear, damage or incorrect settings – see Chapter 9.

7.4 Check tyre tread depths to ensure they comply with regulations

Fault diagnosis overleaf

8   Fault diagnosis – driveshafts and hubs

Symptom	Reason(s)
Knock or clunk when taking up drive	CV joints worn Splined couplings worn Front hub nuts loose or bearings worn
Vibration	Wheel nuts loose Wheels unbalanced (check for security of balance weights and accumulations of mud) CV joints or splined couplings worn
Metallic grating varying with road speed	CV joints worn Wheel bearings worn
Abnormal noise when turning	Differential unit defective CV joints worn Wheel bearings worn

Chapter 8 Braking system

Contents

Specifications

General
Footbrake .... Hydraulic, dual circuit, discs front and drums rear, servo assisted
Handbrake .... Mechanical cable operated to rear wheels only

Front disc brakes

Caliper
Early double piston type (location – rear of wheel centre) .... Girling 14CM or DBA F48 or Bendix 48
Later single piston type (from 1977) (location – front of
wheel centre) .... Teves or DBA 111 AC 48

Brake pads
All early models except 304S .... Abex NS413
Early 304S models .... Abex NS414
All models from 1977 .... Abex NS414
Minimum allowable thickness .... 2.5 mm (0.098 in)

Brake disc
Outside diameter:
    Early models .... 256.5 mm (10.09 in)
    Late models (from 1977) .... 263.0 mm (10.35 in)
Disc thickness (new) – all models .... 10.0 ± 0.1 mm (0.393 ± 0.003 in)
Minimum disc thickness after machining both sides .... 9 mm (0.354 in)
Maximum variation over disc faces .... 0.2 mm (0.0079 in)
Disc run-out on hub (max) – measured 22 mm (0.866 in)
from edge .... 0.07 mm (0.0028 in)

Rear drum brakes
Drum – maximum machining diameter .... 229.6 mm (9.0394 in)
Maximum difference allowable between two drums on the
same axle .... 0.15 mm (0.0059 in)
Maximum allowable ovality .... 0.10 mm (0.0039 in)
Shoe lining width .... 40 mm (1.57 in)
Shoe length:
    Leading shoe .... 231 mm (9.09 in)
    Trailing shoe .... 176 mm (6.92 in)
Shoe lining type .... Ferodo 42

Hydraulic fluid type .... Lockheed 55, Nafic FN3, Peugeot, Stop HD88 or equivalent to SAE J1703

Master cylinder

Make	DBA or Automotive Products
Diameter	19 mm (0.748 in)
Primary/Secondary stroke:	
Early models	15 – 15 mm (0.59 – 0.59 in)
Late models	17 – 13 mm (0.67 – 0.51 in)
Servo unit	Mastervac

Torque wrench settings

	lbf ft	kgf m
Roadwheel nuts	43.4	6.0
Front caliper securing nuts	36.0	5.0
Bleed screw	9.0	1.25
Hydraulic switch	18.0	2.5
Brake pedal pivot	20.0	2.75
Pedal support to bulkhead	3.5	0.5
Mastervac to pedal support	7.25	1.0
Rear brake plate retaining screws	33.0	4.5
Double clamp bolts:		
Normal nut	7.25	1.0
Nyloc nut	11.0	1.5
Handbrake lever nuts	14.5	2.0

1 General description

All Peugeot 304 models have a conventional modern brake system with disc brakes on the front wheels and drum brakes on the rear. The brakes are operated by a servo-assisted hydraulic system having a tandem master cylinder actuated by a suspended foot pedal. Early models were fitted with a single circuit system whilst later models have a dual circuit system. Whichever system is fitted, a brake pressure regulator is incorporated into the circuit to prevent the rear wheels from locking.

The rear brakes can be applied for parking purposes by means of a cable operated handbrake.

Various manufacturers supply system parts and in consequence there is a certain amount of variation in details in system components. In some cases the parts supplied by different makers are not interchangeable or may be interchangeable with qualification. For this reason care is needed when buying spares to get the right parts; it's best to take a sample with you, if possible.

2 Routine maintenance

1 All work undertaken on the braking system, including routine maintenance, must be to the highest standard. It is vitally important to maintain the integrity of the system and to use the right fasteners with correct locking devices where appropriate. Adjustments must be within specified limits where these apply and spare parts must be new or in faultless condition. Absolute cleanliness when assembling hydraulic components is essential. New seals and fresh hydraulic fluid must be used and any fluid drained or removed from the system must be discarded. Remember that your life and possibly the lives of others could depend on these points; if you are in any doubt at all concerning what to do or how to do it, get professional advice or have the job done by an expert.

2 If the brake system tell-tale warning light comes on and the handbrake is not applied, immediately check the level of the brake fluid (see below). If the level is satisfactory check the setting of the handbrake warning switch.

Every 250 miles (400 km) or weekly

3 Thoroughly clean around the hydraulic fluid reservoir cap, remove the cap and check the fluid level. Some reservoirs are made of semi-transparent plastic and the fluid can be seen without removing the cap. However, you should only rely on this check once you have satisfied yourself that an accurate indication of the fluid level is possible. If necessary top up with fresh fluid, but make allowances for the change in level that will occur when the cap, with its switch and float, is refitted. The level in the reservoir will rise to some extent due to displacement by the switch assembly. Check that the vent hole in the filler cap is clear. Any need for regular topping up must be viewed with suspicion and the whole hydraulic system inspected for signs of leaks. A *small*, slow fall in the level as the disc pads wear is normal.

Every 5000 miles (7500 km)

4 Inspect the front disc pads for wear (see Section 5). The grooves in the pads should be visible, indicating that adequate pad material remains.

5 Inspect the rear brake assemblies and check the brake linings for excessive wear. All four shoes will need renewing if the thickness of any one lining is below 2.5 mm (0.1 in).

6 Check the operation of the handbrake. The brakes should lock the wheels when the lever has been moved six to eight notches.

7 Check the clearance between the brake foot pedal and the floor when the brakes are applied, to make sure that the pedal is not bottoming.

Every 10 000 miles (15 000 km) or annually

8 Remove the rear brake drums and carefully clean out the brake dust, **taking care not to inhale it or disperse it.** In addition to repeating the check for wear, inspect the shoe linings for contamination by grease from the bearings or fluid from the hydraulic system. Renewal is essential if they are contaminated and all four shoes will need renewing even if only one is contaminated. If contamination is found, trace the source and take appropriate rectification action. Check the general condition and security of the hydraulic system pipes and hoses.

Every 20 000 miles (30 000 km) or every 2 years

9 Renew the brake fluid in the hydraulic system. Over a period of time the fluid degenerates as the inhibitors, which prevent corrosion and seal deterioration, decay. In addition the fluid absorbs moisture from the atmosphere which is why cans of fresh fluid must be kept tightly sealed. The moisture will affect both the boiling point and the freezing characteristics of the fluid. It is false economy not to change the fluid on a regular basis, and could even be danegrous.

3 Bleeding the hydraulic system

1 The system should need bleeding only when some part of it has been dismantled which would allow air into the fluid circuit, or if the reservoir level has been allowed to drop so far that air has entered the master cylinder. Removal of all air from the fluid circuit is essential if the brakes are to work efficiently and safely.

2 First check all the brake line unions and connections for possible leakage, then remove the reservoir filler cap and check that the fluid level is correct. Check that the vent hole in the cap is clear.

3 Precautions should be taken to protect the body paintwork from possible spillage of brake fluid as the fluid is an efficient paint stripper.

4 You will need a supply of fresh, non-aerated brake fluid of the correct specification; try to leave the tin undisturbed for 24 hours to release air that may be present. A clean glass jar and a length of rubber or plastic tube which will tightly fit the bleed nipples will be needed, as well as a spanner which will fit the bleed screws. Although special rigs for bleeding are available to enable the job to be done single-handed, the best and quickest way is with the help of an assistant to

Fig. 8.1 Adjust rear brakes to position brake shoes maximum distance possible from drum – with adjusters (3) at centre of curve (a) (Sec 3)

Fig. 8.2 Maintain the reservoir fluid level throughout the brake bleeding operation (Sec 3)

operate the brake pedal as required. Apart from opening and closing the bleed screws, the level in the reservoir must be constantly maintained as fluid is pumped out of the system. If you let the level fall, air will get in and defeat the whole object of the exercise. Discard all fluid removed from the system as it is not fit for re-use.

5   Before starting, depress the brake pedal a few times to exhaust any residual vacuum in the servo. Go round the bleed screws and give them all a thorough clean. Put about an inch (25 mm) of brake fluid in the glass jar (photos).

6   Raise and support the car at the rear using safety stands. Put the car in gear and position chocks against the front wheels. Release the handbrake.

7   Where manual adjustment is possible, set the rear brake shoes to position them as far as possible from the drums.

8   Starting at the rear left-hand brake, fit the tubing onto the bleed nipple and immerse the other end in the fluid in the jar. Keep the open end of the tube immersed throughout the bleeding procedure. Unscrew the bleed screw for about half a turn and get your assistant to depress the brake pedal fully, then allow the pedal to return unassisted. Pause for a few seconds and then repeat. To make sure no fluid re-enters the system from the jar it is best to close the bleed

screw when the pedal is fully down and only open it as the pedal starts to be depressed. It is not essential to remove all the air from one brake at a time. If the whole system is to be bled, attend to each wheel for three or four complete pedal strokes and then repeat the whole process. After every three or four pedal strokes replenish the reservoir with fresh fluid – don't reuse the fluid bled from the bleed screws. When no air bubbles can be seen in the jar when the pedal is being depressed tighten the bleed screw before releasing the pedal, remove the tube, wipe up any spilt fluid and fit the dust cap. Note that some Girling LF front brake caliper units have two bleed screws fitted, in which case always bleed the lower one first.

9   Continue until all four brakes have been completed. Test the system by depressing the foot pedal which should offer firm resistance with no suggestion of sponginess. The pedal must not go down under sustained pressure; if it does the seals in the master cylinder are probably leaking, requiring renewal of the seals or of the master cylinder itself if the bores are scored.

10   When bleeding of each brake is completed, readjust the rear brakes as given in Section 4.

11   When the car is next taken onto the road, proceed with caution until you have tried the brakes and found them to be satisfactory.

3.5a Remove dust cap and clean bleed nipple before ...

3.5b ... connecting up bleed tube. Note that in this instance a one-man bleed kit is being used

Fig. 8.3 Move brake adjusters in directions shown so that brake shoes bind on the drums (Sec 4)

Fig. 8.4 Handbrake cable adjustment on earlier models (1) (Sec 4)

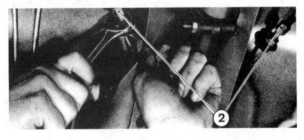

Fig. 8.5 Handbrake cable adjustment on later models (Sec 4)

Fig. 8.6 When adjusting the handbrake cables maintain equal tension on jack lever to retain its relative orientation as shown. On later models the jack lever is situated under the handbrake lever assembly (4) within the car (Sec 4)

4   Brake adjustments

Front disc brakes

1   The front disc brakes are fully self-adjusting in that, as the lining material of the brake pads wears, the pistons move towards the disc and hydraulic fluid will be drawn from the reservoir to compensate. No manual means of adjustment is provided but the brake pads must be inspected periodically for wear and the hydraulic reservoir level must be kept up.

Rear brakes (with external manual adjusters)

2   Raise the car at the rear and support it with safety stands. Put the car in gear and place chocks under the front wheels.
3   Release the handbrake, then working underneath, rotate the brake adjuster on the inside of each brake backplate, so that the brake shoes are felt to bind on the drums.
4   Press hard down on the brake pedal two or three times then working underneath again, slacken off the trailing shoe in each drum assembly.
5   Now loosen off the leading shoe adjuster on each wheel in turn until the wheels are free to rotate but with the shoe as close as possible to the drum. A slight binding of the shoe on the drum is permissible.
6   The trailing shoe must now be retightened against the drum and then loosened off in a similar manner to that of the leading shoes.
7   Apply the footbrake to check its action and then rotate each rear wheel to ensure that they are not binding excessively. If they are, further minor adjustment may be necessary.

Rear drum brakes (automatic adjustment type)

8   As the description implies this type of drum brake is self-adjusting and requires no attention apart from periodical checks for wear and possible hydraulic system leaks or grease contamination.

Handbrake adjustment

9   First raise the hand-lever until the 6th notch in the ratchet is engaged.
10   Jack up the rear of the car and support it with the wheels free, on axle stands or firmly based blocks. Chock the front wheels and engage a gear.
11   Adjustment of each cable is by the adjustment nuts underneath, the two types fitted being shown.
12   Loosen the locknuts and turn the adjusters until, on turning the wheels, the brakes can be felt just starting to bind. Readjust if necessary, so that the jack lever of the handbrake assembly in the car is at right-angles to the fore-and-aft centre-line of the car, by loosening on one adjuster and tightening on the other. Recheck the wheels for binding, which should just be apparent on both sides. Then tighten the cable adjuster locknuts.
13   Check the operation of the handbrake by ensuring that both wheels lock when the hand lever is between the 6th and 8th notch and are free to rotate when it is released.
14   Lower the car to the ground.

5   Disc pads – inspection and renewal

1   Before dismantling any part of the brakes they should be thoroughly cleaned. With a stiff brush, remove as much road dirt as possible and finish off using hot water and a mild detergent (dish washing fluid will do). Do not use paraffin, petrol or other solvents which could cause deterioration of the friction pads or piston seals etc.
2   Use ramps to raise the front of the car, or jack it up and support it on stands. Do not work under a car supported only on the wheel changing jack. Apply the handbrake to prevent movement of the car.
3   Inspection of the front brake disc pads will require removal of the front wheels as the brake calipers are hidden from view by the roadwheel.
4   With the roadwheel(s) removed, the brake pad thickness can be checked. Some pad types are grooved to indicate the remaining depth of friction material. When the groove is not apparent the pads must be renewed. The minimum allowable pad thickness is 2 mm and should any of them be worn down to this thickness, the pads must be renewed as a set (right and left-hand wheels).

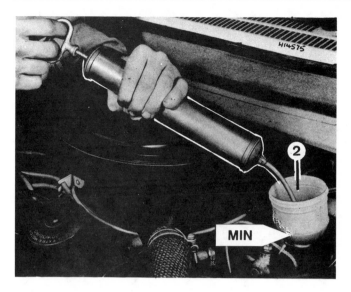

Fig. 8.7 Syphon off the fluid down to the Minimum mark in the reservoir (Sec 5)

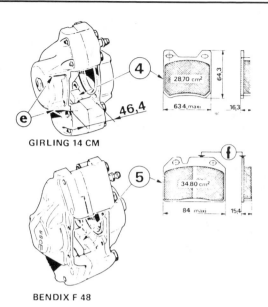

GIRLING 14 CM

BENDIX F 48

Fig. 8.8 Pad and caliper identification features on early models – dimensions given are in mm (Sec 5)

Girling 14 CM – marked G at points e
Bendix F48 – Pads must have white and green reference on back plate (f)

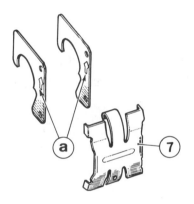

2nd Fitting

Fig. 8.9 Girling 14 CM caliper – refit with shim arrows (a) pointing up (Sec 5)

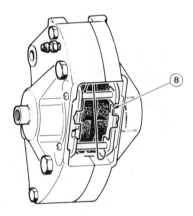

Fig. 8.10 Anti-rattle spring location on the Bendix F48 caliper (Sec 5)

5   To remove and renew the pads you will first need to syphon a small amount of fluid from the brake master cylinder reservoir. Using a clean syringe, remove some of the hydraulic fluid from the reservoir. When new pads are fitted the pistons must be removed back into the cylinders to accommodate the extra thickness and if fluid is not first removed from the system it might overflow with possible damage to the car's paintwork – apart from the mess it will cause. Discard the fluid removed as it is unsuitable for re-use in the system.

6   The caliper type fitted to your model will be one of five types fitted. Earlier models have either a Bendix F48, Girling CM14 or 14LF types fitted, whilst later variants have either a Teves or DBA111 fitted. It is important when renewing the pads or associated components of the calipers that the correct replacements are fitted as some items are not directly interchangeable.

7   For pad removal on DBA111 refer to paragraphs 20 to 29 inclusive. For other models the pad removal and fitting details are basically the same and are as follows.

All brakes (except DBA)

8   Extract the pin retaining clips using a suitable pair of pliers then withdraw the pad securing pins noting that their heads face inwards. The photo sequences shown of pad removal are for the Teves type caliper (photo).

5.8 First remove the pad retaining pins ...

5.9a ... and the damping spring

5.9b Withdraw the pads

5.9c Note the key in the caliper (arrowed) on which the outer pad sits

5.9d The back face of the outer pad (left) has a recess for the caliper key

9   The pads and anti-rattle shims or damping springs can now be withdrawn from the caliper. As they are removed note their orientation to ensure correct reassembly (photos).

10 Inspect the disc friction area. If it is badly scored, cracked or excessively worn, the disc will have to be renewed. Unforunately removal of the disc from the suspension strut can only be undertaken by a Peugeot agent, see Chapter 9. Worn discs can be resurfaced by a specialist garage if the wear is within limits.

11 If the pads are not worn out but have a black, shiny surface, before fitting them roughen the surface with a piece of emery cloth to remove the glaze, but don't overdo it. Pads must be refitted to their original positions.

12 Visually check the condition of the caliper, the hydraulic hose, and the cylinder assembly before fitting the pads. Look carefully for signs of fluid leaks and remove any corrosion and scale. Renew the retaining pins and spring if they are worn or corroded.

13 As previously mentioned, if any new parts are to be fitted, check before fitting that they are the correct replacement as some items are not interchangeable.

14 If fitting new pads remember that all four pads on the front brakes must be renewed at the same time. Before assembling the new pads you will need to press the pistons back into their cylinders to allow the extra pad thicknesses to be accommodated, so watch for fluid

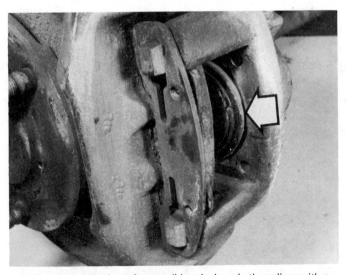

5.14 Compress the piston (arrowed) into its bore in the caliper with a piece of wood

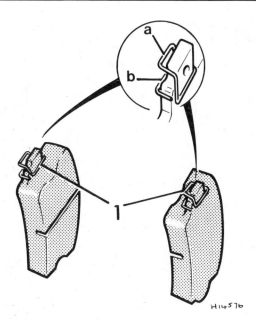

Fig. 8.11 Fit the pad springs, 1, as shown in the inset with the crosspiece, a, over the notch, b (Sec 5, DBA brakes)

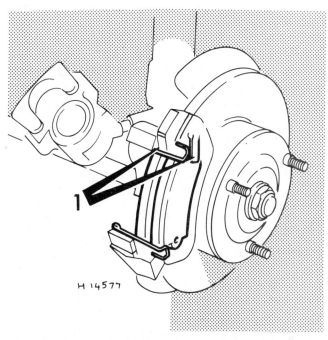

Fig. 8.12 Fit the pads with the springs, 1, to the top (Sec 5, DBA brakes)

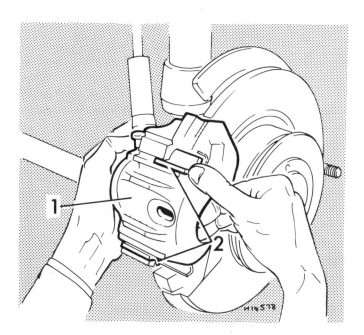

Fig. 8.13 Refitting the cylinder, 1, and the Keys, 2 (Sec 5, DBA brakes)

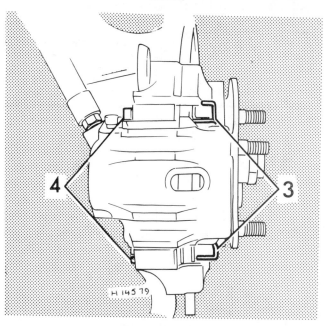

Fig. 8.14 Ensure that the springs, 3, are under the slides and not between the keys and slides, then fit new clips, 4 (Sec 5, DBA brakes)

displacement in the master cylinder reservoir. With a piece of wood, or a similar blunt tool, push the piston back in the caliper cylinder (photo).

15 When refitting the pads on the Girling type calipers, ensure that the anti-rattle shims are fitted with the arrow mark pointing upwards. On the Bendex type caliper locate the anti-rattle spring as shown.

16 With the Teves caliper unit, note that the outer pad has a recess in its backing plate to locate on a key in the caliper.

17 Relocate the pins and fit the new retaining clips to secure them in position.

18 Top up the brake fluid reservoir using fresh fluid and, with the engine running, apply the brakes several times to locate the pistons correctly. Top up the reservoir again on completion if necessary.

19 Remember that new pads need bedding in before they produce full efficiency, so exercise extra caution until they are fully effective.

DBA111 brake calipers

20 To remove the brake pads on this type of caliper, use a pair of long-nosed pliers to remove the clips from the keys and slide the keys out of their slots.

21 With the keys removed, the wheel cylinder can be removed from the caliper and, without disturbing the hose connection, swung to one side out of the way; make sure that the hose is not stressed.

22 Remove the old pads from the caliper and take careful note of the springs fitted to the top ends of the pads, especially how they fit and the way round they are fitted.

23 Refer to paragraphs 10 to 14 inclusive and follow the same procedures as far as they apply to DBA brakes. Examine the slides where the keys fit and remove any burrs with an oilstone, cleaning off any abrasive dust on completion.

24 Assemble the springs to the pads in the same way as originally noted in paragraph 22.
25 Apply a fine film of dry anti-friction agent, to the pad keys and set aside to dry.
26 Hold the pair of pads face to face and, after checking that the springs are correctly fitted, assemble them to the caliper, springs to the top.
27 Refit the cylinder on the caliper and slide the keys home. Make sure that the wire springs locate *under* the slides on the cylinder. They must not be inserted between the keys and the slides.
28 Fit new clips to retain the keys in the slides.
29 Refer to paragraphs 18 and 19 to complete the reassembly procedure.

6 Disc brake calipers – removal and refitting

1 To prevent excessive loss of fluid when the front brake hoses are disconnected, remove the brake reservoir filler cap and seal off the filler neck with a piece of plastic sheeting large enough to accommodate the low level switch float in the cap. Refit the cap tightly. Alternatively, if you can get hold of another filler cap of the right size, block off the vent hole in the cap and fit it to the reservoir, with a seal, in place of the correct filler cap.
2 Slacken the front wheel nuts, then jack up the front of the car and support it on stands or substantial blocks with the wheels free. Apply the handbrake and remove the front wheels.
3 Clean off all the road dirt ffrom the brake units and then disconnect the hydraulic hose from the wheel cylinder of the first unit to be serviced. Plug the end of the hose to stop dirt getting in.
4 Refer to the previous Section and remove the disc pads.
5 Undo the two bolts securing the brake caliper unit to the wheel axle assembly (photo) and remove the unit.
6 Prise free and remove the protection rings from the cylinder bores then position a suitable piece of wood into the pad aperture in the caliper.
7 The inner piston can be removed by applying compressed air through the fluid hose connection in the caliper. The outer piston is

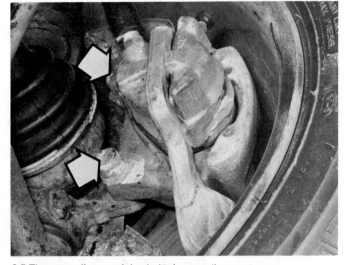

6.5 The two caliper retaining bolts (arrowed)

removed in a similar manner by applying air into the bleed screw hole, having first removed the screw. Be careful not to have your fingers in the way as the pistons are ejected against the wood.
8 Remove the wood block and extract the pistons. The seals can then be removed from the pistons.
9 If the piston(s) is seized in the bore it could be difficult to remove without casuing some damage, but try soaking the assembly with penetrating fluid and leaving it to work. This may do the seal no good but it must be renewed in any case.
10 With the piston removed, extract and discard the seal from its groove in the cylinder bore. Clean all metal parts thoroughly in methylated spirit, but don't use any abrasive cleaning materials, and

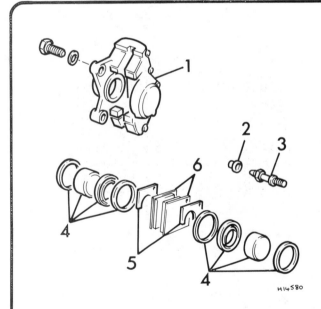

Fig. 8.15 The Girling caliper and piston assembly components (Sec 6)

1 Caliper assembly
2 Bleeder screw cap
3 Bleeder screw
4 Piston and seal components
5 Shims
6 Pads

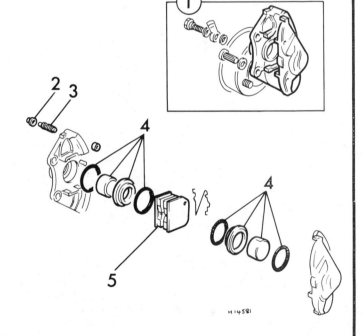

Fig. 8.16 The Bendix Lockheed caliper assembly components fitted to models up to 1977 (Sec 6)

1 Caliper assembly
2 Bleeder screw cap
3 Bleeder screw
4 Piston and seal components
5 Pads

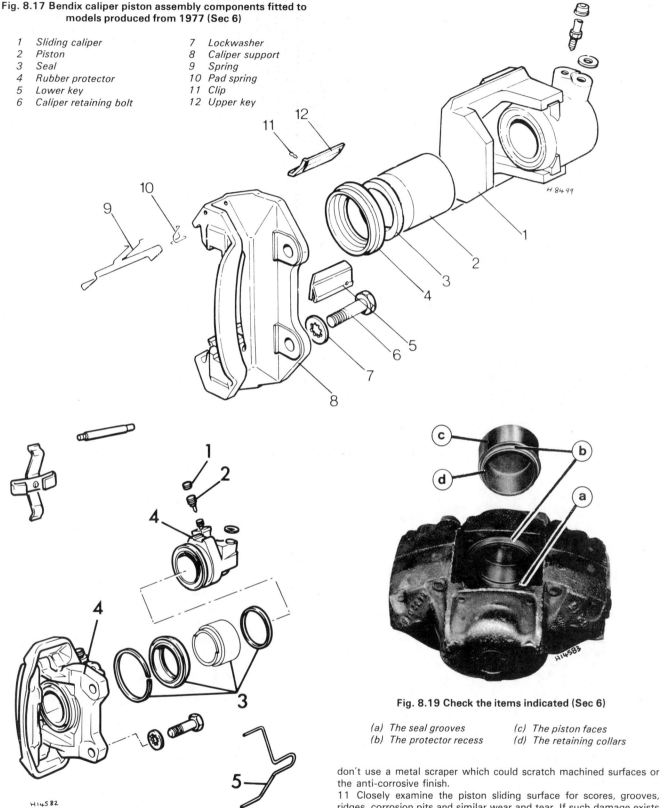

Fig. 8.17 Bendix caliper piston assembly components fitted to models produced from 1977 (Sec 6)

1	Sliding caliper	7	Lockwasher
2	Piston	8	Caliper support
3	Seal	9	Spring
4	Rubber protector	10	Pad spring
5	Lower key	11	Clip
6	Caliper retaining bolt	12	Upper key

Fig. 8.18 The Teves caliper piston assembly fitted to models produced from 1977 (Sec 6)

1	Bleeder screw cap	4	Caliper assembly
2	Bleeder screw	5	Spring
3	Piston and seal components		

Fig. 8.19 Check the items indicated (Sec 6)

(a)	The seal grooves	(c)	The piston faces
(b)	The protector recess	(d)	The retaining collars

don't use a metal scraper which could scratch machined surfaces or the anti-corrosive finish.

11 Closely examine the piston sliding surface for scores, grooves, ridges, corrosion pits and similar wear and tear. If such damage exists the piston must be renewed; on no account attempt to polish or blend out any blemish. Examine all the component parts of the brake assembly for obvious damage, renewing where necessary.

12 Soak the new cylinder seal in fresh hydraulic fluid and lubricate the cylinder bore and the piston with the same fluid. Carefully fit the seal into the cylinder groove and then fit the piston taking care not to damage the seal.

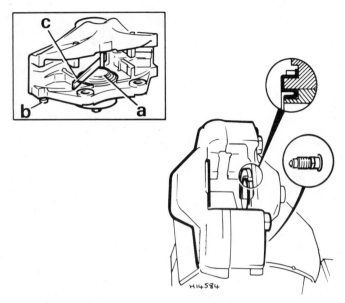

Fig. 8.20 Bendix caliper – align piston face cutaway section (a) with the bleed screw (b) using a straight edge as shown (c) (Sec 6)

13 On the Bendix type caliper unit, position the piston cutaway sections so that they face the bleed screw and the edge is aligned.
14 Wipe the assembly dry with a fluff-free rag and then fit the new rubber dust cover.
15 Refitting of the brake calipers is the reverse of the removal and dismantling sequences, but note the following points:

(a) *When fitting the caliper to the axle clean the threaded holes and the bolt threads thoroughly and coat the bolt threads with thread locking compound. Fit new washers to the bolts and tighten them to the specified torque*
(b) *Fit the brake pads as described in Section 5*
(c) *On DBA111 caliper, remove the bleed screw and prime the wheel cylinder with fresh brake fluid, tipping the cylinder in all directions before installation. Refit the bleed screw*
(d) *Fit a new copper gasket to the hose connector union and when the unit is fitted make sure that the hose is not twisted on reconnection. Check that the hose cannot foul any part of the car when the weight is on the wheels and steering is applied in both directions, lock to lock*
(e) *Remove the piece of plastic or dummy filler cap from the reservoir and bleed the system as described in Section 3*

7   Rear brake drums – removal and refitting

1   With the weight of the car on the whels, slacken the rear wheel retaining nuts.
2   Jack up the rear of the vehicle and support it on axle stands or substantial blocks with the wheels free. Do not work under a car supported only by the wheel changing jack. Chock the front wheels securely, engage a gear, and release the handbrake.
3   Undo the wheel nuts and remove the wheel. Undo and remove the two countersunk screws retaining the brake drum, mark the drum to hub fitted position (chalk or scribe an alignment mark across them), then remove the drum.
4   If the drum resists removal the likely cause is that the brake shoes need retracting. Prise out the plug in the backplate located in the bottom rear area of the plate and insert a screwdriver through the backplate hole. Apply pressure to the handbrake lever within the drum and push the lever sideways to permit retraction of the shoes. Refit the plug in the backplate. Some models differ in that they have the adjusters fitted with external access, in which case use a spanner to release the shoe adjusters.
5   With the drum off, carefully clean out the brake dust so as to

disperse it as little as possible. *It is important not to spread the dust in the atmosphere or to inhale it* as there is a danger to health due to the asbestos content. An old paintbrush and a damp cloth are useful for cleaning the assembly but discard the cloth in a dustbin afterwards.
6   Examine the brake assembly for fluid leaks from the wheel cylinder, grease contamination or leakage from the hub bearings, deterioration of the rubber covers on the cylinder and the general condition of the moving parts. If there are signs of fluid or grease the source must be located and the fault rectified. If the brake linings are contaminated, all four linings on the rear wheels must be renewed. Inspect the linings for wear and if the thickness of the friction material is 0.06 in (1.52 mm) or less, or if it is estimated that it might be worn to that extent before the next servicing, the linings must be renewed. Refer to Chapter 7 for details of renewing the bearings and seals in the wheel hubs.
7   Examine the drum friction face and look for grooving, scores, corrosion or any other obvious damage. If the presence of ridges indicating wear by the shoes is seen, consideration should be given to having the drums skimmed out by a specialist workshop, providing that the wear is within limits and no other damage exists, see Section 10 for details.
8   Refitting the drums is a reversal of the removal procedure. Locate the drum so that the marks made across the faces of the drum and hub align and ensure that both countersunk retaining screws are fully tightened. Refit the wheels but leave the final tightening of the wheel nuts until the weight of the car is on the ground, then tighten to the specified torque.
9   On models fitted with an automatic brake adjustment system depress the brake pedal several times to adjust the brake shoes and then adjust the handbrake as described in Section 4. On manual adjustment models, refer to Section 4 paragraphs 3 to 7 inclusive for readjustment details.

8   Drum brake shoes – inspection removal and refitting

1   The type of drum brake assembly fitted is dependent on year and model and will be of either Bendix or Girling manufacture. The main differences between the types is the adjustment mechanism which will either be of manual, self-adjusting or micrometric adjustment type. The various types are shown in the accompanying illustrations.
2   Remove the brake drums as given in the previous Section.
3   The brake linings should be renewed if they are so worn that the rivet heads are flush with the surface of the lining. If bonded linings are fitted, they must be renewed when the lining material has worn down to 0.06 inch (1.52 mm) at its thinnest part.
4   Depress each shoe holding down spring and detach the anchor plate located at the rear of the brake backplate.

Early manual adjustment drum brakes
5   Ease each shoe from its location slot in the fixed pivot and then detach the other end of each shoe from the wheel cylinder.
6   Note which way round and into which holes in the shoes the retracting springs fit and detach the retracting springs.
7   Lift away the front shoe followed by the operating link.
8   Detach the handbrake inner cable from the rear shoe lever and lift away the rear shoe together with lever.
9   If the shoes are to be left off for a while place a warning on the steering wheel as accidental depression of the brake pedal will eject the pistons from the wheel cylinder.
10 If new shoes are being fitted the levers will have to be transferred.
11 Thoroughly clean all traces of dust from the shoes, backplates and brake drums using a stiff brush. It is recommended that compressed air is not used as it blows up dust which should not be inhaled. Brake dust can cause judder or squeal and therefore, it is important to clean out as described.
12 Check that the pistons are free in the cylinder, that the rubber dust covers are undamaged and in position and that there are no hydraulic leaks.
13 Prior to reassembly smear a trace of Castrol PH Brake Grease on the shoe support pads, brake shoe pivots and on the ratchet pawl teeth, where fitted.
14 Reassembly is the reverse sequence to removal and provided that care was taken to note the location of each part as it was removed no problems will arise.

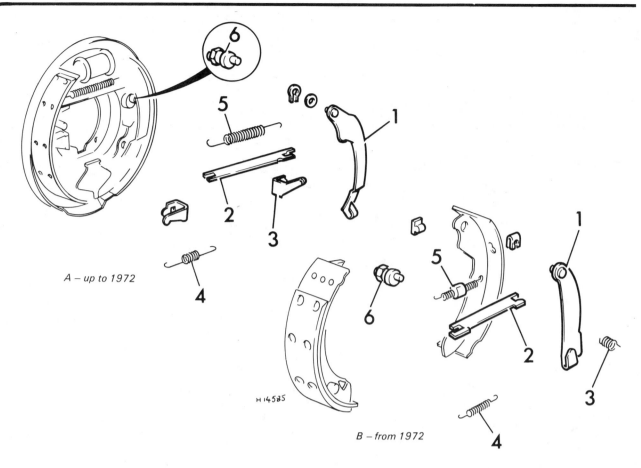

Fig. 8.21 General layout and components of the rear drum brake assemblies with manual adjustment (Sec 8)

1   Lever
2   Parking brake operating
    lever
3   Lateral spring and
    retainer
4   Return spring
5   Pull off spring
6   Eccentric assembly

A – up to 1972

B – from 1972

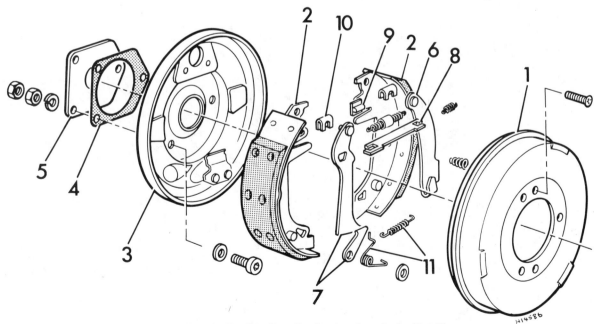

Fig. 8.22 The Bendix self-adjusting drum brake (Sec 8)

1   Drum
2   Shoes
3   Backplate assembly
4   Paper gasket
5   Seal plate
6   Operating lever
7   Brake self-adjuster mechanism
8   Operating link
9   Lateral spring retainer
10 Clip
11 Spring

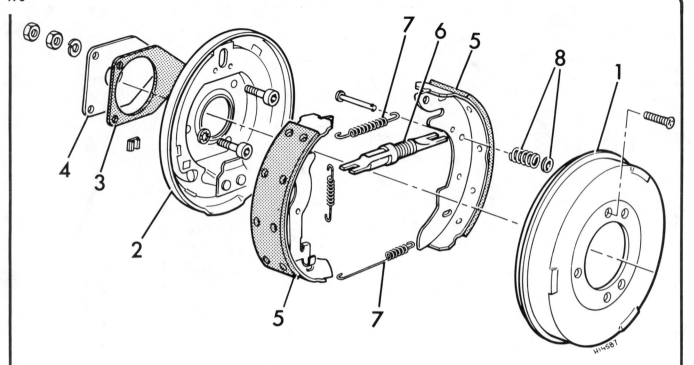

Fig. 8.23 The Girling self-adjusting drum brake components (Sec 8)

1	Drum	3	Paper gasket
2	Backplate assembly	4	Seal plate

5	Brake shoes	7	Return spring
6	Brake self-adjuster mechanism	8	Retaining spring and collar

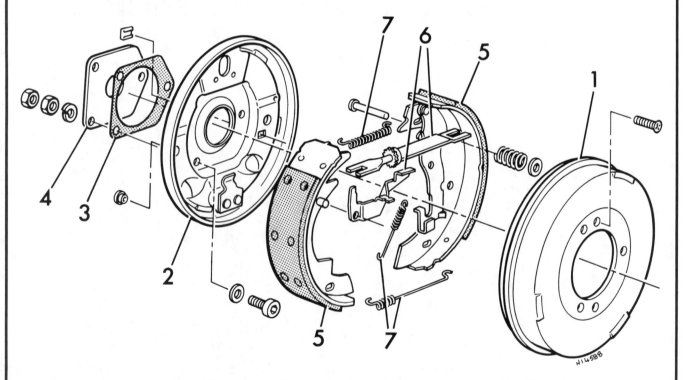

Fig. 8.24 The Girling Micrometric adjuster drum brake components (Sec 8)

1	Brake drum	3	Paper gasket	5	Brake shoes
2	Backplate assembly	4	Seal plate	6	Adjusting mechanism

7	Spring

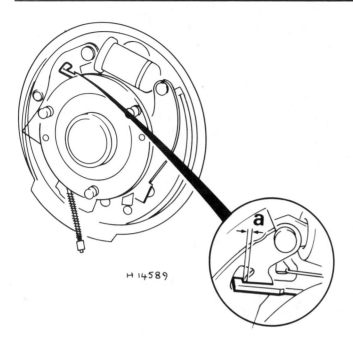

Fig. 8.25 Check the clearance (a) between the horizontal link and the lever (Sec 8)

15 When all is together adjust the handbrake and shoe to drum clearance as described in Section 16 and 4 respectively.

Girling self-adjusting brakes
16 Remove the self-adjusting lever springs and the self-adjusting lever. Note which way springs are fitted as it is possible to fit some the wrong way round on reassembly.
17 Unhook and remove the shoe return springs.
18 Lift out the leading shoe and withdraw the automatic adjusting device.
19 Lift out the trailing shoe. Unhook the handbrake cable and remove the shoe assembly.
20 Clean the assembly thoroughly and inspect for wear and damage. Check the condition of the rubber boots on the cylinder. Any defective parts must be renewed, using new fasteners where appropriate.
21 Brake shoes must be renewed in sets of four, that is, both rear brake assemblies complete. There are three different shoes in the set of four. The two leading shoes are identical and may be fitted to the left or right wheel assemblies. They have their linings riveted, with rivets offset towards the bottom of the shoes. The two trailing shoes are handed by the different positions of the handbrake lever and they have their lining rivets offset towards the top of the shoe.
22 The horizontal links in the self-adjusting device are also handed and they can be identified by the fact that the link for the left-hand brakes is marked with an L and its ratchet wheel nut has no chamfered face. The right-hand link has no identifying letter but the ratchet wheel nut has a chamfered face towards the fork.
23 Before reassembling the shoes apply a little anti-friction agent to the handbrake lever pin on the trailing shoe, taking great care not to contaminate the shoe lining material.
24 Hook the end of the handbrake cable into the bottom fitting on the handbrake lever and fit the trailing shoe to the brake backplate. Fit the retaining pin, spring and washer.
25 Fit the horizontal link of the self-adjusting device, making sure that you have got the correct one. Then fit the leading shoe, engaging it with the link. Fit the shoe retaining pin, spring and washer.
26 Fit the upper and lower shoe return springs making sure that they are the right way round.
27 The diameter across the two linings must now be adjusted to 227.7 mm (8.965 in) and the easy way to do this is to make a simple gauge out of a piece of scrap metal or sheet plastic with a gap of that dimension. Adjust the ratchet wheel nut on the self-adjuster horizontal link to set the linings to fit the gauge.
28 Refit the self-adjusting lever and its spring.

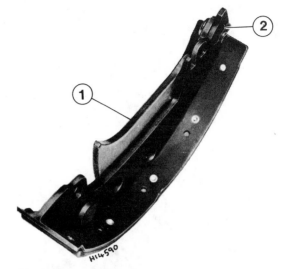

Fig. 8.26 Transfer the adjuster lever, 1, to the shoe using a new clip, 2 (Sec 8)

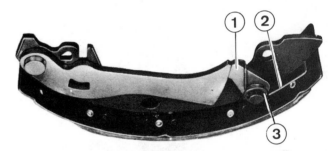

Fig. 8.27 Fit the ratchet, 1, the spring, 2, and a new circlip, 3 (Sec 8)

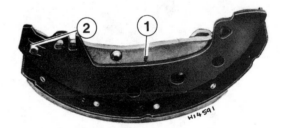

Fig. 8.28 Fit the handbrake lever, 1, and secure with a new clip, 2 (Sec 8)

Fig. 8.29 Fit the horizontal link, 1, and attach the spring, 2 (Sec 8)

8.30a Lubricate the lever pin (arrowed) with Molykote 321 R. Girling later pattern shown

8.30b Fit the brake shoe top return spring

8.30c Fit the horizontal link of the self-adjusting mechanism ...

8.30d ... to both shoes

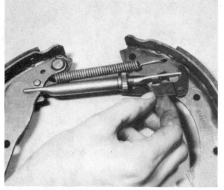

8.30e Fit the self adjuster ratchet ...

8.30f ... and its return spring

8.30g Then fit the brake shoe bottom return spring

8.30h Check that the brake backplate is clean and lightly lubricate the points where the shoes rub with Molykote 321 R

8.30j Fit the shoes to the backplate, engaging the handbrake cable in its lever

8.30k Engage the shoes with the cylinder pistons and, after bedding the assembly down ...

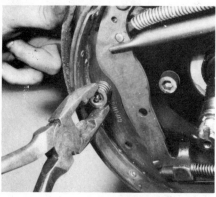

8.30m ... fit the shoe retaining springs, pins and washers

8.31 Use a locally made gauge to check the diameter across the shoe linings

Fig. 8.30 Attach the bottom spring so that it is under the shoes (Sec 8)

Fig. 8.31 Push the lever, 1, towards the hub and connect the horizontal link, 2 (Sec 8)

Girling micrometric adjusting brakes

29 These brakes are similar to the early pattern but they have a different, improved self-adjusting mechanism.

30 The dismantling and reassembling procedure can follow that already described in paragraphs 16 to 28 inclusive, but note that on these brakes the self-adjuster horizontal links have a left-hand thread on the left-hand link and a right-hand thread on the right-hand link. Before installing the links run the ratchet wheel nuts up to the stops on the links, but don't tighten them. The reassembly sequence is shown (photos). Note that the hub is removed for clarity, and the assembly built up off the backplate for the same reason. Assembly can be done on the backplate with the hub in position.

31 On completion of assembly the diameter across the linings must be adjusted to 227.7 mm (8.965 in) using the ratchet wheel nuts on the horizontal links (photo).

Bendix DBA brakes

32 After removing the drum, remove the shoe return spring located under the wheel cylinder and then check the clearance between the horizontal link and the brake shoe lever which should be 0.6 to 0.8 mm (0.024 to 0.032 in). If the clearance is outside this tolerance the worn or damaged parts must be renewed.

33 Remove the brake shoe retaining springs. This can be done using a bolt or an Allen key which will just fit in the conical springs. Push the bolt or key to extend the spring and unhook it from its anchorage. Repeat the procedure on the other shoe. These springs are prone to corrosion and must be renewed on reassembly.

34 Unhook the handbrake cable from the bottom of the handbrake lever, move the other lever towards the hub to disengage the ratchet and then disconnect the horizontal link from it. Allow the ratchet lever to return to its original position and remove the shoe assembly from the backplate.

35 Clean the assembly thoroughly and inspect for wear and damage. Check the condition of the rubber boots on the wheel cylinder. Any defective parts must be renewed, using new fasteners where appropriate.

36 Brake shoes must be renewed in sets of four, that is, both rear brake assemblies complete. These are three different shoes in the set of four. The two trailing shoes are identical and may be fitted to the left or right wheel assemblies. They have their lining rivets offset towards the top of the shoe and they have no pivot pin in the bottom end – only the hole for a pin. The leading shoes have their lining rivets offset towards the bottom of the shoes and the right-hand assembly shoe has a pin protruding to the right, viewed with the lining away from you and the pin at the bottom. The left-hand shoe has the pin protruding to the left when viewed in the same fashion.

37 Providing that it is in good condition, transfer the adjuster lever to the outer face of the new leading shoe using a new clip. Then transfer the ratchet and spring, securing them with a new retaining circlip.

38 Similarly transfer the handbrake lever to the outer face of the new trailing shoe and lock it in place with a new clip.

39 Fit the horizontal link to the trailing shoe with the curved edges

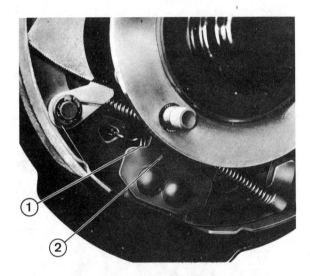

Fig. 8.32 Make sure that the bottom spring, 1, is behind the bracket, 2 (Sec 8)

Fig. 8.33 Fit the spring, 1, and push the adjuster lever, 2, towards the shoe (Sec 8)

Fig. 8.34 Connect the handbrake cable, 1, and fit the shoe retaining springs, 2 (Sec 8)

Fig. 8.35 Adjust the lining diameter by moving the lever A (Sec 8)

facing upwards, and attach the spring on the back. Note that the horizontal links are handed for left and right-hand assemblies.
40 Attach the bottom spring to the two shoes so that it lies underneath the shoes. Offer the assembly to the backplate making sure that the bottom spring lies behind the bottom bracket. Push the adjusting lever towards the hub and connect the horizontal link. Work the assembly into position on the backplate until the upper ends of the shoes rest on the wheel cylinder pistons. Then, using a pair of long-nosed pliers, refit the upper spring. Push the adjusting lever fully forwards against the brake shoe.
41 Lever the handbrake lever forwards and connect the cable to the bottom end.
42 Fit new shoe retaining springs using a long bolt or an Allen key to hook them into their anchorages with their anchor lugs horizontal.
43 Adjust the diameter across the two linings to 227.7 mm (8.965 in) by moving the adjusting lever notch by notch towards the hub.

All rear brakes
44 Give the assembly a final visual check to make sure that all is well, then refit the drums and wheels as described in Section 7 and adjust the handbrake as described in Section 4. As already mentioned for the front brake disc pads, new brake shoes need bedding in before they produce full braking efficiency and you should exercise extra care in driving until they are fully effective.

9 Rear wheel cylinders – removal, overhaul and refitting

1 Jack up the rear of the car and support it on axle stands or substantial blocks. Never work under a car supported only on a wheel changing jack. Chock the front wheels and engage a gear. Remove the brake drum as described in Section 7.
2 Remove the hydraulic reservoir filler cap and seal off the filler neck as described in Section 6, paragraph 1. This will minimise the loss of fluid from the system when the hose connection is undone.
3 Working on the inner side of the brake backplate, brush off all road dirt and clean around the hydraulic hose connection, the bleed screw and the two bolts which secure the wheel cylinder to the backplate (photo 3.5a).
4 Carefully undo the hydraulic line connection to the wheel cylinder, and cover the pipe open end to stop dirt getting in.
5 Unscrew and remove the two wheel cylinder retaining bolts. Unclip the upper shoe return spring and, prising the brake shoes apart at the top, remove the wheel cylinder.
6 If the cylinder has been leaking and the brake linings are contaminated with fluid they must be renewed on *both* rear wheels. This procedure is described in Section 8.
7 Clean off the outside of the cylinder using methylated spirit and take it to a clean work area for dismantling.
8 Pull the rubber boots off each end of the cylinder and carefully extract the pistons, seal cups, and spring. Take careful note of the sequence of assembly of the individual parts and which way round they are fitted.
9 Inspect the cylinder bore carefully for any signs of grooving, scores, corrosion or similar damage. If any damage is present the cylinder must be renewed.
10 Providing that the cylinder is serviceable, clean it thoroughly with methylated spirit – don't use any abrasive material and don't use metal scrapers which could damage the cylinder bore. When clean, wipe the cylinder dry with clean, non-fluffy rag.
11 Sort out the new seals in the repair kit by matching them with the originals and immerse them in clean hydraulic fluid before assembly.
12 Lubricate the cylinder with clean hydraulic fluid and assemble the spring, piston and cup seal. Take care not to damage the seals as you fit them into the cylinder. Fit the rubber boots and then wipe the assembly dry with clean rag.
13 Reassembly of the wheel cylinder to the brake backplate is the reverse of the dismantling procedure, but note the following:

(a) *Take care not to cross-thread the brake pipe union when reconnecting it to the wheel cylinder*
(b) *Refit the brake drum following the procedure described in Section 7*
(c) *Bleed the brake hydraulic system and top up the reservoir remembering to remove the piece of polythene or the dummy filler cap as appropriate. See Section 3 for the procedure for bleeding*

10 Discs and drums – repair by machining

1 Worn discs or drums, providing that the wear has not exceeded the maximum permissible limits and that the components are otherwise fit for use, can be machined to provide an extended lease of life. This work will have to be done by a specialist workshop but it may be cheaper than fitting new items.

Discs
2 First examine the disc for signs of any damage which necessitates renewal. Heavy corrosion, pitting, deep grooves and cracks are the sort of thing which can only be rectified by fitting a replacement disc. If the disc appears sound take a series of micrometer readings to determine

its thickness. The minimum thickness after machining is given in the Specifications. There must be enough metal on the disc to enable it to be machined and remove the defects. After refacing on a machine the disc can continue in use until its thickness is reduced to the minumum specified and then, regardless of its condition, it must be renewed. Another point to note is that the machining process must maintain the original centre-line of the disc which means that the same amount of metal must be removed from each face; if only one face was resurfaced, the centre-line would be offset, resulting in alignment problems with the disc pads. See Specifications for dimensional limits for the discs. Separation of the disc(s) from the front hub assemblies requires the use of specialised tools. Therefore the hub complete with disc and front suspension strut must be removed and taken to a Peugeot dealer for dismantling after which the disc can be refaced or renewed. Refer to Chapter 9 for details of the removal and refitting of the front strut.

Drums

3   As with the brake discs, the brake drums must first be examined for damage which would necessitate renewal such as heavy corrosion, pitting, deep grooves, cracks and excessive ovality. An internal micrometer should be used to take a series of diametrical measurements across the drum lining track. The difference between the largest and smallest diameter indicates the maximum ovality of the drum which must not exceed that specified. The maximum diameter to which the drums can be skimmed out is also given in the Specifications and, as with the discs, there must be enough metal available to be machined out and remove the defects. Also note that the two drums on the same axle must be machined to within 0.15 mm (0.0059 in) of the same internal diameter.

11 Hydraulic fluid pipes – inspection and renewal

1   Periodically, and certainly well in advance of the DoE (MoT) test, if due, all brake pipes, connections and unions should be carefully examined.
2   First examine all the unions for signs of leaks. Then look at the flexible hoses. Later cars have armoured hoses so check that the wire armouring is not broken as it could then endanger the hose itself. Look for chafing, splits and cracks in the rubber, and of course leaks. This is only a preliminary examination of the hoses as exterior condition does not necessarily indicate interior condition which will be considered later.
3   The rigid pipes must be examined equally carefully (photo). They must be brushed clean and inspected for signs of dents or other impact damage, chafing against the structure and corrosion pits. Slight surface corrosion is not necessarily important but deep pitting could

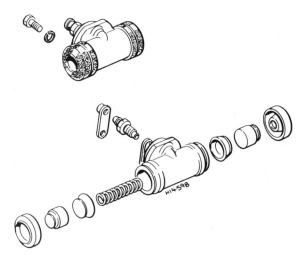

Fig. 8.36 Exploded view of a typical rear brake wheel cylinder (Girling) (Sec 9)

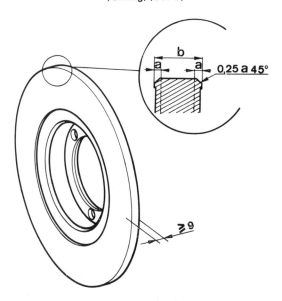

Fig. 8.37 When the disc is reground the amount of material removed, a, must be the same on both sides in relation to the original thickness, b. Minimum thickness after machining is shown in mm (Sec 10)

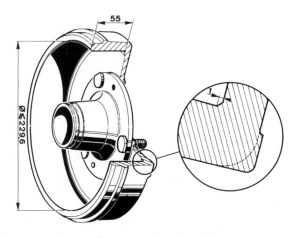

Fig. 8.38 Brake drum maximum skimming dimensions shown in mm (Sec 10)

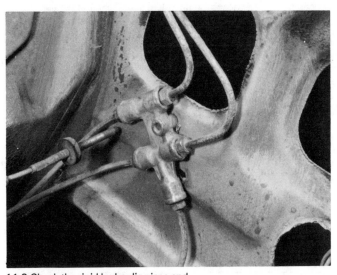

11.3 Check the rigid hydraulic pipes and connections

11.6 Flexible pipe to rigid pipe connections are supported by brackets

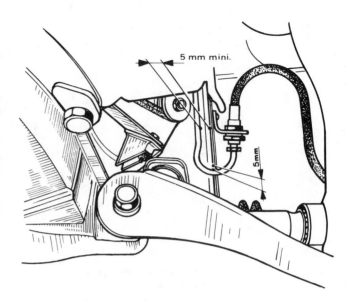

Fig. 8.39 When fitting new pipes and hoses ensure the following clearances (Sec 11)

Front brakes to lower wing valance clearance of 5 mm (0.19 in)
Front brake line to inner wing valance clearance of 5 mm (0.19 in)

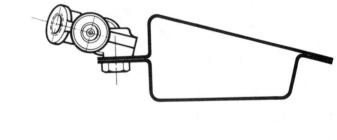

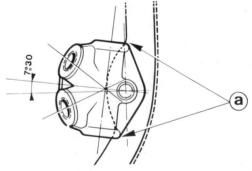

Fig. 8.40 When renewing the four-way union on the engine cradle ensure that it is positioned and secured as shown

lead to leaks and, where present, the piping must be renewed; this is a certain cause for failure of the test. Corrosion and damage to the piping is most likely to occur in those areas under the car body and along the rear suspension arms where the pipes are exposed to the full force of road and weather conditions.

4   If a hydraulic union has to be undone, say to renew a hose, seal the hydraulic reservoir filler neck as described in Section 6, paragraph 1. This will minimise the loss of fluid when the union is undone.

5   Rigid pipe removal is usually straightforward once the unions are undone, but these can give trouble on old cars. The best sort of spanner for the job is a split ring spanner which is like a ring spanner but has a gap in it to permit fitting over the piping. In the absence of this tool a pair of self-gripping pliers is a good alternative. To avoid twisting the pipe, especially when fitting new piping, use two spanners or grips, one to turn the union and the other to hold the fitting to which it is attached.

6   Flexible hoses are always fitted to a rigid support bracket where they join a rigid pipe and the bracket is attached to the structure or rear suspension arm as appropriate. Again use two tools when undoing or connecting the unions and, in cases of difficulty due to corrosion or seizure, give the joint a prolonged soak with penetrating fluid beforehand (photo).

7   Once the flexible hose is removed it can be examined internally. Blow the hose through with air to clear it of fluid and lok down the bore, holding the hose straight with a good light at the other end. Any signs of restrictions in the bore such as wrinkles, blisters, flaking of the lining or similar defects indicate that the lining is breaking up and the hose must be renewed.

8   Rigid pipes which need renewal can sometimes by purchased made up, but the more usual procedure is to get the pipe you want made up by a garage with the necessary equipment. Clearly it is best if you can supply the original pipe as a pattern as then there will be a better chance of getting a good fit when the new one is installed.

9   Refitting of the pipes is a reversal of the removal procedure. Be careful about bending the new rigid pipe when fitting it. Acute bends should have been made by the garage on a pipe bending machine and you should only attempt smooth, large-radiused bends by hand in order to avoid the possibility of kinking or collapse of the pipe. Always clean a new pipe out before fitting, using compressed air or hydraulic fluid.

10   With the pipes refitted and all unions tight remove the plastic seal from the reservoir filler, or the dummy filler cap if one was used, and bleed the system as described in Section 3.

12 Master cylinder – removal and refitting

1   Internal fluid leakage past the seals of the master cylinder will be indiated if the brake pedal slowly moves towards the floor when

pressure is applied and there are no leaks in an otherwise satisfactory system. The seals themselves may be defective or the master cylinder bore may be worn or grooved. In either case the unit will need removing, dismantling and inspecting before the fault can be rectified. The master cylinder is bolted to the front of the brake vacuum servo unit and carries the hydraulic reservoir on top. A repair kit containing all the necessary replaceable items can be obtained from a Peugeot agent.

2   Remember that hydraulic fluid is harmful to paintwork. Try to avoid spillage but if this occurs mop it up immediately. Spread a sheet of plastic and some rags under the master cylinder before undoing unions.

3   Remove the reservoir filler cap and, with a clean syringe, empty the reservoir. Discard the fluid removed as it is unsuitable for re-use.

4   Disconnect the hydraulic pipe connections on the unit and

12.3a Master cylinder and fluid reservoir – earlier models

12.3b Reservoir filler cap, the fluid level warning sender wire and MAX and MIN markings on reservoir body (later models)

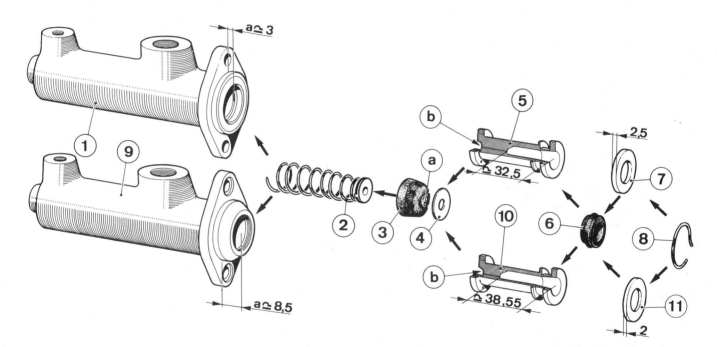

Fig. 8.41 One of two single circuit master cylinder types will be fitted. The repair kits for each are not interchangeable so be sure to obtain the correct kit. The identifying features and parts of each are shown, (dimensions in mm) (Sec 12)

1 Master cylinder
2 Spring
3 Main cup and (a) anchoring nipple
4 Security disc
5 Piston (pistons with no recess must be renewed)
6 Secondary cup
7 Stop washer
8 Snap ring
9 Master cylinder (alternative type)
10 *Piston with recess (b)
11 *Stop washer

*These items applicable to alternative type master cylinder (9) instead of items 5 and 7 which are for cylinder type (1)

carefully push the pipes out of the way sufficiently to permit removal of the unit. Cover the open ends to prevent dirt from getting in.

5   Remove the two nuts and spring washers securing the master cylinder to the servo unit and remove it, wrapped in rags to contain any fluid spillage. Remove the reservoir from the master cylinder and discard the two rubber grommets which must be renewed.

6   As the master cylinder is dismantled take careful note of the sequence of assembly of the various parts and also which way round they are fitted. In many cases a quick sketch will prove more reliable than memory. Depress the piston visible in the cylinder bore and

remove the piston stop. Still depressing the piston, remove the circlip in the end of the bore and remove the piston assembly. If necessary the pistons can be removed by air pressure but restrain the parts from flying out with a piece of rag wrapped round the unit.

7   Clean all metal parts in methylated spirit – never use any abrasive when cleaning hydraulic system fittings and don't use metal scrapers which could score machined surfaces.

8   Sort out the new seals in the repair kit by matching them carefully with the old ones before discarding the old ones. Immerse the new seals in fresh brake fluid before reassembly.

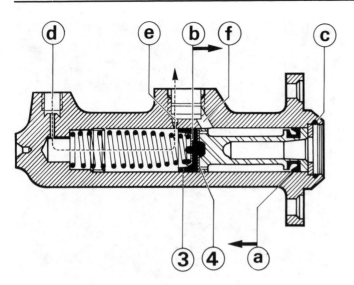

Fig. 8.42 Sectional view of master cylinder – single circuit type (Sec 12)

(a) Secondary cup lip to face as shown
(b) Metal spring cup location
(c) Snap-ring
(d) Outlet orifice
(e) Return orifice
(3) Primary cup
(4) Safety disc

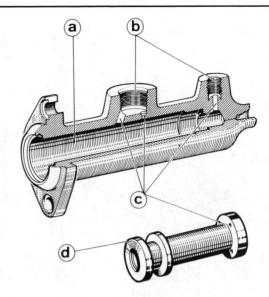

Fig. 8.43 Master cylinder check points (single circuit shown (Sec 12)

(a) Cylinder bore
(b) Threads
(c) Respective supply and return outlets also compensation
(d) Piston orifices

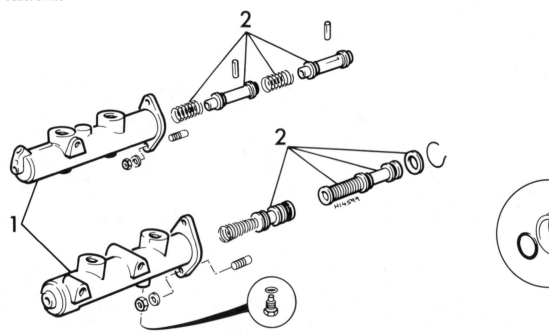

Fig. 8.44 The dual circuit master cylinder fitted to later models will be one of the two types shown (Sec 12)

1   Body

2   Piston and seal assembly

9   Closely inspect all the metal parts for wear, corrosion and obvious damage. Any sign of scoring in the master cylinder bore, however slight, will require renewal, and it is clearly more sensible to renew the whole assembly as a unit if this is necessary.

10 Reassembly is the reverse of the dismantling procedure. Meticulous cleanliness is vital in this work. Wash your hands before starting; wipe all metal components clean, and dry them with fluff-free rag or absorbent kitchen paper. Freely lubricate all parts with clean hydraulic fluid before reassembly. On completion wipe the unit dry before refitting the reservoir using new rubber grommets.

11 Refitting the master cylinder in the car is the reverse of the removal sequence. When refitted, and with the pipe connections

remade, fill the reservoir with fresh hydraulic fluid and bleed the system as described in Section 3.

12 Test the brakes on the next run out, choosing a quiet straight stretch of road and, initially, at low speed. Always check that there is nothing behind before braking.

13 Vacuum servo unit – overhaul

1   It is rare for a servo unit to develop an internal fault and when it is worn out after a long life, renewal of the complete unit is the best remedy.

13.6 Removing the one-way valve from the servo unit

2   Should a fault develop in the unit it should be noticed by the additional effort needed to operate the brakes, but if the fault is progressive it may not be noticed. If you suspect a fault, have the unit checked by your Peugeot agent who will have the necessary equipment to service the unit. The only work feasible on the servo unit for the home mechanic consists of renewing the air filter which is advisable every two years, and renewing the one-way valve which may remedy malfunction if this occurs. First make sure that the new parts can be obtained however.

Air filter renewal
3   The servo unit can remain in position for a filter change. The air filter is located around the input rod and is covered by the rubber boot on the rear wall of the unit.
4   Remove the clip retaining the pivot pin connecting the input rod to the brake pedal and remove the pin. Remove the rubber boot and the filter retainer. The old filter can then be extracted with a hooked tool and discarded.
5   As the filter will not pass over the input rod end fitting, make a diagonal cut along the axis with a sharp knife so that the filter can be opened and fitted onto the input rod. Fit the filter, retainer and boot. Refit the pivot pin and secure with a new clip.

Renewing the one-way valve
6   Loosen the clip and detach the vacuum hose from the one-way valve on the forward face of the unit (photo). The valve can then be extracted by pulling and twisting it from the sealing grommet. It would be worthwhile fitting a new grommet; if it is perished or cracked, renewal is essential. Refit the components in the reverse order. A little hydraulic fluid can be used as a rubber lubricant to aid reassembly.

14 Vacuum servo unit – removal and refitting

1   Slacken the clip securing the vacuum hose to the servo unit and carefully remove the hose from the valve fitting.
2   Undo and remove the two nuts securing the master cylinder to the servo unit and very carefully ease the master cylinder forward to disengage it from the servo unit studs. If you can do this it will save having to disconnect the hydraulic pipelines with the attendant penalty of having to bleed the system. If you find, because of your installation, that you cannot achieve this quick procedure then the master cylinder will have to be removed as described in the previous Section.
3   Remove the spring clip retaining the pivot pin to the foot pedal-to-servo pushrod joint and remove the pivot pin.
4   Undo and remove the four nuts securing the servo unit to the bulkhead and retrieve the four washers. Remove the servo unit from the car.

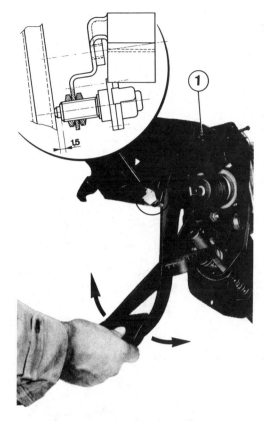

Fig. 8.45 The stop light switch adjustment must provide clearance of 1.5 mm (0.06 in). Also check for free movement of pedal.

For pedal   pivot bolt tightening torque see Specifications (Sec 14)

5   Refitting the servo unit is the reverse of the removal procedure. If the master cylinder had to be removed it will be necessary to bleed the hydraulic system as described in Section 3.
6   On completion, check that the stop light switch adjustment is correct, also the pedal for free movement. Note that the pedal stop is not adjustable and any adjustments that may be necessary are made inside the servo unit (a Peugeot dealer task).

15 Brake compensator – general

1   A brake compensator is fitted in the rear brake hydraulic system and it is located under the car floor just forward of the rear suspension. Its purpose is to maintain equal braking effect on the front and rear wheels and prevent the rear brakes from locking up.
2   If you find that, on applying the brakes, the effect is mainly on the front wheels and that it is impossible to lock the rear brakes without using the handbrake or, alternatively, if you find that the rear brakes invariably lock under heavy braking, it is likely that the compensator is defective.
3   Testing of the compensator will have to be entrusted to a Peugeot dealer since pressure test equipment is necessary. No attempt must be made to dismantle the unit.
4   To remove the compensator, remove the hydraulic fluid reservoir cap and stretch a clean piece of polythene over the aperture, then refit the cap. This will seal the system and prevent leakage from the main supply line to the compensator when it is disconnected.
5   Unscrew and disconnect the hydraulic lines at the compensator unit. Plug or seal the lines to prevent the ingress of dirt.
6   Unbelt and remove the compensator unit.
7   If renewing the unit, be sure to fit a replacement of the correct type for your particular model, (this must be specified at the time of purchase).
8   Refitting of the compensator is a direct reversal of the removal

procedure. When all lines are reconnected, remove the polythene sheet from the reservoir and then referring to Section 3, bleed the brake hydraulic system. It should also be noted that if your model is fitted with an adjustable type of compensator its adjustment must be checked on refitting. Entrust this task to your Peugeot dealer at the earliest opportunity.

16 Handbrake system – general

Handbrake lever – removal and refitting

1   Chock the front wheels and engage a gear. Raise the rear of the car and support it on stands or firm blocks. Release the handbrake.
2   Working underneath the vehicle, loosen off the cable adjusters.
3   Now working within the vehicle, slide the front seats out of the way for access to the handbrake. Then fold back the carpet around the lever unit. On some models you may need to remove the seats to allow

sufficient access. The central gear lever control cover may need to be unfastened and pivoted round as shown (photo). This done, pull the caps from the lever securing nuts and studs each side (photo) and lift the covering away.
4   On early models detach the single primary cable connecting clevis pins from the lever unit. On later models with two cables attached to the lever pull the inner cables forward to detach each of them from the jack lever, (photo).
5   Disconnect the handbrake warning light switch wire (where fitted), then unscrew and remove the handbrake retaining nuts. The handbrake unit can then be lifted clear.
6   Refitting is the reverse of the removal sequence. On completion adjust the cables as described in Section 4.

Handbrake cables (early models) – removal and refitting

7   To remove the primary cable, follow the procedures given in paragraphs 1 to 4 inclusive, then when the primary cable is detached

16.3a Remove the gear lever central cover ...

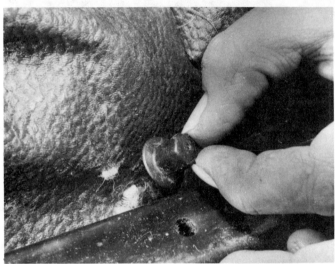

16.3b .. prise free the handbrake unit nut covers/carpet fasteners

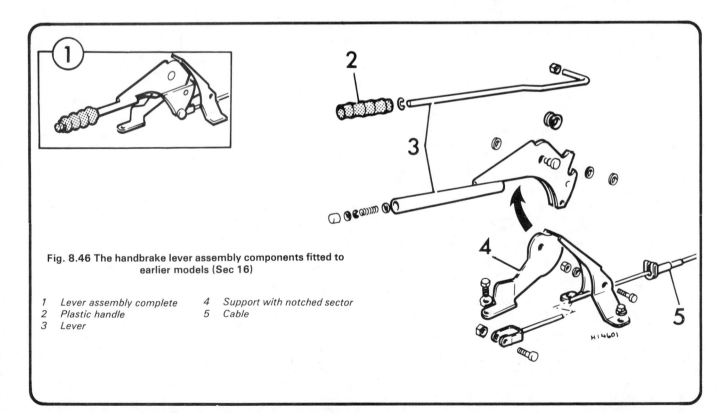

Fig. 8.46 The handbrake lever assembly components fitted to earlier models (Sec 16)

1   Lever assembly complete   4   Support with notched sector
2   Plastic handle   5   Cable
3   Lever

16.4 The cables to jack lever – later models type shown

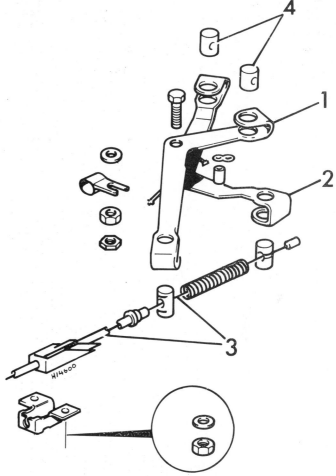

Fig. 8.47 The handbrake jack lever components fitted to the
earliest models (Sec 16)

1 Upper lever
2 Lower lever
3 Primary cable assembly

4 Secondary cable assemblies
   attachment points

from the handbrake lever unit, disconnect the rear end from the jack
lever assembly and pull it through the floor.

8   To remove the securing cables proceed as given in paragraphs 1
and 2, disconnect the cables from the jack lever assembly and then
detach them at the brake shoe operating levers. To do this refer to
Section 7 for brake drum removal details.

9   Refitting of both primary and secondary cables is the reverse of
the removal procedure, but before refitting a cable assembly lubricate
the inner cable in its sheath with a general purpose grease. Leave the
end fitting which attaches to the brake shoe dry, but lubricate the other
pivot points at the jack lever and handbrake.

10 On completion adjust the cables as described in Section 4.

Handbrake cables (later models) – removal and refitting

11 Follow the procedures in paragraphs 1 to 4 above and, referring to
Section 7, remove the brake drums and disconnect the cables from the
shoe operating levers.

12 Withdraw the cable assemblies from the car by pulling them out
of their front end locations and from the rear brake backplates.

13 Refitting is the reverse of the removal procedure but, before
refitting a cable assembly, lubricate the inner cable in its sheath with
a general purpose grease. Leave the end fitting which fits into the
brake shoe lever dry.

14 On completion adjust the cables as described in Section 4.

Fault diagnosis overleaf

17 Fault diagnosis – braking system

Symptom	Reason(s)
Excessive brake pedal travel	Friction linings excessively worn Adjusters seized Disc run-out excessive Hydraulic system defect
Brakes pull to one side	Tyre pressures incorrect Friction linings contaminated on one side Piston or wheel cylinder seized on one side Pads or shoes renewed on one side only Steering or suspension fault
Judder felt through brake pedal and/or steering wheel on braking	Front wheels unbalanced or wheel nuts loose Disc pads excessively worn Disc run-out excessive Disc(s) scored or grooved Caliper mounting bolts loose Brake drum(s) distorted or scored Backplate attachment bolts loose Steering or suspension fault
Brakes binding	Seized hydraulic pistons Handbrake incorrectly adjusted or cable seized Adjusters seized or defective Master cylinder defective
Brake pedal appears spongy or soggy	Air in hydraulic system Master cylinder defective
Excessive effort required to stop vehicle	Servo malfunction Friction linings worn, contaminated or incorrect grade Brake shoes incorrectly fitted New linings not yet bedded in Leakage in one brake circuit
Brake pedal travels to floor with little resistance	Leak in hydraulic system Master cylinder seals defective

Chapter 9 Suspension and steering

Contents

Specifications

Suspension – general

Front suspension .... Independent, coil springs and MacPherson struts with anti-roll bar
Rear suspension .... Independent single pivot trailing arms with coil springs, shock absorber struts and anti-roll bar.

Front wheel alignment unladen

	Up to 1978	From 1977 (August)
Toe-in	2 ± 1 mm	3 ± 1 mm
Camber	0° 30'	0° 50' ± 45'
Castor	0° 30'	40' ± 30'
Kingpin inclination	9° 30'	12° ± 30'

Rear suspension

Trailing arm overhang	54.85 mm (2.15 in)	64.85 mm* (2.55 in)

*To facilitate fitment of new wheels having 45 mm (1.77 in) overhang in place of wheels with 35 mm (1.37 in) overhang previously fitted

Dimensions

Wheelbase	2.59 m (8.5 ft)
Track:	
Front up to 1977	1.32 m (4.4 ft)
Front from 1977	1.37 m (4.49 ft)
Rear	1.29 m (4.23 ft)

Steering

Type	Rack-and-pinion
Steering wheel turns (lock-to-lock)	3.6
Turning circle	10.7 m (34 ft 6 in)

Torque wrench settings

Front suspension and steering

	lbf ft	kgf m
Track control arm balljoint pin clamp bolt	31.0	4.25
Track rod eye bolts (type A)	25.0	3.5
Track rod balljoint locknut (Type B)	33.0	4.5
Track rod to steering rack – 2nd type with ratchet fitting	36.2	5.0
Steering column upper joint nuts	7.2	1.0
Steering wheel nut	33.0	4.5
Steering box to cradle bolts	25.0	3.5
Flector (column lower coupling) bolt:		
Normal (35 mm long) bolt	7.25	1.0
Alternative (38 mm long) bolt with Nyloc nut	11.0	1.5
Front anti-roll bar:		
Bush clamps	7.2	1.0
Link rods on bar	33.0	4.5
Link rods on suspension arm	10.0	1.25
Suspension arm pin nuts	25.0	3.5
Strut (shock absorber) upper mounting nuts	7.2	1.0

Rear suspension

Suspension unit upper mounting nuts	7.2	1.0
Shock absorber lower mounting nut (Nyloc)	40.0	5.5
Trailing arm pivot bolt	80.0	11.0
Handbrake lever mounting nuts	14.5	2.0
Anti-roll bar clamp nuts (Nyloc)	24.0	3.25
Shock absorber lower mounting lug bracket	13.0	1.75

1 General description

The Peugeot 304 has independent suspension at the front and rear. At the front, MacPherson struts incorporate telescopic double-acting hydraulic shock absorbers and coil springs. The struts are located at the top end in the inner wing top structure. At their bottom ends the struts are located by the stub axle and suspension arm assembly. An anti-roll bar is fitted and is located at each end, direct to a single strut suspension arm or indirectly by means of a connecting rod to the wishbone type suspension arm.

The rear axle comprises two independent trailing arms which carry the rear wheel stub axles. Telescopic shock absorbers and coil springs control vertical movements of the wheels and independent wheel movement is limited by an anti-roll bar.

A rack-and-pinion steering unit is fitted and is located at the bottom of the engine bay bulkhead behind the transmission unit.

The majority of the work on the suspension and steering systems which is within the scope of the home mechanic is limited to inspection, removal and refitting procedures as special tools are necessary for overhaul. These are also required in some removal/refit sequences but suggested alternatives, where possible, will help you overcome this problem. Before starting a job read through the instructions and be sure that your tools and facilities will be adequate.

All work undertaken on the steering mechanism must be to the highest standard. It is vitally important to maintain the integrity of the system. Always use the correct fasteners with correct locking devices and renew them where indicated. Any adjustments must be within the specified limits and spare parts must be in new or faultless condition. Your life, and that of others, could depend on these points and if you are in any doubt concerning what to do or how to do it you should get professional advice or have the job done by a skilled expert.

2 Routine maintenance

1 Although the maintenance of the suspension and steering components has been reduced to a minimum it does not mean that it can be ignored completely. A periodic manual and visual check should be made.

2 Inspect the suspension joints and their attachments, including rubber bushes, for security, excessive play or deterioration. The outer track rod balljoint on earlier models was fitted with a grease nipple and this should be lubricated at the specified intervals.

3 Check the steering components and connections for signs of wear and for security.

4 Inspect the shock absorbers for looseness in their mountings and

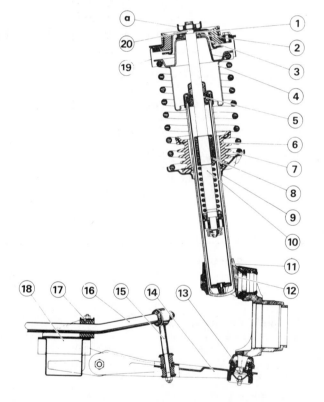

Fig. 9.1 Sectional view of front suspension fitted with the tie-link type anti-roll bar (Sec 1)

1 Upper support comprising the limiting cup (a)	11 Shock absorber body
2 Needle thrust bearing	12 Steering knuckle
3 Spring upper cup	13 Knuckle lower bearing
4 Stop cup	14 Triangle
5 Upper bearing	15 Anti-roll bar link rod
6 Rebound stop	16 Anti-roll bar
7 Spring	17 Rubber bush
8 Detent stop	18 Sub-frame
9 Shock absorber rod	19 Deflector
10 Spring lower cup	20 Nut thrust washer

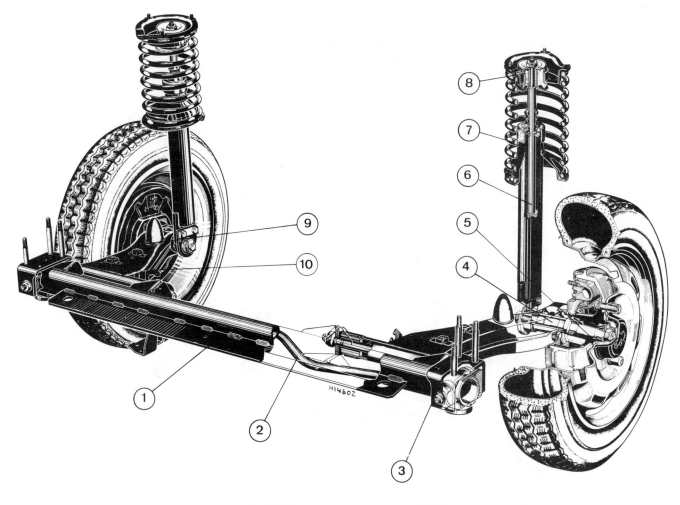

Fig. 9.2 The rear suspension assembly (Sec 1)

1 Rear crossmember
2 Anti-roll bar
3 Crossmember support bracket
4 Stub axle
5 Rear hub
6 Shock absorber strut
7 Coil spring
8 Strut and spring top mounting
9 Stop pad
10 Trailing arm

their rubber bushes for security and deterioration. Look for fluid leakage and, if evident, renew *both* shock absorbers on that axle.
5 Check the tightness of the steering rack attachment bolts, but don't exceed their specified torque. Check the joints for signs of excessive wear and the rack rubber gaiters for splits or leakage. Examine the steering shaft lower flexible joint for wear and fraying.

3 Suspension and steering – testing and examination

1 Because of the construction of these vehicles the suspension cannot be considered in isolation from the steering and vice versa. The safety of the car depends to a very large extent on the steering and suspension components.
2 Any parts which are badly worn, weak or broken must be renewed immediately. Take great care checking the following items. The first list is of those parts which are particularly prone to wear with usage, and the second list is of special check points of those parts which tend to work loose. Check for wear:

(a) Track control arm balljoints
(b) Track control arm rubber bushes
(c) Shock absorbers and mounting bushes
(d) Steering track rod balljoints and inner joints (as applicable)
(e) Rack-and-pinion
(f) Steering column bush

(g) Front and rear hub bearings
(h) Rear trailing arm bushes
(j) Anti-roll bar bushes

All these points can be tested by physically moving the components concerned either by hand or by cautious use of a tyre lever or large screwdriver to see what degree of movement exists. Check for security:

(k) Anti-roll bar
(m) Steering rack mounting bolts
(n) Steering rack-to-column coupling
(p) Shock absorber struts top and bottom mounting
(q) Rear trailing arms

These checks represent only the minimum requirements. When making them be on the alert for any abnormality as different methods of use generate different types of wear and tear on the systems.

4 Front anti-roll bar – removal and refitting

1 The type of front anti-roll bar fitted will depend on the model and year of the vehicle in question. On some models (referred to as type A), the anti-roll bar forms the forward section of the suspension arm each side. In this instance it will be located and secured at each end through the single suspension arm (see photo 4.4). On other models fitted with

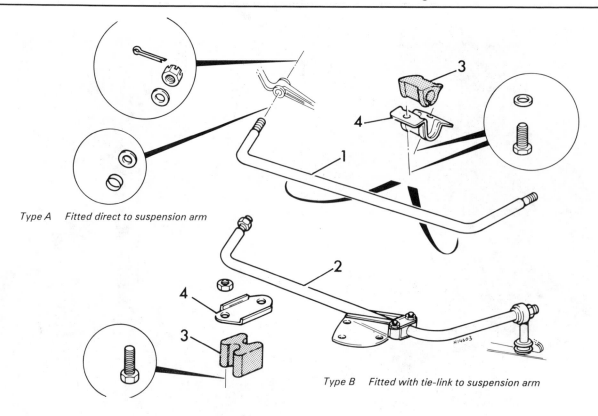

Type A   Fitted direct to suspension arm

Type B   Fitted with tie-link to suspension arm

Fig. 9.3 The two types of anti-roll bar fitted (Sec 4)

1   Anti-roll bar (Type A)   2   Anti-roll bar (Type B)   3   Bush   4   Clamping plate

Note: *Assembly components can differ according to year and model, therefore ensure new components are identical to replaced parts*

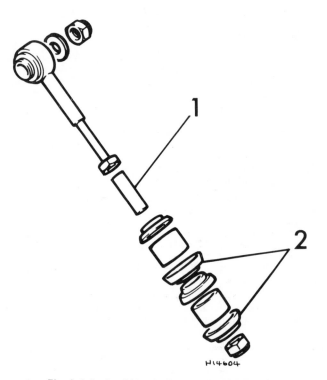

Fig. 9.4 Anti-roll bar tie-link assembly (Sec 4)

1   Spacer   2   Centring cups

a wishbone type of suspension arm, the anti-roll bar is connected at each end to a tie-link which in turn is connected to the wishbone forward arm at its lower end as shown (referred to as type B). In each case the anti-roll bar is located at its forward transversal section to the chassis subframe each side, by a bracket and rubber bushing in which it is allowed to pivot.

2   Removal of the anti-roll bar to renew the rubber mountings, or to renew other suspension components, will require the front end of the vehicle to be raised and supported on safety stands. Check that the handbrake is fully applied and place chocks against the rear wheels.

3   Use a wire brush to clean off the threaded ends of the anti-roll bar and apply some penetrating or light oil to the threads of the bar. Do not get the oil onto the rubber bushings if they are to be renewed.

4   Unscrew and remove the securing nuts from each side at the ends of the anti-roll bar. On some models you will first have to extract the split pin (photo).

5   On type B anti-roll bars you may wish to detach the tie-link assembly. In this case it can be removed together with or separate from the anti-roll bar. Unscrew the nut securing the link to the suspension arm (underneath). If the tie-link assembly is to be detached from the anti-roll bar, the anti-roll bar must be fully detached first.

6   Now unscrew and remove from each side of the anti-roll bar bracket fixing, the bolts/nuts from the forward underside of the chassis sub-frame (photo), and withdraw the anti-roll bar.

7   Check the anti roll bar for any signs of damage or distortion, renewal being the only option should defects be apparent. Renew the bushes if they are worn or defective.

8   Refitting is a reversal of the removal procedure. New split pins or Nyloc nuts must be fitted as applicable.

9   Ensure that the rubber bushes and associated fittings are correctly reassembled.

10   Do not fully tighten the securing nuts/bolts until the vehicle is standing on level ground. Refer to the specifications for the tightening torques.

4.4 Anti-roll bar to suspension arm connection – Type A

4.6 Anti-roll bar to subframe connection

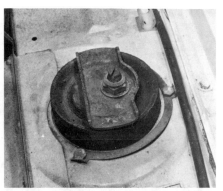

5.6 Suspension strut upper mounting showing two of the three securing bolts and the interconnecting tab washer plate
Note: *Do not remove the central retaining nut and plate*

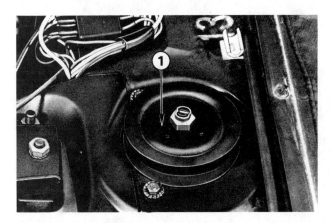

Fig. 9.5 Fixed spring type front suspension identification hole position (1) (Sec 5)

Fig. 9.6 Rotating spring type front suspension identified by limit cup (plate) which must be positioned as shown (Sec 5)

5 Front suspension strut – removal and refitting

1   Raise the front end of the car and support it on axle stands or bolts. Check that the handbrake is firmly applied.
2   Most of the dismantling work is described in Chapter 7, Section 2, paragraphs 2 to 6 inclusive, to which reference should be made, but note that the driveshaft does not have to be withdrawn from the transmission for this operation. In addition you will need to remove the brake caliper and disconnect the steering arm from the track rod.
3   Refer to Chapter 8, Section 6, for details of removing the brake caliper. However, in this case it is not necessary to interfere with the hydraulic system. Don't disconnect the hydraulic hose, but swing the assembly to one side and support it on wire from a convenient point on the structure or engine. Take care not to stress the flexible hose as the assembly is heavy.
4   Disconnect the steering track rod balljoint by removing the nut and using a balljoint separator to extract the pin from the hub assembly (see photo 13.3).
5   Support the bottom of the suspension strut on wooden blocks to take the weight.
6   Unscrew and remove the upper support retaining bolts from the wing valance (photo), then remove the supporting blocks and lower and remove the strut assembly from the vehicle.
7   Refitting a strut unit is a straightforward reversal of the removal procedure, but the following special points should be observed.
8   On models fitted with the fixed spring suspension, the hole (1) shown in Figure 9.5, must be positioned on the engine side when locating the upper support assembly.
9   On models with the 'rotating spring' type suspension ensure that the limit cup is fitted in line with the car.
10 Always use new bolts and double tooth washers to secure the

support assembly to the wing valance and tighten them to the specfied torque setting.
11 With the top end reconnected, the driveshaft can be relocated in the hub (smear Molykote onto the grooved end of the shaft). The anti-roll bar, steering and suspension components can be reconnected as described in the relevant Chapters.
12 If the brake hose to the caliper was disconnected for any reason, top up and bleed the brake hydraulic system as given in Chapter 8 before using the vehicle.
13 Fully tighten the steering and suspension component fastenings to the specified torque settings when the vehicle is lowered and free standing.

6 Front suspension strut – overhaul

Removal and refitting of a suspension spring on the front suspension strut and overhaul of the strut itself, including brake disc renewal, require the use of a number of special tools. Where any of these operations become necessary it is considered that the work should be undertaken by a Peugeot dealer who will have the necessary equipment.

7 Rear anti-roll bar – removal and refitting

1   Raise the vehicle at the rear and support with safety stands. Place the car in gear and chock the front wheels. Release the handbrake.
2   Unhook the handbrake cable each side from the location clips adjacent to the ends of the anti-roll bar.
3   Now remove the anti-roll bar clamp retaining nuts each side and

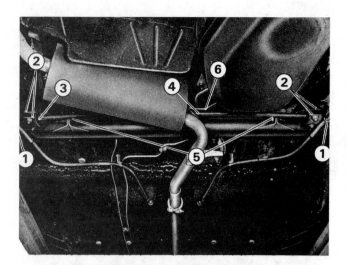

Fig. 9.7 Rear anti-roll bar location (Sec 7)

1   Handbrake cable location   3   Bushes
    clips   4   Anti-roll bar
2   Anti-roll bar clamps   5   Arm bushing shafts

7.3 Rear anti-roll bar retaining clamp

as the anti-roll bar is released and lowered, observe if the identification paint mark remains clearly seen on the left-hand end. If not, mark it for orientation when refitting (photo).
4   If the bar is damaged or worn in any way, it must be renewed.
5   Refit in the reverse order of removal ensuring that the paint mark is on the left-hand side. The bar must fit over the hand brake cable and exhaust. When in position, its central section must be aligned with the bushing shafts. Tighten the clamp nuts to the specified torque setting and check that the bar will not touch the brake cables when they are relocated.

---

8   Rear suspension shock absorber – removal and refitting

1   Working inside the vehicle, remove the trim covering the top end of the shock absorber mounting. To achieve this proceed as follows:

Saloon:
Lift out the rear seat and remove its backrest, then withdraw the rear shelf panel. Raise the end(s) of the rear shelf sound proofing material to give access to the mounting nuts.

Estate models:
Fold down the rear seat backrest and then unscrew the trim cover retaining screw from the top of the shock absorber mounting/housing. Fold over the trim. The shock absorber upper nut is recessed and covered by a rubber plug (photo). **Do not remove this nut!**

Coupe models:
Detach the upholstery from the rear side.
2   Unscrew and remove the shock absorber upper securing nuts.
3   Raise and support the vehicle at the rear, positioning safety stands each side just forward of the rear wheel arches. Place the vehicle in gear and chock the front wheels.
4   Remove the rear wheel(s), then support the hub/drum with a jack.
5   Unbolt and detach the shock absorber from the suspension arm (photo). Compress the shock absorber and remove it from the side concerned complete with the coil spring assembly, which is kept under compression by the upper attachment cup.
6   Removal of the coil spring and overhaul of the shock absorber is best entrusted to your Peugeot dealer since special tools are required, (see following Section).

8.1 Rear shock absorber upper mounting (Estate). Remove the three nuts with shakeproof washers – not the central retaining bolt nut (1) shown with plug removed

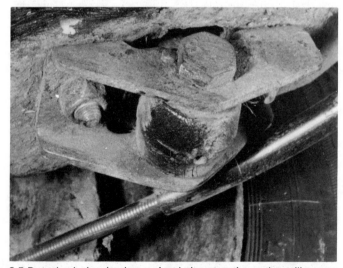

8.5 Rear shock absorber lower pivot bolt connection to the trailing arm

Fig. 9.8 Rear shock absorber upper mounting location on a Saloon – remove only the three upper mounting securing nuts with shakeproof washers (1) (Sec 8)

Fig. 9.9 Support the hub/drum weight with a jack so that suspension arm is horizontal when tightening the shock absorber pivot bolt nut (Sec 8)

7   Refitting is the reversal of the removal procedure. When the lower shock absorber through bolt is in position, locate a jack under the brake drum (handbrake applied) and raise the assembly to enable the three upper cup location studs to pass through their holes in the body. Then fit and tighten the securing nuts to the specified torque setting. Continue to raise the jack so that the spring is under compression. Fit and tighten a new lower attachment Nyloc nut to its specified torque setting.

8   Lower and remove the jack and refit the roadwheel.

9   Refit the trim to the top mounting and lower the vehicle to complete.

9   Rear suspension shock absorber and coil spring – dismantling and overhaul

As mentioned in the previous Section, the dismantling and overhaul of the rear suspension shock absorber and coil spring assembly requires the use of special tools. Therefore any work to be carried out on this assembly must be entrusted to your Peugeot dealer who will have the required equipment.

10   Rear axle complete – removal and refitting

1   Although it is not possible for the home mechanic to renew the rubber bushes in the rear suspension, because of the number and variety of special tools needed, he should be able to remove the complete rear axle or a single trailing arm, if required, using an average tool kit. Removal and refitting of a trailing arm is dealt with in the next Section, but it should be noted that both arms should receive similar servicing to maintain vehicle stability and it might be easier to remove the complete assembly for overhaul by a Peugeot agent.

2   Preferably place the vehicle over a pit or on a ramp, but if neither is available jack the rear of the vehicle up and support it, with the rear axle free, on stands or blocks. Chock the front wheels and engage a gear.

3   Refer to Chapter 8 and seal the brake reservoir. Disconnect the brake hydraulic pipeline at the most suitable point, forward of the axle assembly, depending on the car; this varies with the type of brake compensator installed. Where necessary, unclip the pipeline from the structure to permit removal of the assembly. Seal the open ends of the pipelines to prevent dirt ingress.

4   Remove the rear section of the exhaust system.

5   Working inside the vehicle, remove the rear seat to gain access to

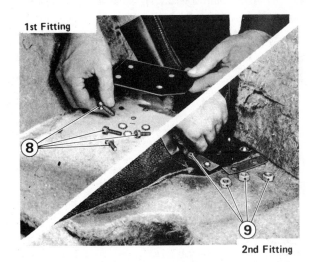

1st Fitting

2nd Fitting

Fig. 9.10 Crossmember securing bolts (1st fitting) or nuts (2nd fitting) removal (Sec 10)

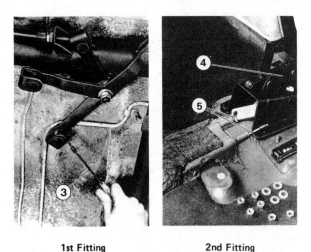

1st Fitting   2nd Fitting

Fig. 9.11 Handbrake cable detachment point – 1st and 2nd fitting types (Sec 10)

the rear crossmember retaining nuts. Unscrew and remove the nuts and washers each side.

6   The handbrake cables will have to be detached at their forward attachment/adjustment fastenings. On models with the later type handbrake cables, detach them from within the vehicle by removing the cover from the handbrake assembly. Unscrew the handbrake mounting retaining nuts, remove the mounting (see Chapter 8). Slacken off the cable adjusters and detach the cables from the handbrake unit.

7   Working underneath the vehicle, on later models pull the handbrake cables through their locations in the floor. On earlier models the cables are detached from the counter lever unit underneath.

8   Jack up the vehicle and locate a block of suitable dimensions under the brake drum of each hub then lower the vehicle onto these blocks to free the studs in each end of the crossmember.

9   Carefully raise the rear end of the vehicle, *keeping the rear wheels in contact with the blocks,* and fully extend the rear springs.

10 Unscrew and remove the pivot bolts from the lower end of each shock absorber (to suspension arm).

11 Check that all attachments to the rear axle are disconnected and not likely to interfere with removal.

12 Remove the blocks from under the wheels and, raising the rear end to clear, remove the rear axle assembly to the rear. Make sure that the car is left in a stable condition on its supports.

13 Refitting the rear axle assembly is a straightforward reversal of the removal procedure, but the following points will need attention:

(a) *Use new Nyloc nuts and plain washers on the studs at each end of the rear crossmember, tightening them to the specified torque*

(b) *Reattach the shock absorber lower pivot bolts to the trailing arm and tighten the fastenings as described in Section 8*

(c) *Reconnect the handbrake cables and the hydraulic lines as given in Chapter 8 and then top up and bleed the hydraulic system and adjust the handbrake also as given in that Chapter*

---

11 Rear suspension (trailing) arm – removal and refitting

1   Raise and support the vehicle at the rear using suitable safety stands positioned just forward of the rear wheel arches. The vehicle should be in gear and the front wheels chocked. Release the handbrake.

2   Remove the roadwheel(s) at the rear and support the weight of the suspension arm by positioning a jack under its rear end.

3   Refer to Section 7 and remove the anti-roll bar.

4   Disconnect the brake hydraulic pipeline at the most suitable point to enable the pipe/hose to be released from its attachment to the suspension arm. Seal off or plug the ends of detached hydraulic pipe lines to prevent fluid leakage and the ingress of dirt into the hydraulic system.

5   Disconnect and detach the handbrake cable from the side concerned at the counterlever end and if necessary refer to Chapter 8, Section 15 for further details.

6   Unbolt and detach the shock absorber lower fixing bolt from the suspension arm pivot lugs.

7   Unscrew and remove the suspension arm pivot bolt/shaft nut(s). The bolt/shaft can be withdrawn using a bar with a slotted end. Use this bar under the bolt head or inner shaft nut and drive out as shown. As the bolt/shaft is withdrawn support and then lever the arm away for removal.

8   With the suspension trailing arm removed it can be cleaned off and if necessary further dismantled. Removal of the brake and hub assemblies is described in Chapters 8 and 7.

9   If a trailing arm or its associated components are to be renewed, check with your Peugeot dealer to ensure that the replacement is suitable for your model. Some modifications were made and where early parts are no longer available if may be necessary to fit an updated component or assembly. When modifying the components fitted to a trailing arm on one side only, it may affect the rear suspension geometry. Check this point with your Peugeot dealer as you may also need to renew the equivalent components on the opposing trailing arm assembly.

10 Commence refitting by locating the shock absorber lugs (yokes)

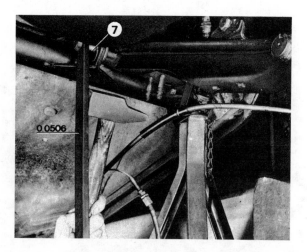

Fig. 9.12 Suspension arm pivot bolt/shaft removal method. The official Peugeot tool number is shown (Sec 11)

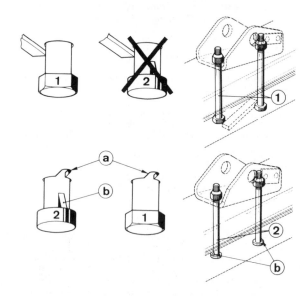

Fig. 9.13 The two shock absorber location lug securing bolts used. The cheese head type bolt must only be used where a location notch exists (Sec 11)

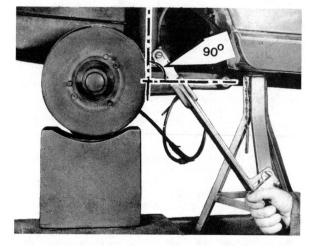

Fig. 9.14 Suspension arm to be at 90° to the shock absorber when tightening the pivot bolt (Sec 11)

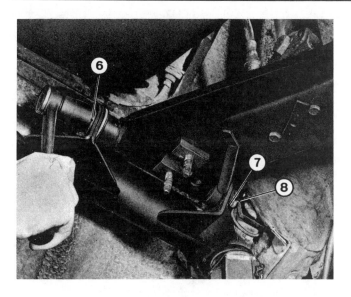

Fig. 9.15 Use new nut 7 and pin 8. Do not torque tighten pivot bolt/shaft until vehicle is free standing 6 (Sec 11)

ensuring that the correct bolts are used. These will be either hexagon or cheese head types. The cheese head type have a boss under the head which locates in a notch for location in the arm. New Nyloc nuts must be fitted to either type of bolt.

11 Raise the suspension arm and support it in a convenient position to engage the shock absorber bottom location eye within the lugs. Fit the pivot bolt from the inside. With the suspension arm positioned at 90° to the shock absorber, fit a new Nyloc nut to the pivot bolt and tighten to the specified torque setting.

12 Locate the forward end of the arm between the pivot lugs and insert the bolt or shaft with a new tab washer at the head (inner) end. The shaft should be lubricated with graphite grease prior to insertion. Fit a new nut to the protruding outer end of the bolt/shaft, but do not fully tighten it yet. Pin the extreme end of the exposed thread.

13 Remove the temporary plugs and reconnect the brake hydraulic line.

14 Reconnect the handbrake cable (referring to Chapter 8).

15 Refit the roadwheel and tighten the retaining nuts to the specified torque, then lower the vehicle so that it is free standing.

16 Enlist the aid of assistants and ask them to sit in the rear of the vehicle whilst you reach underneath and tighten the arm bolt/shaft to the specified torque setting. When tightened, bend the tab washer ears round the bolt head to secure.

17 Ask the assistants to vacate the vehicle then refit the anti-roll bar as described in Section 7.

18 Check that the brake hydraulic line is relocated correctly and then top up the hydraulic fluid reservoir. Bleed the brakes as described in Section 3 of Chapter 8.

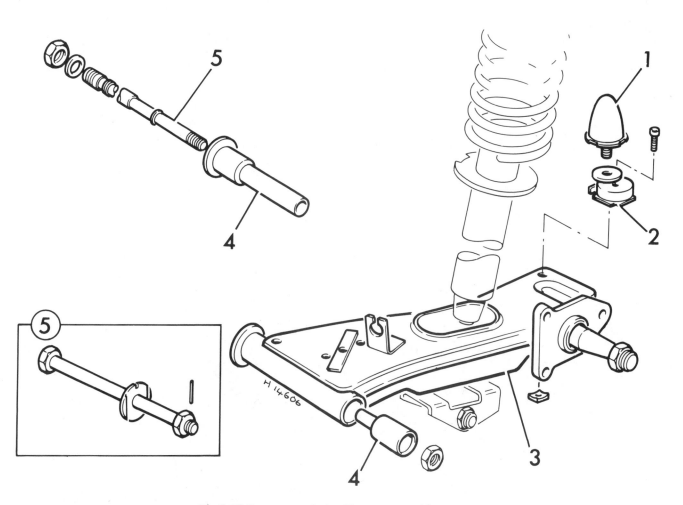

Fig. 9.16 Rear suspension trailing arm assembly components
(Sec 11)

| 1 | Rebound block | 3 | Rear suspension arm | 4 | Bushes | 5 | Articulation shaft |
| 2 | Spacer | | | | | | |

12.1 Remove pad for access to steering wheel retaining nut

12 Steering wheel – removal and refitting

1   Unscrew and remove the two steering wheel pad retaining screws from the underside of the wheel spokes and remove the pad.
2   Centralise the front roadwheels. Unscrew and loosen off the steering wheel retaining nut so that its shoulder is aligned with the top end of the steering column shaft.

3   Use a soft head mallet to tap down on the steering wheel nut whilst simultaneously pressing the steering wheel upwards with your knees. This method should be sufficient to release the wheel and enable it to be withdrawn from the shaft. If it is not, then you will have to use a proper steering wheel puller.
4   Before removing the steering wheel completely remove the nut and make an alignment mark across the top faces of the wheel hub and the column shaft to ensure correct refitting.
5   Refit in reverse order to removal ensuring that the wheel is correctly aligned on the column. Tighten the nut to the specified torque setting. Lock the nut into the shaft groove. If fitting a new steering wheel, position it with the spokes horizontally, with the roadwheels facing straight ahead.

13 Steering column – removal and refitting

Although the steering column was modified in 1972, the basic design has remained the same throughout production and the main components are shown in the diagram. However since the layout of the facia panel and associated controls varies between models and according to gear, the removal and refitting details will differ slightly. This should be obvious as you progress.
1   Disconnect the battery earth lead.
2   Remove the steering wheel as described in Section 12.
3   Remove the steering column lower cover which is secured by seven screws.
4   Detach and remove the soundproofing panel underneath the facia panel.
5   Disconnect the following electrical multi-connectors:

(a)   Steering lock/ignition switch, headlights and indicators switch loom connectors
(b)   The stop-light switch wires on the pedal support noting their connection positions

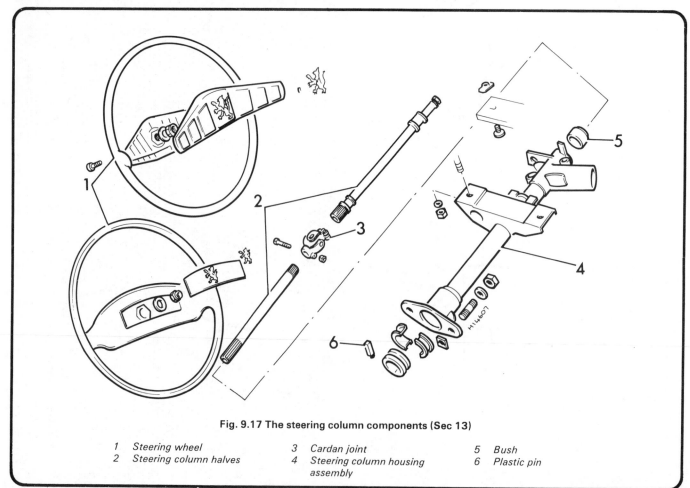

Fig. 9.17 The steering column components (Sec 13)

1 Steering wheel	3 Cardan joint	5 Bush
2 Steering column halves	4 Steering column housing assembly	6 Plastic pin

6 Unscrew and remove the steering column universal joint upper collar bolt (photo).

7 Unscrew and remove the two column lower support bracket securing bolts/nuts.

8 Unscrew and remove the column upper support bracket bolts. In some instances it may be necessary to remove these bolts working from above, in which case you will need to remove the padded facia strip directly in front of the column upper switch lever.

9 The main upper section of the steering column can now be removed.

10 Should it be necessary to remove the lower steering column shaft, disconnect it at its flexible joint connection to the steering box pinion shaft (on the engine compartment side). Unscrew and remove the four bulkhead gaiter retaining plate nuts and withdraw the lower shaft assembly complete with gaiter and plate through the bulkhead.

11 Refitting of the steering column and, if removed, the lower column shaft assemblies is basically the reverse of the removal process.

12 Refer to Section 15 for details on reconnecting the lower shaft to pinion coupling (paragraph 11).

13 The steering column joint bolts, washers, Nyloc nut and the double collar upper screw together with all column mounting lockwashers must be renewed during reassembly.

14 Pre-assemble the column before fully tightening the joint and mounting fastenings to the specified torque settings. Also ensure that the column and steering wheel alignments are correct.

15 When the multi-connectors are reconnected, check the various switch operations before refitting the column lower cover and soundproofing panel.

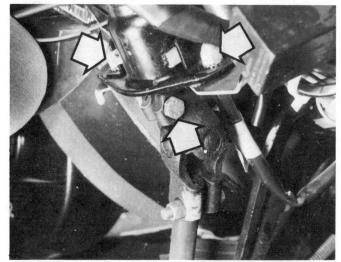

13.6 Remove steering column joint and upper collar bolts (arrowed)

14 Track rods – removal and refitting

1 The earlier model track rod type is shown in the diagram and was fitted to all models up to serial number 4 155 216 (right-hand drive models). This track rod type is available in two lengths, later models fitted with this type being fitted with a longer rod as from serial number 4 031 501 (August 1977), when the track of the front wheels was increased. This design of track rod is referred to as Type A in the text below. A later model track rod type was fitted to all models from serial number 4 155 217 (March 1979). The balljoint on this track rod type does not have a grease nipple fitted as it is sealed for life during manufacture. This design of track rod is adjustable for wheel alignment (toe-in) should it be necessary and is referred to as Type B in the text below.

2 To remove a track rod, first raise and support the car on safety stands at the front. Remove the roadwheel on the side concerned to give greater accessibility.

3 Unscrew and remove the balljoint nut (photo), then using a balljoint separator as shown (photo) release the joint from the steering arm.

4 On the earlier models fitted with the Type A track rod, unbolt and detach the track rod from the connection to the steering rack eye and remove the rod.

5 With the Type B track rod you will need to remove the rubber protection bellows from the end of the steering rack unit. This is secured by a wire clip at each end. Slide the bellows down the rod to gain access to the locknuts at the steering box connection. Loosen off the locknuts and unscrew and remove the track rod.

6 To remove the outer balljoint on the Type A track rod, insert a 2 mm diameter punch through the access hole in the joint and tap the punch to compress and extract the snap-ring. Prise the snap-ring out using a screwdriver as it is compressed by the punch, but make provision for the possible ejection of the joint assembly components as the snap-ring is removed. The various joint components can now be removed for cleaning and inspection. Renew any worn or defective components and reassemble in the reverse order of removal, aligning the pin rod hole. Lubricate the assembly components with grease as they are fitted. Check that the snap-ring is fully located on completion.

7 Outer balljoint removal on the Type B track rod differs in that the joint itself cannot be dismantled. It is removed as a unit from the rod. Before removing the balljoint, measure and note the exposed thread section from the face of the locknut. This will act as a guide for track setting on reassembly. Loosen off the locknut and unscrew the balljoint. Refit in the reverse order to removal and tighten the locknut against the track rod giving the amount of thread protrusion noted on

14.3a Remove the balljoint nut then ...

14.3b ... use balljoint separator to detach

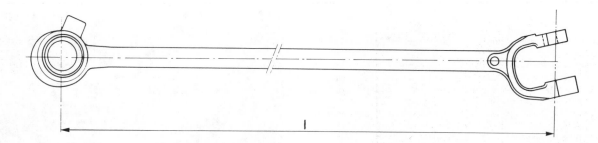

Fig. 9.18 The pre-1979 type track rod identification (Sec 14)

Length (1) between centres up to 1977 was 295.5 mm   *Length (1) between centres from 1977 was 356.68 mm*

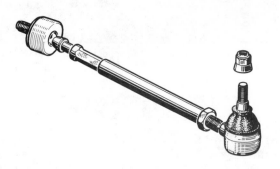

Fig. 9.19 Track rod type fitted from March 1977 (Sec 14)

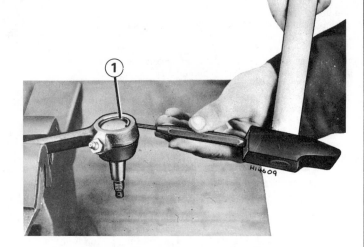

Fig. 9.20 Snap-ring extraction using 2 mm punch through access hole (Type A joint) (Sec 14)

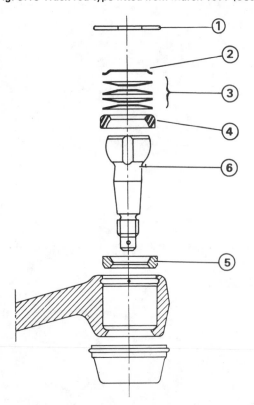

Fig. 9.21 Order of fitting type A balljoint components, note position of pin hole (Sec 14)

Fig. 9.22 Measure and note clearance between nut outer surface (not in the notches) and the bush eye shoulder (Sec 14)

1	Snap-ring	4	Nylon half-cup
2	End cap	5	Steel half-cup
3	Belleville washers	6	Ball head (grease)

Fig. 9.23 Line of eye (9) to be kept horizontal and in line with the subframe when tightening the locknut (Sec 14)

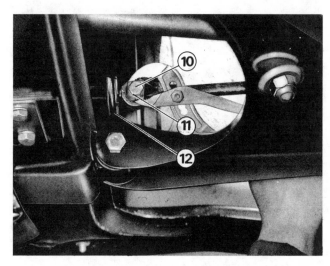

Fig. 9.24 Bend over the lockwasher tabs (11) to lock bolt (10) and clean grease from grooves (12) – Type A rod (Sec 14)

removal. This is only a rough guide since front wheel alignment will have to be rechecked on completion (see Section 15).

8 On the earlier (Type A) track rod models it is advisable at this stage to check the steering rack eye bush for wear. If renewal is necessary, unclip the protection gaiter on the outer edge and compress the gaiter inwards to expose the locknut. Before loosening off the locknut check the nut to eye clearance and make a note of it. Unscrew the eye from the rack. The bush will have to be pressed out and the new bush similarly pressed into the eye. This task is best entrusted to your Peugeot dealer, special tools being required. Refit the eye in the reverse order of removal, setting it at the protrusion noted on removal (about 5.5 mm – locknut to eye shoulder) and with the eye correctly aligned, parallel to the sub-frame. Tighten the locknut to the specified torque wrench setting using the special Peugeot tool number 8.0704Z (J).

9 Refitting the track rods is a reversal of the removal procedure for both Type A and B rods. When reconnecting the Type A rod use a new tab washer with the eye bolt. Bend over the tabs to secure the bolt when tightened.

10 Note that on Type B track rod, the inner connection assembly to the steering rack was modified at serial number 4 194 574 and a ratchet type fitting used in place of the earlier tab washer lock. The two types are not interchangeable so ensure that the correct replacement type is fitted.

11 When rewiring the rubber gaiters, the wire ends must face downwards and outwards (30° to 4.5° from vertical).

12 On completion check the steering action and have your Peugeot dealer check the front wheel alignment at the earliest opportunity since further minor adjustment may be necessary. A basic interior alignment check can be made by referring to Section 15.

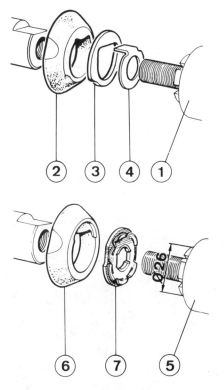

Fig. 9.25 Type B track rod to steering rack locking components used showing the earlier (top) and later (bottom) system (Sec 14)

1	Track rod	5	Track rod
2	Lock stop	6	Lock stop
3	Stop washer	7	Stop washer assembly
4	Tab washer		

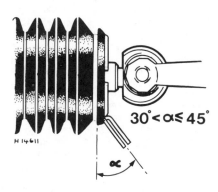

$$30° < \alpha \leqslant 45°$$

Fig. 9.26 Angle of lockwire ends must be as shown (Sec 14)

15.3 Items to be disconnected for removal of steering box
1   Track rods each side (inner or outer end can be detached)
2   Column upper flexible joint and bulkhead plate and gaiter
3   Column lower joint (later type shown)
4   Steering rack bolts to subframe (from underneath)

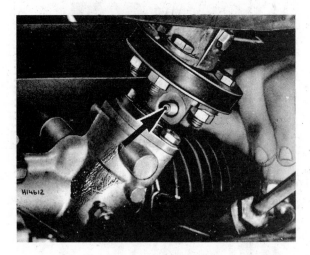

Fig. 9.27 Steering column to pinion coupling showing Flector bolt – fitted to earlier models only (arrowed) (Sec 15)

15 Steering rack-and-pinion unit – removal and refitting

1   Two standards of steering rack-and-pinion assemblies have been fitted to the Peugeot 304, and the principal difference concerns the track rods and their end fittings, the details of which are given in Section 14.
2   To remove the steering rack-and-pinion, first slacken the front wheel nuts and jack up the front of the car. Support it on stands or blocks located at each end of the subframe. Remove the roadwheels.
3   Disconnect the trackrods each side at their inner or outer ends as preferred referring to the previous Section for details (photo).
4   Disconnect the battery earth lead, then working inside the vehicle, loosen off the clamp bolt at the lower end of the steering column flexible joint (see photo 13.6).
5   Remove the steering column to bulkhead seal plate and gaiter which is secured by four nuts. Withdraw the seal and plate up the column.
6   On the engine side of the bulkhead, disconnect the lower column flexible joint coupling to the pinion. On earlier models it is necessary to remove the 'Flector' bolt, whilst on later models unscrew and remove the two upper coupling nuts (photo) from the flexible joint. To ensure correct reassembly make an alignment marking before separating the coupling.
7   Working underneath the vehicle, undo and remove the bolts each side securing the steering rack-and-pinion unit to the subframe.
8   Carefully extract the steering rack-and-pinion assembly.
9   Repair or overhaul of the assembly should be entrusted to a Peugeot dealer who will have the necessary special tools. Inspect the condition of the flexible coupling and, if there is any doubt about it, fit a new one. Use new self-locking nuts if you do this and tighten them to the specified torque. Similarly renew the rubber gaiters if they look tatty or perished. If they were split or leaking grease however, have the assembly checked by a Peugeot dealer as the inner joints may have been contaminated with road dirt. When renewing the gaiters make sure that the wire clips are properly fitted and locate the 'ears' of the clips so that they point downwards when the assembly is installed. Clean the attachment bolt and bolt hole threads.
10   Before refitting the steering rack-and-pinion assembly set the steering wheel to the straight-ahead position and similarly set the rack to the corresponding position.
11   Insert the steering rack-and-pinion assembly into its location. Coat the bolt threads with a locking compound and fit new washers. Do not fully tighten these bolts yet. Assemble the bottom end of the steering

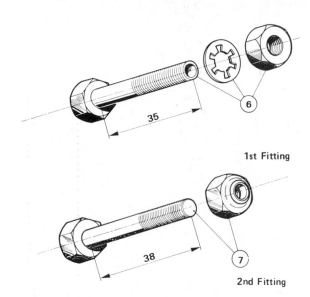

1st Fitting

2nd Fitting

Fig. 9.28 The two Flector bolt types shown with their respective nuts (dimensions shown in mm) (Sec 15)

Fig. 9.29 Fit rod (H4) as shown when tightening the Flector bolt (Sec 15)

column to the flexible coupling using two new self-locking nuts and tighten them to the specified torque. On models where the lower column flexible coupling is secured by a Flector bolt, a new bolt should be used but note that two bolt types are available. When the bolt is in position locate a suitable diameter rod and then tighten the Flector bolt to the specified torque setting. Peen the end of the bolt over to lock it on the final tightening.

12 Tighten the rack-and-pinion unit retaining bolts to the specified torque setting.

13 Engage the steering column anti-theft lock. Move the steering wheel up and down to its limits and position it midway. Tighten the

Fig. 9.30 Special Peugeot spanner for adjustment of the eye bolts

Fig. 9.31 Track rod adjustment on the later models showing locknut (1) and rod (2) (Sec 15)

16.6 End view of steering rack showing the track rod eye bolt with tab washer (1) and the slotted adjuster nut (2)

clamp bolt in the lower flexible joint under the facia to its specified torque.

14 Reconnect the track rods referring to Section 13. On early models with the Type A rods, do not secure the protection gaiters or fully tighten the eye bolt as the track has yet to be checked and possibly adjusted.

15 With the track rods provisionally fitted, refit the roadwheels and lower the vehicle to its normal free-standing position. Now check the front wheels for alignment (toe-in) referring to Section 16. Adjust if necessary to comply with the specified wheel alignment setting for your particular model.

16 Front wheel alignment

1 Accurate front wheel alignment is essential to provide good steering characteristics and maximum tyre life. Much of the alignment accuracy depends on design geometry and the only adjustment available is for the front wheel toe-in.

2 Checking and adjusting toe-in requires accurate equipment not normally available to the home mechanic and it is recommended that the work is done by a properly equipped garage.

3 If the track rod settings have been disturbed, as a result of work on the steering rack-and-pinion assembly for example, an approximate adjustment can be made to enable the car to be taken to a garage for an accurate measurement and readjustment, as required, to be made.

4 The toe-in is the difference between the distances across the car measured at the front rim of the wheels and the rear rim of the wheels at the hub centre height. A gauge can be made up with an adjustable pointer at one end to compare these distances when the wheels are in the straight-ahead position. The toe-in should be as given in the Specifications for your model type depending on whether it is fitted with a Type A or B track rod (see Section 14). The toe-in is checked with the vehicle standing on level ground and with the tyres inflated to their specified pressures.

5 If adjustment is necessary (and remember that with only a small error the car can still be safely taken to the garage for an accurate check) proceed as follows.

Early models

6 These are Type A with no locknuts at the balljoint ends of the track rods. Release the gaiter clip at the inner end of the track rod to permit moving the gaiter back and exposing the inner joint on the track rod. Bend straight the eye bolt lockwasher tabs and unscrew and remove the track rod eye bolt (photo). Loosen off the locknut which has slots in its end face for the location of a Special Peugeot spanner. Without this type of spanner you will have to use grips and/or a punch to loosen off the nut, but take care not to damage it. The inner track rod eye can now be turned in or out to alter the track rod setting. A half turn will alter the toe-in by 1.15 mm (0.045 in). If more than half a turn is necessary, the adjustment must be shared equally between both track rods to maintain turning lock angles. Having achieved the required setting align the inner rod eye so that it is horizontal. Hold it in this position whilst tightening the locknut by inserting a 10 mm rod through the eye so that it can be held in the correct position. Tighten the locknut to the specified torque setting. The procedure is the same on each side. Reconnect the track rod and tighten the eye bolt to the specified torque setting and then bend over the lockwasher tab to secure. When the toe-in is set, reposition the gaiters and their clips. See Section 14 concerning the correct fitment of the gaiter clips.

Later models

7 These are fitted with locknuts at the balljoint ends of the track rods. With the locknuts loose, turn the track rods on the balljoint threads to alter the track rod lengths. A half turn of a rod will alter the toe-in on the related wheel rim by 1 mm (0.0394 in) at the rim. Again, if more than half a turn is necessary to produce the correct toe-in, the adjustment must be equally shared on both track rods. Tighten the locknuts, with the bottom face of the balljoints horizontal, to the specified torque.

8 It is emphasised that this adjustment, in the absence of accurate alignment checking equipment, must be regarded as purely temporary and the car should be taken to a properly equipped garage for precise checks and adjustments to be made at the first opportunity. The same applies if accident or kerb-impact damage is thought to have affected the steering geometry.

17 Fault diagnosis – suspension and steering

Before diagnosing faults from the chart below, be sure that trouble is not due to:
(a) Binding brakes
(b) Incorrect tyre pressures
(c) Inappropriate tyre combinations
(d) Unbalanced wheels or loose wheel nuts
(e) Accident damage

Symptom	Reason/s
Vehicle pulls to one side	Wheel alignment incorrect Steering or front suspension components excessively worn or distorted
Pitching and/or rolling on corners, over pumps and during braking	Shock absorber(s) defective – test by bouncing car at each corner. Poor shock absorber will allow oscillation. Suspension struts or anti-roll bar mountings loose or deteriorated
Excessively stiff steering	Front wheel alignment incorrect Steering column misaligned or binding Front suspension unit(s) defective Rack-and-pinion unit unlubricated or defective
Excessive play at steering wheel	Steering balljoints worn Front suspension swiven joints worn Rack-and-pinion unit worn Rack to track rod joint worn
Wheel wobble and vibration	Front suspension units loose or defective Shock absorber(s) defective Steering balljoints or front suspension swivel joints worn
Car sags at one corner	Coil spring broken or defective Suspension unit loose or defective Shock absorber(s) defective
Excessive or uneven tyre wear	Front wheel alignment incorrect Suspension unit(s) loose or defective Shock absorber(s) defective

Chapter 10 Electrical system

Contents

Specifications

Battery

Type	Lead acid
Voltage	12
Earth terminal	Negative (–)

Dynamo

	Ducellier	Paris-Rhone
Type number	7319G or 7320A (or G) or 7345A	G10 C34 or G10 C46 or G10 C34
Nominal voltage	12	12
Maximum power	330W	330W
Output under 13 volts	25A	25A
Corresponding speed when cold	2500 rpm	2300 rpm
Cut-in speed	1800 rpm	1450 rpm
Cut-in voltage	12.6 ± 0.6V	12.6 ± 0.6V
Drivebelt tension setting (expansion)	102 to 102.5 mm (4.01 to 4.03 in)	

Voltage regulator type

	Ducellier	Paris-Rhone
	8343	YD217

Alternator - single phase types

Make Type	Ducellier		Paris-Rhone	
	Alternator	Regulator	Alternator	Regulator
XL3 engine (with voltmeter)	7533 or 7555	8364	A13M12	AYB21
XL3 engine (without voltmeter)	7559 or 7570	8380A	A13M15	AYB2111
XL5 and XK5 engine (with voltmeter)	512001	8364		AYB21
XL5 engine (without voltmeter)	512002	8373A		AYB21

Alternator - three phase types

	Ducellier		Paris-Rhone	
	Alternator	Regulator	Alternator	Regulator
XL3 engine (with voltmeter and heated rear window)		8364	A13R96 or A12R174	
XL3 and XL3S engine (heated rear window and charge/discharge warning light model)		8364	A13R129 or A13R175	AYB21
XL5 engine (with heated rear window and voltmeter)	513001	8371	A12R13	AYB21
XL5 and XL5S engine (with heated rear window and charge/discharge warning light)		8371	A12R12	AYB21

SEV - Marchal alternator/regulator

XL3 engine (with voltmeter and heated rear window)	71210202/72711302
XL3 and XL3S engine (with heated rear window and charge/discharge warning light)	71210202/72711302 or 71210302/72711303
XL5 engine (with voltmeter and heated rear window)	71210502/72711302
XL5 and XL5S engines (fitted with heated rear window and charge/discharge warning light)	71210602/72711302

Alternator drivebelt tension (expansion) .... 101.5 to 102 mm (3.9 to 4.0 in)

Starter motor

	Ducellier	Paris-Rhone
Type number	6155 or 6178	D8E50
Direction of rotation (from pinion side)	Anti-clockwise	
Bendix adjustment	37 mm (1.456 in)	
Number of pinion teeth	9	

Light bulbs (typical)

	Wattage
Sidelights	5
Headlights	45/40
Direction indicators	21
Reversing light	21
Stoplights	21
Foglights (rear)	21
Rear number plate lights	5
Interior lights (festoon)	4
Boot light (festoon)	4

Fuses

	Rating (amps)
1	5
2	15
3	10
4	15

Torque wrench settings

	lbf ft	kgf m
Starter motor bolts	25.3	3.5
Alternator securing bolt	25.3	3.5
Drivebelt adjuster nut	25.3	3.5
Dynamo drivebelt tension bolt	12.6	1.75

1 General description

The electrical system consists of three major components: the battery, the dynamo (early models only) or alternator and its regulator, and the starter. In addition the remaining electrical equipment can be dividied into three further groups: the lighting system, auxiliary components and instruments and warning light circuits.

The battery supplies a steady amount of current for the starting, ignition, lighting and electrical circuits, and provides a reserve or power when the current consumed by the electrical equipment exceeds that being produced by the dynamo/alternator.

The dynamo/alternator generates electricity in order to maintain the battery in its optimum charged state, and also to ensure that the electrical circuits are supplied with the correct current to enable the auxiliary components to function. The alternator type fitted will be of either single or three phase design dependent on model and electrical circuit fittings. In dynamo equipped models the regulator unit is separate from the generator, whilst for alternator models the regulator is integral with the alternator unit. The function of the regulator is to control the generator output to match the requirements of the electrical system and battery.

The starter motor turns the engine with a pinion which engages with the flywheel ring gear. Due to the amount of current required by the starter, it is necessary to use a separate circuit direct to the battery incorporating special cable.

The electrical system has a negative earth and it is important to check that such items as radios and extra electrical items are connected correctly.

In emergencies it is in order to connect another battery with the aid of 'jumper' leads, but connect the positive terminals first followed by the negative terminals, and remove them in the reverse order.

2.3 The battery clamp bracket and retaining bolt

2 Battery – removal and refitting

1   The battery is located in the engine compartment next to the radiator and access is gained to it by lifting the bonnet.
2   To remove the battery disconnect the negative (earth) terminal, coloured green, first. Unscrw the thumb nut and ease the cable off the battery post, then similarly disconnect the positive terminal, coloured red.
3   Bend the terminal leads away from the battery, then unscrew and remove the battery clamp bolt which retains the battery to the tray.
4   Lift out the battery carefully to avoid spilling electrolyte on the body paintwork.
5   Refitting the battery is a reversal of the removal procedure but, before reconnecting the terminals, clean off any corrosion present and smear them with petroleum jelly.

3 Battery – maintenance and inspection

1   Normal weekly battery maintenance consists of checking the electrolyte level of each cell to ensure that the separators are covered by 10 mm (0.4 in) of electrolyte. If the level has fallen, top up the battery using only purified water. Do not overfill; if a battery is overfilled or any electrolyte spilled, immediately wipe away the excess as electrolyte attacks and corrodes any metal it comes into contact with very rapidly.
2   As well as keeping the terminals clean and covered with petroleum jelly, the top of the battery, and especially the top of the cells, should be kept clean and dry. This helps prevent corrosion and ensures that the battery does not become partially discharged by leakage through dampness and dirt.
3   Once every three months remove the battery and inspect the battery securing bolts, the battery clamp plate, tray and battery leads for corrosion (white fluffy deposits on the metal which are brittle to touch). If any corrosion is found, clean off the deposits with ammonia and paint over the clean metal with an anti-rust/anti-acid paint.
4   At the same time inspect the battery case for cracks. If a crack is found, clean and plug it with one of the proprietary compounds marketed for this purpose. If leakage through the crack has been excessive then it will be necessary to refill the appropriate cell with fresh electrolyte as detailed later. Cracks are frequently caused to the top of the battery case by pouring in purified water in the middle of winter *after* instead of *before* a run. This gives the water no chance to mix with the electrolyte and so the former freezes and splits the battery case.
5   If topping up the battery becomes excessive and the case has been inspected for cracks that could cause leakage, but none are

found, the battery is being overcharged and the voltage regulator will have to be checked.
6   Every three months check the specific gravity with a hydrometer to determine the state of charge and the condition of the electrolyte. There should be very little variation between the different cells and if a variation in excess of 0.025 is present, it will be due to either:

(a)   *Loss of electrolyte from the battery caused by spillage or a leak resulting in a drop in the specific gravity of the electrolyte. The deficiency was probably made up with purified water instead of fresh electrolyte*
(b)   *An internal short circuit caused by buckling of the plates or a similar malady pointing to the likelihood of total battery failure in the near future*

7   The specific gravity of electrolyte for fully charged and fully discharged batteries at different temperatures of the electrolyte is given below.

Specific gravity – battery fully charged	Electrolyte temperature	Specific gravity – battery fully discharged
1.259	43°C (110°F)	1.089
1.263	38°C (100°F)	1.093
1.267	32°C (90°F)	1.097
1.271	27°C (80°F)	1.101
1.275	21°C (70°F)	1.105
1.279	16°C (60°F)	1.109
1.283	10°C (50°F)	1.113
1.287	4°C (40°F)	1.117
1.295	−7°C (20°F)	1.126
1.303	−18°C (0°F)	1.133
1.311	−29°C (−20°F)	1.142

4 Battery – electrolyte replenishment

1   If the battery is in a fully charged state and one of the cells maintains a specific gravity reading which is 0.025 or more lower than the others, and a check of each cell has been made with a voltmeter to check for short circuits (a four to seven second test should give a steady reading of between 1.2 to 1.8 volts), then it is likely that electrolyte has been lost from the cell which shows the low reading.
2   Top up the cell with a solution of 1 part sulphuric acid to 2.5 parts of water. If the cell is already fully topped up, draw some electrolyte out of it with a pipette or you can use a hydrometer as a syringe.
3   When mixing the sulphuric acid and water **never add water to sulphuric acid** – always pour the acid slowly into the water in a glass container. **If water is added to sulphuric acid it will explode.**
4   Continue to top up the cell with the freshly made electrolyte and then recharge the battery and check the hydrometer readings.

5 Battery – charging

1   In winter when heavy demand is placed upon the battery, such as when starting from cold, and much electrical equipment is continually in use, it is a good idea to occasionally have the battery fully charged from an external source at the rate of 3.5 to 4 amps.
2   Continue to charge the battery at this rate until no further rise in specific gravity is noted over a four hour period.
3   Alternatively, a trickle charger charging at the rate of 1.5 amps can be safely used overnight.
4   Specially rapid boost charges which are claimed to restore the power of the battery in 1 to 2 hours are most dangerous as they can cause serious damage to the battery plates through over heating.
5   While charging the battery, note that the temperature of the electrolyte should never exceed 100°F (37.8°C), and, if the battery is being charged in the vehicle, always disconnect both terminals to avoid damage to the alternator.

6 Generator – maintenance

1   Whether a dynamo or alternator is fitted, the equipment has been designed for the minimum amount of maintenance, the only items

subject to wear being the field brushes and the commutator or rotor bearings.

2   The brushes should be examined after about 75 000 miles (120 000 km) usage, and renewed as necessary. The bearings are pre-packed with grease for life during manufacture and should not require further attention.

3   Every 10 000 miles (15 000 km) examine the condition of the generator drivebelt. If it is frayed, cracked or stretched it should be renewed. If satisfactory, check for correct tension. Renewing and tensioning the drivebelt is explained in Sections 13 and 14.

4   Every 5000 miles (7500 km) clean the exterior of the generator with paraffin-moistened rag, particularly around the ventilating holes at the opposite end to the fan (alternator). Also check the wiring connections on the generator and on the regulator, located on the left front wheel bulkhead, for tightness and security.

7   Dynamo – removal and refitting

1   Disconnect the battery lead connections.
2   Detach the wiring connectors at the dynamo and take note of their fitted positions.
3   Loosen off the dynamo retaining strap.
4   Loosen off the drivebelt adjustment sufficiently to enable the belt to be disengaged from the dynamo pulley.
5   Withdraw the dynamo.
6   Refit in the reverse order to removal ensuring that the dynamo drive pulley is correctly realigned to provide the correct belt run and then tighten the retaining strap to secure. Readjust the drivebelt in the manner described in Section 13.

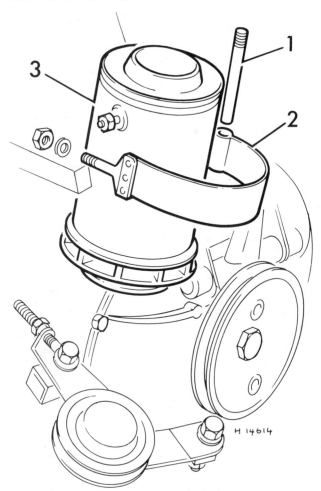

Fig. 10.1 Dynamo location and retaining components (Sec 7)

1   Pivot   3   Dynamo unit
2   Strap

8   Dynamo – dismantling, inspection and reassembly

The dynamo will be of either Paris-Rhone or Ducellier manufacture. Whichever type is fitted the dismantling and reassembly procedure is basically the same. However, make sure that right parts are available for replacement. It is often likely that once the dynamo is past just the replacement of brushes, it is more economic to have the whole unit overhauled or replaced. Overhauling should only be undertaken by qualified auto-electricians. Its total overhaul is not really a home mechanic's task.

Paris-Rhone dynamo

1   Grip the pulley of the dynamo in a vice and loosen the pulley retaining nut. Then remove the nuts from the two tie-rods at the other end of the dynamo to release the commutator end bracket.
2   Remove the commutator end cap and bracket.
3   The brushes may now be removed from the end bracket by pulling back the retaining springs and withdrawing the brushes from their holders.
4   Pull out from the body the armature, pulley and end bearing cap for inspection. The two tie-through-rods should now be loose alongside the armature.

Ducellier dynamo

5   Grip the pulley of the dynamo in a vice and loosen the pulley retaining nut. Then remove the nuts from the two studs at the other end of the dynamo to release the commutator end bracket.
6   Pull off the commutator end cover and bracket.
7   Pull out the armature, pulley and end bearing cap from the body of the dynamo but hold the brushes, still attached to the body, away from the armature to avoid their damage. (Shim steel or feeler blades do this adequately). Place the armature aside for inspection.
8   Remove the brushes from the body of the dynamo by undoing the DYN and EXC terminal nuts and thereby releasing the brush contact wires and the brushes from their seating bodies.
9   Never attempt to release the field coils by dismantling the field terminals of both types of dynamo because an impact screwdriver is necessary. If the dynamo is in need of new field coils it should be replaced as a total unit.
10   Do not dismantle further still at this stage. Examine the carbon brushes. The length of the brushes should be no less than $\frac{7}{16}$ inch. If required fit the correct (not interchangeable type for type) new ones which are supplied with new leads.
11   Examine next the commutator end of the armature. This should not be burnt or scored in any way. First clean it off with a little petrol on a rag. Any traces of pitting, scoring or burring, if slight, can be cleaned off with fine glass paper. Do not use emery paper. Make sure that there are no flat spots, by tearing the glass paper into strips and use it by drawing it round the commutator evenly. Do not try and clean off too much by this method as the commutator must remain circular in section.
12   To test the armature is not difficult but a voltmeter or bulb and 12 volt battery are required. The two tests determine whether there may be a break in any circuit winding or if any wiring insulation is broken down. In the first test the probes are placed on adjacent segments of a clean commutator. All voltmeter readings should be similar. If a bulb is used instead it will glow very dimly or not at all if there is a fault. For the second test any reading or bulb lighting indicates a fault. Test each segment in turn with one probe and keep the other on the shaft. Should either test indicate a faulty armature the wisest action in the long run is to obtain a replacement dynamo altogether. The field coils may be tested if an ohmmeter or ammeter can be obtained. With an ohmmeter the resistance (measured between the terminal and the yoke) should be 6 ohms. With an ammeter, connect it in series with a 12 volt battery, again from the field terminal to the yoke. A reading of 2 amps is normal. Zero amps or infinity ohms indicate an open circuit. More than 2 amps or less than 6 ohms indicates a breakdown of the insulation. Unless you can get the field coils readily repaired it is better to obtain a replacement unit.
13   The drive end bearing should have no play but in the event that it also needs renewal (very rare except where the fan belt has been persistently overtight), first remove the pulley nut and washers and draw off the pulley. Then tap the Woodruff key out of the shaft using a screwdriver under one end. Be careful to guard against it flying off

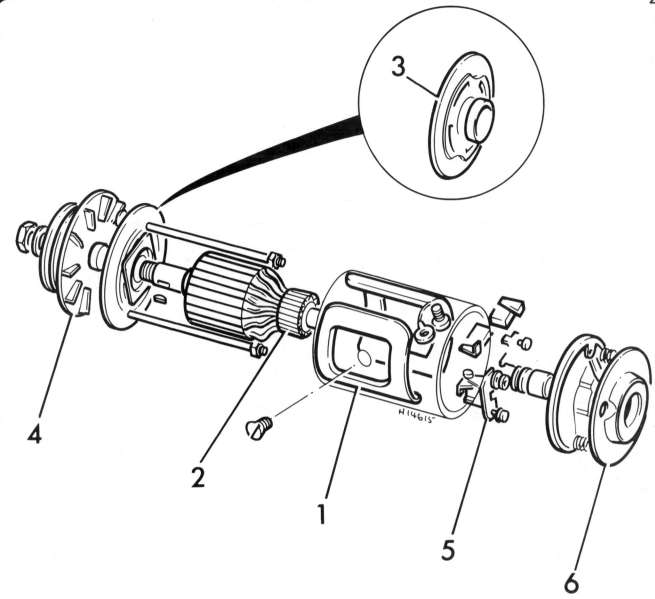

Fig. 10.2 The Ducellier dynamo component parts (typical) (Sec 8)

1	Field coils	3	Endplate and bearing	5	Brush assembly
2	Armature	4	Pulley	6	Cover assembly

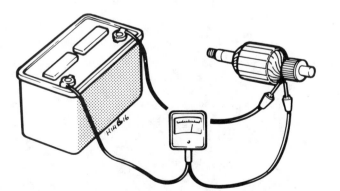

Fig. 10.3 Armature test for open circuit (Sec 8)

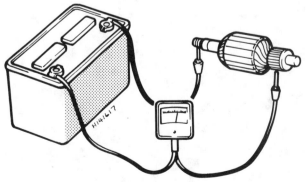

Fig. 10.4 Armature windings insulation test (Sec 8)

and getting lost. If the end cover is now supported across the jaws of a vice, with the armature hanging down, the end of the shaft may be tapped with a soft faced mallet to drive it out of the bearing housing with the bearing. The bearing itself can next be taken off the shaft by the same method. When fitting a new bearing make sure it is thoroughly packed with grease and fit it into the end cover first making sure that the pressure ring and retaining plate are all assembled correctly. Then place the retaining cup over the armature shaft so that the open end faces the armature. Then the end cover may be supported over the vice jaws and the armature carefully tapped through the bearing with a mallet. Refit the spacer, then the Woodruff key, followed by the pulley, washer and nut.

Paris-Rhone dynamo

14 If new brushes have been fitted, make sure that they are a free sliding fit in their holders. If there are any signs of sticking they may be relieved by careful rubbing with a fine file. The bearing face of each brush should be concave to match the commutator. Refit the armature/drive end cover assembly into the main yoke and then prepare to fit the commutator end cover by hooking back the brush springs onto the sides of the brushes which should be drawn back. The brushes will then be held and can be released and the springs brought to bear after the end cover has been assembled. Note that both end covers have locating pips which register in corresponding cut-outs in the yoke. When fitting the commutator end cover, see that the blade terminal of the field coil connection fits in the proper slot and that the insulating sleeve round it is intact. Refit the through bolts and before tightening them right up, check that the end plates are fully and correctly in position. Spin the armature to ensure it is not binding or touching the field coils and then unhook the brush springs and lower the brushes onto the commutator with the springs on top. Finally, place a few drops of engine oil in the oil hole of the commutator bearing bush.

Ducellier dynamo

15 Always refit the armature before refitting the brushes. Refitting the brushes on this dynamo is a simple reversal of their removal even though the armature is in place. Refit the commutator end bracket. See paragraph 14.

9 Alternator – general description

The alternator generates alternating current (AC) which is rectified by diodes into direct current (DC) and is the current needed for charging the battery.

The main advantage of the alternator lies in its ability to provide a high charge at low revolutions. Driving slowly in heavy traffic with a dynamo invariably means no charge is reaching the battery. In similar conditions even with the heater, wiper, lights and perhaps radio switched on the alternator will ensure a charge reaches the battery.

The alternator is of the rotating field ventilated design and comprises principally a laminated stator on which is wound the output winding: a rotor carrying the field windings — each end of the rotor shaft runs in ball race bearings which are lubricated for life.

The rotor is belt-driven from the engine through a pulley keyed to the rotor shaft. A fan adjacent to the pulley draws air through the unit. This fan forms an integral part of the alternator specification. It has been designed to provide adequate airflow with minimum noise, and to withstand the high stresses associated with the maximum speed. Rotation is clockwise when viewed from the drive end. The regulator is set during manufacture and requires no further attention. However, should its operation be faulty it must be renewed as a complete unit.

Where indications show that the charging system is malfunctioning in any way, care must be taken to diagnose faults properly, otherwise damage of a serious and expensive nature may well occur to parts which are in fact quite serviceable.

Apart from the renewal of the rotor slip ring brushes, there are no other parts requiring periodic inspection. Any more detailed testing and inspection of the alternator components is best entrusted to your Peugeot dealer or a qualified automotive electrician.

10 Alternators – safety precautions

The following basic requirements must be observed at all times, therefore, if damage is to be prevented:

1   ALL alternator systems use a NEGATIVE earth. Even the simple mistake of connecting a battery the wrong way round could burn out the alternator diodes in a few seconds.
2   Before disconnecting any wires in the system the engine and ignition circuits should be switched off. This will minimise accidental short circuits.
3   The alternator must NEVER be run with the output wire disconnected.
4   Always disconnect the battery from the car's electrical system if an outside charging source is being used.
5   Do not use test wire connections that could move accidentally and short circuit against nearby terminals. Short circuits will not blow fuses — they will blow diodes or transistors.
6   Always disconnect the battery cables and alternator output wires before any electric welding work is done on the car body. Never earth the wire number 8, marked EXC (field exciter), on the alternator or the regulator.

11 Alternator – removal and refitting

1   Open the bonnet and disconnect the negative battery terminal followed by the positive battery terminal.
2   Note the location of the alternator supply wires, then disconnect them from the rear cover.

9.1 The alternator – Paris-Rhone type shown

9.4 The regulator unit

11.4 Alternator removal

12.2 Removing the brush holder (Paris-Rhone alternator shown)

3   Loosen the adjustment and pivot bolts, swivel the alternator towards the engine and remove the drivebelt from the pulley.
4   Support the alternator and unscrew and remove the adjustment and pivot bolts; the alternator can then be carefully lifted from the vehicle (photo).
5   Refitting the alternator is a reversal of the removal procedure but the alternator wiring should be connected and the nuts tightened before the battery is reconnected.
6   Refer to Section 13 and adjust the drivebelt tension.

12 Alternator brushes – removal, inspection and refitting

1   The alternator brushes are not likely to give trouble unless they have been installed for a long time, when they may show signs of wear. They form part of the field exciter circuit and they bear on plain slip rings on the rotor.
2   Brush removal varies according to alternator type, exploded layouts of the different types fitted being shown in the accompanying

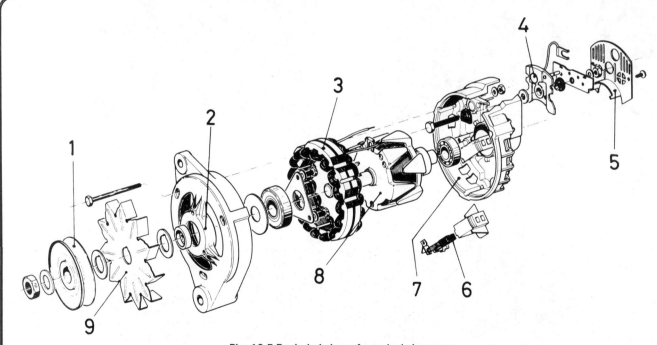

Fig. 10.5 Exploded view of a typical alternator

1 Drive pulley	3 Stator	6 Brushes	8 Rotor
2 Bearing carrier and drive end bracket	4 Isolating diode	7 Diode holders and end cover	9 Fan
	5 Rear end cover		

12.4 Examine the brushes for excessive wear

12.5a SEV alternator brush unit retaining screw and cover

12.5b Remove the cover ...

12.5c ... and extract the brushholder unit ...

12.5d ... to inspect the brushes

diagrams. A more generalized test is given to cover the more commonly fitted alternator types.

3   To remove the brushes, first disconnect the battery leads and then detach the wiring connections to the alternator noting their fitted positions.

4   On the Paris-Rhone type shown (photo), undo the two nuts on the end of the alternator adjacent to wire No 8, marked EXC, and carefully withdraw the brush holder.

5   On other models the brushes will be contained in the diode holder or end cover secured by screws or nuts (photo).

6   Examine the brushes for chipping, smooth contact surfaces, easy fit in the holder and for adequate length. If necessary new brushes should be fitted if they can be obtained but, if not, the alternator should be removed for servicing by a specialist servicing agency. If the brushes do not slide freely in the holders they can be eased slightly with a smooth file but be careful not to make them a loose fit. Clean off all dust and dirt with a petrol-damped soft lint-free rag and wipe the brush slip rings clean.

7   Refitting the brushes is the reverse of the removal procedure, taking care not to damage them when reinserting them in their locations. Make sure that the alternator and battery connections are complete before starting the engine.

Fig. 10.6 Generator drivebelt adjustment (Sec 13)

(5) *Maximum twist of belt 90°* (8) *Retainer nut*
(6) *Adjuster nut* (a) *Mark belt at points shown 100 mm*
(7) *Retainer bolt* *apart when belt tension is slack*

13 Generator drivebelt – tension adjustment

1   Correct tensioning of the generator drivebelt will ensure that it and the generator bearings will have a maximum life expectancy. If the belt is loose, generator performance will be affected and possibly the battery could be discharged. If the belt is too tight it will cause unnecessary generator bearing wear. In either case the belt itself will suffer and its life will be shortened.
2   The drivebelt is tensioned by pivoting the generator out and securing it when the belt is correctly tensioned.
3   To adjust the drivebelt tension first check that it is correctly located in both pulleys. Make two marks on the outer face of the slack belt 100 mm apart (work in metric units for this adjustment) and lightly tighten the pivot bolts and the adjusting link bolts.
4   Pivot the alternator outwards to tighten the drivebelt. You can use a lever to help achieve this but it must be a wooden one and it must be used only at the pulley end of the alternator. Levering on the case or at the end opposite to the drive pulley can easily cause expensive damage.
5   Tighten the belt until the marks on it have stretched to within the specified amount. See Specifications for dynamo or alternator drivebelt tension adjustment. Then tighten all the generator mounting and adjusting link bolts to the specified torque. A rough and ready adjustment of the tension can be made by tightening the belt until you can depress it by finger pressure at a point midway between the two pulleys for about $\frac{1}{2}$ in (say 13 mm), but you will probably get a better belt life by using the measured distance technique which is the Peugeot recommended procedure.

14 Generator drivebelt – renewal

1   On models fitted with separate drivebelts for the generator and cooling system pump/fan, you will have to remove the cooling system drivebelt first as given in Chapter 2, Section 11.
2   Loosen the generator pivot and adjustment bolts, swivel the generator in towards the engine and remove the drivebelt from both pulleys.
3   Fit a new drivebelt and adjust the tension as described in Section 13.
4   Refit and tension the cooling system drivebelt as described in Sections 10 and 11 of Chapter 2.

14.1 Starter motor can be removed from engine once cables are detached and the retaining bolts removed – Paris-Rhone shown

15 Starter motor – general description

The starter motor is located on the clutch housing under the intake manifold and is of the pre-engaged type, having a solenoid mounted on top.
The starting circuit is initially energised when the ignition switch key is turned to the starting position; at this stage current flow through the solenoid coil and the magnetic field produced causes the solenoid plunger to move. Movement of the plunger operates a lever arm which, in turn, slides the starter pinion into mesh with the flywheel ring gear. At the end of its travel the solenoid plunger bridges internal electrical contacts which then direct full battery current to the starter motor causing it to rotate.
When the engine starts, a one-way clutch on the starter armature shaft allows the pinion to spin on the shaft and be driven by the flywheel, thus avoiding damage to the starter which could occur if it was driven by the engine. As soon as the starter key is released, the solenoid coil is de-energised and a spring returns the solenoid plunger to the rest position. At the same time the lever arm disengages the starter pinion from the flywheel ring gear. As the solenoid plunger returns under the spring load, the electrical contacts are opened and the starter motor is de-energised.

16 Starter motor – removal and refitting

1   Disconnect the battery earth terminal cable.
2   Access to the starter is difficult and it will pay to remove the air cleaner and, if you still have difficulty in reaching the terminals on the starter solenoid, the intake manifold as well (Chapter 3).
3   Unscrew and remove the nut securing the heavy supply cable on the starter solenoid terminal and remove the cable and the thinner, positive lead mounted with it. Unscrew and remove the small nut securing the ignition switch cable to the solenoid terminal and remove the cable. Leave the terminal nut securing the feed to the starter motor on the remaining terminal done up.
4   Unscrew and remove the three retaining bolts securing the motor to the clutch housing and carefully remove the starter from the engine. Take care to avoid damaging the flywheel ring gear.
5   Refitting the starter motor is the reverse of the removal procedure. Tighten the retaining bolts to the specified torque.

17 Starter motor – dismantling and reassembly

1   The dismantling, inspection and reassembly procedure is similar for both the Paris-Rhone starter motor (described below and shown in accompanying photos) and the Ducellier starter motor.

17.2a The brushes can be checked through the housing 'inspection window'

17.2b Pull back on the retainer spring to enable brush to be withdrawn

17.3 Remove the end cover

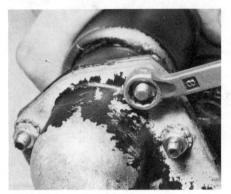
17.5a Unscrew the nuts and ...

17.5b ... remove the solenoid

17.6a Withdraw the armature braking assembly noting how spring is engaged in the slot of the end cover ...

17.6b ... then remove the spring

17.7a With the cover/brush holder unit removed ...

17.7b ... note the washers and shims on the armature shaft

2   Before dismantling the complete starter motor look at the brushes by removing the inspection window cover from the main body. The brushes can then be extracted after pulling back the retainer springs as shown (photo). Withdraw each brush in turn from its holder. If the brushes are very worn or sticky in their holders or their wiring is defective, then this is perhaps all that is required in the way of repairs. If the starter motor is to be fully dismantled proceed as follows.

3   Unscrew and remove the two retaining nuts from the end cover and detach the cover (photo).

4   Unscrew and remove the solenoid unit wire retaining nuts.

5   Unscrew the four solenoid retaining nuts and remove the solenoid (photo), detaching the rod from the operating lever.

6   Remove the armature braking assembly (photo) noting the order of fitting and how the spring locates into the shouldered flange and hole in the end cover (photo).

7   Now remove the armature cover/brush holder retaining nuts and

withdraw the cover (photo). Note the washers on the armature shaft (photo) and remove them.

8   Extract the solenoid actuating lever pivot pin clip (photo) withdraw the pin (photo). Then withdraw the drive pinion housing with through bolts.

9   Remove the lever fork and thrust guide pads from the shifter (photo), and withdraw the armature unit.

10   Clean and inspect the various components for signs of excessive wear or damage. If the commutator or field coils are suspected of malfunction, have them checked by an automotive electrician.

11   Clean the armature with a petrol dampened cloth and examine the commutator segments. If they appear glazed or dirty, wrap a piece of glass paper, (not emery cloth), round the segments and lightly clean them. If the segments are badly worn or show signs of obvious overheating, have the assembly checked by a specialist.

12   Check the commutator spindle bush for excessive wear, also the

17.8a Remove the lever pivot securing clip ...

17.8b ... then extract the pin to ...

17.8c ... allow the lever fork to be freed and withdraw the pinion housing

17.9 Remove the fork and thrust pads

17.10 Clean and inspect the armature unit

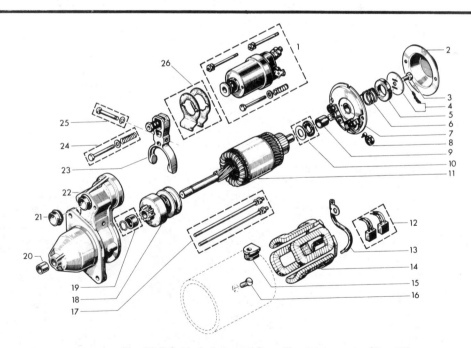

Fig. 10.7 Exploded view of Ducellier starter motor (Sec 17)

1 Solenoid	8 Brush spring	15 Contact	21 Plug
2 End cover	9 End bush	16 Field coil retaining screw	22 Drive end bracket
3 Bolt	10 Insulating spacers	17 Through bolts	23 Engagement lever
4 Spacer	11 Commutator	18 Drive cog	24 Drive lever bolt and spring
5 End bush	12 Brushes	19 Bush and washer	25 Pivot bolt
6 Spring	13 Brush wire contact	20 End bush	26 Lever plates
7 Brush holder plate	14 Field coils		

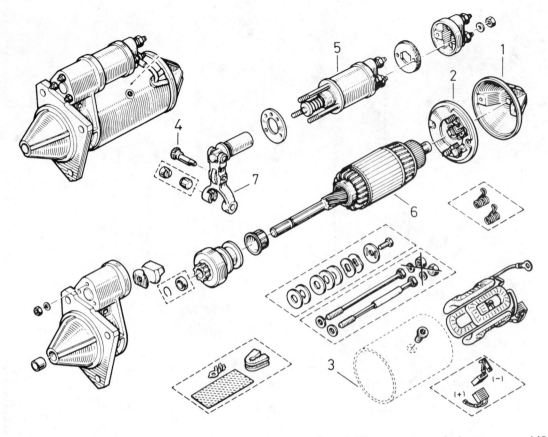

Fig. 10.8 Typical Paris-Rhone starter motor — exploded view (detail differences may exist between types) (Sec 17)

1 Cap	3 Body	5 Solenoid	7 Fork
2 Bearing plate	4 Fork bearing pin	6 Armature	

bearing at the pinion end, and renew them if necessary. The pinion assembly is secured by means of a snap-ring or roll pin.

13 If the brushes are to be renewed, they will have to be cut and re-soldered at the post/field coil end. Be sure to refit the insulating sleeve on the field coil brush wire.

14 Reassembly of the starter motor is a reversal of the dismantling procedure. It is important to reassemble the shim washers in their original positions. Retract the brushes from their holders when fitting the endplate.

18 Fuses

1 The fuse panel is located under a removable plastic cover on top of the right-hand wing valance (photo). Open the bonnet and unclip the cover of the fuse box for access.

2 There are four positions for fuses in the panel which are numbered from front to rear. The circuits protected by each fuse are as follows:

Fuse No.	Rating	Services
1	5A	Front/rear side lights, boot and tell-tale, rear number plate lights, facia lights
2	15A	Door courtesy lights, tailgate light, horns, cigar lighter, clock, rear screen heater, hazard warning light
3	10A	Direction indicators
4	15A	Electro magnetic cooling fan, heater/ventilator, windscreen washer/wiper, stop lights, fuel gauge, water temperature gauge, warning lights and accessories

3 A blown fuse suggests a fault in the circuit concerned and this must be checked and rectified when renewing the fuse.

19 Headlights — removal, bulb renewal and refitting

1 Disconnect the battery earth lead.

2 Lift the spring-retained catch at the top of the headlight unit and pull the top of the light unit forwards. Prise free the lower retainers with a screwdriver and withdraw the light (photos).

3 To remove the bulb first disconnect the terminal connector from the back of the bulb. Lift the two springs retaining the bulb in the headlamp and remove the bulb by easing it out of its location (photos).

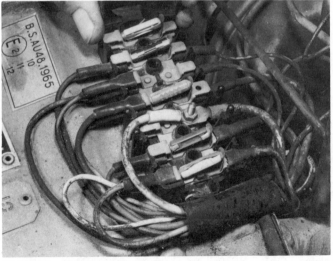

18.1 The fuse block shown with the cover removed

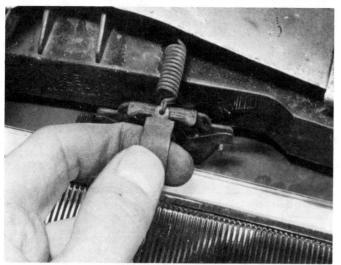

19.2a Lift spring catch clear at top of light unit ...

19.2b ... and prise free lower retainers

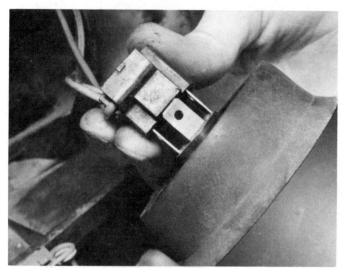

19.3a Detach the wiring terminal connector ...

19.3b ... prise free the retaining clip each side ...

19.3c ... and extract the bulb

4   Refit the new bulb following the reverse procedure but make sure that the locating notch in the bulb flange is mated with that in the headlamp. If halogen bulbs are used take care not to touch the glass with your fingers – use the protective sleeve supplied with the bulb. If by accident the glass is touched, clean it using alcohol (methylated spirit). Some bulb mountings can be adjusted for left or right-hand drive traffic. Check that the slider clip on the headlamp fitting, if applicable, is moved to the correct position.

5   Refitting the headlamp unit is the reverse of the removal procedure and provided that the adjustment screws have not been disturbed, it will not be necessary to adjust the headlamp alignment.

20 Headlights – alignment

1   Accurate alignment of the headlamps is essential for your own safety and that of other road users. Alignment is best done by a garage with the necessary optical alignment equipment; the job is quick and inexpensive.

2   Temporary adjustment can be made, if this should be necessary, using the adjustment screws provided at each headlamp. At the centre top is a single screw for vertical adjustment of the beam and at the base there are two further screws for horizontal adjustment. Adjust the beams so that, with dipped beam selected, each beam shines straight

ahead and slightly below the horizontal. Have the beams properly adjusted at the first opportunity.

3 A further adjustment is provided to permit lowering the headlamp beams when the car is heavily loaded. This loading causes the tail end to settle with the result that, even with dipped beams selected, the headlamps shine upwards causing annoyance and possibly danger to oncoming drivers. This can be corrected by using the rocking lever behind each headlamp top retaining clip. With the right-hand side of the lever (viewed from the driver's position) pressed down, the lamp is in the normal load position. When the left-hand side of the lever is depressed, the headlamp is rocked slightly down to the heavy load position.

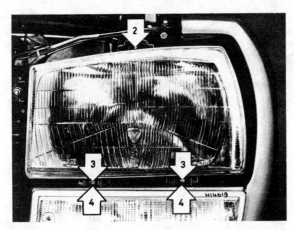

Fig. 10.9 Headlight adjustment is made by adjuster screws (Sec 20)

(2) Vertical adjustment
(3) Horizontal adjustment
(4) Lower unit retaining lug positions

21 Rear light clusters – bulb renewal

1 Unscrew and remove the lens retaining screws and then carefully pull the lens free so that the rubber seal is not distorted or broken (photos).
2 The bulbs can now be removed for renewal.
3 If renewing a bulb, be sure to replace it with one of equal rating (see Specifications). Check operation of new bulb before refitting the lens.
4 The light unit itself is secured by screws which are accessible once the lens is removed. Other types are secured by a nut on the inside of the boot panel.
5 Refit in reverse order of removal sequence.

22 Rear number plate lights – bulb removal and renewal

1 The rear number plate lights are housed in the rear bumper(s). On the single rear bumper type, remove the thumb screw underneath to withdraw the unit to enable the lens to be detached and the bulb removed for renewal. On the two section bumper type, access to the bulb(s) is obtained on removal of the lens which is secured by two screws (photos).
2 Depress and rotate the bulb to remove it.
3 Refit in the reverse order and check that the light(s) operate on completion.

23 Front side lights and direction indicators – bulb renewal

1 Unscrew and remove the lens retaining screws and then remove the lens.
2 The bulbs in the unit concerned can now be removed by pressing and twisting to release from the bayonet fixing holder (photo).

20.3 The headlamp beam load adjustment lever

21.1a The rear light lens removed for access to bulbs (Estate) ...

21.1b ... and Saloon variants

22.1a Rear number plate light with lens removed for bulb replacement (Estate model)

22.1b Rear number plate light unit removal (Saloon) ...

22.1c ... enables lens withdrawal for bulb renewal

23.2 Front side/indicator light unit lens removed for bulb renewal

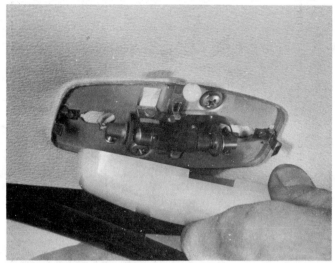

24.2 Remove lens for renewal of the festoon bulb – interior light

24.4a Remove the upper facia trim securing screws underneath ...

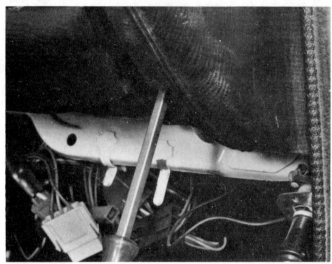

24.4b ... and at the side for ...

24.4c ... renewal of the heater/ventilation control panel light

3   Refit in the reverse order of removal renewing the lens seal if it is defective. Check the operation of the lights on completion.

24 Interior lamp bulbs and heater control panel illumination bulb – renewal

Interior light bulbs
1   The two interior lamps are mounted on the left and right-hand sides of the roof lining. To renew a bulb, first remove the lamp lens by gently prising it out of its mounting with a blunt knife, taking care not to mark or damage the roof lining.
2   The festoon type bulb is removed by easing it out of its two spring clips (photo).
3   Refitting the bulb and lens is a reversal of the removal procedure, but make sure that the bulb is firmly held in its clips; if necessary gently bend the clips inwards slightly to increase security. Test the lamp on completion.

Heater control panel illumination bulb
4   Access to this panel light is made in one of two ways. On the earlier types fitted with a 'high mounted' heater control panel, remove the upper facia trim which is secured by three screws underneath in the middle (photo) and a single screw at each end at the sides (photo).

24.5 Typical control panel light and holder removed for renewal

25.2 Rocker switch removal

25.3 Trim removal may be necessary for access to some switches

25.4 Switch knobs can be pulled free

25.8 The indicator flasher unit (typical)

25.11 The boot light switch (1) and bulbholder (2)

Pull the trim panel clear so that you can disconnect the wires to the light unit which is attached to the plastic lens strip integral with the panel within its cavity. The bulbholder and bulb can then be removed for checking or replacement. Refit in the reverse order of removal.

5   On later models where the control panel is beneath the line of the instrument panel you will need to either reach up (if possible) behind the panel to pull the bulbholder free from its control panel location or remove the panel itself. This entails pulling free the control knobs, removing any switches from the panel (or disconnecting their wires) and where necessary detaching the panel fastenings. With the panel withdrawn, the bulb and/or its holder can be removed for renewal.

6   Refit in reverse and check operation.

25 Switches – removal and refitting

1   Various types of switches are fitted to the facia panel and their removal and refitting is dependent on the switch type. Whenever a switch is to be removed the battery earth lead should first be disconnected.

2   Rocker switches are secured by plastic clips which are an integral part of the switch. To remove this type of switch you will need to reach under the panel and compress the retaining clip each side of the switch body whilst simultaneously pushing the switch outwards from the panel aperture. When it is withdrawn the switch can be detached from its wiring connector(s) as shown in the photo. Refit this switch by reconnecting the wire connector and simply press the switch into its aperture until the securing clips are heard to snap open.

3   Access to some switch types is not particularly good and it may be necessary to remove an adjacent fitting or panel/trim to achieve removal (photo).

4   With push/pull/twist type switches, pull the knob from the switch shaft to gain access to the securing nut. Unscrew the nut using a suitable box spanner (photo). With some switch types the securing nut will be on the underside of the panel. On removing the switch, detach the wiring to it. Refit in the reverse order of removal.

5   On completion check the switch concerned and any other switches or controls which may have been removed or disconnected.

Cigar lighter

6   Having disconnected the battery earth lead, remove the heater control panel quarter surround on the side of the cigar lighter. This is secured by two nuts on the underside of the facia (photo).

7   Reaching up under the control panel unscrew the cigar lighter securing nut and remove the bracket. The cigar lighter unit can then be withdrawn through its location aperture and the wires detached for full removal.

8   Refit in the reverse order to removal and check operation is satisfactory on completion.

Flasher unit switch

9   The flasher unit is located under the facia, its location depending on model. If it is not readily seen from underneath the facia assembly you will have to remove the instrument panel for access to it (photo). When accessible (and having disconnected the battery), detach its wiring connector/s and note their locations for correct refitting, then remove the unit from its fastening.

10   Refit in reverse order and check operation of indicators on completion. It should be noted that the flasher unit is delicate and therefore must be handled with care and not dropped. It is not repairable or adjustable.

Boot light switch

11   Disconnect the battery earth lead.

12   Raise the boot lid and then prise free the plastic cover from the side of the boot, just below the drain channel. The switch and the bulb are now accessible for inspection, removal and refitting (photo).

26 Steering column switches – removal and refitting

1   Disconnect the battery earth lead.

2   Remove the steering wheel as detailed in Chapter 9, Section 12.

26.3 Remove the column lower cover screws

26.4 Upper column cover securing screws

26.5a The wiper/washer switch retaining bolt and the indicator switch securing screw on later models

26.5b Note how coil spring is fitted round column – indicator switch on earlier models

3   The upper and lower column half covers can now be removed. First remove the lower cover by unscrewing the retaining screws, the number of which is dependent on model (photo).

4   To remove the upper half cover you will need to first prise free the cover to instrument panel fillet trim to gain access to the cover lower retaining screws. Remove the cover screws at the bottom and top, and lift the cover clear. Owing to the angle of the lower securing screws you may find it necessary to remove the instrument panel on some models in order to release these screws (photo).

5   To remove the switch(es) unscrew the single securing bolt or screw, detach the switch wiring, noting the connections and remove the switch concerned. On earlier models when removing the indicator switch, note how the coil spring is located around the steering column (photos).

6   Refit in the reverse order of removal and check operation of the switch(es) on completion.

27   Instrument panel and clock – removal and refitting

A methodical work procedure is necessary and careful note should be taken of such details as cable runs, location and length of fastening screws and bolts, earth connections, fitting details of individual parts and so on. Written notes and sketches are well worth making, particularly if there is likely to be a time gap between removal and refitting. Due to variations between models, and progressive modifications resulting from improvements, it is not possible to give a detailed procedure to cover all possibilities but the broad procedure which applies to the two most common types is given below.

GL type models

1   Disconnect the battery earth lead.

2   Removal of the front seats at this point will allow a relative improvement in working comfort during the subsequent operations when detaching the under facia items.

3   Remove the steering wheel as described in Chapter 9, Section 12.

4   Remove the heater control panel quarter surround trim which is secured by two nuts on the underside of the facia (photo).

5   Unbolt the upper steering column to facia fixing to enable the column to be lowered.

6   Remove the column upper cover to instrument panel fillet moulding.

7   Unscrew and remove the instrument panel securing screws underneath and then partially withdraw the panel unit sufficiently to

27.7a Remove the instrument panel securing screw each side of the column underneath the facia

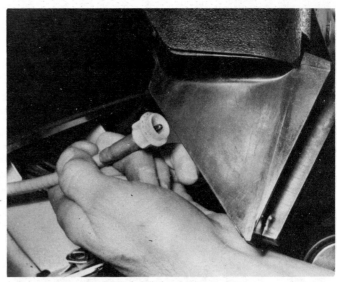

27.7b Detach the speedometer drive cable connection

27.8 Removing an instrument panel bulb

27.9a Remove the instrument panel cover screws ...

27.9b ... and prise free the catches

27.9c Do not damage the printed circuits (arrowed)

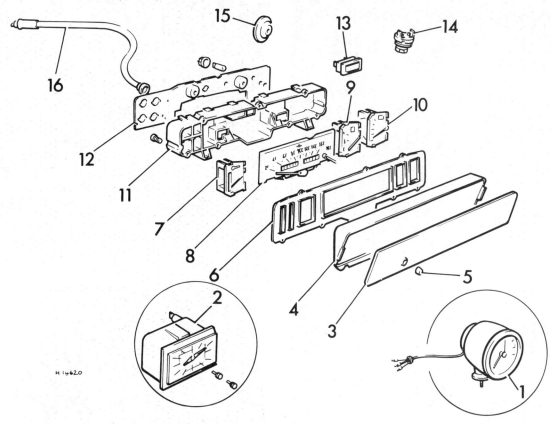

Fig. 10.10 Instrument panel assembly components – up to 1972
(Sec 27)

1	Tachometer Coupe (Cabriolet)	5	Trip recorder zeroing knob	9	Fuel gauge	13	Contacter
2	Clock	6	Frame	10	Voltmeter	14	Rheostat switch
3	Glass	7	Thermometer	11	Instrument cluster body	15	Grommet
4	Instrument cluster visor	8	Speedometer	12	Printed circuit	16	Speedometer cable

detach the speedometer cable and the wiring multi-connectors from the panel rear face. Withdraw the instrument panel (photos).

8   The instrument panel bulbs can now be removed by simply twisting and pulling the holders free (photo). The bulbs can then be removed from their holders for inspection and renewal.

9   Removal of the instrument units can be achieved after separating the outer panel cover from the unit. To do this remove the retaining screws and prise free the plastic catches, but take care as the unit is separated not to break the printed circuits (photos).

10 Reassembly and refitting of this instrument panel is a reversal of the removal procedure. Take care to ensure that the wiring connections are securely made. Attach these and the speedometer cable prior to fully inserting the panel unit into position. Check the operation of the various instruments on completion.

Other models

11 Disconnect the battery earth lead.

12 Prise free the facia moulding on the right-hand side then remove it to the right disengaging its left-hand end tag, as shown (photo).

13 Prise free the fillet moulding directly in front of and between the steering column upper cover and the instrument panel (photo).

14 Unscrew and remove the two instrument panel securing screws from underneath the facia panel assembly (photo). You will have to unclip and remove the soundproofing panel first for access to these screws.

15 The instrument panel can now be partially withdrawn to enable the speedometer cable and the electrical lead multi-connectors to its rear face to be detached. The panel can then be fully withdrawn (photo).

27.12 Remove facia moulding

27.13 Prise free the fillet moulding

27.15 Withdraw the instrument panel – early type shown

27.16 Bulbholder removal from early type instrument panel rear face

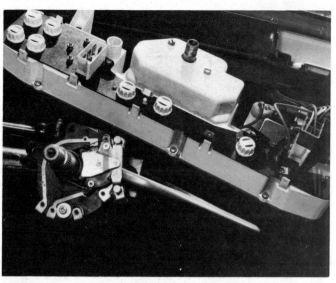

27.17 Instrument panel rear face showing bulb locations and assembly securing screws

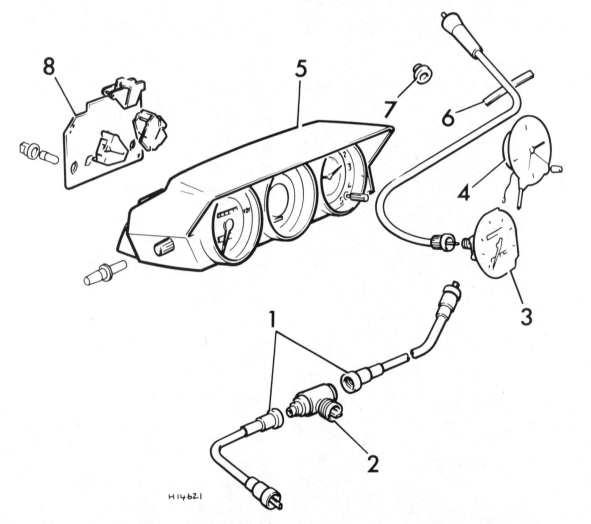

H14621

Fig. 10.11 Instrument panel assembly components from 1972 (typical) (Sec 27)

1 Speedometer cable	3 Speedometer	5 Instrument cluster	7 Grommet
2 Power take-off	4 Clock	6 Strap	8 Gauge assembly and printed circuit

27.19 Remove clock from facia panel ...

27.20 ... and then detach the wires or bulbholder

28.2 Windscreen wiper blade removal from arm

29.2 Windscreen wiper arm securing nut

16 Untwist and remove the bulbholders for bulb checking and renewal (photo).

17 To dismantle the panel you will need to remove the surround retaining screws. When separating, take care not to damage any of the circuits or the instruments themselves (photo).

18 Reassembly and refitting of the instrument panel is a reversal of the removal procedure. Check that all wiring connections are securely made and check the circuits and instruments for satisfctory operation on completion.

Clock

19 To remove the clock unit prise free with a thin blade between the clock surround and facia to withdraw the unit. If possible reach behind the clock to push it free simultaneously (photo).

20 Disconnect the wire and bulbholder or wire at holder connector, to completely remove clock or to change the bulb (photo).

21 Refit in reverse order of removal.

28 Windscreen wiper blades – removal and refitting

1 The windscreen wiper blades should be frequently checked for

deterioration and as soon as they fail to wipe the windscreen effectively without leaving smears they should be renewed. Wipe the blades clean with a damp cloth occasionally to help prolong their life.

2 To remove a blade assembly, lift the wiper arm off the windscreen and squeeze the clip in the assembly hinge fitting (photo). Slide the blade assembly off its arm.

3 Refitting a wiper blade assembly is the reverse of the removal procedure. Ensure that the clip is fitting correctly.

29 Windscreen wiper arms – removal and refitting

1 Before removing a wiper arm, turn the windscreen wiper switch on and off to ensure that the arms are in their normal parked position parallel with the bottom edge of the windscreen.

2 Lift the hinged cap at the bottom end of the wiper arm and remove the arm retaining nut. Lift the arm fully to release its catch and withdraw it from the drive spindle (photo).

3 Refitting a wiper arm is the reverse of the removal procedure. Make sure that the wiper blades are parallel with the bottom edge of the windscreen on refitting and operate the wipers on completion to check that their sweep is correct. (Wet the windscreen first if it is dry to avoid damage to the wiper blades).

30 Windscreen wiper mechanism – fault diagnosis and rectification

1   Should the windscreen wipers fail or work very slowly, check the electrical connector to the motor for security and check the wiring for breakage, loss of insulation which could cause a short-circuit, and for adequate earthing. If all appears in order, check the motor current consumption by connecting an ammeter into the circuit and turning on the wiper switch. Current flow should not exceed 5 amps. The ignition switch and wiper switch must be on, of course.
2   If no current is available at the motor, check fuse No 4 by switching on the heater fan (ignition on) which will confirm the fuse as fit or otherwise. If satisfactory use a 12 volt test lamp and, by reference to the wiring diagrams, trace the current supply from the fuse to the motor connection.
3   Should the wiper motor take a very high current, check the wiper arms and linkages for free movement; if in order the motor will have to be removed for further investigations. Similarly if the motor takes a very low current and the battery is fully charged, the motor will have to be removed.

31 Windscreen wiper mechanism – removal and refitting

1   Disconnect the battery earth terminal and remove the windscreen wiper arms as described in Section 29.
2   Remove the five scuttle air intake grille panel retaining screws and lift the panel clear for access to the motor and operating arms (photo).
3   To remove the motor unit, unscrew the linkage support plate retaining bolts (photo).
4   Remove the motor cover.
5   Detach the windscreen washer tubes and the motor wires at the connectors and then lift the motor unit out (photo).
6   To detach the motor from the linkage support plate, prise free the pivot snap-ring (photo) and unscrew the three motor retaining bolts with star washers.
7   Refitting the motor assembly to the linkage mechanism is essentially the reverse of the removal procedure. Similarly, refitting the wiper mechanism to the car is also the reverse of the removal procedure, but the following points should be noted:

   (a) Lubricate all moving parts sparingly before installation
   (b) Reconnect the earth wire to the plate if it was disconnected (photo)
   (c) Ensure that the wires and washer hoses are correctly fitted and secure before refitting the grille
   (d) Check operation of motor before fitting the wiper arms then when they are in position ensure that they park correctly to complete

32 Windscreen washer reservoir and pump unit

1   Both the windscreen washer reservoir and its pump unit are housed within the right-hand wing cavity and access to them is obtained after removing the headlight unit on that side – see Section 19 (photo).
2   The reservoir is secured by means of a strap, the fastening bolt of which is attached to the wing valance, access being from the top (photo). If removing the reservoir, syphon off any remaining washer fluid, detach the fastening strap and the connecting hose from the pump unit. Withdraw the unit through the headlight aperture.
3   To remove the pump unit, detach the wire connector, and the connecting hose to the reservoir. Plug the hose to prevent leakage. Detach and remove the pump from the wing valance.
4   Refitting of both reservoir and pump unit is a reversal of the removal process. Check operation on completion, but prior to refitting the headlight unit.
5   Malfunction is usually due to blocked spray nozzles. If the pump can be heard running and, with fluid in the reservoir, there is no spray from the nozzles, they should be cleared with a piece of thin wire or a pin. Other causes of failure to spray are blocked, kinked or disconnected pipes. In winter failure may be due to water freezing in the pipes or in the reservoir; use of a proprietary windscreen washer antifreeze (see below) will prevent this problem.

31.2 Intake grille retaining bolt and washer

31.3 Linkage support plate bolt removal

31.5 Windscreen wiper motor location – note the washer tubes

31.6 The wiper motor to linkage support plate retaining bolts

31.7(b) Earth wire location under washer retaining bracket nut

32.1 Windscreen washer reservoir and pump unit location in the right-hand wing valance cavity

32.2 Reservoir strap securing bolt

33.1 The twin horns (shown with radiator removed)

6   Should the pump fail to run when switched on, and the wipers confirm that power is available, gain access to the pump and unplug the electrical connection. Connect a 12V test bulb across the electrical connection. Connect a 12V test bulb across the feed wire and the earth wire and check for power availability. If the bulb lights then the pump motor must be renewed. If the bulb fails to light, trace the circuit back, using the wiring diagrams and the test bulb, until the cause of the failure is located.

Note: *Never use standad cooling system antifreeze in the washer system as the car paintwork could be damaged and, in any case, the windscreen will not be cleaned. Special windscreen washer additives to aid windscreen cleaning and to prevent freezing in winter are available from most garages and accessory shops.*

33 Horns

1   Twin horns are fitted and they are mounted between the front grille and the radiator, (photo). They are accessible once the grille is removed.
2   If the horns fail to operate disconnect the supply lead and, using a 12V test lamp, check that power is available. If not, trace the cause using the wiring diagrams and the test lamp.

3   If the horns fail to operate with a confirmed power supply, check that they have a good earth to the structure. If this is sound then the defect must be in the horns although it is unlikely for both to fail at the same time.

4   Substitution of a known satisfactory horn will confirm the circuit. Defective horns will have to be renewed as they are not adjustable or repairable.

34 Radios and tape players – fitting (general)

A radio or tape player can be an expensive item to buy and will only give its best performance if fitted properly. It is useless to expect concert hall performance from a unit that is suspended from the dash panel on string with its speaker resting on the back seat or parcel shelf! If you do not wish to do the installation yourself there are many in-car entertainment specialists who can do the fitting for you.

Make sure the unit purchased is of the same polarity as the car and ensure that units with adjustable polarity are correctly set before commencing installation.

It is difficult to given specific information with regard to fitting, as final positioning of the speakers and aerial is entirely a matter of personal preference. However, the following paragraphs give guidelines to follow, which are relevant to all installations.

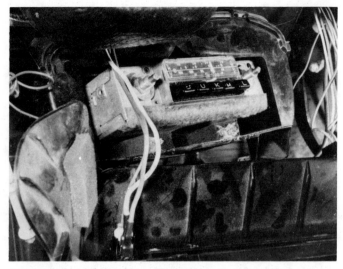

34.0 Radio location aperture – GL Estate

Radios

Most radios are a standardised size of 7 inches wide, by 2 inches deep – this ensures that they will fit into the radio aperture provided in most cars. The Peugeot 304 is equipped to acept a radio in the console directly beneath the heater/ventilator control panel but your radio might need an adaptor mounting plate for it to be fitted. It would be best to consult a dealer in this respect if you are in any doubt. The set must be securely fitted and properly earthed.

Use the radio manufacturer's instructions when wiring the radio into the car's electrical system. The power supply should come from an accessories feed, that is, one which is energised when the ignition switch is turned to the A position. Fuse No 4 supplies this circuit but it is rated at 15 amps and, to provide adequate protection for the radio, you must fit an in-line fuse in the power supply lead rated at the value recommended by the set manufacturer, usually about 2 amps.

The type of aerial used, and its fitted position, is a matter of personal preference. In general the taller the aerial, the better the reception. It is best to fit a fully retractable aerial – especially if a mechanical car-wash is used or if you live in an area where cars tend to be vandalised. In this respect electrical aerials which are raised and lowered automatically when switching the radio on or off are convenient, but more likely to give trouble than the manual type.

When choosing a site for the aerial the following points should be considered:

(a)   The aerial lead should be as short as possible – this means that the aerial should be mounted at the front of the car
(b)   The aerial must be mounted as far away from the distributor and HT leads as possible
(c)   The part of the aerial which protrudes beneath the mounting point must not foul the roadwheels, or anything else
(d)   If possible the aerial should be positioned so that the coaxial lead does not have to be routed through the engine compartment
(e)   The plane of the panel on which the aerial is mounted should not be so steeply angled that the aerial cannot be mounted vertically (in relation to the 'end-on' aspect of the car). Most aerials have a small amount of adjustment available

Having decided on a mounting position, a relatively large hole will have to be made in the panel. The exact size of the hole will depend upon the specific aerial being fitted, although, generally, the hole required is of $\frac{3}{4}$ inch (19 mm) diameter. Try to get hold of a tank-cutter of the relevant diameter as this is the best tool for making holes in sheet metal. This tool needs a small diameter pilot hole drilled through the panel through which the tool clamping bolt is inserted. To avoid slipping with the drill and scratching the car finish, stick a piece of adhesive tape over the spot you wish to drill and drill through the tape – it can be removed after you have made the hole. You can also cut the hole by drilling a hole and filing to size with a round or half-round file, but this takes longer and requires more energy. When the hole has

been made the raw edges should be de-burred with a smooth file and then treated with an anti-corrosion preparation to prevent rusting.

Fit the aerial according to the manufacturer's instructions. If the aerial is very tall, or if it protrudes beneath the mounting panel for some way, it is worth considering fitting a stay between the aerial and the vehicle under the panel. This stay or brace can be made up from slotted metal strip available in most accessory shops. The stay must be securely bolted or screwed in place for it to be of any use. For best reception it is advisable to fit an earth lead between the aerial and the vehicle frame – this is essential if you have made a good job of anti-corrosion treatment when making the hole as the aerial will be insulated from earth.

It will probably be necessary to drill one or two holes through bodywork panels in order to feed the aerial lead into the interior of the car. Where this is the case ensure that the holes are fitted with rubber grommets to protect the cable, and to stop possible entry of water.

The Peugeot-installed radio available as an optional extra on the 304 has a wing or roof-mounted aerial. The roof type aerial is located in the centre front end of the roof with the aerial lead running down the windscreen pillar to the radio console.

If you aim to fit stereo equipment, the two speakers will probably be 'pod' types which are best located on the shelf behind the rear seat. The pads can be secured to the mounting panel with self-tapping screws.

When connecting a rear-mounted speaker to the radio, the wires should be routed through the vehicle beneath the carpets or floor mats – preferably the middle, or along the side of the floorpan, where they will not be trodden on by passengers. Make the relevant connections as directed by the radio manufacturer.

By now you will have several yards of additional wiring in the car, use PVC tape to secure this wiring out of harm's way. Do not leave electrical leads dangling. Ensure that all new electrical connections are properly made (wires twisted together will not do) and completely secure.

The radio should now be working, but before you pack away your tools it will be necessary to 'trim' the radio to the aerial. If specific instructions are not provided by the radio manufacturer, proceed as follows. Find a station with a low signal strength on the medium-wave band, slowly turn the trim screw of the radio in, or out, until the loudest reception of the selected station is obtained – the set is then trimmed to the aerial.

Tape players

Fitting instructions for both cartridge and cassette stereo tape players are the same and in general the same rules apply as when fitting a radio. Tape players are not usually prone to electrical interference like radio – although it can occur – so positioning is not so critical. If possible the player should be mounted on an 'even-keel'. Also, it must be possible for a driver wearing a seat belt to reach the unit in order to change or turn over tapes.

For the best results from speakers designed to be recessed into a panel, mount them so that the back of the speaker protrudes into an enclosed chamber within the car (eg door interiors or the boot cavity).

To fit recessed type speakers in the front doors first check that there is sufficient room to mount a speaker in each door without fouling the latch or window winding mechanism. Hold the speaker against the skin of the door, and draw a line around the periphery of the speaker. With the speaker removed draw a second 'cutting' line, within the first, to allow enough room for the entry of the speaker back, but at the same time providing a broad seat for the speaker flange. When you are sure that the cutting line is correct, drill a series of holes around its periphery. Pass a hacksaw blade through one of the holes and then cut through the metal between the holes until the centre section of the panel falls out.

Deburr the edges of the hole and then paint the raw metal to prevent corrosion. Cut a corresponding hole in the door trim panel – ensuring that it will be completely covered by the speaker grille. Now drill a hole in the door edge and a corresponding hole in the door surround. These holes are to feed the speaker leads through – so fit grommets. Pass the speaker leads through the door trim, door skin and out through the holes in the side of the door and door surround. Refit the door trim panel and then secure the speaker to the door using self-tapping screws. **Note:** *If the speaker is fitted with a shield to prevent water dripping on it, ensure that this shield is at the top.*

Pod type speakers can be fastened to the shelf behind the rear seat, or anywhere else offering a corresponding mounting point on each side of the car. If the pod speakers are mounted on each side of the shelf behind the rear seat, it is a good idea to drill several large diamater holes through to the boot cavity beneath each speaker – this will improve the sound reproduction. Pod speakers sometimes offer a better reproduction quality if they face the rear window – which then acts as a reflector – so it is worthwhile to do a little experimenting before finally fixing the speaker.

35 Radios and tape players – suppression of interference (general)

To eliminate buzzes and other unwanted noises costs very little and is not as difficult as sometimes thought. With a modicum of common sense and patience and following the instructions in the following paragraphs, interference can be virtually eliminated.

The first cause for concern is the generator. The noise this makes over the radio is like an electric mixer and the noise speeds up when you rev up (if you wish to prove the point, you can remove the drivebelt and try it). The remedy for this is simple; connect a 1.9mF – 3.0mF capacitor between earth, probably the bolt that holds down the generator base, and the *large* terminal on the alternator to which are connected wires 1 and 4. This is most important for if you connect it to the small terminal, you will probably damage the generator permanently.

A second common cause of electrical interference is the ignition system. Here a 1.0mF capacitor must be connected between earth and the 'SW' or '+' terminal on the coil. This may stop the tick-tick-tick sound that comes over the speaker. Next comes the spark itself.

The Peugeot 304 is fitted with suppressed ignition plug leads and you should get no interference from that source, but if the leads have been renewed at some time with non-standard leads this may not apply.

There are several ways of curing interference from the ignition HT system. One is to use carbon film HT leads but these have a tendency to snap inside and you don't know then why you are firing on only half your cylinders. So the second, and more successful method is to use resistive spark plug caps of about 10 000 ohm to 15 000 ohm resistance. If, due to lack of room, these cannot be used, an alternative is to use 'in-line' suppressors – if the interference is not too bad, you may get away with only one suppressor in the coil-to-distributor line.

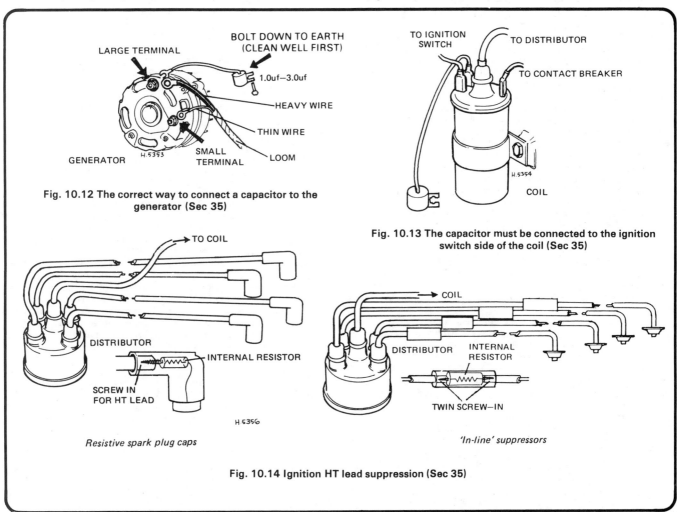

Fig. 10.12 The correct way to connect a capacitor to the generator (Sec 35)

Fig. 10.13 The capacitor must be connected to the ignition switch side of the coil (Sec 35)

Resistive spark plug caps

'In-line' suppressors

Fig. 10.14 Ignition HT lead suppression (Sec 35)

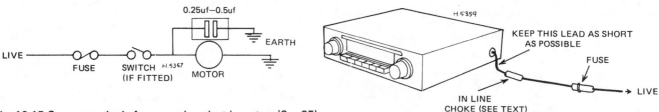

Fig. 10.15 Correct method of suppressing electric motors (Sec 35)

Fig. 10.16 An in-line choke should be fitted into the line supply lead as close to the unit as possible (Sec 35)

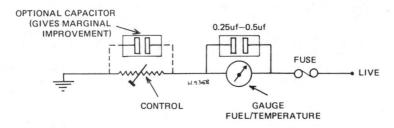

Fig. 10.17 Method of suppressing gauges and their control units (Sec 35)

If the interference does continue (a 'clacking' noise) then doctor all HT leads.

At this stage it is advisable to check that the radio is well earthed, also the aerial, and to see that the aerial plug is pushed well into the set and that the radio is properly trimmed (see preceding Section). In addition, check that the wire which supplies the power to the set is as short as possible and does not wander all over the car.

At this point the more usual causes of interference have been suppressed. If the problem still exists, a look at the causes of interference may help to pinpoint the component generating the stray electrical discharges.

The radio picks up electromagnetic waves in the air; now some are made by radio stations and other broadcasters and some, not wanted, are made by the car. The home made signals are produced by stray electrical discharges floating around the car. Common producers of these signals are electric motors; ie, the windscreen wipers, electric screen washers, electric window winders, heater fan or an electric aerial if fitted. Other sources of interference are flashing turn signals, and instruments. The remedy for these cases is shown in Fig. 10.15 for an electric motor whose interference is not too bad and Fig. 10.16 for instrument suppression. Turn signals are not normally suppressed. In recent years, radio manufacturers have included in the line (live) of the radio, in addition to the fuse, an 'in-line' choke. If your installation lacks one of these, put one in as shown in Fig. 10.17.

All the foregoing components are available from radio shops or accessory shops. For a transistor radio, a 2A choke should be adequate. If you have an electric clock fitted this can be suppressed by connecting a 0.5mF capacitor directly across it as shown for a motor in Fig. 10.18.

If, after all this, you are still experiencing radio interference, first assess how bad it is, for the human ear can filter out unobtrusive unwanted noises quite easily. But if you are still adamant about eradicating the noise, then continue.

As a first step, a few 'experts' seem to favour a screen between the radio and the engine. This is OK as far as it goes, literally! – for the whole set is screened and if interference can get past that then a small piece of aluminium is not going to stop it.

A more sensible way of screening is to discover if interference is coming down the wires. First, take the live lead; interference can get between the set and the choke (hence the reason for keeping the wires short). One remedy here is to screen the wire and this is done by buying screened wire and fitting that. The loudspeaker lead could be screened also to prevent 'pick-up' getting back to the radio – although this in unlikely.

Without doubt, the worst source of radio interference comes from the ignition HT leads, even if they have been suppressed. The ideal

way of suppressing these is to slide screening tubes over the leads themselves. As this is impractical, we can place an aluminium shield over the majority of the lead areas. In a vee- or twin-cam engine, this is relatively easy but for a straight engine the results are not particularly good.

Now for the really difficult cases, here are a few tips to try out. Where metal comes into contact with metal, an electrical disturbance is caused which is why good clean connections are essential. To remove interference due to overlapping or butting panels you must bridge the join with a wise braided earth strap. The most common moving parts that could create noise and should be strapped are, in order of importance:

(1) Silencer-to-frame
(b) Exhaust pipe-to-engine block and frame
(c) Air cleaner-to-frame
(d) Front and rear bumpers-to-frame
(e) Steering column-to-frame
(f) Bonnet or boot lids-to-frame

These faults are most pronounced when (1) the engine is idling, (2) labouring under load. Although the moving parts are readily connected with nuts, bolts, etc, these do tend to rust and corrode, thus creating a high resistance interference source.

In conclusion, it is pointed out that it is relatively easy, and therefore cheap, to eliminate 95 per cent of all noises, but to eliminate the final 5 per cent is time and money consuming. It is up to the individual to decide if it is worth it. Please remember also, that you will not get concert hall performance from a cheap radio.

Finally at the beginning of this Section are mentioned tape players; these are not usually affected by interference but in a very bad case, the best remedies are the first three suggestions plus using a 3 – 5 amp choke in the 'live' line and in difficult cases screen the live and speaker wires.

Note: *If your car is fitted with electronic ignition, then it is not recommended that either the spark plug resistors of the ignition coil capacitor be fitted as these may damage the system. Most electronic ignition units have built-in suppression and should, therefore, not cause interference.*

36 Heater unit – removal and refitting

Before deciding that the heater unit has to be removed owing to a malfunction or unsatisfactory performance, a check can be made of

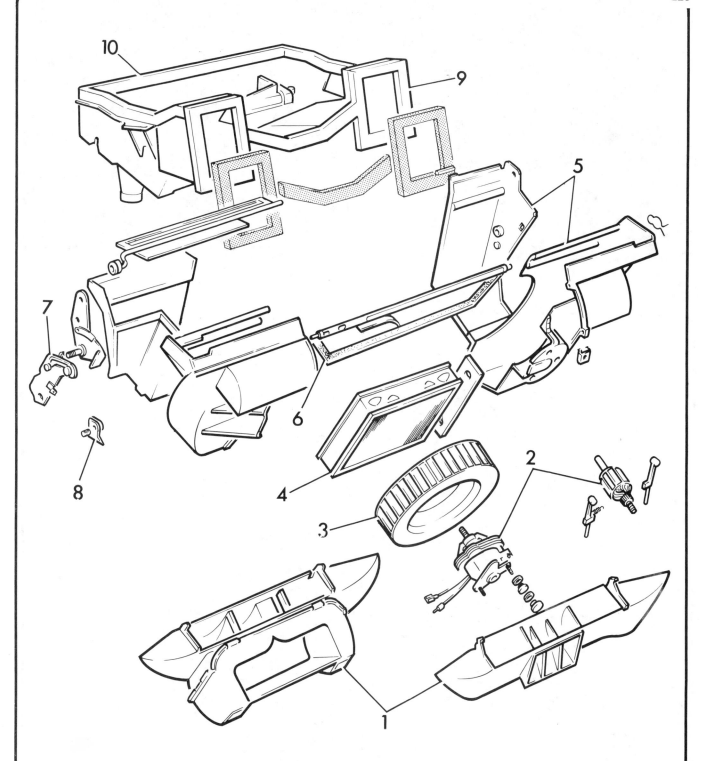

Fig. 10.18 The heater unit components (Sec 36)

1 Air diffuser (two types)
2 Fan motor assembly
3 Blower fan
4 Heater matrix
5 Housing assembly
6 Air intake flap
7 Cam lever
8 Air distribution shutter
   quadrant
9 Dash cowl water separator
10 Cowl

36.0 The heater coolant thermostat unit

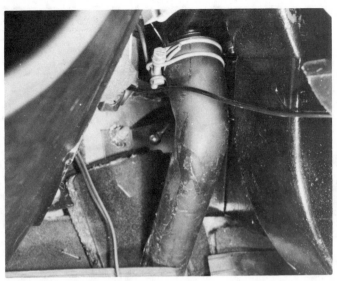

36.4 Detach the heater hoses

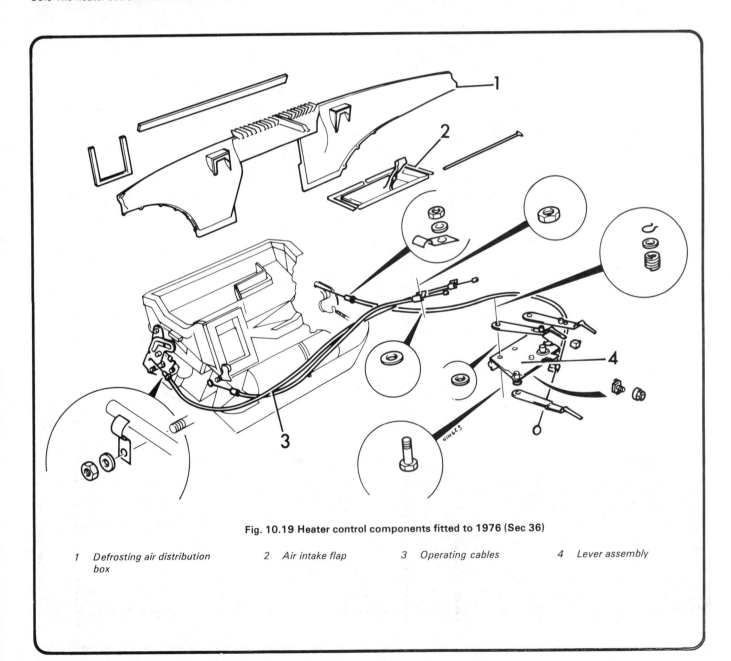

Fig. 10.19 Heater control components fitted to 1976 (Sec 36)

1   Defrosting air distribution
    box

2   Air intake flap

3   Operating cables

4   Lever assembly

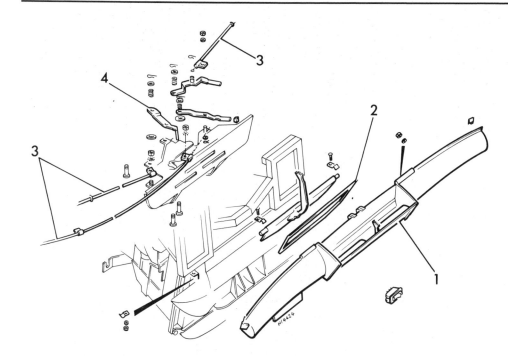

Fig. 10.20 Heater control components fitted from 1976 (Sec 36)

1   Defrosting air distribution box
2   Air intake flap
3   Operating cables
4   Lever assembly

the thermostatic valve unit (photo). You will have to drain the cooling system to remove it, but this will be necessary anyway should the heater unit assembly have to be removed. If on removal the thermostat is found to be operational then the heater unit must be at fault and can be removed as follows.

1   Disconnect the battery earth lead and then drain the cooling system with the heater valve open. Refer to Chapter 2 for details.

2   Access to the heater unit and its controls is dependent on the model and the type of facia and trim fittings. Whilst with some models it is not necessary to remove very much in the way of trim and associated fittings, models like the GL Estate require the radio control panel and its inner support panel to be removed.

3   The heater and ventilation control cables will also have to be disconnected and access depending on model can be very restricted and again necessitate the removal of the control panel itself and/or associated fittings. Details are given elsewhere in this Chapter.

4   The heater unit itself is secured by two nuts each side. When these nuts are removed, disconnect the heater/ventilation ducts, the coolant supply and return hoses (photo). Check that any associated fittings, wiring and trim are detached and out of the way before removing the heater unit.

5   Once removed the heater unit can be cleaned externally and then dismantled for inspection. The most likely causes of trouble will be either the blower motor or the matrix. Access to both requires at least partial dismantling of the unit.

6   As with the radiator, repair to the matrix is best entrusted to a specialist or the unit simply renewed.

7   If the blower motor is malfunctioning it can be dismantled to

inspect the wiring, brushes and commutator. If any parts are in need of renewal it is most unlikely that they will be readily available and you may have to renew the motor complete. Alternatively an automotive electrician may be able to undertake repairs to it, but the cost may well equal that of a new unit.

8   Reassembly and refitting is a reversal of the removal procedure. Ensure that all electrical and coolant hose connections are securely made. On completion top up the cooling system and run the engine up to its normal operating temperature. Check that the heater and ventilation controls are operating satisfactorily and that there are no signs of leaks from the intake and outlet hoses.

37 Heater/ventilation control panel (GL models) – removal and refitting

1   Disconnect the battery earth lead.

2   Disconnect the windscreen wiper switch, the choke control and the cigar lighter. Remove corner trim if necessary for rear access (photo).

3   Prise free the heater and ventilation control knobs (photo).

4   The heater/ventilator control panel can now be detached and withdrawn. The panel light and bulbholder can be removed by reading upwards from underneath the panel and simply pulling it free.

5   Refit in the reverse order to removal. Check that all controls and switches function on completion.

37.2 Disconnect the control switches

37.3 Prise the knobs free

37.4 Removing the ventilation/heater control facia panel

Fault diagnosis – electrical system

Symptom	Reason(s)
Starter motor fails to turn engine	Battery discharged Battery connections loose or corroded Starter motor connections, or earth straps, loose or broken Solenoid wiring loose or broken Ignition/starter switch defective Solenoid defective Starter motor defective
Starter motor turns engine slowly	Battery discharged Battery connections loose or corroded Starter motor connections, or earth straps, loose or damaged Starter motor defective
Starter motor spins without turning engine	Pinion actuating lever maladjusted Starter pinion or ring gear damaged
Starter motor noisy or rough on engagement	Mounting bolts loose Starter pinion or ring gear damaged
Battery will not hold charge	Battery connections loose or corroded Electrolyte level low Dynamo/alternator drivebelt slack Dynamo/alternator connections loose Short-circuit draining battery (isolate battery and see if charge retained) Battery defective internally Dynamo/alternator or voltage regulator defective
Ignition (no-charge) warning light stays on with engine running	Dynamo/alternator drivebelt slack or broken Dynamo/alternator or voltage regulator defective
Ignition (no-charge) warning light fails to come on	Light bulb blown Bulbholder or printed circuit damaged Wiring disconnected or broken Dynamo/alternator or voltage regulator defective
Fuel and/or temperature gauges give no reading	Wiring disconnected or broken No 4 fuse blown (other systems on that fuse will also fail) Gauge or sender unit faulty (earth wire at sender with ignition on – full gauge reading indicates defective sender, no reading indicates defective gauge or wiring)
Fuel or temperature gauges read maximum continuously	Lead shorting to earth Sender unit defective
Lights fail to come on	Bulb(s) blown Fuse blown (check other circuits on same fuse) Wiring disconnected or broken Earth fixing loose or corroded Switch defective
Lights very dim	Battery discharged Connections or earth mounting loose or corroded Incorrect wattage bulb fitted Bulb decayed with age Reflector or glass tarnished or dirty (if applicable)
Direction indicators fail to work	Bulb blown (failure, or excessively rapid operation, on one side only) Flasher unit disconnected, defective or inadequately earthed (failure on both sides) Direction indicator switch defective
Electrical component failure – general	Fuse blown (check other components served by same fuse) Wire broken or disconnected Multi-pin connector unplugged or pin(s) corroded Switch defective Earth return defective (wire broken, component mounting loose or corroded)

For windscreen wiper or horn faults refer to Sections 30 or 33 respectively

Key to wiring diagram (Fig. 10.21)

NB Left-hand drive shown

A to Z	Connectors	J.R.	Fuel gauge
A.C.	Cigar lighter	J.Tr.	Fuel gauge tank unit
A.C.S.	Seat belt buzzer		
AI.	Distributor with condenser	L.	Sidelight
Alt.	Alternator	L.C.	Heated rear window
Amp.	Ammeter	L.E.	Instrument panel light
A.T.C.	Buzzer (ignition key indicator)	L.V.D.	Right-hand window winder motor
AV.	Horn	L.V.G.	Left-hand window winder motor
Bie.	Battery	M.	Earth
Bo.	Ignition coil	Ma.	Headlight flasher control
Bo.P.	Preheater plug	M.C.A.	Brake power assistance pressure switch
Br.	Connecting terminal	M.C.E.	Fuel pressure switch
		M.C.F.	Braking system monitoring pressure switch
C.A.	Horn switch	M.C.H.	Oil pressure switch
Cap.P.	Sensor	Mo.	Clock
C.C.E.	Solenoid valve control case		
C.Cli.	Direction indicator flasher unit	P.B.	Inspection light plug
C.E.V./L.V.	Windscreen wiper/windscreen washer switch	P.E.	Fuel pump
Cli.	Direction indicator	P.E.V.	Windscreen wiper pedal switch
Com.	Lighting switch	P.F.	Brake pad
Conac.	Scuttle mounted twin switch	Pl.	Interior light with switch
Cor.	Relay case	Pl.2	Rear interior light (derived versions)
Co.R	Regulator condenser	Pl.D.	Right-hand interior light
Coup.	Coupling	Pl.G.	Left-hand interior light
Cr.	Connector	P.L.V.	Windscreen washer pump
C.R.	Idling cut-out	Pl.R.	Relay plate
C.S.	Diesel engine cut-out control	Pog.	Gear shift lever with built-in switch
C.T.	Rev counter	P.R.	Reversing light
C.T.P.	Preheater warning light switch	Pr.	Headlight
		Pr.C.	Full beam/dipped beam headlight
Dem	Solenoid type starter	Pr.H.	Halogen headlight
DIR.AV.	Horn and direction indicator switch	Pr.R.	Full beam headlight
Dyn	Dynamo	P.T.	Water temperature pick-up
E.C.	Boot lid	R.A.E.V.	Alternator and windscreen wiper relay
E/Ce.	Ashtray light	R.A.L.	Headlight flasher relay
E.Cl.	Heater lighting	R.A.P.	Anti-pollution system relay
E.Co.	Control lighting	R.Bie	Battery switch
E.I.	Interior lighting	R.C.S.	Seat belt relay
E.I.D.	Right-hand interior light	R.D.	Starter relay
E.I.G.	Left-hand interior light	Reg.	Regulator
E.P.B.D.	Right-hand fascia panel light	R.E.V.	Windscreen wiper relay
E.P.B.G.	Left-hand fascia panel light	R.F.E.V.	Windscreen wiper fixed relay
E.P.P.	Number plate light	Rh.	Instrument panel lighting rheostat
E.V.	Windscreen wipers	Rh.Co.	Control lighting rheostat
E.Va.	Solenoid valve	Rh.V.Cl.	Heater fan rheostat
E.V.P.	Glove compartment light	R.L.C.	Heated rear window relay
		R.L.F.	Brake fluid reservoir
F.(n)	Fuse	R.P.	Preheater relay
F.L.	Sidelights	R.Ph.	Headlight relay
F.P.	Door mounted lights	R.Pr.	Spotlight relay
F.Pr.	Headlight fuse	R.T.	Warning light resistance
F.R.	Side mounted direction indicator repeater	R.V.E.	Electric fan relay
F.S.	Parking light		
		S.	Stop light
Gov.	Governor		
		T.	Windscreen wiper timer
H.E.	Oil pressure and water temperature warning light	T.C.	Charge/discharge warning light
		T. Cli.	Direction indicator repeater light
I.A.	Davauto switch or Neiman steering lock	T.C.S.	Seat belt warning light
I.A.D.	Ignition, steering lock and starter switch	T.D.	Hazard warning flasher repeater
I.C.F.	Brake warning light switch	Te.E.	Water temperature warning light
I.Cli.	Direction indicator switch	T.E.	Fuel pressure warning light
I.C.P.	Pressure drop indicator	T.H.	Oil pressure warning light
I.C.S.	Seat belt switch	Th.E.	Water temperature indicator
I.D.	Hazard warning light switch	Th.T.	Water temperature switch
I.E.C.	Boot light switch	Th.V.D.	Electro-magnetic fan temperature
I.E.V.	Windscreen wiper switch	Th.V.D.E.	Electro-magnetic fan temperature switch on cooling system
I.E.V./L.V.	Windscreen wiper/windscreen washer control switch	Th.V.D.H.	Electro-magnetic fan temperature switch on lubrication system
I.E.V.P.	Glove compartment light switch	Th.V.E.	Electric fan temperature switch
I.F.M.	Handbrake switch	T.L.	Sidelight warning light
I.F.S.	Parking light switch	T.L.C.	Heated rear window warning light
I.L.C.	Heated rear window switch	T.Ph	Headlight warning light
I.L.V.D.	Right-hand window winder switch	T.P.	Preheater warning light
I.L.V.G.	Left-hand window winder switch	T.S.	Choke warning light
I.P.	Door switch	T.S.F.	Brake safety warning light
I.P.AV.	Front door switch	T.V.	Gear shift gate
I.P.AR.	Rear door switch		
I.P.D.	Starter preheater switch	V.Cl.	Heater/ventilator fan
I.P.M.	Neutral switch	V.Cl.C.	Additional heater/ventilator fan
I.P.P.	Passenger presence switch	V.D.	Electro-magnetic fan
I.P.R.	Reversing light switch	V.E.	Electric fan
I.S.	Stop light switch	+ a.c.	Feed after ignition switch
I.S.D.	Starter safety cut-out	+ p.	Permanent feed
I.T.S	Choke warning light switch		
I.V.	Rear flap switch		
I.V.Cl.	Heater/ventilator fan switch		
I.V.Cl.C	Additional heater/ventilator fan switch		

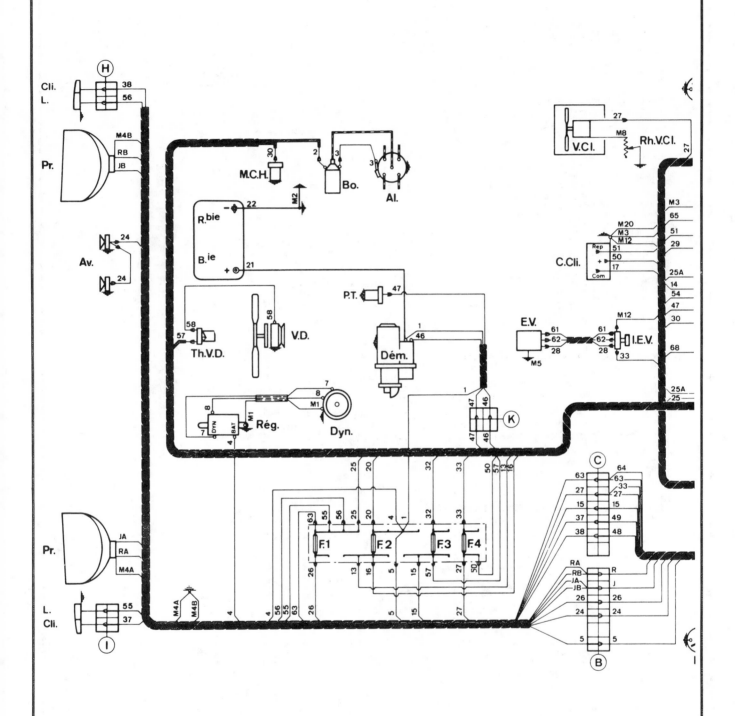

Fig. 10.21 Wiring diagram – 304 Saloon up to serial number 304 A01-3 084 000 (July 1970)

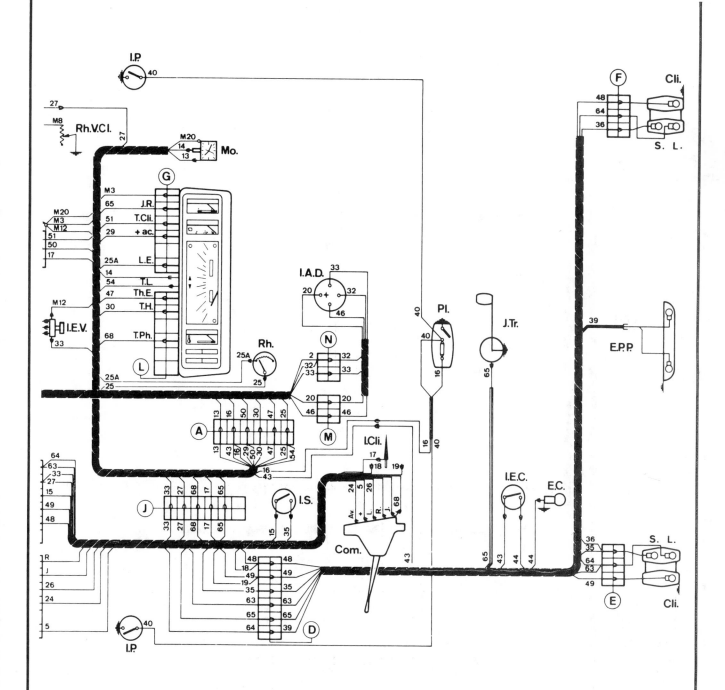

NOTE – *Wire* **50** *is connected since March 1970 on fuse* **F4**
(with lead **27***) instead of* **F3**

Fig. 10.21 Wiring diagram – 304 Saloon up to serial number 304 A01-3 084 000 (July 1970) (continued)

304 A01 – From 3 084 001 to 3 143 544

304 D01 – From the beginning of series up to 3 143 487

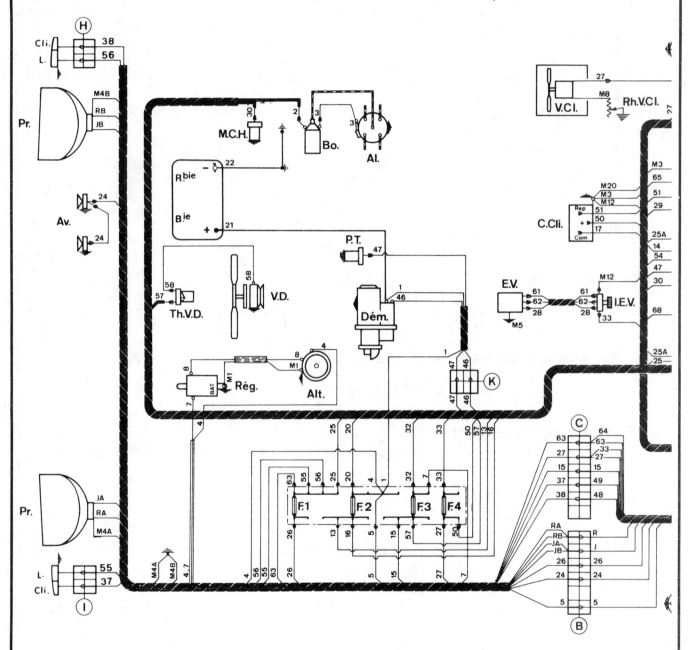

Fig. 10.22 Wiring diagram – Saloon and Estate from July 1970 to January 1971
(For coding refer to Figure 10.21 key)

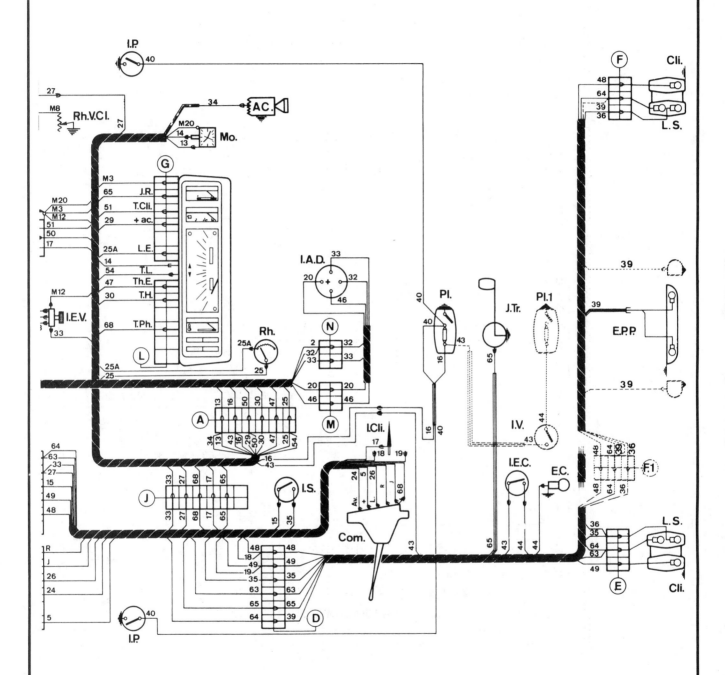

Fig. 10.22 Wiring diagram – Saloon and Estate from July 1970 to January 1971 (continued)

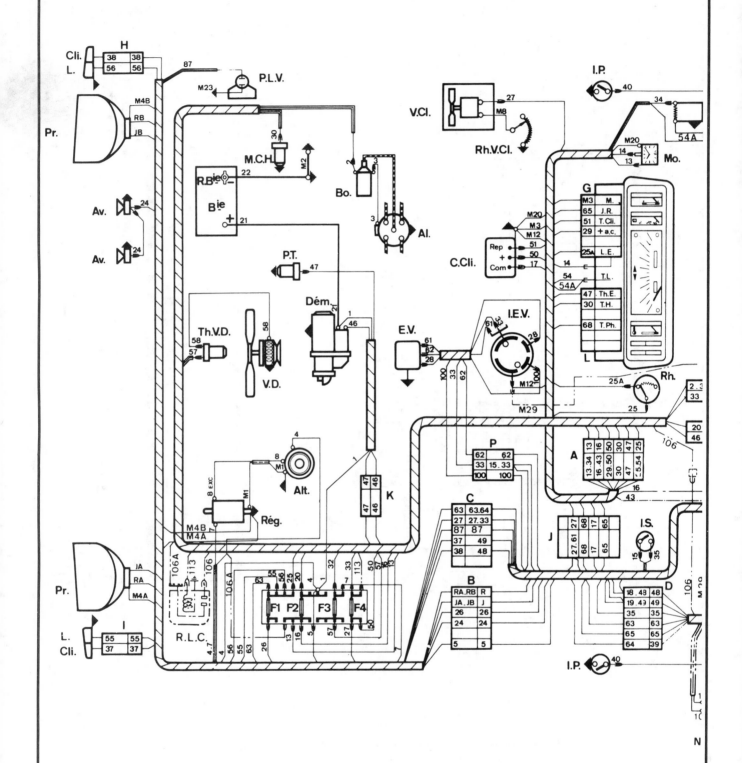

304 A01 – From 3 143 545 to end of series
304 D01 – From 3 143 488 to 3 354 000

Fig. 10.23 Wiring diagram – Saloon and Estate from January 1971 to July 1972
(For coding refer to Figure 10.21 key)

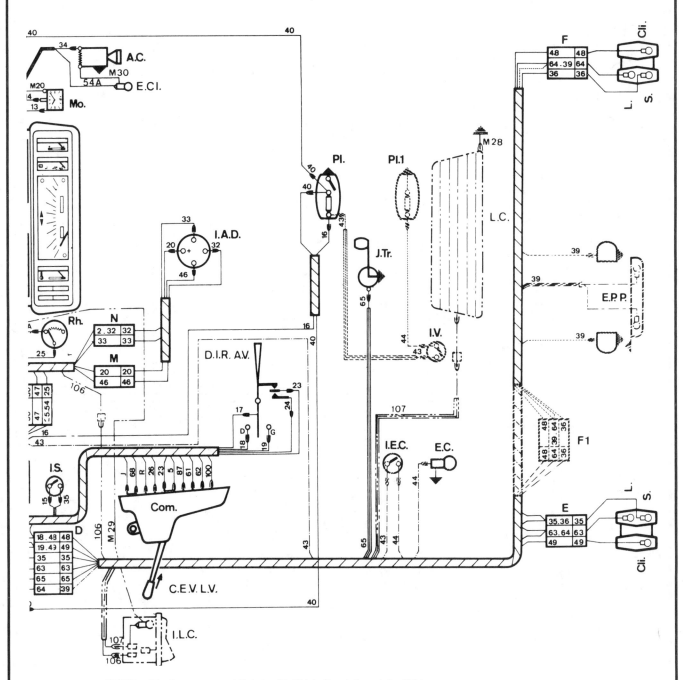

NOTE – *The heater control lighting (E.Cl.) is fitted since July 1971.*

– *The heated rear window (L.C.), with relay (R.L.C.) and switch (I.L.C.), is fitted as an optional extra since July 1971.*

Fig. 10.23 Wiring diagram – Saloon and Estate from Janaury 1971 to July 1972 (continued)

304 D01 – 3 354 001

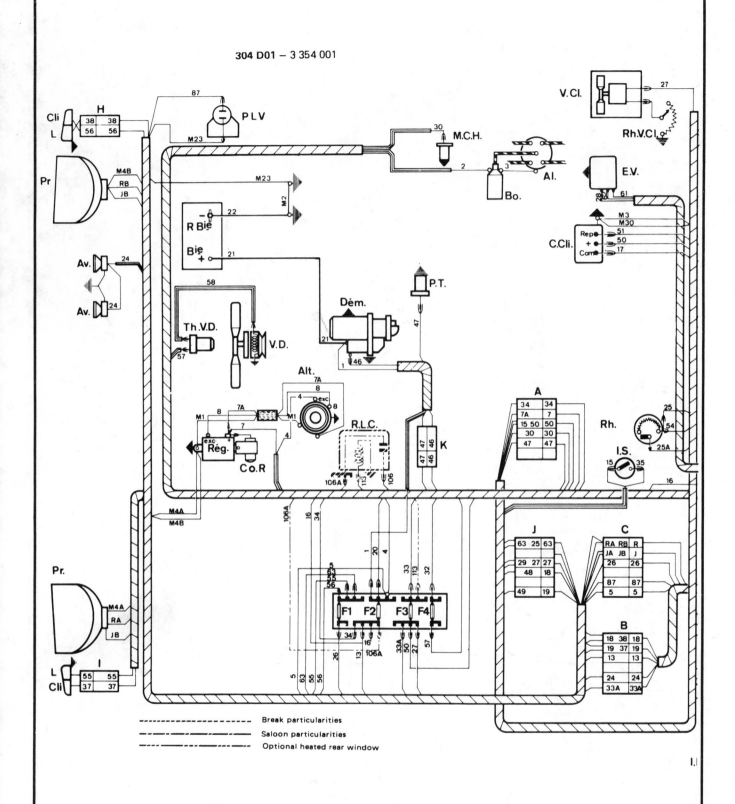

Break particularities
Saloon particularities
Optional heated rear window

Fig. 10.24 Wiring diagram – Saloon and Estate from July 1972 (for coding refer to Figure 10.21 key)

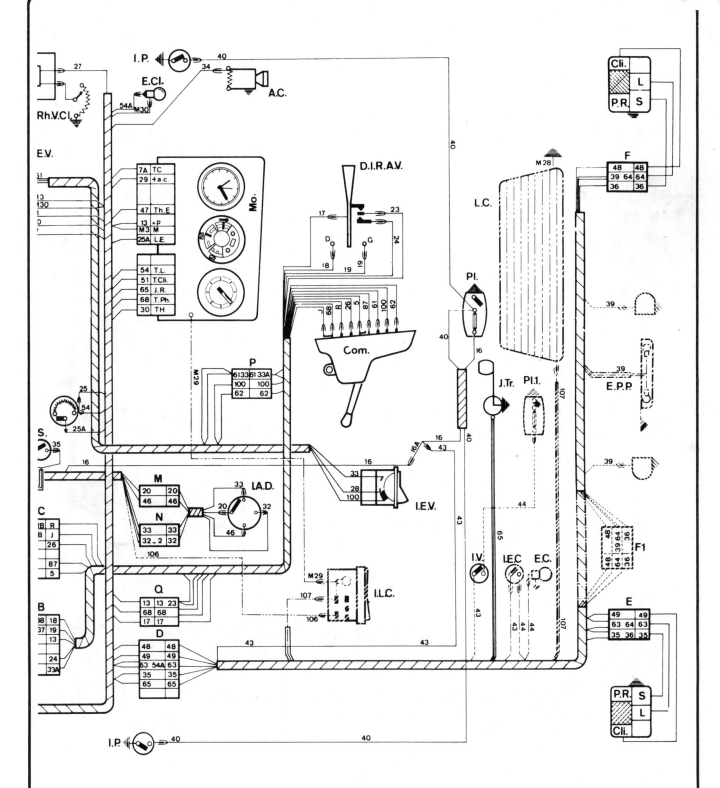

Fig. 10.24 Wiring diagram – Saloon and Estate from July 1972 (continued)

N.B. - *The condenser* (Co.R.) *is not fitted with triphased alternator* (optional *heated rear window*).

238

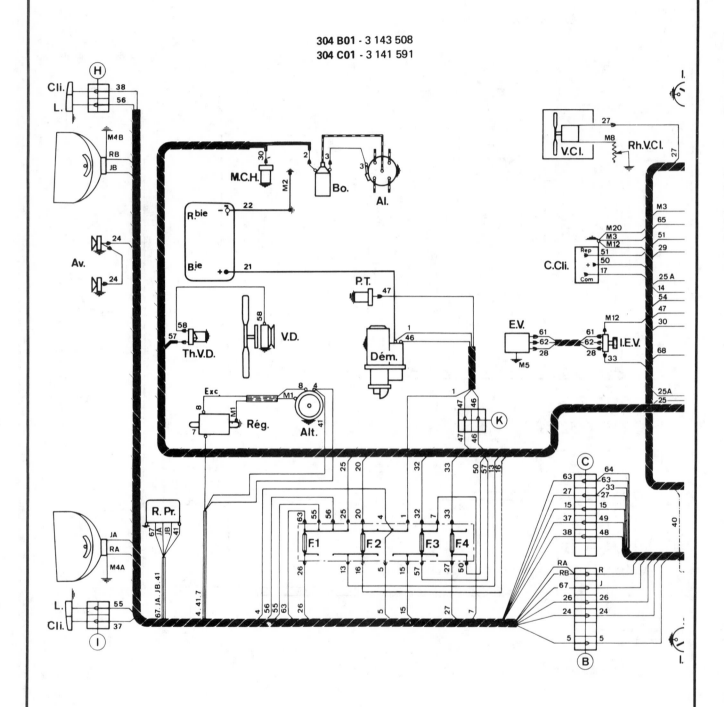

Fig. 10.25 Wiring diagram – Coupe and Convertible up to January 1971 (for coding refer to Figure 10.21 key)

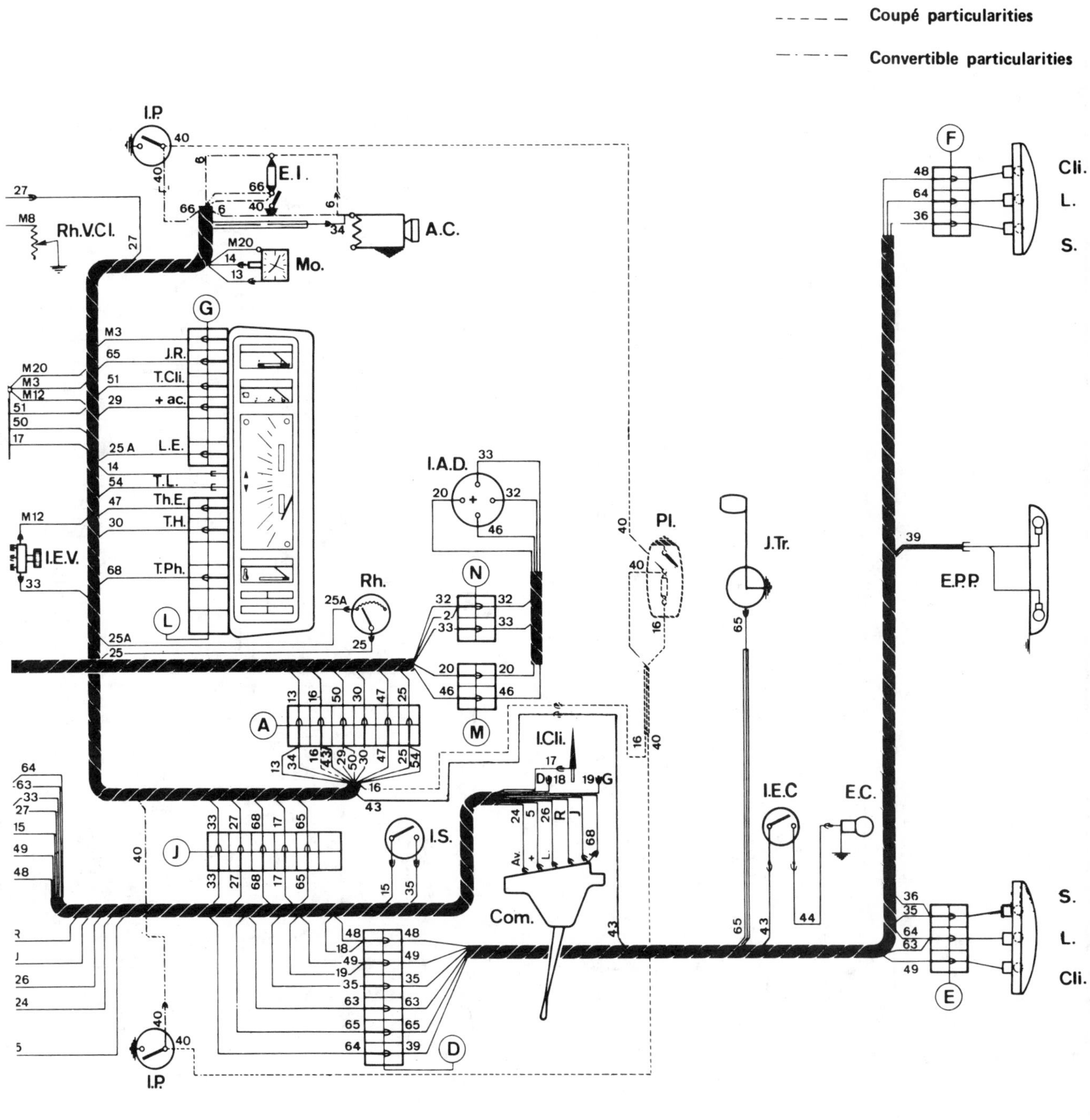

Fig. 10.25 Wiring diagram – Coupe and Convertible up to January 1971 (continued)

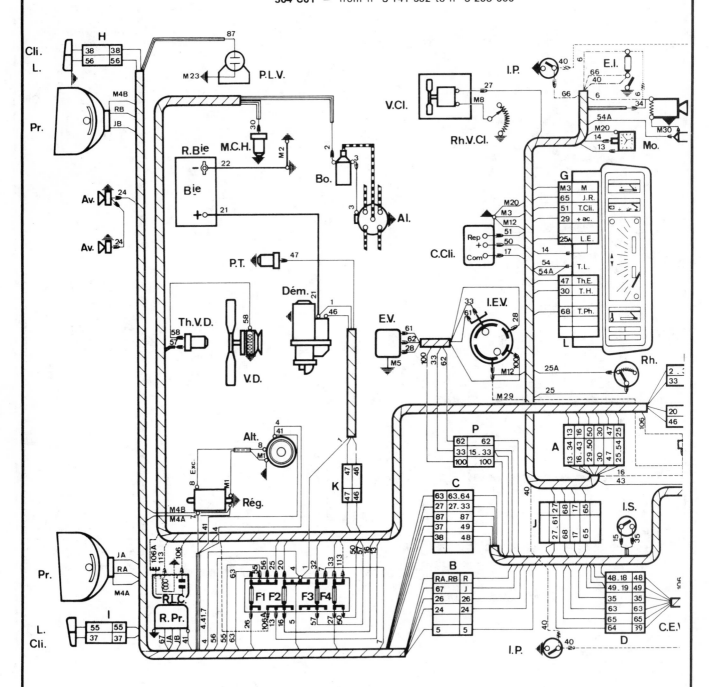

304 **B01** — from n° 3 143 509 to n° 3 298 000
304 **C01** — from n° 3 141 592 to n° 3 298 000

Fig. 10.26 Wiring diagram – Coupe and Convertible from January 1971 to March 1972
(For coding refer to Figure 10.21 key)

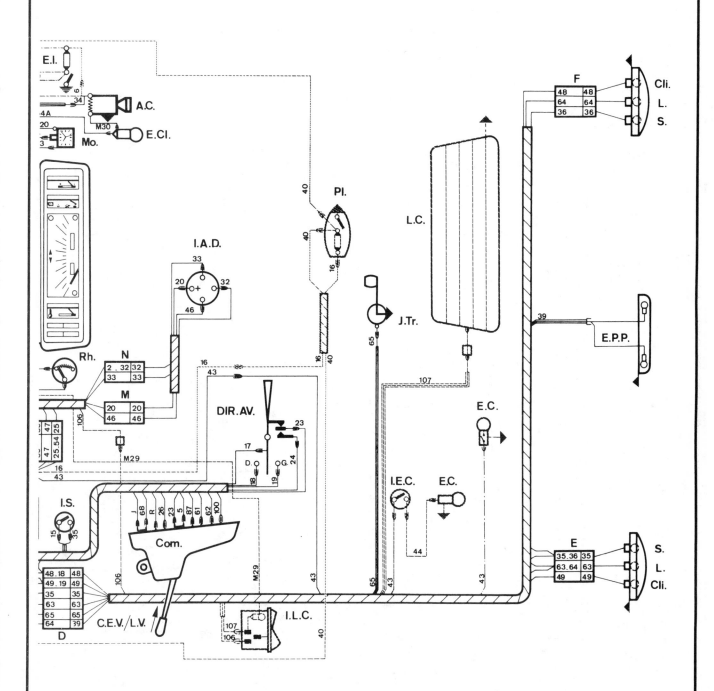

--------- Coupé particularities
— · — · — · — Convertible particularities

NOTE – *On convertible, the switch (I.E.C.) is incorporated in the light (E.C.) since may 1971*
     – *The heater control lighting (E.CI) is fitted since July 1971*
     – *The heated rear window (L.C.) with relay (R.L.C.) and switch (I.L.C) is fitted as an optional extra on Coupes since July 1971.*

Fig. 10.26 Wiring diagram – Coupe and Convertible from Janaury 1971 to March 1972 (continued)

From March 1972 to July 1972 :

3 04 B01 - From 3 298 001 to end of series
304 C01 - From 3 398 001 to 3 354 000
304 B02 - From 3 298 001 to 3 354 000
304 C02 - From 3 298 001 to 3 354 000

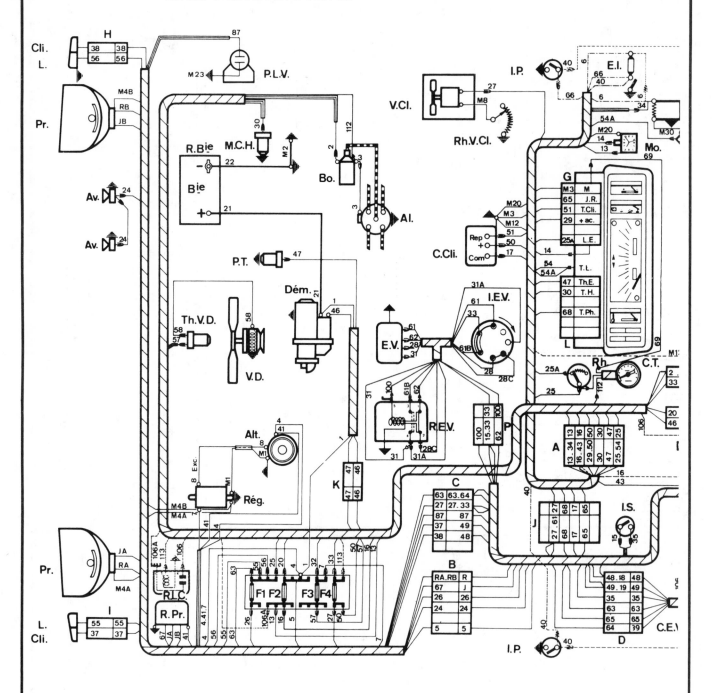

Fig. 10.27 Wiring diagram – Coupe and Convertible from March 1972 to July 1972
(For coding refer to Figure 10.21 key)

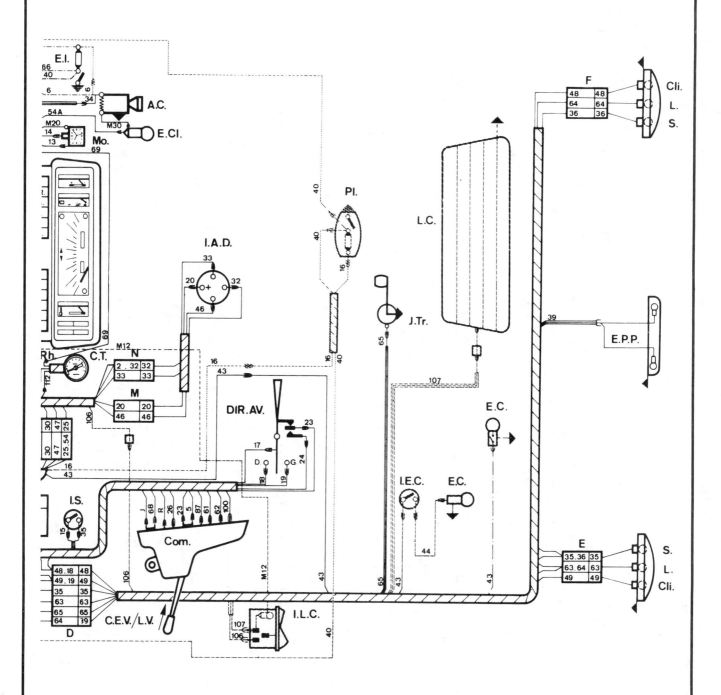

N.B. - *The rev-counter (C.T.) is only fitted on 304 "S" models.*

Fig. 10.27 Wiring diagram – Coupe and Convertible from March 1972 to July 1972 (continued)

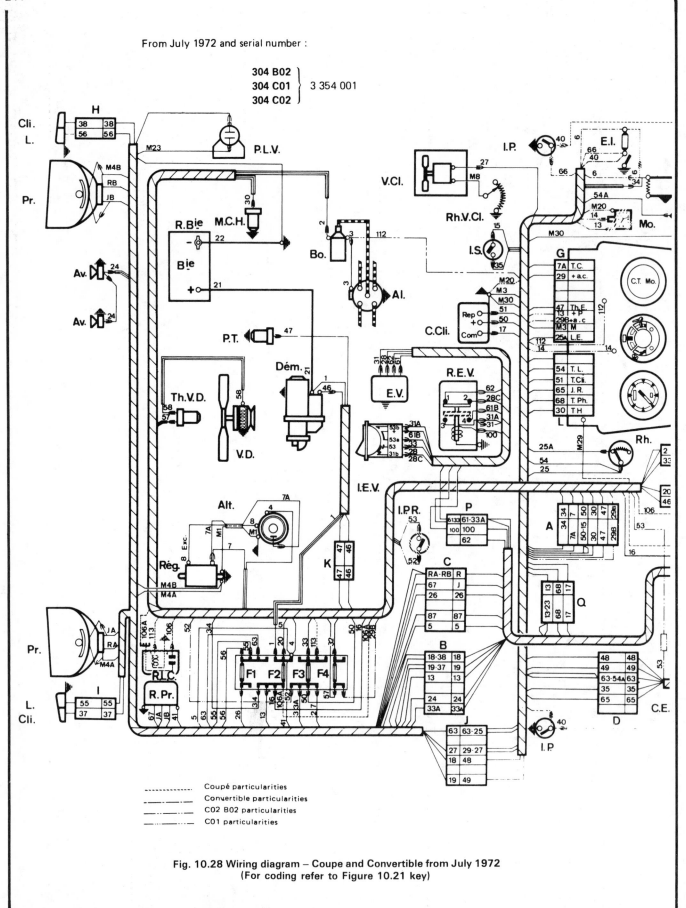

Fig. 10.28 Wiring diagram – Coupe and Convertible from July 1972
(For coding refer to Figure 10.21 key)

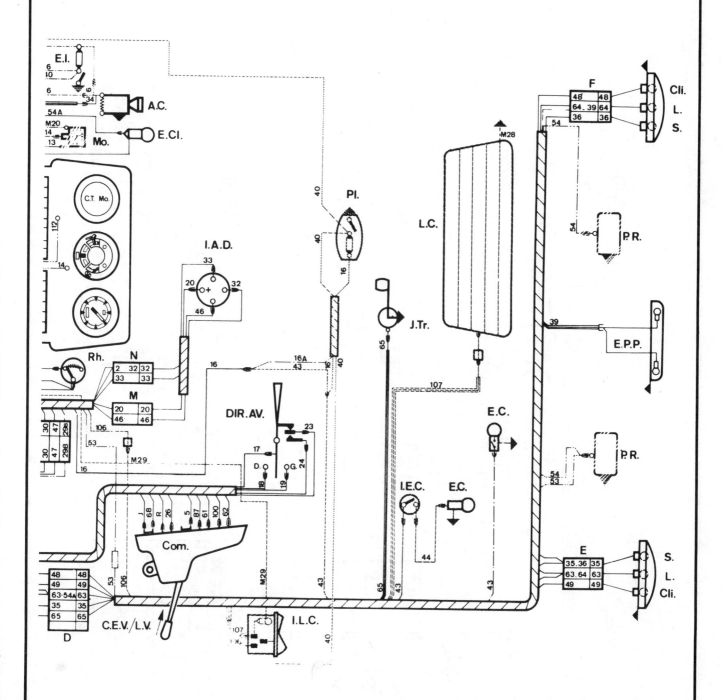

N.B. - *The rev-counter (C.T.) is only fitted on 304 "S" models.*

Fig. 10.28 Wiring diagram – Coupe and Convertible from July 1972 (continued)

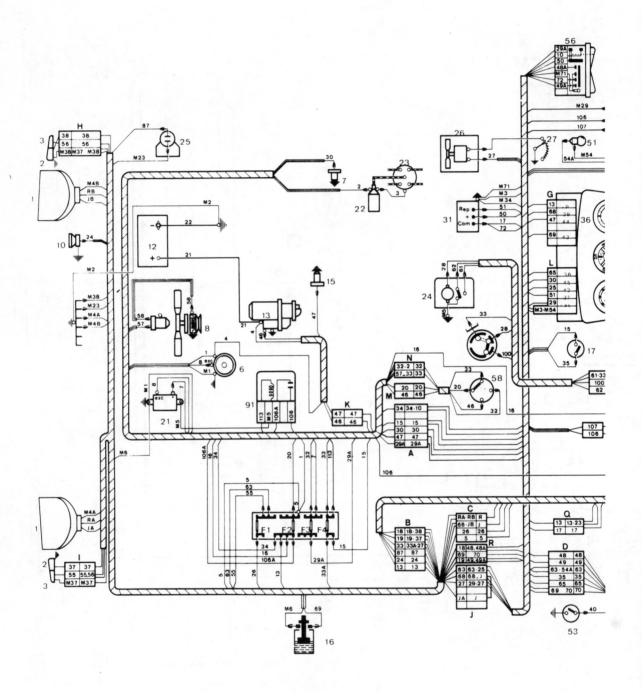

Fig. 10.29 Wiring diagram – 304 GL (later models)
(For coding refer to page 250)

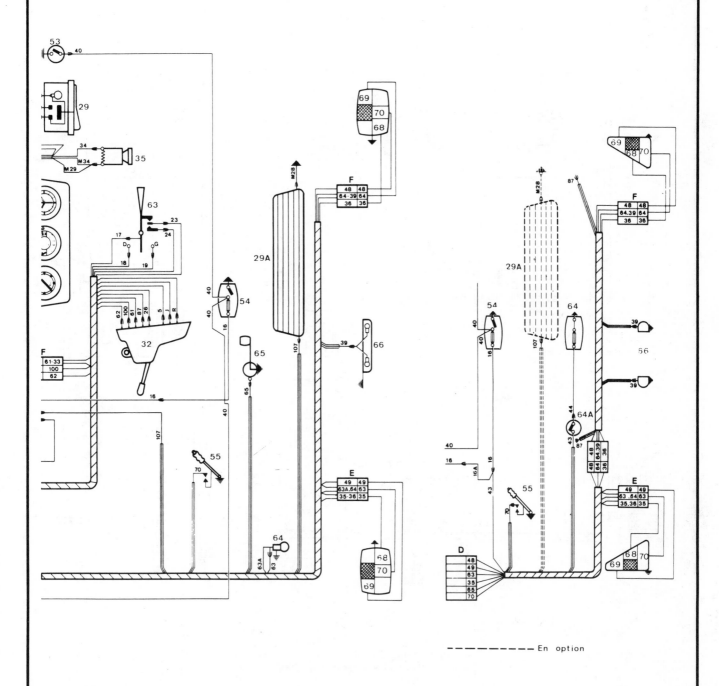

Fig. 10.29 Wiring diagram – 304 GL (later models) (continued)

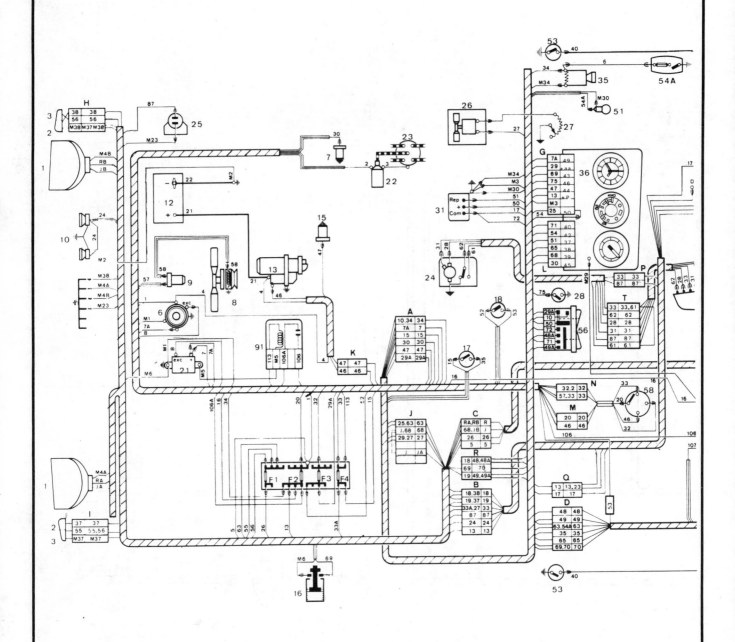

Fig. 10.30 Wiring diagram – 304 SL (later models)
(For coding refer to page 250)

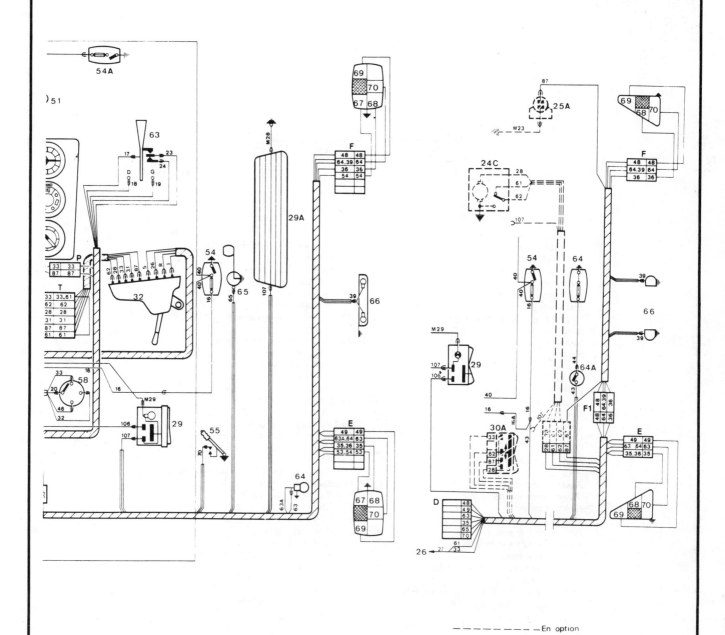

Fig. 10.30 Wiring diagram – 304 SL (later models) (continued)

Key to wiring diagrams 10.29 and 10.30

1	Headlamps	36	Clock
2	Front direction indicators	37	Tell-tale direction indicators
3	Front sidelight	38	Fuel gauge
4	Direction indicator tell-tale	39	Tell-tale headlamps
6	Alternator	40	Tell-tale, hazard warning
7	Oil pressure switch	41	Tachometer
8	Electromagnetic fan	42	Tell-tale, side-lights
9	Electromagnetic fan thermostat	43	Brakes system warning light
10	Horn	44	Water temperature gauge
11	Headlamps relay	45	Oil pressure warning light
12	Battery	46	Tell-tale-choke
13	Starter	49	Charge indicator
15	Water temperature transmitter	50	Fascia lighting
16	Brake fluid reservoir	51	Heater controls lighting
17	Stoplights switch	53	Front door switch
18	Reversing lights switch	54	Interior lighting
21	Voltage regulator	54A	Fascia lower light
22	Coil	55	Handbrake tell-tale switch
23	Distributor	56	Hazard warning lights switch
24	Front windscreen wiper	58	Anti-theft lock
24C	Rear screen wiper	63	Combined switch – direction indicators/horns
25	Front windscreen washer pump	64	Boot light
25A	Rear screen washer pump	64A	Tailgate light switch
26	Heater blower	65	Fuel gauge unit
27	Heater blower rheostat	66	Rear number plate lighting
28	Choke tell-tale switch	67	Reversing light
29	Heated rear screen switch	68	Stop light
29A	Heated rear screen	69	Rear direction indicator
30A	Rear screen wiper/washer switch	70	Rear light
31	Direction indicators unit	91	Relay
32	Combined switch; lights – screen wash/wipe	+p	Continuous feed
33	Headlamps flasher relay	+ac	Feed when switched-on
35	Cigar lighter	+aa	Feed to accessories

Chapter 11 Bodywork and fittings

Contents

1 General description

The Peugeot 304 body and underframe are of integral steel construction and during manufacture it is given an electrophoresis anti-corrosion treatment. Four basic styles have been produced, these being the Saloon, Estate, Coupe and Convertible.

Apart from the normal cleaning, maintenance and minor body repairs, there is little that the DIY owner can do in the event of structural defects caused by collision damage or possibly rust. This Chapter is therefore devoted to the normal maintenance, removal and refitting of those parts of the vehicle body and associate components that are readily dismantled.

Although the underbody is given a protective coating when new, it is still likely to suffer from corrosion in certain exposed areas or where road dirt deposits can congeal. Light corrosion can be treated as described in Section 2 but severe rusting of a structural area in the underbody must be repaired by your Peugeot dealer or competent vehicle body repair shop.

2 Maintenance – bodywork and underframe

1   The general condition of a vehicle's bodywork is the one thing that significantly affects its value. Maintenance is easy but needs to be regular. Neglect, particularly after minor damage, can lead quickly to further deterioration and costly repair bills. It is important also to keep watch on those parts of the vehicle not immediately visible, for instance the underside, inside all the wheel arches and the lower part of the engine compartment.
2   The basic maintenance routine for the bodywork is washing – preferably with a lot of water, from a hose. This will remove all the loose solids which may have stuck to the vehicle. It is important to flush these off in such a way as to prevent grit from scratching the finish. The wheel arches and underframe need washing in the same way to remove any accumulated mud which will retain moisture and tend to encourage rust. Paradoxically enough, the best time to clean the underframe and wheel arches is in wet weather when the mud is thoroughly wet and soft. In very wet weather the underframe is usually cleaned of large accumulations automatically and this is a good time for inspection.

3   Periodically, it is a good idea to have the whole of the underframe of the vehicle steam cleaned, engine compartment included, so that a thorough inspection can be carried out to see what minor repairs and renovations are necessary. Steam cleaning is available at many garages and is necessary for removal of the accumulation of oily grime which sometimes is allowed to become thick in certain areas. If steam cleaning facilities are not available, there are one or two excellent grease solvents available which can be brush applied. The dirt can then be simply hosed off.
4   After washing paintwork, wipe off with a chamois leather to give an unspotted clear finish. A coat of clear protective wax polish will give added protection against chemical pollutants in the air. If the paintwork sheen has dulled or oxidised, use a cleaner/polisher combination to restore the brilliance of the shine. This requires a little effort, but such dulling is usually caused because regular washing has been neglected. Always check that the door and ventilator opening drain holes and pipes are completely clear so that water can be drained out. Bright work should be treated in the same way as paintwork. Windscreens and windows can be kept clear of the smeary film which often appears, by adding a little ammonia to the water. If they are scratched, a good rub with a proprietary metal polish will often clear them. Never use any form of wax or other body or chromium polish on glass.

3 Maintenance – upholstery and carpets

1   Mats and carpets should be brushed or vacuum cleaned regularly to keep them free of grit. If they are badly stained remove them from the vehicle for scrubbing or sponging and make quite sure they are dry before refitting. Seats and interior trim panels can be kept clean by wiping with a damp cloth. If they do become stained (which can be more apparent on light coloured upholstery) use a little liquid detergent and a soft nail brush to scour the grime out of the grain of the material. Do not forget to keep the headlining clean in the same way as the upholstery. When using liquid cleaners inside the vehicle do not over-wet the surfaces being cleaned. Excessive damp could get into the seams and padded interior causing stains, offensive odours or even rot. If the inside of the vehicle gets wet accidentally it is worthwhile taking some trouble to dry it out properly, particularly where carpets are involved. *Do not leave oil or electric heaters inside the vehicle for this purpose.*

4   Minor body damage – repair

The photographic sequences on pages 254 and 255 illustrate the operations detailed in the following sub-sections.

Repair of minor scratches in bodywork

If the scratch is very superficial, and does not penetrate to the metal of the bodywork, repair is very simple. Lightly rub the area of the scratch with a paintwork renovator, or a very fine cutting paste, to remove loose paint from the scratch and to clear the surrounding bodywork of wax polish. Rinse the area with clean water.

Apply touch-up paint to the scratch using a fine paint brush; continue to apply fine layers of paint until the surface of the paint in the scratch is level with the surrounding paintwork. Allow the new paint at least two weeks to harden; then blend it into the surrounding paintwork by rubbing the scratch area with a paintwork renovator or a very fine cutting paste. Finally, apply wax polish.

Where the scratch has penetrated right through to the metal of the bodywork, causing the metal to rust, a different repair technique is required. Remove any loose rust from the bottom of the scratch with a penknife, then apply rust inhibiting paint to prevent the formation of rust in the future. Using a rubber or nylon applicator fill the scratch with bodystopper paste. If required, this paste can be mixed with cellulose thinners to provide a very thin paste which is ideal for filling narrow scratches. Before the stopper-paste in the scratch hardens, wrap a piece of smooth cotton rag around the top of a finger. Dip the finger in cellulose thinners and then quickly sweep it across the surface of the stopper-paste in the scratch; this will ensure that the surface of the stopper-paste is slightly hollowed. The scratch can now be painted over as described earlier in this Section.

Repair of dents in bodywork

When deep denting of the vehicle's bodywork has taken place, the first task is to pull the dent out, until the affected bodywork almost attains its original shape. There is little point in trying to restore the original shape completely, as the metal in the damaged area will have stretched on impact and cannot be reshaped fully to its original contour. It is better to bring the level of the dent up to a point which is about $\frac{1}{8}$ in (3 mm) below the level of the surrounding bodywork. In cases where the dent is very shallow anyway, it is not worth trying to pull it out at all. If the underside of the dent is accessible, it can be hammered out gently from behind, using a mallet with a wooden or plastic head. Whilst doing this, hold a suitable block of wood firmly against the outside of the panel to absorb the impact from the hammer blows and thus prevent a large area of the bodywork from being 'belled-out'.

Should the dent be in a section of the bodywork which has a double skin or some other factor making it inaccessible from behind, a different technique is called for. Drill several small holes through the metal inside the area – particularly in the deeper section. Then screw long self-tapping screws into the holes just sufficiently for them to gain a good purchase in the metal. Now the dent can be pulled out by pulling on the protruding heads of the screws with a pair of pliers.

The next stage of the repair is the removal of the paint from the damaged area, and from an inch or so of the surrounding 'sound' bodywork. This is accomplished most easily by using a wire brush or abrasive pad on a power drill, although it can be done just as effectively by hand using sheets of abrasive paper. To complete the preparation for filling, score the surface of the bare metal with a screwdriver or the tang of a file, or alternatively, drill small holes in the affected area. This will provide a really good 'key' for the filler paste.

To complete the repair see the Section on filling and re-spraying.

Repair of rust holes or gashes in bodywork

Remove all paint from the affected area and from an inch or so of the surrounding 'sound' bodywork, using an abrasive pad or a wire brush on a power drill. If these are not available a few sheets of abrasive paper will do the job just as effectively. With the paint removed you will be able to gauge the severity of the corrosion and therefore decide whether to renew the whole panel (if this is possible) or to repair the affected area. New body panels are not as expensive as most people think and it is often quicker and more satisfactory to fit a new panel than to attempt to repair large areas of corrosion.

Remove all fittings from the affected area except those which will act as a guide to the original shape of the damaged bodywork (eg headlamp shells etc). Then, using tin snips or a hacksaw blade, remove all loose metal and any other metal badly affected by corrosion. Hammer the edges of the hole inwards in order to create a slight depression for the filler paste.

Wire brush the affected area to remove the powdery rust from the surface of the remaining metal. Paint the affected area with rust inhibiting paint; if the back of the rusted area is accessible treat this also.

Before filling can take place it will be necessary to block the hole in some way. This can be achieved by the use of zinc gauze or aluminium tape.

Zinc gauze is probably the best material to use for a large hole. Cut a piece to the approximate size and shape of the hole to be filled, then position it in the hole so that its edges are below the level of the surrounding bodywork. It can be retained in position by several blobs of filler paste around its periphery.

Aluminium tape should be used for small or very narrow holes. Pull a piece off the roll and trim it to the approximate size and shape required, then pull off the backing paper (if used) and stick the tape over the hole; it can be overlapped if the thickness of one piece is insufficient. Burnish down the edges of the tape with the handle of a screwdriver or similar, to ensure that the tape is securely attached to the metal underneath.

Bodywork repairs – filling and re-spraying

Before using this Section, see the Sections on dent, deep scratch, rust holes and gash repairs.

Many types of bodyfiller are available, but generally speaking those proprietary kits which contain a tin of filler paste and a tube of resin hardener are best for this type of repair. A wide, flexible plastic or nylon applicator will be found invaluable for imparting a smooth and well contoured finish to the surface of the filler.

Mix up a little filler on a clean piece of card or board – measure the hardener carefully (follow the maker's instructions on the pack) otherwise the filler will set too rapidly or too slowly.

Using the applicator apply the filler paste to the prepared area; draw the applicator across the surface of the filler to achieve the correct contour and to level the filler surface. As soon as a contour that approximates to the correct one is achieved, stop working the paste – if you carry on too long the paste will become sticky and begin to 'pick up' on the applicator. Continue to add thin layers of filler paste at twenty-minute intervals until the level of the filler is just proud of the surrounding bodywork.

Once the filler has hardened, excess can be removed using a metal plane or file. From then on, progressively finer grades of abrasive paper should be used, starting with a 40 grade production paper and finishing with 400 grade wet-and-dry paper. Always wrap the abrasive paper around a flat rubber, cork, or wooden block – otherwise the surface of the filler will not be completely flat. During the smoothing of the filler surface the wet-and-dry paper should be periodically rinsed in water. This will ensure that a very smooth finish is imparted to the filler at the final stage.

At this stage the 'dent' should be surrounded by a ring of bare metal, which in turn should be encircled by the finely 'feathered' edge of the good paintwork. Rinse the repair area with clean water, until all of the dust produced by the rubbing-down operation has gone.

Spray the whole repair area with a light coat of primer – this will show up any imperfections in the surface of the filler. Repair these imperfections with fresh filler paste or bodystopper, and once more smooth the surface with abrasive paper. If bodystopper is used, it can be mixed with cellulose thinners to form a really thin paste which is ideal for filling small holes. Repeat this spray and repair procedure until you are satisfied that the surface of the filler, and the feathered edge of the paintwork are perfect. Clean the repair area with clean water and allow to dry fully.

The repair area is now ready for final spraying. Paint spraying must be carried out in a warm, dry, windless and dust free atmosphere. This condition can be created artificially if you have access to a large indoor working area, but if you are forced to work in the open, you will have to pick your day very carefully. If you are working indoors, dousing the floor in the work area with water will help to settle the dust which would otherwise be in the atmosphere. If the repair area is confined to one body panel, mask off the surrounding panels; this will help to minimise the effects of a slight mis-match in paint colours. Bodywork fittings (eg chrome strips, door handles etc) will also need to be masked off. Use genuine masking tape and several thicknesses of newspaper for the masking operations.

Before commencing to spray, agitate the aerosol can thoroughly, then spray a test area (an old tin, or similar) until the technique is mastered. Cover the repair area with a thick coat of primer; the thickness should be built up using several thin layers of paint rather than one thick one. Using 400 grade wet-and-dry paper, rub down the surface of the primer until it is really smooth. While doing this, the work area should be thoroughly doused with water, and the wet-and-dry paper periodically rinsed in water. Allow to dry before spraying on more paint.

Spray on the top coat, again building up the thickness by using several thin layers of paint. Start spraying in the centre of the repair area and then, using a circular motion, work outwards until the whole repair area and about 2 inches of the surrounding original paintwork is covered. Remove all masking material 10 to 15 minutes after spraying on the final coat of paint.

Allow the new paint at least two weeks to harden, then, using a paintwork renovator or a very fine cutting paste, blend the edges of the paint into the existing paintwork. Finally, apply wax polish.

5 Major body damage – repair

1 If damage is limited to the major replaceable components, namely doors, boot lid, bonnet, front wings, or bumpers, repair is a simple matter of renewing the component(s) concerned. However it is more likely that major body damage will involve the basic unit structure. In this case repairs must be undertaken by a properly equipped body repair shop with hydraulic straightening facilities and welding equipment.
2 Extensive damage to the body may distort the structure and in this case precision alignment checking equipment will be necessary to measure the degree and location of the distortion and to check the structure after repair. As a distorted chassis can result in unstable and even dangerous handling characteristics, as well as excessive wear to tyres and suspension or steering components, it is imperative that remedial work is only undertaken by specialists.

6 Hinges, door catches and locks – maintenance

1 Periodically oil the hinges of the bonnet, the boot lid and the doors with a drop or two of light oil. A good time to do this is just after washing the car, especially if a detergent wash has been used.

2 Oil the bonnet release mechanism and catches at the same time.
3 Do not overlubricate door latches and strikers as it is only too easy to stain clothing. A non-staining lubricant for these areas can be obtained from accessory shops if you have a problem in this area but normally, minimal lubrication, wiping off all surplus, suffices.
4 On convertible models the hood frame hinges should occasionally be treated to a small amount of light oil, but do not get the oil onto the hood material itself or the car's upholstery.

7 Bonnet – removal and refitting

1 Open the bonnet and prop it on its stay.
2 Mark round the hinges at the rear of the bonnet to show their correct location and thus facilitate reassembly. Undo and remove the upper hinge bolt and nut securing the stay to the bonnet and hold the bonnet up with the aid of an assistant.
3 Undo and remove the bolts securing the hinges to the bonnet and carefully remove the bonnet. Park it in a safe place where it can't get damaged, knocked down or blown down (photo).
4 Refitting is simply a reverse of the removal procedure, making sure that the hinges align with the marks made on removal. Check the fit of the closed bonnet and oil the hinges, stay pivots and catches on completion.

8 Bonnet release catch and cable – removal and refitting

1 Raise and support the bonnet.
2 There are two bonnet release catches, one housed in each wing valance. Removal of either catch requires the headlight on the side concerned to be removed. Headlight removal is described in Chapter 10.
3 Disconnect the catch release cable from the catch on the side concerned. When working on the nearside catch you will also need to disconnect the cable to the right-hand catch (photo).
4 Remove the catch retaining nuts and extract the catch from the wing valance.
5 Refitting of the catch is a reversal of the removal procedure, but before refitting the headlight and shutting down the bonnet check that the cable adjustment at the catch end will fully release and operate the catch through its full movement.
6 If the main release cable is to be renewed, release it from the catch attachment and pull the inner cable through from within the car. Refit by using the above procedure in reverse, lubricating the cable as it is fitted. Check its adjustment as described in paragraph 5.

7.3 The bonnet hinge bolts. Mark hinge position outline before removing to facilitate correct reassembly

8.3 Bonnet catch showing retaining nuts and the cable attachment

This sequence of photographs deals with the repair of the dent and paintwork damage shown in this photo. The procedure will be similar for the repair of a hole. It should be noted that the procedures given here are simplified — more explicit instructions will be found in the text

In the case of a dent the first job — after removing surrounding trim — is to hammer out the dent where access is possible. This will minimise filling. Here, the large dent having been hammered out, the damaged area is being made slightly concave

Now all paint must be removed from the damaged area, by rubbing with coarse abrasive paper. Alternatively, a wire brush or abrasive pad can be used in a power drill. Where the repair area meets good paintwork, the edge of the paintwork should be 'feathered', using a finer grade of abrasive paper

In the case of a hole caused by rusting, all damaged sheet-metal should be cut away before proceeding to this stage. Here, the damaged area is being treated with rust remover and inhibitor before being filled

Mix the body filler according to its manufacturer's instructions. In the case of corrosion damage, it will be necessary to block off any large holes before filling — this can be done with zinc gauze or aluminium tape. Make sure the area is absolutely clean before...

...applying the filler. Filler should be applied with a flexible applicator, as shown, for best results; the wooden spatula being used for confined areas. Apply thin layers of filler at 20-minute intervals, until the surface of the filler is slightly proud of the surrounding bodywork

Initial shaping can be done with a Surform plane or Dread-nought file. Then, using progressively finer grades of wet-and-dry paper, wrapped around a sanding block, and copious amounts of clean water, rub down the filler until really smooth and flat. Again, feather the edges of adjoining paintwork

The whole repair area can now be sprayed or brush-painted with primer. If spraying, ensure adjoining areas are protected from over-spray. Note that at least one inch of the surrounding sound paintwork should be coated with primer. Primer has a 'thick' consistency, so will fill small imperfections

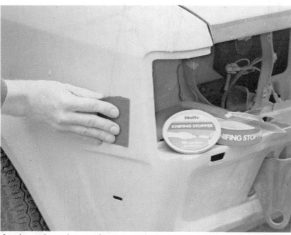

Again, using plenty of water, rub down the primer with a fine grade of wet-and-dry paper (400 grade is probably best) until it is really smooth and well blended into the surrounding paintwork. Any remaining imperfections can now be filled by carefully applied knifing stopper paste

When the stopper has hardened, rub down the repair area again before applying the final coat of primer. Before rubbing down this last coat of primer, ensure the repair area is blemish-free — use more stopper if necessary. To ensure that the surface of the primer is really smooth use some finishing compound

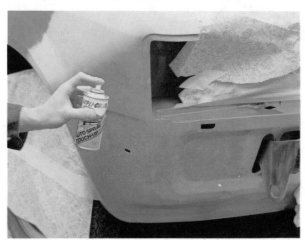

The top coat can now be applied. When working out of doors, pick a dry, warm and wind-free day. Ensure surrounding areas are protected from over-spray. Agitate the aerosol thoroughly, then spray the centre of the repair area, working outwards with a circular motion. Apply the paint as several thin coats

After a period of about two weeks, which the paint needs to harden fully, the surface of the repaired area can be 'cut' with a mild cutting compound prior to wax polishing. When carrying out bodywork repairs, remember that the quality of the finished job is proportional to the time and effort expended

256

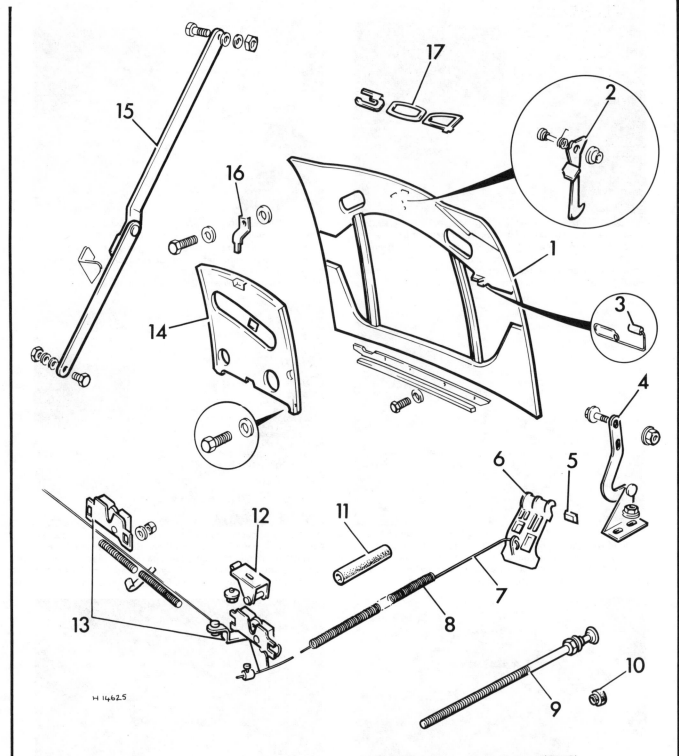

Fig. 11.1 Exploded view of the bonnet with its stay hinge and release catch mechanisms (Sec 8)

H 14625

1 Bonnet	6 Release lever	10 Rubber grommet	14 Sound proofing board
2 Catch lock	7 Cable inner	11 Rubber tube	15 Prop
3 Spring	8 Cable outer	12 Striker	16 Retainer
4 Hinge assembly	9 Cable assembly	13 Catch	17 Name plate
5 Rubber rest			

9.2 Front grille retaining screws at top are removed ...

9.3 ... then lift grille from its lower mounting location holes

10.2 Remove the door catch release screw

10.3a Remove retaining screw and ...

10.3b ... lift out the escutcheon panel

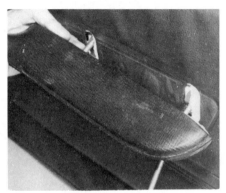

10.4a Remove armrest screws, the two shown ...

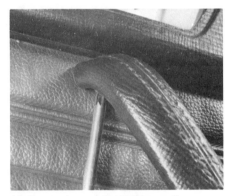

10.4b ... and one under the door pull section

10.5 Remove the window winder handle

10.6 Prise the trim panel away from door to release clips

7 The connecting cable between the catches can be removed after detachment from each catch. Refit in reverse and check the adjustment on completion to ensure that both catches are fully operational as given in paragraph 5.

8 On completion refit and check the headlights for correct operation and adjustment as given in Chapter 10.

9 Front grille – removal and refitting

1 Raise the support the bonnet.

2 Unscrew and remove the three grille retaining screws from its top edge each side (photo).

3 Carefully lift the grille out, releasing it from its peg location holes at the bottom.

4 Refit in the reverse order of removal, renewing the rubber peg location grommets if necessary.

10 Door trim panel – removal and refitting

1 Removal and refitting of a door trim panel is a similar procedure for all four doors.

2 Unscrew and remove the catch retaining screw, slide the catch up to remove it (photo).

3 Remove the escutcheon panel which is secured by a single screw (photo).

4 Remove the armrest which is secured by three screws (photo).

5 To remove the window winder handle, press escutcheon in, prise free the clip and withdraw the handle (photo).

6 Use a screwdriver with a wide blade, or a similar tool such as a blunt knife, and carefully insert it between the trim panel and the door. Apply leverage to prise the plastic clips retaining the trim panel to the door, and work round the panel until all clips are removed and the panel can be taken off the door (photo).

7 Refitting is a simple reversal of the removal procedure. Engage the

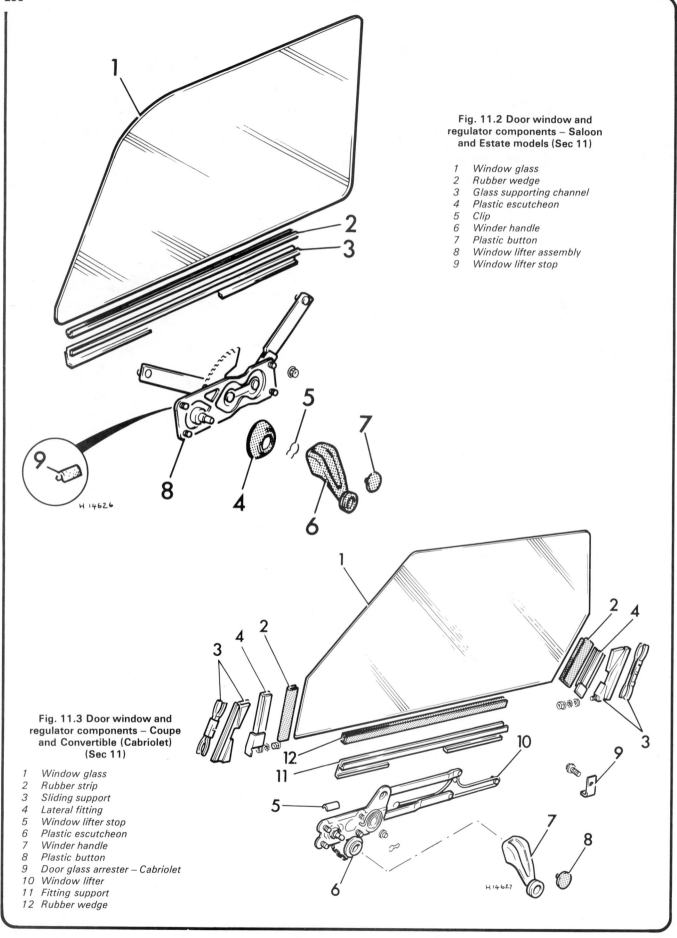

Fig. 11.2 Door window and
regulator components – Saloon
and Estate models (Sec 11)

1 Window glass
2 Rubber wedge
3 Glass supporting channel
4 Plastic escutcheon
5 Clip
6 Winder handle
7 Plastic button
8 Window lifter assembly
9 Window lifter stop

H 14626

Fig. 11.3 Door window and
regulator components – Coupe
and Convertible (Cabriolet)
(Sec 11)

1   Window glass
2   Rubber strip
3   Sliding support
4   Lateral fitting
5   Window lifter stop
6   Plastic escutcheon
7   Winder handle
8   Plastic button
9   Door glass arrester – Cabriolet
10 Window lifter
11 Fitting support
12 Rubber wedge

H 14627

trim panel clips by pressing them into their retainers. When refitting the window winder handle first fit the retaining clip to the handle, fit the washer to the spindle and then fit the handle. Check its position, which should be clear of the seat occupant's knees when the door is shut and the window is wound fully up.

11 Door window – removal and refitting

1 Despite minor differences between the front and rear door window installations, the removal and refitting procedure is similar for all. The front left door window installation which is described here can be adopted for the others.
2 First remove the trim panel as described in the previous Section.
3 Unscrew and remove the door latch retaining nuts and then remove the latch unit from within the door panel, disengaging the operating rod as it is withdrawn.
4 Wind the window down then unscrew the window winder regulator bolts. Manoeuvre the regulator within the door to free the winder arms from the runner channels and remove the regulator unit.

Tilt and remove the window pulling it upwards through the door, taking care not to jam it or apply bending loads to it.
5 Clean and examine the winder mechanism for wear. As individual spare parts are not likely to be available for repairs, renewal of the complete assembly is the only feasible remedy. Lubricate all moving parts before refitting (photo).
6 Refitting the window and winder mechanism is a reversal of the removal procedure. Make sure that the window seals are bedded down and secure in their retaining clips when fitted. Check the window operation before refitting the door trim panel and fittings.

12 Door lock and striker plate mechanisms – removal and refitting

1 Access to these mechanisms and their fastenings is from within the door panel so first remove the door panel as described in Section 10.
2 Both the door lock barrel and striker latch release are secured by sliding clips as shown in the photo.

11.3 General view of inner door panel with trim removed showing door catch and window winder mechanism retaining screws

11.5 Lubricate the window winder runner channels on assembly

12.2 View into door cavity showing lock barrel and striker latch with retaining clips

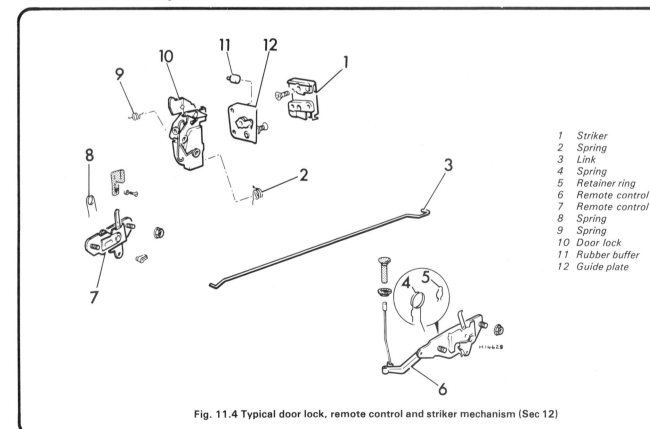

1 Striker
2 Spring
3 Link
4 Spring
5 Retainer ring
6 Remote control
7 Remote control
8 Spring
9 Spring
10 Door lock
11 Rubber buffer
12 Guide plate

Fig. 11.4 Typical door lock, remote control and striker mechanism (Sec 12)

3   To withdraw the lock barrel, remove its sliding clip and detach the barrel to lock retainer. Withdraw the barrel outwards from the door.

4   To remove the door handle, withdraw the sliding clip, release the handle fastenings within the door and remove the handle. The plunger is secured to the handle by a clip which when prised free allows the plunger and spring assembly to be released.

5   The striker plate is secured by three screws which normally require the use of a special Peugeot tool to release them. If you are able to borrow the tool or you have a suitable alternative screwdriver remove the screws. Detach the striker plate to lock, and connecting rod attachments. Then remove the plate (photo).

6   Refit in the reverse order to removal, renewing any defective components or fastenings. Check the lock for satisfactory operation prior to refitting the door trim panel.

13 Doors – removal and refitting

1   Both front and rear doors can be removed in the same manner. First open the door to be removed and support it underneath, but don't lift it.

2   The upper and lower hinge pins have plastic caps in their ends. When the caps are removed, a special Peugeot tool can be fitted to remove the pins but, in the absence of the tool, the pins can be carefully drifted out although this is more difficult. Remove the roll pin in the door stay before removing the hinge pins.

3   Refitting the door is a direct reversal of the removal procedure. Use new hinge pins if the old ones are worn and lubricate them before assembly. Check the door for closing and alignment on completion.

4   Adjustment of door fit is made on the door half of the hinges, which are bolted into the door by two bolts each. Before disturbing the hinge bolts scribe a line round the hinge brackets to act as datum for subsequent reference.

5   The door latch is secured by two countersunk bolts and a special

12.5 The door striker showing the three retaining screws

male six-pointed screwdriver bit to fit a socket wrench is needed to adjust the latch position.

14 Boot lid – removal and refitting

1   Raise the boot lid and mark around the hinges to outline their fitting positions for guidance when refitting (photo).

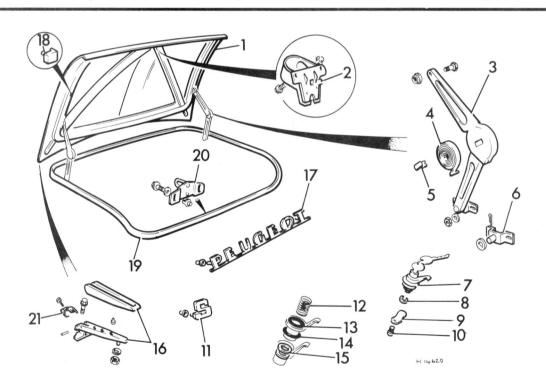

Fig. 11.5 Boot lid assembly components – Convertible (Cabriolet) model (Sec 14)

1 Boot lid	7 Lock barrel assembly	12 Plunger spring	17 Name plate
2 Lock assembly	8 Ring	13 Rubber O-ring	18 Rubber buffer
3 Compensator assembly	9 Finger	14 Rubber gasket	19 Reinforced rubber strip
4 Spring	10 Bolt	15 Felt retaining washer	20 Lock staple
5 Pin	11 Letter plate	16 Hinge assembly	21 Trim
6 Bridge plate			

2   Get an assistant to support the lid whilst you unscrew and remove the hinge bolts, then remove the lid. On the Convertible (Cabriolet) model you will need to detach the compensator to lid pivot, and the external hinges. These are secured by screws which when removed allow lid removal. Note the gasket between the hinge and the lid.

3   Refitting is a direct reversal of the removal procedure, but slight adjustment may be necessary on completion.

15   Boot lid lock and latch – removal and refitting

1   Open the boot lid, then unscrew the lock barrel nut, between the rear panel and latch support. Withdraw the lock.

2   To remove the latch unscrew the retaining nuts and detach the latch from the support strut (photo).

3   Refit in the reverse order of removal and check operation.

16   Tailgate lock and latch – removal and refitting

1   Open the tailgate and prise free the tailgate trim panel to gain access to the lock mechanism.

2   Prise free the retaining clip to withdraw the lock unit on Estate models. On the Coupe model the lock assembly is secured by two bolts and the lock barrel by the finger bolt and/or snap ring (photo).

3   The latch on Estate models is secured by special Peugeot screws

14.1 Boot lid hinge – Saloon. Bolt holes are slotted to allow any adjustments to be made

15.2 The boot lid latch – Saloon models

16.2 The tailgate lock unit on the Estate model. Retaining clip of lock barrel is arrowed

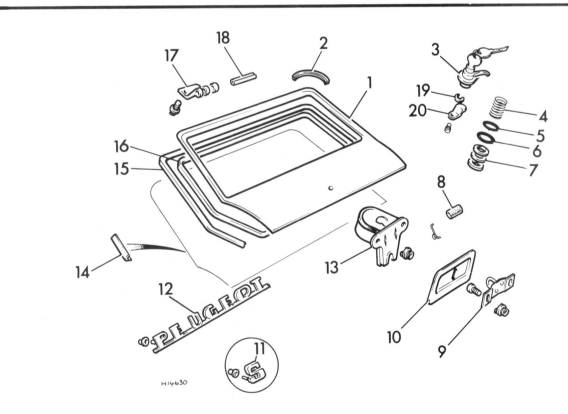

Fig. 11.6 The tailgate assembly components – Coupe model (Sec 16)

1	Tailgate assembly	6	Rubber gasket	11	Name plate	16	Reinforced rubber strip
2	Support	7	Washer	12	Name plate	17	Tailgate hinge arm
3	Lock barrel assembly	8	Rubber tube	13	Lock assembly	18	Pivot pin
4	Spring	9	Lock staple	14	U-piece	19	Ring
5	O-ring	10	Plastic concealer	15	Strip	20	Finger

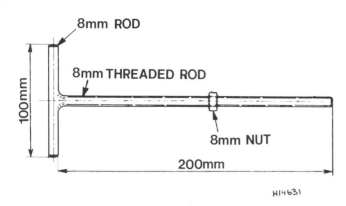

Fig. 11.7 The suggested tool necessary for tailgate torsion bar removal on the earlier models (Sec 17)

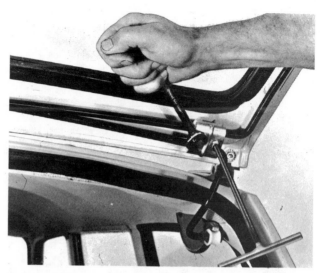

Fig. 11.8 Remove the inner torsion bar screw each side (Sec 17)

and may require a special Peugeot tool for their removal, but you may find a suitable alternative screwdriver will release them.

4   Refitting is a reversal of the removal procedure. Check lock operation before refitting the trim panel.

17 Tailgate – removal and refitting

1   Tailgate removal necessitates detachment of the torsion bars (of the stabilizer mechanism). To do this two special service tools must be borrowed from your Peugeot dealer or made up to the dimensions shown in Figure 11.7. This is of utmost importance because the torsion bar roller thrust loading on the cam is 36 to 45 lbf (80 to 100 kgf) on each side of the tailgate and damage could result if they are not released in the correct manner. Having borrowed or made the tools (two of the type illustrated are required) proceed as follows.
2   Fully open the tailgate and prop it up in this position using a suitable length of bar or wood so that the torsion bar rollers are not resting on their thrusts which limit the stabilizer cams travel.
3   Unscrew and remove the torsion bar casing securing screws each side and remove the casing.
4   Now fit the special service tools into the outer holes vacated by the casing screws each side, to a depth not exceeding 15 mm (0.58 in) or you will damage the outer tailgate panel. Tighten the locknut on each service tool to the torsion bar flanges.
5   Now unscrew and remove the inner torsion bar flange screw each side.
6   Now, progressively and simultaneously, unscrew the service tool locknut on each side whilst preventing the tool from turning. This allows the flanges to move and enable the torsion bars to be loosened.
7   When the torsion bars are completely loosened off, the service tools, torsion bars and their flanges can be withdrawn.
8   Remove the prop and get an assistant to support the tailgate whilst you unscrew and remove the tailgate hinge screws each side, then remove the tailgate.
9   Refitting is a reversal of the removal procedure. Relocate the torsion bars using the service tools. On completion remove the prop and check the operation of the tailgate and the torsion bar action.

18 Bumpers – removal and refitting

Front bumpers

1   Unscrew and remove the retaining bolt at the end of the bumper each side within the wheel arch.
2   Unscrew the main support bracket from within the bumper cavity working from underneath, whilst supporting the bumper by hand. Withdraw the bumper noting the rubber spacers on each corner between the bumper and body (photo).
3   Refit in reverse order of removal, but check the alignment of the bumper before fully tightening its fastenings.

17.2 The tailgate hinges on the Estate

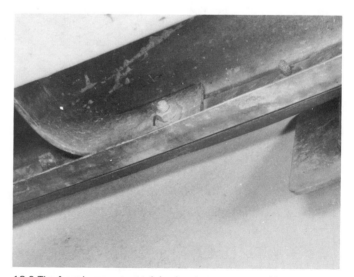

18.2 The front bumper to retaining bracket nut on one side

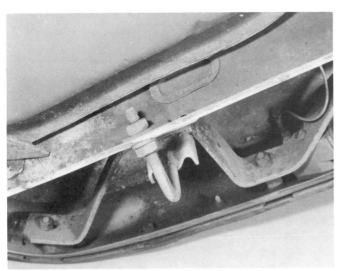

18.4 Rear bumper retaining bracket and tow hook – Estate models

Rear bumpers

4 Working underneath the vehicle unscrew and remove the bumper to support bracket retaining nuts. Owing to their exposed position you may well find them corroded in position. If so, wire brush them clean and soak in penetrating oil to assist removal (photo).

5 On removal of the bumper detach the number plate light lead(s) at their connectors.

6 Refitting of the rear bumper(s) is a reversal of the removal procedure, but check the alignment of the bumper before fully tightening the fastenings. Check the operation of the number plate light(s) on completion.

19 Windscreen – removal and refitting

1 If you are unfortunate enough to have a windscreen shatter or should you wish to renew your existing windscreen, fitting a replacement is one job that is best left for the specialist windscreen fitters. For the owner who wishes to do the job himself the following procedure can be used.

2 Cover the bonnet, the facia and the front seats with plastic sheeting to prevent accidental damage and then remove the windscreen wiper blades and arms as described in Chapter 10.

3 If the screen has shattered remove the remaining crystals of glass from the rubber weatherstrip surround and clean out all visible glass crystals from the facia, ducts, floor and so on. Remove the weatherstrip from the car.

4 Remove the metal trim strip from the weatherstrip surround. This depending on the model, is retained by two or three joint clips which must be slid to one side so that the metal trim can be carefully prised free from the rubber moulding. If the metal trim is bent or distorted during removal it will have to be renewed.

5 If the screen is intact it must be pressed out of the mounting flange and you will need the help of an assistant. Sit in the left-hand seat, to provide more freedom, and with a cloth pad interposed, put your feet on one corner of the screen and exert a progressive pressure. At the same time your assistant, working outside, should prise the screen and seal out of the car flange aperture using wide-bladed, blunt tools. Work progressively, and don't rush the job, until the top and side edges are free and then the panel and weatherstrip can be removed from the car.

6 Check the aperture flange in the car to ensure that it is free from buckles and dents and that all traces of hardened sealer are removed from both sides of the flange. Clean and examine the weatherstrip and if it is damaged, perished or hardened, renew it.

7 Using a suitable sealer, obtainable from windscreen specialists or motor accessory shops, fill the weatherstrip inner groove and assemble the weatherstrip to the windscreen, remembering that the groove for the metal trim strip must be outside.

8 You will now need a length of stout cord, such as washing line, sufficiently long to wrap around the outer groove of the weatherstrip and overlap by a metre (say a yard). Fit the rope into the grooves so that the ends overlap at the bottom centre.

9 Locate the windscreen and weatherstrip assembly on the bottom flange of the aperture and make sure that the rope ends are inside the car. Soapy water can be used to lubricate the rubber weatherstrip as it is fitted to the flange.

10 With your assistant outside pressing on the panel, start pulling on one end of the cord to lift the weatherstrip over the flange. Work round the panel until halfway is reached and then start on the other end of the rope and work round until the rope is free and the weatherstrip fitted over the flange. Where necessary ease any ill-fitting area of rubber into place with a screwdriver.

11 A suitable sealant should now be applied between the weatherstrip and the outside of the car. This can be obtained in containers with a nozzle which permits extruding the sealant under the rubber lip. Apply the sealant all round the weatherstrip.

12 Refit the trim strip, starting with the bottom piece, and use a screwdriver to prise open the groove in the weatherstrip as the trim strip is pressed into place. Fit the side/top pieces and slide the top joint into position. Clean off all surplus sealant from the windscreen, weatherstrip and car body and then refit the windscreen wiper arms and blades.

Conversion factors

Length (distance)
Inches (in)	X	25.4	= Millimetres (mm)	X	0.0394	= Inches (in)
Feet (ft)	X	0.305	= Metres (m)	X	3.281	= Feet (ft)
Miles	X	1.609	= Kilometres (km)	X	0.621	= Miles

Volume (capacity)
Cubic inches (cu in; in^3)	X	16.387	= Cubic centimetres (cc; cm^3)	X	0.061	= Cubic inches (cu in; in^3)
Imperial pints (Imp pt)	X	0.568	= Litres (l)	X	1.76	= Imperial pints (Imp pt)
Imperial quarts (Imp qt)	X	1.137	= Litres (l)	X	0.88	= Imperial quarts (Imp qt)
Imperial quarts (Imp qt)	X	1.201	= US quarts (US qt)	X	0.833	= Imperial quarts (Imp qt)
US quarts (US qt)	X	0.946	= Litres (l)	X	1.057	= US quarts (US qt)
Imperial gallons (Imp gal)	X	4.546	= Litres (l)	X	0.22	= Imperial gallons (Imp gal)
Imperial gallons (Imp gal)	X	1.201	= US gallons (US gal)	X	0.833	= Imperial gallons (Imp gal)
US gallons (US gal)	X	3.785	= Litres (l)	X	0.264	= US gallons (US gal)

Mass (weight)
Ounces (oz)	X	28.35	= Grams (g)	X	0.035	= Ounces (oz)
Pounds (lb)	X	0.454	= Kilograms (kg)	X	2.205	= Pounds (lb)

Force
Ounces-force (ozf; oz)	X	0.278	= Newtons (N)	X	3.6	= Ounces-force (ozf; oz)
Pounds-force (lbf; lb)	X	4.448	= Newtons (N)	X	0.225	= Pounds-force (lbf; lb)
Newtons (N)	X	0.1	= Kilograms-force (kgf; kg)	X	9.81	= Newtons (N)

Pressure
Pounds-force per square inch (psi; lbf/in^2; lb/in^2)	X	0.070	= Kilograms-force per square centimetre (kgf/cm^2; kg/cm^2)	X	14.223	= Pounds-force per square inch (psi; lbf/in^2; lb/in^2)
Pounds-force per square inch (psi; lbf/in^2; lb/in^2)	X	0.068	= Atmospheres (atm)	X	14.696	= Pounds-force per square inch (psi; lbf/in^2; lb/in^2)
Pounds-force per square inch (psi; lbf/in^2; lb/in^2)	X	0.069	= Bars	X	14.5	= Pounds-force per square inch (psi; lbf/in^2; lb/in^2)
Pounds-force per square inch (psi; lbf/in^2; lb/in^2)	X	6.895	= Kilopascals (kPa)	X	0.145	= Pounds-force per square inch (psi; lbf/in^2; lb/in^2)
Kilopascals (kPa)	X	0.01	= Kilograms-force per square centimetre (kgf/cm^2; kg/cm^2)	X	98.1	= Kilopascals (kPa)

Torque (moment of force)
Pounds-force inches (lbf in; lb in)	X	1.152	= Kilograms-force centimetre (kgf cm; kg cm)	X	0.868	= Pounds-force inches (lbf in; lb in)
Pounds-force inches (lbf in; lb in)	X	0.113	= Newton metres (Nm)	X	8.85	= Pounds-force inches (lbf in; lb in)
Pounds-force inches (lbf in; lb in)	X	0.083	= Pounds-force feet (lbf ft; lb ft)	X	12	= Pounds-force inches (lbf in; lb in)
Pounds-force feet (lbf ft; lb ft)	X	0.138	= Kilograms-force metres (kgf m; kg m)	X	7.233	= Pounds-force feet (lbf ft; lb ft)
Pounds-force feet (lbf ft; lb ft)	X	1.356	= Newton metres (Nm)	X	0.738	= Pounds-force feet (lbf ft; lb ft)
Newton metres (Nm)	X	0.102	= Kilograms-force metres (kgf m; kg m)	X	9.804	= Newton metres (Nm)

Power
Horsepower (hp)	X	745.7	= Watts (W)	X	0.0013	= Horsepower (hp)

Velocity (speed)
Miles per hour (miles/hr; mph)	X	1.609	= Kilometres per hour (km/hr; kph)	X	0.621	= Miles per hour (miles/hr; mph)

Fuel consumption*
Miles per gallon, Imperial (mpg)	X	0.354	= Kilometres per litre (km/l)	X	2.825	= Miles per gallon, Imperial (mpg)
Miles per gallon, US (mpg)	X	0.425	= Kilometres per litre (km/l)	X	2.352	= Miles per gallon, US (mpg)

Temperature
Degrees Fahrenheit = (°C x 1.8) + 32   Degrees Celsius (Degrees Centigrade; °C) = (°F - 32) x 0.56

*It is common practice to convert from miles per gallon (mpg) to litres/100 kilometres (l/100km), where mpg (Imperial) x l/100 km = 282 and mpg (US) x l/100 km = 235

Index